sex; by John Money, who shows the importance of pornography in sex education; and by Harold I. Lief, who discusses obstacles to a complete sex education program.

A section on the brain and therapeutic strategy includes papers by Arthur W. Epstein on models for altered brain states and psychopathology such as fetishism, transvestism, and exhibitionism; by Ursula Laschet on the use of drugs in treating sex offenders; by Arthur Zitrin *et al.* correlating brain serotonin levels and sex behavior; by Robert J. Stoller on the need for coordination of psychological and biological sex research; and by Richard Green on the psychosocial development of transsexuals and homosexuals.

Describing recent animal research on sexual behavior, Arnold A. Gerall tells of studies showing that mammals possess bisexual potentiality. Gordon D. Jensen offers a fascinating comparison of sexual behavior in monkeys and humans. Knut Larsson discusses the importance of studying animal sexual behavior in the social context; and Paul D. MacLean, recipient of a special award, presents new findings on brain function in squirrel monkeys with special reference to evolutionary implications of the findings for human behavior.

Joseph Zubin, who writes a historical foreword on the role of the APPA in providing a platform for the sexual revolution, is Chief of Biometrics Research for the New York State Department of Mental Hygiene. John Money is Professor of Medical Psychology and Pediatrics at The Johns Hopkins Hospital.

contemporary sexual behavior: critical issues in the 1970s

AMERICAN PSYCHOPATHOLOGICAL ASSOCIATION

Officers for 1970–71

Milton Greenblatt, M.D., President	Boston, Massachusetts
Alfred M. Freedman, M.D., President-Elect	New York, New York
Henry Brill, M.D., Vice President	West Brentwood, New York
Max Fink, M.D., Secretary	New York, New York
Arnold Friedhoff, M.D., Treasurer	New York, New York
Jonathan O. Cole, M.D., Councillor	Boston, Massachusetts
Fritz A. Freyhan, M.D., Councillor	New York, New York

Committee on Program

Joseph Zubin, Ph.D.	New York, New York
John Money, Ph.D.	Baltimore, Maryland

contemporary sexual behavior: critical issues in the 1970s

edited by Joseph Zubin
and John Money

Based on the proceedings
of the sixty-first annual
meeting of the American
Psychopathological
Association

The Johns Hopkins University Press
Baltimore and London

The Johns Hopkins University Press, Baltimore, Maryland 21218
The Johns Hopkins University Press Ltd., London

Library of Congress Catalog Card Number 72-4013
ISBN 0-8018-1431-6

Library of Congress Cataloging in Publication data
will be found on the last printed page of this book.

Contents

part III:
Integration of Clinical
and Behavioral Approaches

part IV:
The Brain and
Therapeutic Strategy
in Sex-behavioral Pathology

part V:
Sex Education for
the Professional

Foreword

This is the last time my name will appear as editor of the proceedings of the American Psychopathological Association. After 33 years of serving either as an officer or as a member of the program committee and coeditor, I lay aside my duties with a sigh of relief but with a feeling of satisfaction that the Association has survived the vicissitudes of the last 60 years and has made notable contributions to the ever-shifting front of psychopathology.

Before dealing with the current symposium, I would like to give an overview of the nature of the symposia which the Association has sponsored, their place in the development of psychopathology, and the innovative thrust which they have exerted over the past six decades. The history of the Association has been recorded, at least in part, elsewhere (Hamilton 1945, 1947; Zubin 1965). It has not always been as vigorous and lusty as it is now, but it has been in the forefront of developments in psychopathology. The Association was an outgrowth of the monthly meetings of the Psychopathic Club in Morton Prince's home in Boston at the turn of the century. It was organized in 1910, during the meetings of the American Neurological Association, by neurologists who were dissatisfied with exclusive emphasis on the organic and by psychiatrists (alienists) who were equally dissatisfied with the stress on institutional administration to the exclusion of the psychological aspects of behavior. It was the first group to welcome the newly developing psychoanalytic theory in this country. Psychoanalysis had its proponents as well as its critics in the Association, and the pages of the *Journal of Abnormal and Social Psychology*, which Morton Prince had founded as the organ of the Association from 1910 to 1925, were filled with the controversies which took place at the meetings. "(This long connection was finally terminated when it seemed to Prince unwise to jeopardize the eclectic character of the *Journal* by continuing it as the 'official' organ of a society that had by 1925 many other outlets for its productions.) In announcing the affiliation in 1910 Prince expressed the hope that medical practitioners would now find the *Journal* more serviceable than ever. At the same time he felt obliged to apologize to the general reader, whose sensibilities he feared might be hurt by the inclusion of franker studies in sexual pathology. Such studies, he explained, would henceforth be necessary owing to the new discoveries of Sigmund Freud. But there seem to have been no protests at the *Journal's* departure from decorum (Allport 1938, p. 5)."

Then in 1911 the psychoanalytic subgroup founded the American Psychoanalytic Association, but loyalty to the American Psychopathological Association was such that the majority retained their membership in both associations. The remaining group veered more toward the American Neurological Association than toward the Medico-Psychological Association (later the American Psychiatric Association). At one meeting an attempt was made to dissolve the Association and incorporate with the larger group. This was voted down by a narrow margin through the efforts of a psychologist, L. Eugene Emerson, and the life of the Association was maintained.

By 1938 Dr. Samuel Hamilton had become an active leader in the Association and he persuaded a group of younger men, including me, to join. My first effort was to organize a one-session symposium on the question: "Are mental diseases on the increase?" This was a successful session, but as all of the contributors published their papers in various journals the impact of the meeting was dissipated. Such symposia had been held at previous annual meetings, but not very often; most meetings were devoted to contributed papers on diverse topics with no central focus, and interest in the Association lagged.

At one memorable meeting, in the early forties only Sam Hamilton, Paul Hoch, and I were present to listen to Father Moore who was holding forth. We decided there and then that the only way to revive the Association was to select a central issue in psychopathology, develop around it a well-planned symposium in which the topic would be studied from several points of view, and publish the proceedings as a unit in either a journal or a book. The first symposium, held in 1944 and devoted to "Trends of Mental Disease," was a tentative move in that direction. It was published

in 1945 under the imprimatur of the Association under my editor-
ship as the first symposium of the Association. Then followed the
succession of symposia which are recorded on page 455 of this
volume. I had joined the armed forces in the meantime, leaving me
little time for the work of the Association, but, nevertheless, managed to participate in the program committee until 1948 when
Paul Hoch and I joined forces as editors. In the meantime, Grune
and Stratton had become our publishers.

Interestingly enough, our first joint venture was "Psychosexual
Development in Health and Disease" in which Kinsey and Beach
were notable participants. Kinsey was just beginning his work and
not many associations were willing to sponsor a platform for such
a revolutionary development. The experimental attitude toward
programming, which since 1944 had become our policy, permitted
us to undertake this symposium. It was a good venture both scientifically and financially. It was well received by the scientific
public and went into several editions. Our next venture,
"Anxiety," was also favorably received, since there had been no
previous attempt to integrate the findings in this field; this volume
became a textbook for students and workers and went into three
editions. There followed several more epoch-making symposia:
"Depression" in 1952 antedated the current interest in depression
coming in the wake of the drug era; "Psychiatry and the Law"
preceded the revision of the mental hygiene laws in this country as
well as in New York State. Paul Hoch and I kept our fingers on the
pulse of psychopathology in this country, and as each new movement began we afforded it a ready platform. In this way "Mental
Retardation," "Social Psychiatry," and "Psychopathology of Adolescence" were given a hearing in recent years as the work in each
field began to break new ground.

The current symposium is another example of the readiness of
our Association to afford a dispassionate platform for controversial issues. It is noteworthy that the Association began with an
interest in Freud's newly developing concepts in 1910, picked up
the second sexual revolution spearheaded by Kinsey in 1948, and
now has picked up Masters' and Johnson's third revolution.

In our symposium on "Anxiety," Paul Tillich pointed out that
the then current problems of society stemmed from the decline in
the institutions which society had developed to contain or assuage

anxiety. Religion, the family, and vocational goals had begun to show cracks in their structure, but nothing was then said about marriage, law and order, youth revolt, etc. At that time it was contended that the cracks in the structure were not so much at fault as the lack of techniques either to repair them or to replace them. It reminds one of the story told by an anthropologist who had asked an old Indian brave whether he would be willing to spend a night in the cemetery. "Yes," replied the brave, "I would spread my holy beans around me and sleep like a pig." The young braves refused the invitation. Why? Apparently they had lost faith in the beans but had nothing with which to replace them. Whether co-marital sex will ever come to replace monogamy is an open question, but one which the Association in its experimental approach to programming could hardly afford to dismiss, especially because of the presumed critical role of sex in psychopathology. Furthermore, co-marital sex without infidelity is a practice which Mohammedans and Eskimos have practiced for a long time without apparent noxious results. Whether the teaching by means of what we designate today as pornographic materials will have a salutary influence on sexual behavior remains to be seen, but, here again, this revolutionary approach could hardly be omitted from consideration. The medical care afforded today by most obstetricians may perhaps be influenced by Alice Rossi's impassioned plea for revision. Here, again, I believe that the American Psychopathological Association has lived up to its role as the "conscience of psychopathology" and offered a platform for innovative concepts in current issues on the psychopathological scene.

In the scientific models for the etiology of psychopathology with which our Association has concerned itself over the years, there have been two polar opposites. As in physics, where the two poles are field theories versus atom or particle theories, so in psychopathology we have the contrast between the ecological model on the one hand and the genetic on the other. The ecological model essentially stipulates that man's behavior is the result of the forces which impinge upon him—social, cultural, economic, and physical. At the other end of the spectrum we have the genetic model which, paraphrasing Freud, states that genetics is fate. Since both of these extreme positions are occupied by straw men these days, we need the developmental and learning theory models which lean toward the ecological but do not ignore the genetic and the internal environment and neurophysiological models which, though leaning toward the genetic, do not eschew the ecological forces (Zubin 1969).

In the light of these models, what can we say about the contributions of this symposium? It is quite clear that the internal environment model (endocrinology and neurochemistry) can do much to help us understand how psychosexual behavior takes place and why it goes wrong on anatomic, neurophysiological, or endocrinological levels. But the psychosexual revolution that has taken place has been fed by ecological winds rather than by biological changes. Certainly the altered views of sex differences are influenced more by changes in the ecological than in the biological sphere.

It is interesting to note that although text books have dealt with the psychopathology of sex, few, if any, authentic textbooks have dealt with normal sex until recently. Colored photographs of sex abnormalities are frequently presented in textbooks, while presentations of normal sex are taboo. It is high time that we removed these taboos so that both children and adults can receive appropriate education about a major function of their bodies which, even today, still remains clouded in mystery and ignorance.

If one regards sexual behavior as analogous to other "emotional" responses, such as fear or joy, it is interesting to note how the two ends of the spectrum—the ecological and the genetic—must interact to produce genuine sexual experience and behavior. For example, adrenaline alone will not produce fear in the absence of the cognitive component of fear, nor will euphoric cognition induce joy if the physiological component is inhibited by drugs (Zubin & Katz 1964). Similarly, fullsome sex behavior cannot exist in its anatomical and physiological components alone, anymore than it can exist by merely viewing pornography cognitively. The results of stimulating the "sex centers" in the brain are no more like genuine sexual behavior than is the behavior of the voyeur, though both may lead to orgasms.

Despite the similarities between fear and sex as responses, there is a very important difference. Fear can be experienced alone, even though it represents an interaction between the physiological and cognitive components, and can even be experienced without specific external stimulation in the form of anxiety. Lone sexual behavior is hardly a substitute for the interaction between the two participants in both the physiological and cognitive spheres, and perhaps this interaction is the most important aspect of the process. No wonder Freud, perhaps mistakenly, considered mental disorders as caused by instinctive sexual disturbance. The delicate balance in interpersonal relationships required in the sexual act is truly impossible with certain mental disorders, since they are essentially disorders of interpersonal relationship. Thus, even though sexual disturbance may not be a cause, its failure may serve as a sensitive thermometer of the presence of a mental disorder.

In closing my remarks, I would like to express my great debt to the late Paul H. Hoch, with whom I coedited 17 of the 26 volumes for the Association, to Dr. Henry Stratton of Grune and Stratton, who published 26 of our first 27 volumes, and to the Association itself. When I entered the field of psychopathology, under the academic tutelage of the late Carney Landis and the practical tutelage of the late Samuel Hamilton, psychopathology was largely a descriptive field. Textbooks of psychiatry and of abnormal psychology in those days had the distinction of consisting of case histories only and no numerical data. The only numbers in the books were page numbers. Coming from the discipline of psychology and statistics I began to search for more objective, quantitative knowledge. The multidisciplinary character of this Association permitted me to learn how one can integrate the findings of various disciplines in a quantitative way. This is what kept me interested in the Association despite the severe demands it made on my time. These demands paid off, and I owe the little advance we have made in our work in biometrics research to the inspiration, knowledge, and encouragement afforded by the splendid fellowship of the Association. Therefore, to the present and former members I tender my warmest thanks for advice, counsel, and guidance, as well as warm friendship throughout these years. I also look forward to future symposia, knowing that the new hands into which program making will fall will carry on the tradition of being ever alert to new trends and fearless in providing platforms for innovative, if still unproven, approaches to psychypathology.

Finally, I must express my sincerest thanks to John Money who is largely responsible for the current symposium. Like its predecessor of thirteen years ago, in which Kinsey participated, it bids well to break new ground and become a classic.

JOSEPH ZUBIN

Leonia, New Jersey
February 7, 1971

REFERENCES

Allport, G. W. The Journal of Abnormal and Social Psychology: An editorial. *Journal of Abnormal and Social Psychology* 1938, 33: 3-13.

Hamilton, Samuel W. Notes on the history of the American Psychopathological Association 1910-1931. *Journal of Nervous and Mental Disease* 1945, 102: 30-53.

———. The American Psychopathological Association. *Journal of Clinical Psychology* 1947, 3: 200-2.

Zubin, Joseph. Paul H. Hoch's contribution to the American Psychopathological Association. *Comprehensive Psychiatry* 1965, 2: 74-77.

———. The biometric approach to psychopathology—revisited. In J. Zubin & C. Shagass (eds.), *Neurobiological aspects of psychopathology.* New York: Grune & Stratton, 1969, pp. 281-309.

Zubin, J., & Katz, M. Psychopharmacology and personality. In D. Byrne & P. Worchel (eds.), *Personality change.* New York: John Wiley & Sons, 1964, pp. 367-95. Reprinted in: *International Journal of Psychiatry* 1966, 2: 640-75.

Preface

The American Psychopathological Association (APPA) has dealt with the problems of sexual behavior at three points in its history. The first was its role in the formation of the American Psychoanalytic Association, which developed as a spin-off from the APPA in 1912. On that occasion Morton Prince warned the readers of the official journal of the Association (*Journal of Abnormal and Social Psychology*) not to be dismayed to see the journal publish papers on sex in the wake of Freud's new ideas. The second occasion was the symposium in 1949 on "Psychosexual Development in Health and Disease" which was organized in response to the early epoch-making work of Kinsey. The present symposium is the third occasion.

A comparison of the table of contents of the 1949 symposium with that of the current symposium reveals the interesting fact that there is no overlap in authors, nor in the sections nor chapter titles. It is as if an entirely new field had arisen during the last two decades. In the 1949 symposium an entire section was devoted to the psychoanalytic approach; in the current volume only one paper deals with psychoanalysis under the title: "Psychoanalysis and physical intervention in the brain: the mind-body problem again." The new developments in the current volume are on prenatal hormones and subsequent sexual dimorphism of behavior; brain function and sexual behavior; maternalism and women's sexuality; sex, marital status, and family structure; sex education; and the psychophysiological aspects of the sexual act and treatment of its disturbances.

As was the case with the editors of the 1949 symposium, the present editors feel the need for pointing out that they could not cover the entire field. Thus the following topics are known to have been omitted through lack of time, despite a three-day program, or unavailability of speakers: postconceptional reversal of chromosomal determinants of morphologic and behavioral sex in fish and amphibia; prenatal medicational and other effects on subsequent sexual behavior in mammals; radiographic brain studies and sexual behavior in mammals; pheromonal or odiferous stimulation of sexual response in subhuman primates and human beings; effects of precocious and delayed puberty in human beings; adult gonadotropic and gonadal hormone levels and homosexual versus heterosexual gender identity; the phenomenon of falling in love; psychedelic drugs and enhancement of erotic experience; and ethnosexologic studies of sexual pairing and mating. No doubt there are other new branches on the tree of sexual research which were too young to have yet been perceived by the program organizers when they planned the program that became the table of contents of this volume.

It has always been the function of The American Psychopathological Association to envisage the impact of new developments on normal and abnormal behavior. In its forward-looking programs it has provided platforms for topics before they reached the stage of general professional interest and long before they reached the stage of popular acceptance: it anticipated the currently widespread scientific interest in depression by about a decade in its 1951 symposium; the current interest in diagnosis and prognosis in its 1953 symposium on "Current Problems in Psychiatric Diagnoses"; the current interest in addiction in the 1957 symposium on "Drug Addiction and Habituation"; the present interest in the problems of the aged in the 1961 symposium on "Psychopathology of Aging." Now, in keeping with this forward-looking tradition it is providing a ready platform for the burgeoning renewal of scientific interest in sexual behavior.

One published symposium, however, should just be the beginning. Public support for research in the traditionally sensitive areas of human sexuality is still difficult to obtain. The determinants of sexual incompatibility between couples must be sought, even if that research runs contrary to current mores, such as requiring the observing of a videotape of a couple during coitus. Systematic studies of infantile and juvenile sexual play in relation to normal adolescent psychosexual development are also needed. The sexual behavior of homosexuals needs to be investigated further. The old taboos against sex must give way so that publicly funded scientific research can be expanded into all areas of normal and abnormal sexual behavior.

ACKNOWLEDGMENT

The editors are grateful to Miss Karen M. Olson of our staff for her expert editing of the manuscripts. The editors, as well as the contributing authors, stand in her debt for the masterful efficient preparation of this volume for publication.

JOHN MONEY
JOSEPH ZUBIN

part I

Recent Animal
Research on
Sexual Behavior

chapter 1

Influence of Perinatal Androgen on Reproductive Capacity*

Arnold A. Gerall†

At the meeting of this Association six years ago, Dr. William C. Young outlined a theory of sexual differentiation which he hoped would integrate biological and behavioral approaches in reproduction (Young 1967). Whatever the shortcomings of this theory, it has served as an important contemporary impetus for research and the generation of empirical relationships. Drawing an analogy from mammalian embryological research (Burns 1942; Jost 1957), it was proposed that differentiation of the neural substrate of sexual behavior follows principles similar to those governing development of various secondary reproductive organs (Phoenix et al. 1959). Mammalian peripheral organs destined to participate in reproduction are viewed as passing through a stage during which they

*The original research cited was supported by Research Grant HD 00867-09 from the National Institute of Child Health and Human Development, USPHS.
†Tulane University, New Orleans, Louisiana.

1

possess bisexual potentiality. In the absence of hormonal influences, these organs tend to develop into female structures regardless of genetic sex. Androgen is assumed to act as a biological "organizer" which enhances male and suppresses or disrupts female sexual structural and behavioral differentiation. According to this view, ovarian, in contrast to testicular, secretion has no permanent influence on the development of sexual characteristics. In this presentation, data from studies manipulating the amount of androgen circulating during the perinatal period in both sexes will be reviewed partly to illustrate the heuristic value of Young's hypothesis, but also because they have direct relevance to current research and application. The studies will be presented in the order of amount of androgen injected. Second, the role of estrogen, particularly with reference to modifications produced by perinatal androgen, will be considered. The overview will be limited to rodents, but while species differences certainly exist many of the implications concerning androgen effects on development have been found relevant among diverse types of subjects.

Relatively large amounts of androgen, approximately equivalent to the effectiveness of 1.0 mg testosterone propionate (TP), administered to female rats and guinea pigs during development have been shown to increase significantly their capacity to exhibit male copulatory responses. When provided with androgen during adulthood, perinatally androgenized females not only mount estrous females but also exhibit all other responses in the male's copulatory repertoire (Gerall 1966; Gerall & Ward 1967; Phoenix et al. 1959; Ward 1969; Whalen & Robertson, 1968). They are fully capable of executing intromission and ejaculatory patterns. Some of these female rats, for example, ejaculate about seven times during a long test period (Ward 1969); each ejaculation is followed by a refractory period of similar duration to that shown by genetic males (Ward 1969; Whalen & Robertson 1968). Females in which androgen injections are initiated approximately six days before birth and continued postnatally have well-developed seminal vesicles and coagulating glands and, subsequent to ejaculation, eject fluid which forms vaginal plugs. Those injected with androgen only postnatally do not have these organs, but still exhibit the behavioral components characteristic of ejaculation.

Given TP later in life, all of these perinatally androgenized females have clitorises which assume penile appearance and proportions. While some question exists as to whether the masculine behaviors of intromission and ejaculation shown by these androgenized females should be attributed to sensory feedback from the hypertrophied clitoris or direct modification of the central nervous system, it is clear that the data are consistent with the expectation of the hypothesis outlined by Young. Feminine behavioral capacities of animals receiving large amounts of perinatal androgen are minimal or completely absent when endogenous or exogenous ovarian hormones are available. They do not show cyclic physiological or behavioral characteristics, nor do they respond with more than a slight lordotic reflex when mounted by vigorous males, even when provided with large amounts of estrogen and progesterone.

While effects on sexual differentiation produced by high levels of perinatal androgen are dramatic and informative, a large amount of meaningful data can be gathered from studies using lower dosages. Although not producing the degree of masculinization described above, amounts of androgen having the potency equivalent to or greater than 100 μg TP administered on any one of the first eight days after birth systematically alter female reproductive capacity. The following modifications are reliably obtained: tonic rather than phasic gonadotrophic release, polyfollicular ovaries with few, if any, corpora lutea, persistently cornified vaginal epithelium, refractory lordotic responses, and absence of the typical four-day estrous cycle (Barraclough 1961; Barraclough & Gorski 1961; Harris & Levine 1965; Segal & Johnson 1959; Whalen & Edwards 1967). The relationships between dosage of androgen injected on the fifth postnatal day and receptivity, locomotor activity, and uterine weight are shown in Figures 1 to 3. These data were obtained from animals ovariectomized after puberty and provided with controlled hormone replacement. Receptivity was measured in mating tests with vigorous males which mounted each female ten times during each session. All experiments reveal essentially the relationship shown in Figure 1, in which the decrease in receptivity below control level is greatest in those subjects receiving the largest amount of TP neonatally. Gen-

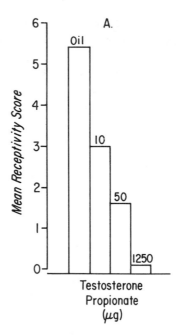

Fig. 1. *Mean receptivity scores obtained during 5 mating tests in which the subjects were mounted 10 times. The experimental groups were females injected with either oil, 10, 50, or 1250 µg testosterone propionate when 5 days old and ovariectomized after puberty. Each subject was injected with estrogen and progesterone before each of the tests (Gerall & Kenney 1970).*

eral activity, shown in Figure 2, was measured in a Wahmann apparatus in which the animal lived continuously. The rate of increase in activity, particularly at the higher replacement dosage of estradiol benzoate (EB), again was greatest in the oil-injected and least in the most neonatally androgenized subjects. As in the case of behavioral measures, morphological changes, for example, uterine responsiveness, can be ordered on the basis of the amount of neonatally administered TP. As shown in Figure 3, uterine weight obtained from spayed animals injected for five days with 3.3 µg EB was lowest in the 1250 µg TP and highest in the oil-injected females. Whether morphological or functional phenomena are being examined, it is apparent that suppression of normal responsiveness to circulating hormones is graded and proportional to the amount of androgen present neonatally (Gerall & Kenney 1970; Mullins & Levine 1968; Harris & Levine 1965).

There is disagreement as to which hormones have diminished efficacy in perinatally androgenized females. Clemens et al. (1969) have suggested that utilization of progesterone is altered, whereas studies from our laboratory have revealed that reactivity to estrogen is depressed. Examples of estrogen's lower effectiveness are shown in Figures 2 and 4 for the end points of activity and receptivity. For both behavioral measures, the slope of the dose-response function is greatest for the oil- and least for the 1250 μg TP-injected subjects. Although subjects receiving large quantities of androgen neonatally appear to be incapable of utilizing any amount of exogenous estrogen, those receiving lower dosages show greater responsiveness with increasing dosage of EB.

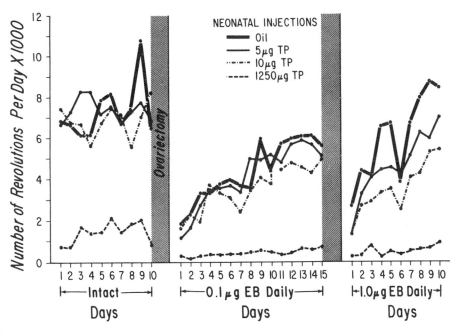

Fig. 2. *Mean number of revolutions run each day by neonatally androgenized subjects while intact and after ovariectomy and institution of daily injections of either 0.1 or 1.0 μg estradiol benzoate (Gerall et al. 1972).*

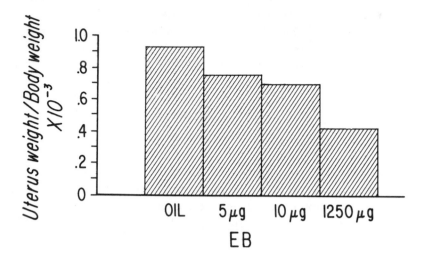

Fig. 3. *Weight of a standard 5 mm section of uterus expressed as a ratio of body weight obtained in rats injected neonatally with either oil or different amounts of testosterone propionate when 5 days old. All subjects were injected daily for 5 days with 3.3 µg estradiol benzoate before uterus was removed (Gerall et al. 1972).*

These and other data establish that estrogen, when present alone or with progesterone, is less potent in androgenized than in normal females. Whether progesterone sensitivity is altered as systematically as that of estrogen remains to be demonstrated.

When less than 50 µg TP is injected on approximately the fifth day of age, females have normal reproductive functions after reaching puberty; however, these terminate at a much earlier age than in nontreated animals (Gorski 1968; Swanson & van der Werff ten Bosch 1964). The duration of normal processes has been shown to be inversely proportional to the amount of neonatal androgen (Napoli & Gerall 1970). The occurrence of persistent vaginal estrus in intact animals, which is one way of identifying the onset of the anovulatory, acyclic syndrome, can be seen in Figure 5, where the percentage of subjects losing normal female capabilities increases directly both with age and the amount of androgen injected neonatally. Kenney (1970) has obtained evidence that behavioral receptivity also declines in minimally androgenized females much faster than in oil-injected subjects. Thus, on both physiological and behavioral levels, normal function precedes the onset of the sterile conditions in low-dosage androgenized females.

An attempt has been made to determine whether the onset of dysfunction is hastened by hormones, particularly estrogen, circulating in the animal about the time of puberty, or, conversely, whether it is independently controlled by intrinsic factors within the central nervous system or peripheral organs. Results obtained from two studies testing the hypothesis that estrogen interacts with the effects of neonatal androgen are shown in Figures 6 and 7. In the first experiment, subjects receiving 50 µg or less TP when five days old were administered either 10 µg EB daily from 26–30 or 26–35 days of age or oil during these ages. As shown in Figure 6, estrogen circulating just before puberty increased the num-

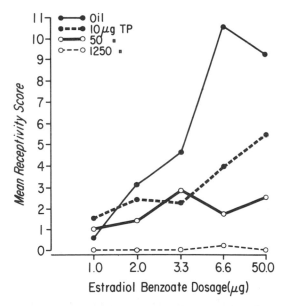

Fig. 4. *Mean receptivity score of neonatally androgenized subjects obtained in mating tests, each preceded by different dosages of estradiol benzoate and the same dosage of progesterone (Gerall & Kenney 1970).*

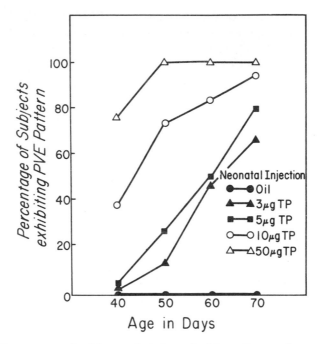

Fig. 5. *Percentage of subjects administered either oil or various amounts of testosterone propionate on the 5th day of life having persistent vaginal estrus (PVE) when 40–70 days of age. PVE is defined as having cornified cells 8 out of 9 days (Napoli & Gerall 1970).*

ber of neonatally treated animals showing persistent vaginal estrus at each age examined over that obtained with oil (Napoli & Gerall 1970). However, estrogen given at this period also induced precocious puberty. Thus, it might be argued that the endogenous timing process is merely started sooner in these subjects and, hence, the period of normal function also ends sooner than in subjects given oil. Although a definitive interpretation of these results is not possible at this time, the empirical meaning is clear. When present shortly before and during puberty, estrogen accelerates processes associated with suppressing female reproductive functions in animals that have received minute amounts of androgen neonatally. This conclusion is supported by the second study (Kenney 1970) using a factorial design in which females were injected with oil, 10 or 20 μg testosterone on the fifth day of life, and ovariectomized either when one day or 40 days old. Thus, one-half of the subjects had ovaries and presumably estrogen circulating before puberty. No animals had ovaries after 40 days of age. After typical hormone replacement they were given mating tests with vigorous males. The results, depicted in Figure 7, revealed that the 10 and 20 μg testosterone-treated animals with ovaries until puberty exhibited lower levels of behavior than peers receiving the same amounts of androgen but spayed neonatally. On the other hand, subjects receiving oil neonatally, as shown in Figure 7, had higher receptivity scores if their ovaries were present for 40 days. Thus, prepuberal estrogen in physiological amounts, although inhibitory for androgenized females, is facilitatory for nor-

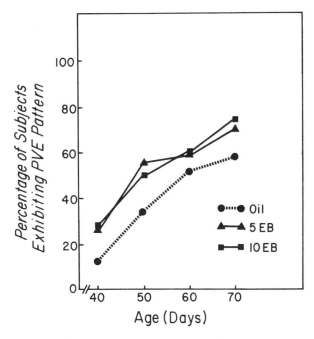

Fig. 6. *Percentage of neonatally androgenized subjects meeting the persistent vaginal estrous (PVE) criterion of 8 out of 9 days of cornified cells in each of 3 groups having either oil or 10 μg estradiol benzoate injected daily from 26 - 35 days of age (Napoli & Gerall 1970).*

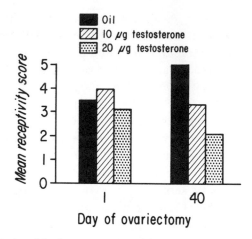

Fig. 7. *The relationship between receptivity scores and both age of ovariectomy and amount of neonatal androgen. Each subject was injected with 6.6 µg estradiol benzoate and 40 hrs later with 0.5 mg progesterone before each test (Kenney 1970).*

mal females as measured by the effectiveness of estrogen and progesterone in mediating mating behavior.

The hypothesis presented by Young provides a useful and perhaps not intuitively obvious evaluation of the generality of the results described above. According to it, female reproductive patterns should be exhibited by genetic males if testicular androgen is eliminated during their developmental period. Many studies have now been performed in which rats have been castrated neonatally, and, in general, the results confirm the expectation that, when given estrogen and progesterone, they manifest the female mating pattern more readily than intact males (Gerall et al. 1967; Grady et al. 1965). Also, the ease with which these lordotic patterns can be elicited following estrogen and progesterone injections is diminished as a function of the time the testes remain after birth (Grady et al. 1965). In our studies (Hendricks 1969; Thomas & Gerall 1969; Gerall et al. 1967), however, even those males castrated within six hours after birth, while showing extensive female lordotic and soliciting patterns, do so with a lower frequency and intensity than genetic females. We have suggested that this is because the testes are functional before birth in the rat and probably secrete sufficient androgen to induce partial differentiation of the fetus in a masculine direction. If the basic tendency of mammals is to develop female behavioral capacities and if the secretions of the fetal testes only slightly alter this tendency, then the male rat castrated soon after birth should exhibit some of the characteristics of minimally androgenized females. One of the major characteristics of these androgenized females is that their physiological and behavioral reproductive capacities decline more rapidly than those of nonhormone exposed animals as they grow older. As indicated above, it also appears that estrogen circulating after puberty accelerates the rate of loss of function. Analogously, it would be anticipated that after attaining puberty the neonatally castrated male would exhibit lordotic responses when provided with estrogen and progesterone. But the quality and frequency of these responses should decline relatively quickly as a function of age. This expectation was confirmed in a study performed by Dunlap et al. (1972), in which male rats were castrated within 12 hours after birth and differed only in the age at which a series of female mating tests was initiated. The results shown in Figure 8 indicate that initial and maximum receptivity levels are higher for younger animals. After reaching the maximum within approximately four tests, the receptivity in all animals decreases during succeeding mating tests. If the level of receptivity were a function of age only, then mean receptivity decline rates should not differ for any of the groups after their initial conditioning series. As shown in the inset as well as in the original data presented in Figure 8, the rate of decline is greater after the maximum is reached in those animals that received the larger number of estrogen and progesterone injections. Thus, it appears that exposure to estrogen increases the rate of decline beyond that which would be anticipated from an aging factor alone. Females given the same series of tests exhibit no decrease in receptivity after reaching a maximum level.

A more direct demonstration that estrogen interacts with perinatal androgen in the male is being provided by a study now in progress in our laboratory. Experimental males were castrated within 24 hours after birth and injected when five days old with

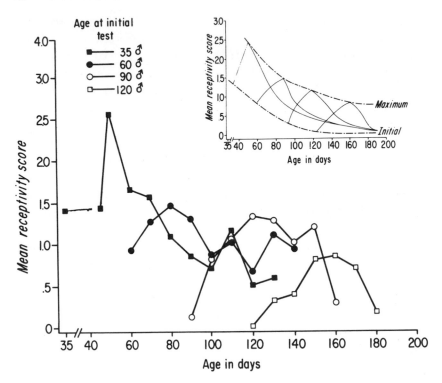

Fig. 8. *Mean receptivity score obtained by neonatally castrated males as a function of their age at the initiation of the tests. Each subject was injected with estradiol benzoate and progesterone before each test. The inset consists of a series of curves which closely conform to the data and represent female receptivity exhibited by castrated males as a function of chronological age and experience with hormones and testing procedures (Dunlap et al 1972).*

either oil or testosterone. One-half of the subjects in each of the groups had ovaries implanted soon after birth; these were removed 40 days later. A long series of mating tests separated by at least one week were initiated at 58 days of age, each preceded by the same priming dosages of estrogen and progesterone. Receptivity of animals injected with testosterone and implanted with ovaries uniformly reached a maximum level in three tests, but declined during the next three tests to a level indicating that lordotic responses were rarely evoked. After six tests, receptivity in subjects obtaining postnatal testosterone but without an ovary was beginning to decline. All other groups were still displaying high levels of receptivity at the time of the seventh test. While the series is not yet completed, it appears that the combination of perinatal androgen and prepuberal estrogen is a condition for causing a rapid decline in female receptivity.

In conclusion, most of the data currently available are congruent with the hypothesis that mammalian organisms possess bisexual potentiality. Masculine behavior potential in both genetic sexes is fully developed when androgen is present during fetal and neonatal periods. The female component of the bisexuality is either suppressed or disrupted systematically according to the amount of androgen circulating during fetal or neonatal periods. Large dosages cause complete absence of normal female physiological and behavioral capacities. Microgram amounts of perinatal androgen, however, manifest their effects at varying periods after puberty. It is suggested that each target organ, including the brain, uterus, etc., possesses an intrinsically controlled critical period for responding to ovarian hormones. In proportion to the amount present during development, androgen apparently shortens this period of responsiveness. Estrogen present during adolescence and maturity appears to potentiate the limiting effects on female capacity produced by perinatal androgen. However, in genetic females, which do not have androgen present during development, ovarian secretions have a facilitatory effect on, at least, the intensity of their behavioral receptivity manifested during their first few postpuberal exposures to estrogen and progesterone.

REFERENCES

Barraclough, C. A. Production of anovulatory sterile rats by single injections of testosterone. *Endocrinology* 1961, 68: 62–67.

Barraclough, C. A., & Gorski, R. A. Evidence that the hypothalamus is responsible for androgen-induced sterility in the female rat. *Endocrinology* 1961, 68: 68–79.

Burns, R. K. Hormones and the differentiation of sex. In G. S. Avery et al. (eds.), *Survey of Biological Progress*, vol. 1. New York: Academic Press, 1942, pp. 233–66.

Clemens, L. G., Hiroi, M., & Gorski, R. A. Induction and facilitation of female mating behavior in rats treated with low doses of testosterone propionate. *Endocrinology* 1969, 84: 1430–38.

Dunlap, J. L., Gerall, A. A., & Hendricks, S. E. Female receptivity in neo-natally castrated males as a function of age and experience. *Physiology and Behavior* 1972, 8: 21-23.

Gerall, A. A. Hormonal factors influencing masculine behavior of female guinea pigs. *Journal of Comparative and Physiological Psychology* 1966, 62: 365-69.

———. Effects of early postnatal androgen and estrogen injections on the estrous activity cycles and mating behavior of rats. *Anatomical Record* 1967, 149: 97-104.

Gerall, A. A., & Kenney, A. McM. Neonatally androgenized females' respon-siveness to estrogen and progesterone. *Endocrinology* 1970, 87: 560-66.

Gerall, A. A., Hendricks, S. E., Johnson, L. L., & Bounds, T. W. Evaluation of the effects of early castration in male rats on adult sexual behavior. *Journal of Comparative and Physiological Psychology* 1967, 64: 206-12.

Gerall, A. A., Stone, L. S., and Hitt, J. C. Neonatal androgen suppresses fe-male responsiveness to estrogen. *Physiology and Behavior* 1972, 8: 17-20.

Gerall, A. A., & Ward, I. L. Effects of prenatal exogenous androgen on the sexual behavior of the female albino rat. *Journal of Comparative and Physiological Psychology* 1967, 62: 370-75.

Gorski, R. A. Influence of age on the response to paranatal administration of a low dosage of androgen. *Endocrinology* 1968, 82: 1001-04.

Grady, K. L., Phoenix, C. H., & Young, W. C. Role of the developing rat testis in differentiation of neural tissue mediating sexual behavior. *Journal of Comparative and Physiological Psychology* 1965, 57: 177-82.

Harris, G. W., & Levine, S. Sexual differentiation of the brain and its experi-mental control. *Journal of Physiology* 1965, 181: 379-400.

Hendricks, S. E. Influence of neonatally administered hormones and early gonadectomy on rats' sexual behavior. *Journal of Comparative and Physi-ological Psychology* 1968, 69: 408-13.

Jost, A. The secretory activities of fetal endocrine glands and their effect upon target organs. *Macy Foundation Conference on Gestation* 1957, 3: 129-71.

Kenney, A. McM. The effects of neonatal androgen and duration of ovarian tenancy on reproductive behavior and physiology of the adult female rat. Dissertation, Tulane University, 1970.

Mullins, R. F., Jr., & Levine, S. Hormonal determinants during infancy of adult sexual behavior in the female rat. *Physiology and Behavior* 1968, 3: 333-38.

Napoli, A., & Gerall, A. A. Effect of estrogen and anti-estrogen on reproduc-tive function in neonatally androgenized female rats. *Endocrinology* 1970, 87: 1330-36.

Phoenix, G. H., Goy, R. W., Gerall, A. A., & Young, W. C. Organizing action of prenatally administered testosterone propionate on the tissues mediating mating behavior in the guinea pig. *Endocrinology* 1959, **65**: 369–82.

Segal, S. J., & Johnson, D. C. Inductive influence of steroid hormones on neural system. *Archives d'Anatomie Microscopique et de Morphologie Experimentale* 1959, **48**: 261–65.

Swanson, H. E., & van der Werff ten Bosch, J. J. The early-androgen syndrome: its development and the response to hemi-spaying. *Acta Endocrinologica* 1964, **45**: 1–12.

Thomas, C. N., & Gerall, A. A. Effect of hour of operation on feminization of neonatally castrated male rats. *Psychonomic Science* 1969, **16**: 19–20.

Ward, I. L. Differential effect of pre- and postnatal androgen on the sexual behavior of intact and spayed female rats. *Hormones and Behavior* 1969, **1**: 25–36.

Whalen, R. E., & Edwards, D. A. Hormonal determinants of the development of masculine and feminine behavior in male and female rats. *Anatomical Record* 1967, **157**: 173–80.

Whalen, R. E., & Robertson, R. T. Sexual exhaustion and recovery of masculine copulatory behavior in virilized male and female rats. *Psychonomic Science* 1968, **11**: 319–20.

Young, W. C. Prenatal gonadal hormones and behavior in the adult. In J. Zubin and H. F. Hunt (eds.), *Comparative Psychopathology, Animal and Human*. New York: Grune and Stratton, 1967, pp. 173–81.

chapter 2

Human Sexual Behavior in Primate Perspective*

Gordon D. Jensen[†]

Ethology, originally the study of animals in their natural environments, is now broadened to include the study of man (Crook
1970). Human ethology views man as a member of the animal
kingdom, and tracing the origin of human sexual behavior in nonhuman primates is one aspect of human ethology. Human behavior
in modern society is, in part, the result of a slow process of evolution from our ape ancestors. When we view our own behavior in
the perspective of evolution (Hamburg 1970; Washburn 1968) and
enrich our knowledge of man from studies in the new field of
human ethology, we can better understand how man came to be

*This investigation was supported by General Research Support Grant RR 05684
from the General Research Support Branch, Division of Research Resources, National
Institutes of Health. I thank G. Mitchell, C. B. Koford, D. G. Lindburg for help in the
preparation of this manuscript.
†Gordon D. Jensen, M.D., School of Medicine, University of California, Davis.

what he is today. Insights from animal studies continue to tumble many treasured old concepts about man. Nonhuman forms of life take on greater importance. Most all students of human behavior now realize that "the proper study of mankind" is not man but all of nature.

In the past ten years we have learned a lot about the sexual behavior of various nonhuman primates, particularly monkeys and baboons. Dr. Jane van Lawick-Goodall (1965, 1968) has published the most detailed observations so far on man's closest primate relatives, the chimpanzees. For eleven years she has made continuous observations of a community of wild chimpanzees in the Gombe Stream Reserve, Tanzania, Africa. A Japanese primatologist working in another part of Africa studied the social and sexual behavior of a group of wild champanzees (Sugiyama 1969). Extensive studies of the sexual behavior of chimpanzees are now in progress at the Gombe Stream Reserve.

Of all the species of monkeys and apes, chimpanzees most resemble man. Many chimpanzee postures, gestures, and facial expressions have a surprisingly human quality. These similarities probably also appear in sexual expression. I am going to describe sexual behavior in chimpanzees and monkeys and compare it with human sexual behavior. Statements about chimpanzees are derived from van Lawick-Goodall's reports unless otherwise cited.

In any general consideration of primate behavior, it is important not to become conveniently oversimplistic and believe that all ape and monkey behavior is much alike. There are over 200 living nonhuman primate species, and among them there are great differences in behavior patterns and social structure. There are relatively few generalizations that can be made. Even one species can present various behavior patterns, depending upon habitat. For example, African green monkeys living in the open grasslands show a stronger mother-infant bond than the same species living in forest areas (Gartlan & Brain 1968). The discovery of a number of such intraspecies differences has led to the suggestion that social structure in many primate species is habitat-determined rather than species-specific (Gartlan 1968). Several different wild Japanese monkey groups have adopted specific behavior patterns, such as washing their sweet potatoes before eating. Such behavior patterns have been seen first in one or two individuals and then have been gradually acquired by all group members. Because they have been passed on from generation to generation they have been called precultural behaviors (Kawamura 1963). There are some differences in the social behavior of wild chimpanzees living in the areas studied so far (Reynolds & Reynolds 1965; Sugiyama 1969; van Lawick-Goodall 1968). Whenever I generalize about chimpanzees or other nonhuman primates, I expect that there will be exceptions as there are in man.

Chimpanzees, like all nonhuman primates, have intermittent sexuality. Female chimpanzees are attractive to males and sexually receptive for only about six days in the midportion of the 35-day menstrual cycle. This period, called estrus, is clearly marked by the large swelling of the sex skin of the genital area. The human female's more or less continual sexual receptivity is not found in any other primate.

Chimpanzees show relatively little courtship behavior. There are two courtship display behaviors used only in the sexual contexts, beckoning and tree-leaping. The beckoning male stands upright facing the female, extends his arm out in front and draws it swiftly down to his body. The tree-leaping display is a series of leaps and swings through the branches in an upright position while he faces in the general direction of the female. Two displays are used in both aggressive and sexual contexts. One is called the swagger. The male with hair erect stands upright on his two feet as he swaggers in a rather confident, aggressive way toward the female. This behavior is a threat in agonistic situations. A glaring look is another display. Occasionally a high-ranking male induces a female to approach and present for copulation by simply glaring at her. All of these displays work very well. Females respond to 82 percent of approaches or courtship displays of mature males by presenting for copulation. They either remain crouched while the male approaches or actually run toward him and present.

Preliminaries to copulation are relatively minor for chimpanzees. In about 50 percent of the copulations the males simply suddenly approach the female and copulate. In the other 50 percent, males display relatively brief courtship behavior. However, chimpanzee males often inspect females prior to copulation by inserting their finger into her vagina and smelling it. Male squirrel monkeys typically make frequent olfactory inspection of females prior to copulation (Latta et al. 1967). Humans clearly distinguish themselves among the primates in the long duration and complexity of their sexual foreplay.

Generally males take the initiative in sexual behavior, but in 15 percent of the copulations van Lawick-Goodall observed females clearly approached and solicited the males. In Sugiyama's group of wild chimpanzees, females initiated most of the copulations. It would be interesting to determine how frequently the human female initiates sexual encounters. Perhaps a bias for male initiation has obscured the true incidence of human female initiation.

For copulation chimpanzees use only a single position. The receptive female presents herself by crouching low, buttocks high. The male approaches from behind, and he may grasp her waist with one or both hands. Humans use a similar position for copulation, but it is relatively uncommon. Man's preference for the face to face position may be related to our upright posture and to the evolution of the human female's secondary sexual organs on the ventral surface of the body (Morris 1967). In humans the vulva is also situated more ventrally than it is in the chimpanzee, and this makes ventro-ventral copulation more feasible. It is interesting that pygmy chimpanzees, like man, copulate in the ventro-ventral position. The pygmy chimpanzee's vulva and sex swelling is more ventrally placed than in the common chimpanzee. The fact that man has hundreds of copulation positions attests to the powerful role of the human cerebral cortex in modifying basic sexual behavior.

During copulation the male chimpanzee thrusts only 5 to 25 times. One such sequence culminates in ejaculation. Both man and chimpanzee have a single mounting episode. They differ from most macaque monkeys and baboons, who have a series of copulations. Between each copulation the male baboon loses his erection, but a minute or two later he is suddenly rearoused and promptly mounts the female again. A dozen or so mounts in a series culminate in ejaculation.

Some chimpanzee males give a soft audible pant at the end of copulation, sounds heard only in this context. These respiratory sounds may be analogous to the respiratory changes in human orgasm (Masters & Johnson 1966). This is one reason to doubt that the human is the only orgasmic animal.

The nature of the social situation affects chimpanzee sexual behavior. Copulation is most likely to occur when the males are socially stimulated. For example, they become excited when two groups meet or when they arrive hungry at a favorite food source. In the excitement the males make vigorous charging displays in which penile erection is frequently seen. If there is a receptive female in the group, copulations frequently occur.

Rank or status plays a role in primate sexuality. Sugiyama's (1969) data suggest that when a series of chimpanzee males copulate with the same female, the higher ranking males generally take precedence over lower ranking ones. Adolescent males appear to avoid copulating with mature females when older males are present.

The inhibitory effect of a higher ranking male has been well demonstrated in the laboratory with rhesus monkeys (Alexander & Perachio 1970). When a male is alone with a receptive female he will copulate freely, but he is totally inhibited when a higher ranking male is introduced. On the other hand, introduction of a subdominant male increases the monkey's sexual potency in some respects.

The inhibitory effect of dominant males may have a parallel in instances of human sexual inadequacy, particularly impotence. It may arise because the human has the unique ability to fantasize, and fantasies can trigger sexually inhibitory affects such as anxiety and fear. If a male has a fantasy involving a more dominant person of either sex, such a fantasy could have an effect comparable to that which the actual presence of a higher ranking animal has for the monkey or chimpanzee. Impotence could be the consequence of this kind of fantasy. Persons who are unable to control their thoughts or fantasies would be expected to have particular difficulty and develop a fear of inadequacy. Perhaps fantasies are a major cause of sexual inhibition which triggers the fears of inadequacy that Masters and Johnson (1970) have identified as the greatest known deterrent to effective sexual functioning.

Chimpanzees are sometimes promiscuous, to use an anthropomorphic term. Females in estrus may be followed by half a dozen or more adult males and copulate with numerous males. Van Lawick-Goodall has for example observed a female copulate a dozen times with a dozen different males in the same number of minutes. Promiscuity is characteristic of most species of non-human primates. On the other hand, chimpanzee couples some-times stay together for days or weeks during the female's estrus period (Bower 1971). A similar relationship is seen in some ba-boons and macaque monkeys (Hall & DeVore 1965); it is called a consort relationship (Carpenter 1942). In man the consort pattern has been extended by marriage customs, and other cultural forces discourage any remaining evolutionary-acquired inclinations to promiscuity.

A consort pair of chimpanzees is probably entirely secretive in sexual behavior. Monkeys and baboons are less secretive during their consort relationships. The lower ranking males tend to wait until higher ranking males are not around and higher ranking males mate openly within the group. A comparison of primates empha-sizes the fact that secrecy during copulation is already developed to some extent in the nonhuman primates, but it is most highly developed in man. Since sexual privacy, like the incest taboos, is virtually pancultural, why in the course of evolution has man ac-quired this characteristic? It is well known that humans are excep-tionally sensitive to extraneous stimuli when engaged in sexual behavior. A male can lose his erection when disturbed by a door slamming or the lights being turned on (Masters & Johnson 1970). Perhaps the main function of seclusion is a reduction of distracting stimuli, and cultural taboos serve to reinforce the seclusion behav-ior.

Secrecy would appear disadvantageous to the learning of nor-mal sexual behavior. Hamburg (1970) has pointed out that obser-vation in a social context is a principal mode of learning for chim-panzees and monkeys. For example, infants watch their mother and then repeatedly attempt the same thing. An infant picks up and eats bits of food which the mother drops while eating. Infant chimpanzees also imitate adults' sexual behavior. Further, secrecy may produce culturally engendered concepts that sexual behavior is wrong or bad.

In human societies, cultural taboos inhibit incest. In chimpan-zee communities, males also refrain from certain incestual relations. Van Lawick-Goodall has never seen a male chimpanzee mate with his mother. Rhesus monkeys also appear to have a mother-son "incest taboo" (Sade 1968). Chimpanzee and monkey siblings have been observed to copulate. Chimpanzee and monkey fathers probably do not know which offspring are their own, and they probably mate with their genetic daughters; however, one case of father-daughter "incest taboo" has been observed in monkeys (Alexander 1970). These observations suggest that we may have overlooked some basic noncultural factors in the processes regulating human incest.

Gender role behavior in chimpanzees develops in the first year of life. Although an infant must be three years of age in order to survive without his mother's help, and a chimpanzee does not reach physical sexual maturity until about nine years of age, a male infant of one year can already perform a nearly complete repertoire of copulatory behaviors. Mounting and thrusting is particularly common during play. This sexual behavior, like rough and tumble play, is probably inborn and male-hormone regulated.

A number of important primate studies all point to the prenatal period and the first year of life as the crucial and definitive period for sex differentiation. Experimental studies of rhesus monkeys by Goy (1970) have shown that some masculine and feminine behaviors are determined prenatally, in a sense, imprinted by the balance of sex hormones. By injecting mother monkeys with testosterone during early pregnancy, pseudohermaphroditic and masculinized female infants were produced. When these females grew up they showed more rough and tumble play than normal females, and they were more masculine in other social behaviors, compared with females who had not been exposed to high levels of androgen in utero. Studies of Harlow and his colleagues at the University of Wisconsin have shown dramatically how the first six months after birth are a crucial period for normal sexual development. Infant monkeys raised in social isolation grew up to be totally inadequate in sexual behavior (Mason 1960). Observations of these disturbed monkeys suggested the therapeutic potential of a younger monkey (Arling et al. 1969). Harlow (1970) has rehabilitated monkeys raised for six months in social isolation by giving them access to a normal female infant much younger than they. Male infants exposed to the female "psychotherapist" develop normal rough and tumble play, a characteristic social behavior of males that would otherwise not develop. This experiment is not yet complete, but the results so far suggest that treated infants will develop normal sexual behavior later in life. I believe that this demonstration of social rehabilitation in infant monkeys has important implications for the treatment of social deviations in human children.

In my own laboratory I have studied mother-infant development in pigtailed macaque monkeys and found a number of ways in which mothers treated their male and female offspring differently (Jensen et al. 1968). In the early weeks of life mothers and their male infants showed greater maternal independence; mothers became increasingly punitive of their male infants, and they carried them, cradled them, and retained them less than they did females. Mothers of males directed more of their own total behavior toward the environment. The differences in maternal behavior suggest that the mother plays a role of instigator of the greater independence which is typical of males. Similar results have been obtained with rhesus monkeys. Mitchell (1968) found that three- to six-month-old male and female infants differed significantly in behavior toward their mothers; the males pulled and bit more. These findings support the general observation that male infants are rougher on their mothers than are females. Mitchell and Brandt (1970) characterize mothers of males as "punishers" and mothers of females as "protectors." Infants begin to behave differently in the early months of life; the males can be characterized as "doers" and the female infants as "watchers."

One of our experimental studies involved raising infant monkeys with their mothers in two different environments (Jensen et al. 1967). One environment was highly restricted (a bare cage in a sound proof room) and was called deprived. The other environment was relatively rich in stimuli. Infants growing up in the deprived environment showed slower development of independence from their mothers. The deprived environment affected male infants more adversely than it did females. Males did significantly more thumb sucking and bit their mothers more. Male infants also were rougher on their mothers in terms of hitting, pushing, shoving, yanking, jerking, and grabbing than were female infants in the privation environment. The analyses suggest that male infant monkeys more than females need a rich environment for healthy development and for the prevention of deviant behavior, and support the notion that males are more delicately balanced and more susceptible to deviation under conditions of environmental deprivation than females (Jensen 1969).

Studies of infant gender-role differentiation in monkeys and humans are complementary. This area of research also shows how concepts derived from primate research can reorient and enrich views on human development. An accumulating body of studies of human development parallels these monkey studies and supports the concept that human gender role differentiation occurs prenatally and from environmental factors operative in the first two or three years of life. This concept contrasts with classical psychoanalytic theory that gender role differentiation occurs primarily during the Oedipal period. Ehrhardt (1971) studied the development of human females who had been exposed to excessive amounts of androgen because early in the program hormones had been administered to their mothers to prevent miscarriage. This situation parallels Goy's monkey studies and the results were similar. These androgen-affected females developed significantly greater amounts of masculine play and masculine interests when compared with normal control subjects. A number of clinical studies of pseudohermaphroditic children (Hampson 1965) and transsexuals (Green & Money 1969) support the concept that gender role identity becomes fixed by two to three years of age. Studies of infant development have shown sex differences as early as three to four months of age (Bell & Costello 1964; Kagan & Lewis 1965; Zelazo 1967). Kagan (1969) believes that human mothers unconsciously or instinctively have one "program" for female infants and another different "program" for male infants and that they put one of these into effect as soon as their child is born.

The patterns of arousal and copulation in male chimpanzees and humans are comparable in several respects which suggest a similar sexual arousal mechanism.* First, male chimpanzees and

*Beach (1956) proposed a sexual arousal mechanism in rats, and Missakian et al. (1969) suggested a comparable mechanism in rhesus monkeys.

humans have a single bout of arousal and copulation which leads to ejaculation. Second, as with the chimpanzee, human sexual behavior is increased by exciting social situations. Third, behaviors used in aggressive contexts and for dominance display are also used in sexual contexts. The chimpanzee's swagger with hair erect and his stare are used for both aggression and sex display. We know that some human males are often quite aggressive in sexual behavior. Fourth, males are susceptible to inhibition of sexual behavior. The lower ranking chimpanzee waits for higher ranking ones, and adolescent males are even more inhibited by an adult male. I would suggest that an inhibiting effect of dominant males exists in the human male. If man and chimpanzee do have a similar sexual arousal mechanism we should expect that studies of chimpanzees will be particularly relevant to our understanding of ourselves.

The continual sexuality of man contrasts sharply with the seasonal sexuality of most nonhuman primates. We do not have a sexual season; the human female is sexually receptive throughout the year. Several factors may account for this difference. First, monkeys living in nature apparently have clear-cut seasonal hormonal fluctuations which control the estrous cycles (Conaway & Koford 1964). The change in food supply brought about by the rainy season may be an essential controlling factor. Second, the human cerebral cortex exerts a high degree of influence over sexual receptivity. Third, the human female has permanently enlarged breasts. These permanent sex swellings, to use zoomorphic terminology, correlate with continual receptivity. The breasts may be an important factor in stimulating human males to continual sexual behavior (Morris 1967). Although humans do not have a clear-cut seasonality of sexual behavior, they do show a slight but significant tendency toward seasonality of births (Cowgill 1969). The yearly variation in peak of births throughout the world (e.g., the two hemispheres have opposite seasons) suggests that the tendency toward human birth seasonality is determined by meteorological factors.

There is evidence that in monkeys the male sexual response is closely tied to the state of the female sexual activity. Experimental studies of free-ranging rhesus monkeys have shown how the male's sexual activity is stimulated by the presence of sexually active females (Vandenbergh 1969). During the nonbreeding season sexually quiescent males were returned to a sexually active state by exposure to females who had been brought into estrus artificially with the administration of estrogen. Similarly, male rhesus monkeys in the laboratory have been activated sexually by endocrine stimulation of females (Herbert 1967). These studies show that females communicate their endocrine state to males and point out how female sex hormones exert control over male sexual behavior.

Human females apparently communicate their sexual state to other females by means of social interaction (McClintock 1971). A group of women, either roommates or closest friends living in a college dormitory, were found to have a significant increase in synchronization of menses over a one-year period. This appeared to be mediated by social interaction rather than by weather or diet. Monkeys have a breeding season, which means some synchronization of cycles. Reproductive timing in macaque monkeys is attributed to a number of factors, including rainfall, temperature, food availability, latitude, population structure, infant survival, and disturbances in the social group (Koford 1965; Vandenbergh & Vessey 1968). One primate species, a lemur, is an extreme example of sexual synchrony. Most all mature females apparently are likely to mate at the same time by the light of a full moon (Jolly 1966). The female sexual synchronization of humans and monkeys is probably caused by various factors, and we should not be surprised to find some factors in common for monkeys and humans.

As man is hypersexual when compared with monkeys and apes, we need to determine the adaptive value of this characteristic. How does it enhance survival, comfort, or status? Some scientists say that man's perennial sexuality cements the pair-bond between husband and wife and thereby insures the family unit (Morris 1967). I would suggest that hypersexuality permits a greater reproductive rate, which in turn permits a society to deliberately select males to enhance its strength. Studies of some primitive tribes living today in South America (Nccl 1970) suggest that prehistoric man had a surplus of births and practiced infanticide, favoring males. The skeletal remains of adult fossil man show a sex ratio of 125 males to 100 females (Vellois 1961). For early man, as with primitive man today, the preponderance of males could have served the needs of warfare and hunting, thereby enhancing the strength of the group and promoting its survival. Early in human evolution hypersexuality may have facilitated hyper-aggression.

An observation of chimpanzees suggests a link between sexuality and aggression, since aggression among chimpanzees appears to be at a peak during the sexual season (Sugiyama 1969). Perhaps man's perennial and high level of sexual activity is a contributing factor to his perennial and high level of aggression.

Although man is not an ape, he once was one. We should expect that human sexual behavior is basically determined by the same processes that govern such behavior in the primates living today. These biologic processes have not entered sufficiently into our theories and ideas for understanding man. Primate studies can enrich psychiatry by providing perspective and reorientation.

REFERENCES

Alexander, B. K. Parental behavior of adult male Japanese monkeys. *Behaviour* 1970, 36: 270–85.

Alexander, M., & Perachio, A. A. An influence of social dominance on sexual behavior in rhesus monkeys. *American Zoologist* 1970, 10: 294.

Arling, G. L., Ruppenthal, G. C., & Mitchell, G. D. Aggressive behavior of the eight-year old nulliparous isolate female monkey. *Animal Behaviour* 1969, 17: 109–13.

Beach, F. A. Characteristics of masculine "sex drive." In M. R. Jones (ed.), *Nebraska symposium on motivation*. Lincoln: University of Nebraska Press, 1956.

Bell, R. Q., & Costello, N. S. Three tests for sex differences in tactile sensitivity in the newborn. *Biologia Neonatorum* 1964, 7: 335–47.

Bliss, G. Testosterone and behavior. Paper presented at the Psychiatric Research Society Meeting, San Diego, California, February 1971.

Bower, H. Lecture presented to a Short Course in Primate Behavior, University of California, Davis, June 26, 1971.

Carpenter, C. R. Sexual behavior of free ranging rhesus monkeys *Macaca mulatta. Journal of Comparative Psychology* 1942, 33: 113–42.

Conaway, C. H., & Koford, C. B. Estrous cycles and mating behavior in a free ranging band of rhesus monkeys. *Journal of Mammalogy* 1964, 45: 577–82.

Cowgill, U. M. The season of birth and its biological implications. *Journal of Reproduction and Fertility* 1969, Supplement 6: 89–103.

Crook, J. H. Social organization and the environment: aspects of contemporary social ethology. *Animal Behaviour* 1970, 18: 197–209.

Ehrhardt, A. A. Maternalism in fetal hormonal and related syndromes. In J. Zubin & J. Money (eds.), *Contemporary sexual behavior*. Baltimore: Johns Hopkins University Press, 1973.

Gartlan, J. S. Structure and function in primate society. *Folia Primatologica* 1968, 8: 89 –120.

Gartlan, J. S., & Brain, C. K. Ecology and social variability in *Cercopithecus aethiops* and *C. mitis*. In P. C. Jay (ed.), *Primates studies in adaptation and variability*. New York: Holt, Rinehart and Winston, 1968.

Goodall, J. Chimpanzees of the Gombe Stream Reserve. In I. DeVore (ed.), *Primate behavior field studies of monkeys and apes*. New York: Holt, Rinehart and Winston, 1965.

Goy, R. W. Experimental control of psychosexuality. *Philosophical Transactions of the Royal Society of London Biological* 1970, 259: 149–62.

Green, R., & Money, J. (eds.) *Trans-sexualism and sex reassignment*. Baltimore: The Johns Hopkins Press, 1969.

Hall, K. R. L., & DeVore, I. Baboon social behavior. In I. DeVore (ed.), *Primate behavior field studies of monkeys and apes*. New York: Holt, Rinehart and Winston, 1965.

Hamburg, D. Recent evidence on the evolution of aggressive behavior. *Engineering and Science* 1970, 33: 15–24.

Hampson, J. L. Determinants of psychosexual orientation. In F. A. Beach (ed.), *Sex and behavior*. New York: John Wiley, 1965.

Harlow, H. F., & Suomi, S. J. Induction and treatment of psychotherapeutic states in monkeys. *Proceedings National Academy of Science* 1970, 66 (abstract).

Herbert, J. Neural and endocrine stimuli from the female and the sexual behavior of the male rhesus monkey. *Acta Endocrinologica (Kbh)* 1967, supplement 119, 47 (abstract).

Jensen, G. D. Environmental influences on sexual differentiation. In N. Kretchmer and D. N. Walcher (eds.), *Environmental influences on genetic expression biological and behavioral aspects of sexual differentiation*. Washington, D.C.: U.S. Government Printing Office, 1969.

Jensen, G. D., Bobbitt, R. A., & Gordon, B. N. Sex differences in social interaction between infant monkeys and their mothers. In J. Wortis (ed.),

Recent advances in biological psychiatry, IX. New York: Plenum Press, 1967.

————. Sex differences in the development of independence of infant monkeys. *Behaviour* 1968, 30(1): 1-14.

Jolly, A. *Lemur behavior—A Madagascar field study.* Chicago: University of Chicago Press, 1966.

Kagan, J. Discussion on Hamburg, D. A. Sexual differentiation and the evolution of aggressive behavior in primates. In N. Kretchmer and D. N. Walcher (eds.), *Environmental influences on genetic expression biological and behavioral aspects of sexual differentiation.* Washington, D.C.: U.S. Government Printing Office, 1969.

Kagan, J., & Lewis, M. Studies of attention in the human infant. *Merrill Palmer Quarterly* 1965, 11: 95-127.

Kawamura, S. The process of sub-culture propagation among Japanese macaques. In C. H. Southwick (ed.), *Primate social behavior.* Princeton, New Jersey: D. Van Nostrand, 1963.

Koford, C. B. Population dynamics of rhesus monkeys on Cayo Santiago. In I. DeVore (ed.), *Primate behavior field studies of monkeys and apes.* New York: Holt, Rinehart and Winston, 1965.

Latta, J., Hopf, S., & Ploog, D. Observation on mating behavior and sexual play in the squirrel monkey (*Saimiri sciureus*). *Primates* 1967, 8: 229-46.

Mason, W. A. The effects of social restriction on the behavior of rhesus monkeys: I. Free social behavior. *Journal of Comparative and Physiological Psychology* 1960, 53: 583-89.

Masters, W. H., & Johnson, V. E. *Human sexual response.* Boston: Little, Brown, 1966.

————. *Human sexual inadequacy.* Boston: Little, Brown, 1970.

McClintock, M. K. Menstrual synchrony and suppression. *Nature* 1971, 229: 244-45.

Missakian, E. A., Del Rio, L. R., & Myers, R. E. Reproductive behavior of captive male rhesus monkeys (*Macaca mulatta*). *Communications in Behavioral Biology* 1969, part A., nos. 4-6: 231-35.

Mitchell, G. Attachment differences in male and female infant monkeys. *Child Development* 1968, 39: 611-20.

Mitchell, G., & Brandt, E. M. Behavioral differences related to experience of mother and sex of infant in the rhesus monkey. *Developmental Psychology* 1970, 3(1): 149.

Morris, D. *The naked ape.* New York: McGraw-Hill, 1967. (Republished: New York: Dell Publishing, 1969.)

Neel, J. V. Lessons from a "primitive" people. *Science* 1970, 170(3960): 815–22.

Reynolds, V., & Reynolds, F. Chimpanzees of the Budongo Forest. In I. DeVore (ed.), *Primate behavior field studies of monkeys and apes.* New York: Holt, Rinehart and Winston, 1965.

Sade, D. S. Inhibition of son-mother mating among free-ranging rhesus monkeys. In J. H. Masserman (ed.), *Science and psychoanalysis Vol. XII Animal and human.* New York: Grune & Stratton, 1968.

Sugiyama, Y. Social behavior of chimpanzees in the Budongo Forest, Uganda. *Primates* 1969, 10: 197–225.

Vandenbergh, J. G. Endocrine coordination in monkeys: male sexual responses to the female. *Physiology and Behavior* 1969, 4: 261–64.

Vandenbergh, J. G., & Vessey, S. Seasonal breeding of free-ranging rhesus monkeys and related ecological factors. *Journal of Reproduction and Fertility* 1968, 15: 71–79.

van Lawick-Goodall, J. The behaviour of free-living chimpanzees in the Gombe Stream Reserve. *Animal Behaviour Monographs* 1968, I (Part 3).

Vellois, H. V. The social life of early man: the evidence of skeletons. In S. L. Washburn (ed.), *Social life of early man.* Chicago: Aldine, 1961.

Washburn, S. L. Behavior and the origin of man. *Rockefeller University Review* 1968, Jan.–Feb.: 10–19.

Zelazo, P. R. Differential three month old vocalizations to sex of strangers. Paper presented at the International Congress of Psychology, London, 1967.

chapter 3

Sexual Behavior: The Result of an Interaction*

Knut Larsson†

In experimental work on animals one has become used to thinking of the sexual behavior of the male and that of the female as two different, entirely independent patterns of responses. Sexual behavior, however, is an essentially social phenomenon. The presence or absence of the male mating pattern, as well as its organization and orientation, take place as responses to the female. Similarly, the female's lordotic response, acceptance or rejection of the male, and various invitation movements occur as responses to stimuli provided by the male. The occurrence of a particular sexual response as well as the physiological state of the participants are therefore best understood and investigated within a social context.

*The work was supported in part by grants from the Swedish Council for Research in Social Sciences and the National Bank of Sweden.

†Knut Larsson, Ph.D., Institute of Animal Behavior, Rutgers University; now at Department of Psychology, Goteborg University, Goteborg, Sweden.

Some experimental evidence will be reviewed, demonstrating the importance of studying sexual behavior within the social perspective of two mutually interacting individuals, rather than as a study of two independently acting individuals. The presence and behavior of the male will be shown to influence the physiological state of the female, and, conversely, the behavior of the female will be shown to determine the behavior and physiological condition of the male. Two examples show the extent to which the behavior of the female and of the male are usually coordinated during mating. One example is derived from a study by Beach on "coitus interruptus" in dogs (Beach 1970). The other, reported by Diakow (1971), shows how deficits in the sensory feedback from the female during mating in cats affect the male's behavior pattern.

BEHAVIORAL COORDINATION BETWEEN THE MALE AND THE FEMALE DURING COITUS

During mating, dogs form a genital lock; the penis is swollen within the vagina and cannot be withdrawn until detumescence begins. Normally a lock may last 15 to 30 minutes. Occasionally, however, coitus may be interrupted spontaneously before locking has occurred (Beach 1970). Under this condition a drastically changed behavior pattern appears. Normally the female is calm and stands practically motionless as locking takes place. When coitus is interrupted within one or two minutes after insertion, the female becomes hyperactive. She races around the male in tight circles, prancing in front of him, barking at him, licking his erected penis, and repeatedly mounting him. The male, in turn, exhibits a phantom lock. For 5 to 15 minutes he stands nearly motionless with his back arched, his tail erect, and exhibits rhythmic contractions, showing little or no response to environmental stimulation.

Beach explained these observations in the following way. The estrous dog reacts to the chasing male by developing a high level of sexual excitement, a condition further intensified when the penis is inserted into the vagina. The pressure exerted against the vaginal walls by the swelling penis has an inhibitory influence on the neural mechanisms previously responsible for the female's hyperactivity; the female calms down. If this stimulation continues for about 5 minutes the intense state of arousal abates and interruption of coitus no longer disturbs the animal. If, by contrast, coitus is interrupted within a few minutes after insertion, the hyperactivity persists.

The male reaches a maximal level of arousal fairly quickly, within 15 to 25 seconds. During this period erection is completed and ejaculatory contractions are initiated. If the male is interrupted before this period is ended, his behavior changes in a manner similar to that of the female under the same circumstances. He becomes hyperactive, mounting the female repeatedly. If, however, insertion has lasted long enough for rhythmical contractions to begin and is then interrupted, a series of events is triggered similar to those occurring during normal coitus, including a sort of coma-like unresponsiveness to the environment.

The observations reported by Diakow (1971) involved mating behavior in cats. Normally the male cat grasps the female's neck and then mounts her. After repeated mounts insertion takes place. Each mount is terminated by the female who throws the male off while she hisses and shows aggressive behavior. This hissing is not as intense as the copulatory call following ejaculations. After each mount she proceeds to roll about on the floor, alternately stretching and flexing her trunk muscles and twisting violently from side to side. During this after-reaction to mating, the female is completely unreceptive to the male and may even attack him if he tries to mount her.

Diakow desensitized parts of the female genital organs by interrupting surgically those branches of the pelvic plexus that innervate the vagina and parts of the uterus. She observed that following the operation the female showed much less vigorous rubbing and rolling behavior. The copulatory call, normally occurring after ejaculation has taken place, was recorded less frequently. Most interesting was the finding that the male often was not dislodged after the intromission. He remained on the back of the female even after ejaculation (as evidenced by sperm in the urogenital sinus of the female) and after withdrawal of the penis. After a short period of time, still remaining on her back, the male made several more insertions and ejaculations.

These two examples may serve as demonstrations of the mutual dependency of the male and the female for successful copulation, a dependency which is usually not revealed unless the normal mating pattern is spontaneously or experimentally interrupted. In the case of the dog, interruption of coitus drastically changes the performances both of the male and the female, the extent of the disturbances varying with the particular phase of activity in which the interruption occurs. In the female cat interruption of the sensory inflow from the genital organs causes behavioral changes which, in turn, alter the normal copulatory behavior of the male.

Realizing how intimately coordinated the behaviors of the female and the male usually are during copulation, we will proceed to consider evidence showing that the physiological state of the female is influenced by the presence and behavior of the male.

REPRODUCTIVE FUNCTION OF THE FEMALE AS DETERMINED BY EXTEROCEPTIVE STIMULATION FROM THE MALE

Social Influences upon the Estrous Cycle

According to the traditional view the female laboratory mouse shows a regular estrous cycle, being in heat every fourth or fifth day, unless pregnancy, lactation, or pseudopregnancy occur. Recent evidence has shown, however, that this picture is incomplete. The cycle is highly flexible and reflects the social conditions under which the female is living.

Bruce (1965) has shown that when female mice are housed individually they usually come into heat every 5 to 6 days. When housed in small groups of 3 or 4 they tend to develop pseudopregnancy, and when they are kept together in large groups of 25–30 they develop a state of constant diestrus (Whitten 1958, 1959). A mutual suppression of the cycle thus takes place. Whitten (1959) presented a male confined within a wire basket to a group of female mice, all of which were in diestrus. Within 3 to 4 days most of the females exhibited estrous behavior. Not only does introduction of a male terminate the state of diestrus induced by other females, but the cycles shorten and become more regular. In a variation of the above experiment Bruce (1962) removed an encaged male from a group of 30 females which had been exposed to the male for a period of time. The regular cyclicity previously induced by the male was abolished, and in 7 of the females the cycle was entirely suppressed.

The male can also be used as a contraceptive. This most dramatic effect of the presence of a male was demonstrated by Bruce in a series of papers (Bruce 1959, 1961, 1962, 1963; Bruce & Parrott 1961; Parkes & Bruce 1961). If a recently mated female is exposed to a male other than the stud male, pregnancy is blocked and estrus returns 4 to 5 days after mating. Exposure to other females does not interfere with pregnancy (Bruce 1959). As with the estrous cycle, proximity is sufficient for the occurrence of pregnancy-block; direct contact is not necessary. Unlike the social effects on the estrous cycle, which are most likely to occur within the strain, strain differences are important for the occurrence of pregnancy-block. Presenting the recently mated females with males from several different strains, Parkes and Bruce (1961) found that a high proportion of blocked pregnancies occurred whenever the stud male and presented male belonged to different strains. The strain which the female belonged to was not a relevant factor. Pregnancy-block is most easily induced during the first days after mating. The effect is thereafter less easily provoked and is totally abolished after the sixth day (Bruce 1961).

The critical stimulus for pregnancy-block as well as synchrony of the estrous cycle appears to be odor. Females made anosmic by removal of the olfactory lobes were immune to exposure to alien males (Bruce & Parrott 1961). Pregnancy-block also occurred when the newly mated female was housed in a box earlier vacated by a strange male of the same or a different strain. Marsden and Bronson (1964) induced estrous synchrony by placing male urine on the nose of the female, and a similar effect was obtained by exposing mice to a stream of air from a group of male mice (Whitten, Bronson, & Greenstein, 1968).

The presence of a male also influences the onset of sexual maturation. Vandenbergh (1967) compared the development of sexual maturity in one group of female mice that had been isolated since weaning with another group that either had been reared together with an adult male or with an adult female. Sexual maturity as evidenced by vaginal opening, first estrus, or first mating was hastened in those groups where the pups had been exposed to an adult, the accelerated maturation being particularly marked in the group reared with the male. Even in this case the effect seemed to be stimulated by odor (Vandenbergh 1969).

Estrous synchrony and olfactory block to pregnancy have been demonstrated in the deer mouse (Bronson & Marsden 1964; Elefteriou, Bronson, & Zarrow 1962; Marsden & Bronson 1964), but not in other species except for the house mouse. However, recent evidence has been reported that girls living close together in dormitories tend to show synchronized menstrual cycles and to have shortened cycles when exposed to males (McClintock 1971). This suggests that the menstrual cycle in the human female is vulnerable to exteroceptive stimulation as is the estrous cycle of the mouse. The frequency with which psychological disturbances may result in an abrupt alteration of menstrual function, causing irregular uterine bleeding or amenorrhea, is another indication of its vulnerability (Rakoff 1968).

Effects of the Male's Copulatory Behavior on the Hormonal Condition of the Female

Using rats as the experimental animal, Adler, in a series of elegant studies, has demonstrated how the hormonal condition of the female may vary according to successive phases of the male's copulatory pattern (Adler 1969; Adler, Resko, & Goy 1970; Adler & Zoloth 1970; Wilson, Adler, & Le Boeuf 1965).

The male rat ejaculates after a series of repeated mounts and dismounts. The number of intromissions preceding ejaculation varies between 3 and 30. After ejaculation the male loses all sexual interest for awhile. He may then mount the female again and ejaculate a second time. It is easy to imagine the series of intromissions as representing a means by which the sexual excitement of the male is increased until it culminates in ejaculation. Adler (1969) demonstrated, however, that the series of intromissions preceding ejaculation also has a specific function for the female. He compared two groups of females, one in which the females received a high number of intromissions and another in which the females received only a few intromissions. Pregnancy occurred in 84 percent of the females in the high intromission group and in only 20 percent of the low intromission group. Further experiments showed that for conception to occur the female must receive a minimal number of two intromissions. Implantation of eggs in the uterus would not occur with less than this number of intromissions, suggesting that the multiple intromissions induced the hormonal state that is a prerequisite for ovum implantation. The intromissions also facilitate sperm transport. Without at least one intromission before ejaculation the sperm do not pass from the vagina into the uterus.

How does the male's series of intromissions work to bring about these effects? Since progesterone, together with estrogen, is the hormone mainly responsible for egg implantation, it is possible that the intromissions induce secretion of progesterone and that a certain number of intromissions is necessary for a sufficient amount of progesterone to be secreted. This hypothesis was confirmed by Adler, Resko, and Goy (1970). They measured the amount of progesterone in the plasma after mating and found a higher quantity secreted after the female had received multiple intromissions than after no intromissions.

Since the pre-ejaculatory phase in the male sexual behavior has a specific effect on female reproductive function, one might ask if the postejaculatory phase of sexual inactivity also influences the female cycle. This was demonstrated in a recent study by Adler and Zoloth (1970). If immediately after ejaculation a female was placed with a new male and intromissions took place within 15 minutes, sperm transport and subsequent pregnancy was inhibited. A similar effect could be obtained by manual stimulation of the vagina, showing the importance of direct vaginal stimulation. The results demonstrated that the period of rest following ejaculation ensures the female the tranquility that is necessary for fertilization to take place.

Ovulation Induced by Copulation

In some species (e.g., the rabbit and the cat) ovulation is not induced "spontaneously" but as a response to copulation. The reflexogenically induced ovulation is perhaps the best known example of the importance of the male/female interaction and has served as a model for research on the mechanism for ovulation in mammals (Everett 1961). Diakow (1971), in her previously mentioned studies on the cat, found that cervical denervation tended to abolish this response. Stimulation of the vagina and cervix with a glass rod failed to induce ovulation in 6 of 9 denervated cats while the same stimulation caused ovulation in 7 out of 10 sham-operated females. The results suggest that ovulation takes place as a response to specific stimulation of the vagina and cervix, rather than as a consequence of a sexual excitement, as was previously believed (Brooks 1937).

Conclusion

Examples from experiments with mice and rats give remarkable evidence that stimuli associated with the male may alter the physiological conditions of the female. In mice the presence of a male was sufficient to influence the estrous cycle, and the normal course of pregnancy might be interrupted by the mere odor of a male. In rats the physiological condition of the female was altered with successive phases of the male's mating pattern.

Two kinds of stimuli, odor and touch, were effective in influencing and coordinating the behavior of the male and the female. Odor influenced the general social situation by causing females to respond sexually to males, whereas tactile stimulation had more specific effects in adjusting the ongoing sexual activity of two individuals. The physiological mechanisms by which these effects are mediated have not been sufficiently explained, but in all probability they are of a neuroendocrine nature.

THE BEHAVIOR OF THE MALE AS DETERMINED BY THE PHYSIOLOGICAL CONDITION OF THE FEMALE

Studies on Rats

The receptive female rat shows a highly characteristic behavior; an essential component is the lordosis display. With her feet firmly planted on the floor and her rear legs slightly spread, she depresses her lumbar region so that her belly nearly touches the substrate, raising the perineum to a nearly vertical position. In this way her genital region is exposed and made readily accessible to the male. The fully receptive female, when not engaged in lordosis, also shows an increased locomotor activity, including various kinds of invitation responses. Adopting a stiff-legged, hopping gait she alternately approaches the male and moves away from him presenting her anogenital area.

We have studied two of the various qualities in the female that make her attractive to the male: locomotion and odor (Sodersten & Larsson, unpubl.). The importance of the locomotor activity of the female was demonstrated in the following way. Female rats, brought into heat by injections of estradiol-benzoate (10µg/kg) 48 hours before testing and progesterone (0.4 mg/animal) 6 hours before testing, were injected with a tranquilizer, tetrabenazine (10 mg/kg). While maintaining the animals in a state of receptivity, tetrabenazine, in the dosage injected, more or less immobilizes the females. Thirty minutes after the drug injection the female was presented with a highly sexually experienced and normally active male. The behavior was observed until the male had ejaculated once and had started a second series of copulations. Testing was interrupted if ejaculation did not occur within 30 minutes after the first intromission had been attained or if the copulatory activity was not resumed within 20 minutes after ejaculation. Each male was tested six times, half of the tests were with a tetrabenazine-treated female and half of the tests were with a saline-treated female.

The following behavior was recorded: (1) intromission latency—latency between presentation of the female and first intromission; (2) ejaculation latency—latency between first intromission and ejaculation; (3) postejaculatory interval—interval between ejaculation and next intromission; (4) mounts—mounting of the female with pelvic thrusting; (5) intromission—mounting with vaginal penetration.

Table 1 shows the results of this experiment. When males were presented with a sedated female the ejaculatory latency was prolonged fourfold and the postejaculatory interval was doubled. No statistically significant changes were observed in the number of mounts and intromissions preceding ejaculation. In addition to

Table 1. *Sexual behavior of 13 male rats presented with sexually receptive females treated with estrogen and progesterone alone (control) or, in addition, with tetrabenazine (experimental)*

	Experimental Median	Control Median	p
Intromission latency (in min)	3.6	0.5	$< .05$
Ejaculation latency (in min)	26.2	7.3	$< .02$
Post-ejaculatory interval (in min)	11.3	6.1	$< .02$
Mounts before ejaculation	5.0	4.5	NS
Intromissions before ejaculation	5.0	8.0	NS

Note: Medians refer to the performances during three tests under each condition. Comparisons were performed by help of the Wilcoxen T-test.

these quantitative changes in the behavior, qualitative alterations were observed, the males displaying an increased number of head mounts.

The results of this experiment demonstrated the role the female's locomotor activity plays in the male's responses. In the presence of a more or less immobilized female the male displays much less sexual activity, and his mounting attempts become less adequately directed.

Olfactory stimuli, presumably associated with the female, play an important role in sexually activating the male. Following anosmia the animals become less likely to engage in mating, and the response latencies tend to be prolonged. The impairment may have several different causes. In the absence of smell the males may be less aroused sexually, they may be more easily emotionally disturbed, or they may simply have difficulty in finding the female. To get a more detailed picture of the behavior deficits occurring in the anosmic male, an experimental situation was arranged in which the female was tethered so that the male had to search for her. Furthermore, by recording the proximity of the female to the male in terms of approaches and withdrawals, an attempt was made to measure her attractiveness to the male versus his ability to locate her.

Participating in this experiment were 10 intact male rats and 18 males made anosmic by removal of the olfactory bulbs. All animals showed preoperatively a consistently high level of sexual activity. Mating was observed under two different experimental conditions. In one series of tests the mating arena was a large cage, 1 1/2 X 1 1/2 meters. While the male could move freely in the arena, the receptive female was tethered by a string in the midst of the arena, allowing her to move within a diameter of 40 cm. In a second series of tests mating took place in a cage, 40 X 40 cm. Although tethered, the female had access to all parts of the cage. Testing was interrupted (1) if intromission had not taken place within 15 minutes after the presentation of the female; (2) if the male did not ejaculate within 45 minutes after the initial intromission; or (3) if intromissions were not resumed within 15 minutes after ejaculation. The animals were allowed only one ejaculation.

In addition to the behavior recorded in the previous experiment the following measures were used: (1) Visit: a series of mounts and/or intromissions interrupted by no behavior other than autogenital grooming and investigation of the genitals of the female. A visit was defined as that initiated at the time of the first mount and ended at the time of the last mount when the male left the female; (2) mounts per visit: number of mounts and/or intromissions per visit; (3) intervisit interval: time from the onset of one visit to the onset of the succeeding visit; (4) time out: time between the last mount of one visit and the first mount of the next visit; (5) intermount interval: time between the mounts and/ or intromissions during one visit.

Table 2 shows the number of animals that, under the various conditions of testing, displayed at least one mount, intromission, or ejaculation. When tested in the small cage no statistically significant decrease took place in the number of anosmic animals showing the various response patterns, but in the large cage fewer anosmic animals showed intromissions and ejaculations than the control group. A detailed picture of the behavioral changes occurring in the mating pattern is shown in Table 3. The behavior

Table 2. *Sexual performances of intact and anosmic males in a large cage (1.5 × 1.5 m) compared to a small cage (0.4 × 0.4 m)*

| | Large Cage | | | Small Cage | | |
	Experimental	Control	*p*	Experimental	Control	*p*
Mount	14	10	NS	18	10	NS
Intromission	12	10	< .05	16	10	NS
Ejaculation	11	10	< .03	13	10	NS
Number of subjects	18	10		18	10	

NS $p > .05$

Note: The figures indicate the number of animals that displayed, under the various conditions, at least 1 mount, 1 intromission, or 1 ejaculation. Group comparisons were performed by help of the Fisher exact probability test.

exhibited by the anosmic animals in the large arena differed significantly in all components measured. The response latencies to the female were prolonged, and the ejaculation was preceded by a greater number of mounts and intromissions, suggesting a lowered excitatory effect of each response to the female. Similar changes were observed when the males mated in the small cage, although

Table 3. *Sexual performances in intact (N:10) and anosmic (N:21) male rats when presented with a tethered sexually receptive female*

| | Experimental | Control | |
	Median	Median	*p*
Intromission latency (in min)	0.5	0.2	< .002
Ejaculation latency (in min)	25.7	2.7	< .002
Post-ejaculatory interval (in min)	8.2	4.4	< .002
Mounts before ejaculation	11.0	2.5	< .002
Intromissions before ejaculation	10.0	7.0	< .02

Note: The figures refer to performances in three tests.

under this condition the contact latencies of the anosmic animals were within the range of the control animals.

By studying in more detail the approaches of the male toward the female, we expected to obtain some indication of whether or not the impaired sexual performances were due to orientation difficulties. Counting the frequency of approaches of the male to the tethered female ("visits" to the area within which the female could move), we observed that the anosmic rats made many more visits to the female than the intact rats did (Table 4). During each visit, however, the anosmic males performed fewer mounts than the normal rats. The intervisit interval was the same for the operated and the unoperated animals. Whereas the intact males tended to stay in the vicinity of the female and make several repeated mounts before leaving her, the anosmic males were constantly running in and out of the area of the female.

These observations do not support the hypothesis that the impaired sexual activity of the anosmic males is due to orientation difficulties. In the absence of olfactory cues the male becomes more reluctant to mount the female and shows increased difficulty in attaining ejaculation, as evidenced by the large number of mounts and intromissions preceding ejaculation and the lowered

Table 4. *Sexual performances and approach-withdrawal behavior toward a female tethered in the midst of the large cage*

Behavior component	Experimental Median	Control Median	p
Visits	14	4	$< .002$
Mounts and intromissions per visit	1.4	2.5	$< .02$
Intervisit interval (in min)	0.8	0.8	NS
Time out (in min)	0.7	0.6	$< .05$
Intermount interval (in min)	0.1	0.2	NS
Number of subjects	16	10	

Note: Group comparisons were performed by the Mann–Whitney U-test.

incidence of ejaculation. These effects of anosmia are particularly marked when mating is performed in a large arena, giving the male less opportunity to meet the female. The anosmic male, after having encountered the female and mounted her, tended to with-draw quickly as if he were afraid of her.

In summary, the sexual behavior of the male rat cannot be correctly accounted for without due consideration of the female. The locomotor activity displayed by the receptive female increases the opportunities of contacts with the male and may in addition increase the intensity of the visual, auditory, and olfactory stimu-lation provided by her. The smell of the female appears to play a particularly important role in eliciting and maintaining the male's sexual activity.

Studies on Rhesus Monkeys

Like most other nondomesticated mammals, rhesus monkeys show a seasonal variation in reproductive function. During part of the year the gonads regress, and the sexual activity diminishes or is totally abolished. This rhythm is supposed to be determined by seasonal variation in temperature—humidity, food, and other en-vironmental factors—while little attention has been given to the social environment. In an attempt to study the influence of social factors upon the seasonal variation in endocrine function Vanden-bergh (1969) performed the following experiment.

The animals participating in the study belonged to a troop of free-ranging rhesus monkeys living in island colonies near Puerto Rico. The monkeys show a distinct seasonal variation in reproduc-tion. During the nonmating season the testes regress and mating ceases. Four males were removed from this population and placed in outdoor cages adjacent to but visually isolated from 3 ovariecto-mized females, which were placed in similar cages. The design of the experiment was to monitor the behavioral and endocrine states of the males for 16 days before the females received estrogen replacement therapy and for the 16 days after daily treatment of the females with estrogen. Testicular biopsies were taken before and after the males were exposed to estrogen-treated females. In addition, mating was observed in daily testing during both periods of exposure.

During the prehormone period only occasional mounts were observed. After the females received estrogen, mounts and ejaculations occurred. The copulatory behavior was similar to that described for normal mating, but sperm was not found until the end of the posthormone period. It thus appeared that the females elicited a behavioral climax in the males which was indistinguishable from normal copulatory behavior, but which was not accompanied by actual insemination until late in the posthormonal period. Furthermore, the male's testes were relatively inactive before observations began and after exposure to ovariectomized females. Following exposure to estrogen-treated females, testicular size, seminiferous tubule diameter, and sex skin redness increased in each of the males.

The sexual reactivation of otherwise sexually inactive males by estrous females indicates (1) the important role hormones play in the expression of primate sexual behavior; (2) that females communicate their endocrine state to males; and (3) the existence of a system for the synchronization of mating activities between the sexes.

As far as the first problem is concerned estrogen appears to be the hormone responsible for making the females attractive to the males. This conclusion is substantiated by the observations of Michael and of Herbert of the interaction between the male and the female rhesus monkey during mating (Herbert 1970; Michael 1968). A gonadectomized female does not provoke the male to any mounting attempts, while estrogen treatment restores his interest in her.

A second problem is related to the mechanisms by which the females communicate their endocrine state to the male. The female rhesus monkey displays a great variety of response patterns aimed at stimulating the male to mount. She looks at him, orients her body toward him, reaches out for him, and approaches him. Particularly conspicuous is her presenting behavior—displaying her anogenital region toward him, sometimes backing up close to his face. It might be assumed that gonadectomy decreases the amount of invitation responses, thereby providing the male with less stimulation. This, however, does not seem to be the case. An increase in the number of presentations is sometimes seen even after gonadectomy (Herbert 1970). A second guess might be that the critical factor is the bright red color of the "sexual" skin around the vagina, which turns whitish in the absence of estrogen. However, application of estrogen to the skin area, although making the skin red, does not affect the behavior of the male (Herbert 1966).

A third guess is that estrogen influences the vaginal epithelium, thereby changing its consistency and perhaps its odor. This hypothesis appears to be the correct one. Application of estrogen directly into the vagina resulted in resumption of the sexual activity of the male (Herbert 1966). The crucial stimulus for this seems to be odor. Michael and Keverne (1968) showed that the male was attracted to the female by distant olfactory cues.

While estrogen appears to be particularly important for the attractiveness of the female to the male, androgen seems to be a critical factor in determining her state of receptivity. In an unsuccessful attempt to increase the females' attractiveness, Herbert and Trimble (1967) injected the females with testosterone. The males remained as little interested in the females as before, but the testosterone-treated females exhibited a great increase in the number of presentations. Further systematic experiments confirmed this observation and suggested that androgen, secreted by the adrenal glands, determines the level of receptivity of the female. Suppression of the ACTH secretion by dexamethasone sodium phosphate (Everitt & Herbert 1969) or adrenalectomy (Herbert 1970) resulted in a diminished number of presentations by the female and an increased number of rejections of the male.

CONCLUSIONS

After surveying evidence from the testing of a variety of species and of a fair sampling of sexual behavior patterns, we have found it to be of critical importance for an understanding of reproductive function to conceive of sexual behavior as the result of an interaction between the male and the female. The male responds to stimuli provided by the female, while the female is dependent upon appropriate stimulation from the male. The female acts according to her physiological state which is, in turn, determined in part by the behavior of the male. The behavior exhibited by one partner thus generates physiological changes in the other, and an organized pattern of behavioral and physiological responses emerges. Depending upon the characteristics of the reproductive pattern of a given species, there is a variety in stimuli influencing the behavior and the particular phase influenced by these stimuli.

From another point of view, this survey indicates the importance of the study of sexual behavior as a social phenomenon, implying more than the synchrony of two behavioral patterns exhibited by independently acting individuals. The organization of sexual behavior is not additive in a simple sense, but represents an integrated series of behavioral patterns which are inseparable, descriptively, causally, and functionally.

REFERENCES

Adler, N. T. Effects of the male's copulatory behavior on successful pregnancy of the female rat. *Journal of Comparative and Physiological Psychology* 1969, 69: 613-22.

Adler, N. T., Resko, J. A., & Goy, R. W. The effect of copulatory behavior on hormonal change in the female rat prior to implantation. *Physiology and Behavior* 1970, 5: 1003-07.

Adler, N. T., & Zoloth, S. R. Copulatory behavior can inhibit pregnancy in female rats. *Science* 1970, 168: 1480-82.

Beach, F. A. Coital behavior in dogs. IX. Sequelae to "Coitus interruptus" in males and females. *Physiology and Behavior* 1970, 5: 263-68.

Bronson, F. H., & Marsden, H. M. Male-induced synchrony of estrus in deer mice. *General Comparative Endocrinology* 1964, 4: 634-37.

Brooks, C. M. The role of the cerebral cortex and of various sense organs in the excitation and execution of mating activity in the rabbit. *American Journal of Physiology* 1937, 120: 544-53.

Bruce, H. M. An exteroceptive block to pregnancy in the mouse. *Nature* 1959, 184: 105.

———. Time relations in the pregnancy-block induced in mice by strange males. *Journal of Reproduction and Fertility* 1961, 2: 138.

The author wishes to thank George Delrymple, Carol Diakow, Harvey Feder, Joan Herrmann, and Jay Rosenblatt for their helpful comments and criticism during the preparation of this paper. He also appreciated the opportunity to read the prepublication manuscript of Dr. Diakow on effects of genital desensitization. Contribution No. 120 from Institute of Animal Behavior.

_____. The importance of the environment on the establishment of pregnancy in the mouse. *Animal Behavior* 1962, **10**: 389–90.

_____. Olfactory block to pregnancy among grouped mice. *Journal of Reproduction and Fertility* 1963, **6**: 451–60.

_____. The influence of environment on behaviour, with special reference to reproduction in mice. *Cosmet. Toxicol.* 1965, **3**: 193–98.

Bruce, H. M., & Parrott, D. V. M. Role of olfactory sense in pregnancy-block by strange males. *Science* 1961, **131**: 1526.

Diakow, C. Effects of genital desensitization on mating behavior and ovulation in the female cat. *Physiology and Behavior* 1971, **7**: 47–54.

Elefteriou, B. E., Bronson, F. H., & Zarrow, M. X. Interaction of olfactory and other environmental stimuli on implantation in the deer mouse. *Science* 1962, **137**: 764.

Everett, J. W. The mammalian female reproductive cycle and its controlling mechanisms. In W. C. Young (ed.), *Sex and luteal secretions*. Baltimore: Williams & Wilkins, 1961, pp. 497–555.

Everitt, B. J., & Herbert, J. Ovarian hormones and sexual preference in rhesus monkeys. *Journal of Endocrinology* 1969, **43**: 31.

Herbert, J. The effect of oestrogen applied directly to the genitalia upon the sexual attractiveness of the female rhesus monkey. *Excerpta Medica International Congress*, Series III 1966: 212.

_____. Neural and hormonal factors concerned in sexual attraction between rhesus monkeys. *Proceedings of the 2nd International Congress on Primates* 1968, **2**: 41–49.

_____. Hormones and reproductive behaviour in rhesus and talapin monkeys. *Journal of Reproduction and Fertility*, Suppl. 1970, **11**: 119–40.

Herbert, J., & Trimble, M. R. Effect of oestradiol and testosterone on the sexual receptivity and attractiveness of the female rhesus monkey. *Nature* 1967, **216**: 165–66.

Marsden, H. M., & Bronson, F. H. Estrous synchrony in mice: alteration by exposure to male urine. *Science* 1964, **144**: 1469.

McClintock, M. K. Menstrual synchrony and suppression. *Nature* 1971, **229**: 244–45.

Michael, R. P. Gonadal hormones and the control of primate behavior. In R. P. Michael (ed.), *Endocrinology and human behaviour*. London: Oxford University Press, 1968, pp. 69–93.

Michael, R. P., & Keverne, E. B. Pheromones in the communication of sexual status in primates. *Nature* 1968, **218**: 746–49.

Parkes, A. S, & Bruce, H. M. Olfactory stimuli in mammalian reproduction. *Science* 1961, **134**: 1049–54.

Rakoff, A. E. Endocrine mechanisms in psychogenic amenorrhoea. In R. P. Michael (ed.), *Endocrinology and human behaviour.* London: Oxford University Press, 1968, pp. 139–60.

Vandenbergh, J. G. Effect of the presence of a male on the sexual maturation of female mice. *Endocrinology* 1967, 81: 345–49.

––––––. Endocrine coordination in monkeys: male sexual responses to the female. *Physiology and Behavior* 1969, 4: 261–64.

Whitten, W. K. Modification of the oestrus cycle of the mouse by external stimuli associated with the male. *Journal of Endocrinology* 1958, 17: 307–13.

––––––. Occurrence of anoestrus in mice caged in groups. *Journal of Endocrinology* 1959, 18: 102–7.

Whitten, W. K., Bronson, F. H., & Greenstein, J. A. Estrus-inducing pheromone of male mice: transport by movement of air. *Science* 1968, 161: 584–85.

Wilson, J. R., Adler, N., & Le Boeuf, B. The effects of intromission frequency on successful pregnancy in the female rat. *Proceedings of the National Academy of Science* 1965, 53: 1392–95.

chapter 4

Special Award Lecture: New Findings on Brain Function and Sociosexual Behavior

Paul D. MacLean*

Near the turn of mid-century when I began experimental work on forebrain mechanisms of emotional behavior, I was puzzled by the lack of direct evidence of a representation of sexual functions. It was as though nature, a master playwright and producer, had staged a new production and inadvertently overlooked a part for one of the main actors!

In a series of brain stimulation studies on the squirrel monkey it became evident that there was a fairly extensive representation of elemental sexual functions in the forebrain. A brief review of the published findings will serve to introduce another phase of my research concerned with forebrain mechanisms underlying species-specific forms of sociosexual behavior. The work deals specifically

*Paul D. MacLean, M.D., Chief, Laboratory of Brain Evolution and Behavior, National Institute of Mental Health, Bethesda, Maryland.

with the effects of brain lesions on an inborn, genital display of the squirrel monkey that has important communicative value in social and sexual activities. Finally, I will discuss some evolutionary implications of the findings in regard to human behavior.

BACKGROUND CONSIDERATIONS

In its evolution (Figure 1) the human brain expands in hierarchic fashion along the lines of three basic patterns that may be characterized as reptilian, paleomammalian, and neomammalian (Mac-Lean 1962, 1964a, 1967). Although radically different in chemistry and structure, the three cerebrotypes establish extensive interconnections and function together as a triune brain (MacLean 1970). There is evidence, however, that each cerebrotype is capable of operating somewhat independently.

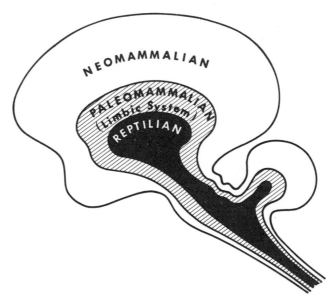

Fig. 1. *The primate brain evolves and enlarges along the lines of three basic patterns that may be characterized as reptilian, paleomammalian, and neomammalian. The limbic system, which is largely a paleomammalian derivative, occupies an intermediate position in the hierarchy (MacLean 1967).*

The main counterpart of the reptilian forebrain in mammals is represented by the striatal complex, comprising the corpus striatum (caudate nucleus + putamen) and globus pallidus. It has been traditional to assign purely motor functions to these large ganglia. The display studies to be described emphasize the need for challenging this established pedagogical view. At our new field Laboratory of Brain Evolution and Behavior, near Poolesville, Md., we plan to test the hypothesis that the mammalian striatal complex provides an intelligence for such genetically constituted forms of behavior as selection of homesite, establishing and defending territory, hunting, homing, mating, breeding, forming social hierarchies, and similar behavior. Comparative observations suggest that this particular counterpart of the reptilian forebrain may also account for a predisposition to obsessive-compulsive, ritualistic, superstitious, and imitative behavior.

The rudimentary reptilian cortex is presumed to have undergone expansion and differentiation in the lost animal forms that were antecedent to lower mammals. The degree to which the cortex had advanced in earliest mammals is a matter of speculation. In all existing lower and higher mammals most of the cortex with primordial features is found in a convolution which Broca (1878) called the great limbic lobe because it surrounds the brainstem. In 1952 I suggested the term "limbic system" as a suitable designation for the limbic cortex and structures of the brainstem with which it has primary connections (MacLean 1952). This paleomammalian derivative is anatomically and functionally an integrated system. It has been found to play an important role in emotional behavior, and shortly I will summarize evidence that it is directly involved in sexual functions.

The hallmark of the neomammalian brain is a refined cortex called neocortex which mushrooms late in evolution and culminates in man, providing the essential neural substrate for reading, writing, and arithmetic. Mother of invention and father of abstract thought, it promotes the preservation and procreation of ideas.

Elaborating in 1949 (MacLean 1949) on the Papez theory of emotion (Papez 1937), I presented a diagram suggesting that the limbic cortex derives and acts upon information in terms of emotional feelings compounded of internally and externally derived experience. Inputs from all the intero- and exteroceptive systems were shown converging on the hippocampal formation, and on the basis of indirect clinical evidence one input was labeled "? sex." By that time the forebrain had been extensively explored by electrical stimulation, but there was no direct evidence of sexual responses. Penfield (Penfield & Jasper 1954) who had stimulated a great part of the medial and lateral cortex in man had never elicited signs or symptoms of a sexual nature.

Figure 2 shows three main subdivisions of the limbic system which I have focused upon in brain stimulation studies. The two subdivisions innervated via the amygdala (No. 1) and septum (No. 2), respectively, are closely linked to the olfactory apparatus, as well as to the hypothalamus and other structures of the brainstem. Note, on the contrary, that the major pathway (No. 3) to the third subdivision bypasses the olfactory apparatus. What is a possible explanation of this situation? I will return to this question when describing the display studies.

Electrical stimulation within the first subdivision of the limbic system—the frontotemporal portion—was found to elicit alimentary, searching, aggressive, and defensive responses (MacLean 1952). These findings, together with other kinds of evidence, suggested that this portion of the limbic system is concerned with behavior that insures self-preservation (MacLean 1952, 1958, 1962, 1964a).

Since the classical studies of Klüver and Bucy in 1939, it had been known that bilateral ablations, including the structures of the first subdivision (amygdala and rostral parts of the hippocampal gyrus and hippocampus), gave "release" in monkeys to bizarre sexual behavior. In an investigation of the second subdivision of the limbic system, we found that afterdischarges induced by electrical stimulation of the septum or caudal hippocampus of male cats resulted in enhanced pleasure and grooming reactions and sometimes penile erection (MacLean 1957). Similar effects were seen following local chemical stimulation of these structures by cholinergic agents (MacLean 1957). These manifestations which are seen in courtship behavior suggested that this subdivision of the limbic system is involved in expressive and feeling states that are conducive to sociability and the procreation of the species.

CEREBRAL REPRESENTATION OF ELEMENTAL
SEXUAL FUNCTIONS

The findings in the cat led me to a systematic study in awake, sitting squirrel monkeys in which we used a closed-system, stereotaxic technique for exploring the brain millimeter by millimeter looking specifically for sexual responses. I will first summarize the findings on penile erection and then the observations on seminal discharge.

In the brainstem above the level of the hypothalamus there were two nodal regions in which stimulation elicited full penile erection (MacLean & Ploog 1962). (Erection was graded on a six-point scale, ranging from ± to 5+.) One of these regions was co-extensive with the medial septopreoptic area which in Figure 3 would lie rostroventral to and inferior to the anterior commissure (AC). The other was located in the core of the medial dorsal nucleus (MD). There was evidence that the major effector pathway from this locus first followed the inferior thalamic peduncle (ITP) and then joined the medial forebrain bundle (MFB). The major effector pathway from the medial septopreoptic region was also traced into the medial forebrain bundle. Stimulation along the course of this bundle through the hypothalamus was highly effective in eliciting erection. At the level of the midbrain the pathway was followed laterally into the substantia nigra, from which it descended through the ventrolateral pons and entered the medulla just lateral to the exit of the 6th nerve (MacLean, Denniston & Dua 1963).

In anticipation of a statement about sociosexual functions of the third subdivision, it should be noted that stimulation at points along the course of its major pathway (Figure 2, No. 3) results in genital tumescence (MacLean & Ploog 1962). Strongly positive points are found in the thalamic tubercle, which is formed by the forward extension of the anterior thalamic nuclei.

Anatomically the anterior thalamic nuclei, which project to the cingulate gyrus, articulate with core elements of the medial dorsal nucleus that are connected with the posterior part of the gyrus rectus. As shown in Figure 4, strongly positive loci for penile erection were found in the pre- and subcallosal cingulate cortex, as

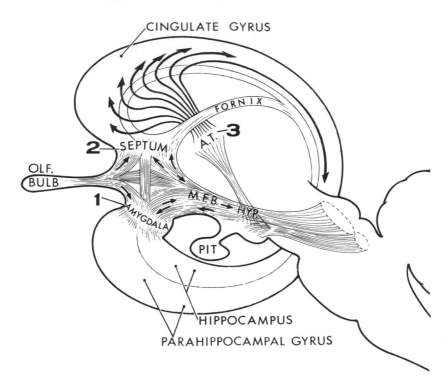

Fig. 2. *Diagram of three corticosubcortical subdivisions of the limbic system. Note how the major pathway of the third subdivision (No. 3) bypasses the olfactory apparatus. See text regarding evolutionary and sociosexual implications. Abbreviations: HYP, hypothalamus; M.F.B., medial forebrain bundle; OLF, olfactory; PIT, pituitary (after MacLean 1958).*

well as in the limbic cortex in the caudal part of gyrus rectus (Dua & MacLean 1964). The related thalamocortical structures involved in genital tumescence are diagrammed in Figure 3.

Except for the insular cortex overlying the claustrum, we have explored virtually all of the limbic cortex and systematically stimulated the amygdala (see below). In some instances partial erection has been observed during hippocampal after-discharges induced by hippocampal stimulation (MacLean, Denniston, Dua, & Ploog 1962).

We have also explored the greater part of the parasagittal frontal, parietal, and occipital neocortex. We have not, however, examined wide areas of the cortex of the lateral convexity. Large parts of the striatal complex remain to be explored. We cannot exclude the possibility that pallidal and striatal pathways entering the subthalamus and substantia nigra are involved, but a limited survey of the striatal complex itself has yielded negative results.

PSEUDO-ORGASTIC EFFECTS AND SEMINAL DISCHARGE

Stimulations at positive loci in the septum and anterior thalamus (MacLean, Denniston, Dua, & Ploog 1962; MacLean & Ploog 1962), as well as in the medial frontal cortex (Dua & MacLean 1964), recruited potentials in the hippocampus, leading in some

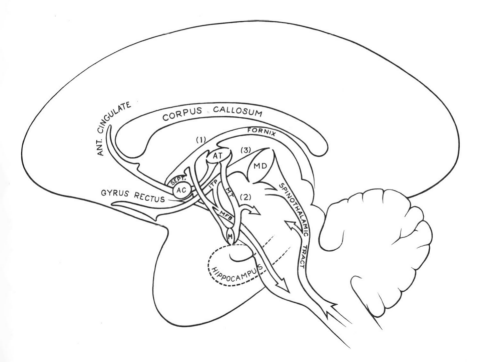

Fig. 3. *Anatomical diagram to aid visualization of cerebral circuits that are involved in elemental sexual functions. Abbreviations: AC, anterior commissure; AT, anterior thalamic nuclei; ITP, inferior thalamic peduncle; M, mammillary bodies; MD, medial dorsal nucleus; MFB, medial forebrain bundle; MT, mammillothalamic tract; SEPT, septum (MacLean 1962).*

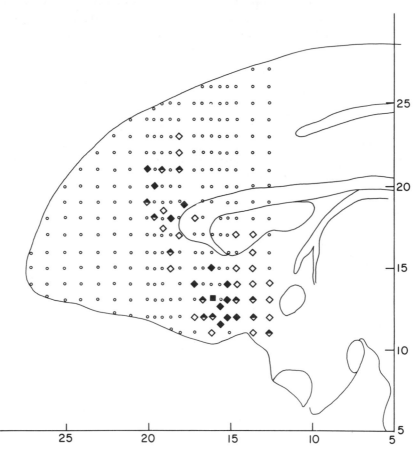

Fig. 4. *Diagram of medial frontal lobe of squirrel monkey with diamond and square symbols indicating loci at which electrical stimulation resulted in penile erection. Squares give added information that stimulation was followed by hippocampal afterdischarges. White, half-black, and solid black symbols refer, respectively, to gradations of erection of 1+, 2–3+, 4–5+. Rows of small circles overlie regions explored and found negative. Marginal scales in millimeters give distances forward and above zero axis of stereotaxic atlas (Dua and MacLean 1964).*

instances to hippocampal afterdischarges. During these after-discharges the erection might become throbbing in character, but despite the orgastic appearance, ejaculation was never observed under these conditions. Seminal discharge, sometimes preceding erection, occurred only when stimulation involved loci that proved upon reconstruction to lie along the course of the spinothalamic pathway and its medial ramifications into the caudal intralaminar region of the thalamus (MacLean, Dua, & Denniston 1963) (Fig-ure 3). Stimulations resulting in seminal discharge were accom-panied by quasi-pruritic scratching of the genitalia, but if the mon-key were prevented from touching itself, emission containing motile sperm could still be elicited. The thalamic structures in-volved in seminal discharge and apparently in genital sensation, lie in close proximity to and possibly articulate with that part of the midline thalamus that is nodal for penile erection (Figure 3).

From experiments of this kind a picture is beginning to form of brain structures involved in sensorimotor aspects of elemental sexual functions.

OROSEXUAL IMPLICATIONS

In regard to orosexual functions it is significant that slow-frequency stimulation of parts of the amygdala may result in sali-vation and chewing, followed almost a minute later by penile erec-tion (MacLean 1962). The long latency of the genital response is apparently attributable to recruitment of neural activity in struc-tures that are closely related to the amygdala, such as the nearby septopreoptic region (see Figure 2). It is not uncommon to ob-serve penile erection in animals and human infants when they are being fed. The close relationship of oral and sexual functions is presumably due to the olfactory sense which, dating far back in evolution, plays an indispensable role in both feeding and mating. The *lemur fulvus*, a prosimian form with a well developed ol-factory apparatus, has a greeting display in which the male and female mutually lick the anogenital region (Andrews 1964). Here one can see the primitive origins of a behavior that seems to have become a fascination in some of the current literature and screen plays. In the neocortex the representation of the body is such that the head and tail stand at opposite poles like north and south. But in the limbic lobe, head and tail are brought into proximity by the olfactory sense. Nature evidently was not thinking in terms of legal standards of morality when she designed the paleomammalian brain. Civilized man suspected that the world was round before Columbus sailed to America, but how could he have visualized that the limbic lobe was a closed ring and that in sailing an olfactory course in one direction the head would be reached by way of the tail and vice versa (MacLean 1968)?

It is relevant to aggressive and violent forms of sexual behavior that pathways from the amygdala and septum converge near a locus in the hypothalamus involved in angry and defensive behavior. At loci between the two arrows in Figure 5, stimulation elicited agonistic and genital manifestations (see legend). In Figure 6 I have used the shield of Mars to indicate points at which stimulation elicits oral responses and his sword as a symbol for genital responses. As the symbols are followed caudally from the amygdala and septum we see a reconstitution of the warrior Mars in the hypothalamus, recalling that fighting may be a preliminary to both feeding and mating.

NEURAL SUBSTRATE OF GENITAL DISPLAY BEHAVIOR

As already mentioned, one variety of lemurs has a greeting display in which the snout and olfactory sense come actively into play in mutual licking of the anogenital region. Such a display is in striking contrast to that of a monkey intermediate on the phylogenetic scale of primates. Our observations on the small South American squirrel monkey have revealed that this animal has a genital display which depends on visual rather than olfactory communication (MacLean 1962; Ploog & MacLean 1963). In view of this difference it deserves emphasis that in the evolution of the primate brain the septal region undergoes no dramatic changes, whereas structures comprising the third subdivision of the limbic system (Figure 2) increase in size and become most prominent in man. Elsewhere I have suggested that this transformation may reflect, in part, a shifting of emphasis from olfactory to visual influences in sociosexual behavior. This inference is partly based on experi-

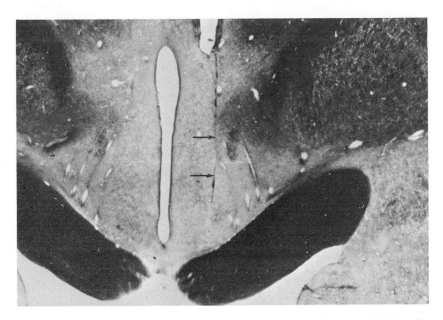

Fig. 5. *Gliosis shows track of an electrode that passed just medial to the pallidohypothalamic tract where it loops over the fornix. Stimulation at locus 1 millimeter above upper arrow resulted in 4+ erection. Stimulation at site of upper arrow elicited agitated behavior, cackling vocalization, and partial erection. As electrode descended toward lower arrow, stimulation resulted in loud vocalization and biting. Rebound erection occurred after stimulation was terminated.*

ments testing the effects of brain lesions on the natural display behavior of the squirrel monkey (MacLean, in press).

In the remainder of this paper I will describe some recent experiments of a similar kind that promise to shed light on the functions of the striatal complex, about which so little has been learned in the past 150' years. If, for example, large bilateral lesions are made in the caudate, putamen, or globus pallidus without damage to the internal capsule, the usual examination may reveal no significant changes in the animal's behavior. It is inconceivable that these large ganglia are of as little importance as ablation experiments suggest.

For these reasons the effects of pallidal lesions on the innate sexually related display behavior of the squirrel monkey are of

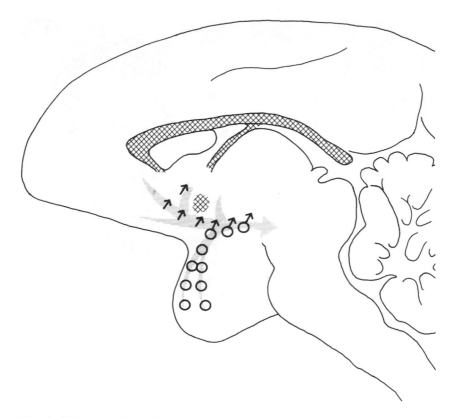

Fig. 6. *Diagram of medial view of squirrel monkey's brain illustrating functional relationship of amygdala and septal pathways involved in oral and genital functions. The shield of Mars (○) is used as a symbol for oral responses and his sword (↑) for genital responses. Symbols for shield cluster in the amygdala region and those for sword in the septal region. Followed caudally, sword and shield unite in anterior hypothalamus, portraying a reconstitution of the warrior Mars at a locus where electrical stimulation elicits angry and defensive behavior (MacLean 1964a).*

particular interest. First, a word about the display. In the communal situation male squirrel monkeys utilize an aggressive genital display in an attempt to dominate other males. Figure 7 illustrates a typical encounter between two males. The displaying monkey vocalizes, spreads one thigh, and directs the fully erect penis toward the head or chest of the other animal. The display is seen in its most dramatic form when a new male is introduced into an established colony of squirrel monkeys (MacLean, in press). Within seconds all males begin to display to the strange monkey, and if the new male does not remain quiet with its head bowed, it will be viciously attacked. We have found that the incidence of display among males in a colony is a better measure of dominance than the outcome of rivalry for food (Ploog & MacLean 1963). It is of interest to note that the display is commonly accompanied by grinding of the teeth, recalling that penile erection and bruxism have been observed in man during periods of REM (rapid eye movement) sleep (Fisher, Gross, & Zuch 1965) that have been correlated with dreaming. It is a remarkable parallel that, as seen

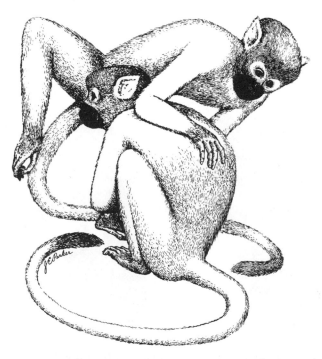

Fig. 7. *Posture of genital display of squirrel monkey in aggressive encounters with males or prior to attempts at copulation with females (Ploog & MacLean 1963).*

in reptiles and lower forms, the display of this primate is the same in courtship as in the show of aggression.

A variation of the display is also used as a form of social greeting, and I have described one variety of squirrel monkey that will regularly display to its reflection in a mirror (MacLean 1964*b*). Ploog, Hopf, and Winter (1967) have since observed that without exposure to any animal other than its own mother, the infant squirrel monkey will display as early as the second day of life to another monkey, clearly indicating that the display is an innate form of behavior. Figure 8 shows two common subspecies with which we have worked. We informally refer to the mirror displaying animal as the "gothic" type because above the eye the ocular patch suggests the peak of a gothic arch. We call the other type "roman" because the patch is round like a roman arch.

For investigating primate behavior the mirror display test has special interest because it depends on visual rather than olfactory

Fig. 8. *Two varieties of squirrel monkeys informally identified as "gothic" and "roman" types because of the pointed and rounded shape of the ocular patch above the eye. Both types of monkey have a greeting display, but only the gothic type will consistently display to its reflection in a mirror (MacLean* 1964b).

or other cues. With daily testing most gothic-type monkeys living visually isolated will consistently display to their reflections in a mirror. This provides a reliable means of obtaining pre- and post-operative scores. Figure 9 shows a typical protocol sheet, recording the latency and magnitude of the erection, and the other most common behavioral manifestations—vocalization, spreading of the thigh(s), scratching, and urination. All testing is done in the home cage with a mechanical contrivance for exposing a full-length mirror for 30 seconds.

Using this test, I have observed the effects of lesions in various parts of the brain on the autonomic and somatic components of the display in more than 70 monkeys. There have been numerous cases in which large bilateral lesions of the brain have had no perceptible effect on the display. Figure 10 shows an interesting example. In this case a large bilateral lesion was placed in the amygdala.

Bilateral lesions of the globus pallidus that avoid injury to the internal capsule do not result in perceptible motor deficits. I have found, however, in four monkeys that pallidal lesions result in a statistically significant decline in display behavior. Figure 11 shows the performance curve in a pilot animal. Following the initially placed lesions depicted below the curve, display was performed at a 100 percent level. When additional lesions were placed more posteriorly in the globus pallidus, there was no longer any inclination to display. As indicated by the graph of planimetric measurements in Figure 12, about one-third of the globus pallidus was destroyed on one side, and a smaller amount on the other. Without an appropriate test it might have been concluded that these monkeys were not significantly affected by the brain lesions.

CONCLUSION

The findings in the experiments just described suggest that the striatal complex may be part of a neural repository for species-specific forms of behavior illustrated in the present experiments by a genital display variously used in a show of aggression, in courtship, and in greeting.

Eliot Howard (1929), the English naturalist, emphasized that the establishment of territory was a necessary preliminary to

PRE-OP TESTING
TO MECH. MIRROR

#762
Z-THREE

U.S. GOVERNMENT PRINTING OFFICE : 1968 O—323—822

Trial #	Date 1969	Time	Pos	Er	Lat	Ur	Voc	TS	Scr	Cue	Time exp			Comments
1	10/16	11:07	↑	5+	7"	+	+	+	O	E	30"			RG
2	10/19	9:52	↑	5+	8"	⊕	+	+	O	E	30"			RG
3	10/19	1:45	↑	5+	5"	+	+	+	O	E	30"	PULLED ON PENIS		RG
4	10/20	10:11	↓	5+	10"	+	+	+	O	E	30"			RG
5	10/20	2:04	↑	5+	9"	+	+	+	O	E	30"			RG
6	10/21	11:07	↑	5+	5"	O	+	+	O	E	30"			RG
7	10/21	5:03	↑	5+	6"	+	+	+	O	E	30"			RG
8	10/22	11:25	↑	5+	5"	⊕	+	+	O	E	30"			RG
9	10/22	2:22	↑	5+	4"	+	+	+	O	E	30"			RB
10	10/23	12:44	↑	5+	5"	+	+	+	O	E	30"			RB
11	10/23	2:20	↑	5+	5"	+	+	+	O	E	30"			RB
12	10/23	4:43	↑	5+	5"	+	+	+	O	E	30"			RB
13	10/24	11:44	↑	5+	6"	O	+	+	O	E	30"			RB
14	10/24	2:20	↑	5+	9"	+	+	+	O	E	30"			RB
15	10/27	9:24	→	5+	3"	O	+	+	O	E	30"			RG
16	10/27	1:18	→	5+	7"	+	+	+	O	E	30"			RB
17	10/28	10:52	→	5+	6"	+	+	+	O	E	30"			RG
18	10/28	2:38	→	5+	7"	+	+	+	+	E	30"			RG
19	10/29	10:17	⇐	5+	5"	+	+	+	+	E	30			RG
20	10/29	2:06	→	5+	5"	+	+	⊕	⊕	E	30			RG
21	10/30	4:34	→	5+	5"	+	+	+	⊕	E	30"			RG
22	10/30	1:29	⇐	5+	6"	+	+	+	⊕	E	30"			RG
23	10/31	11:08	→	5+	6"	+	+	+	O	E	30			RG
24	10/31	4:37	↑	5+	6"	+	+	+	+	E	30"			RG
25	11/1	10:56	↑	5+	4"	+	+	+	O	E	30"			RG
26	11/1	2:47	→	5+	5"	+	+	+	O	E	30"			RB
27	11/2	10:42	→	5+	5"	+	+	+	O	E	30"			RG
28	11/2	1:37	→	5+	4"	+	+	+	O	E	30"			RG

Fig. 9. *Typical protocol sheet illustrating manner of scoring mirror display behavior of squirrel monkeys. Testing two times a day, observer notes magnitude and latency of erection, as well as other components of the display, namely, vocalization (VO), thigh-spread (TS), scratching (SCR). Arrows in column labeled position (POS) indicate direction of monkey's movements in cage during 30-second exposure to a full-length mirror.*

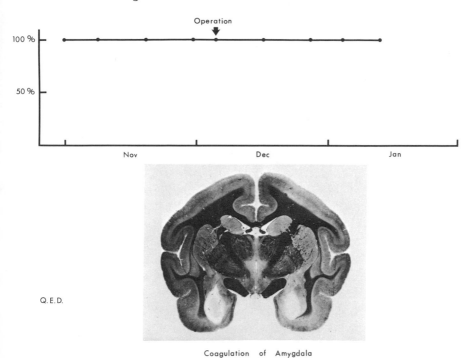

Coagulation of Amygdala

Fig. 10. *It has been found that large bilateral lesions in many parts of the brain may result in no change in an animal's display behavior. The performance curve in the case of this monkey (Q.E.D.) shows that large bilateral lesions of the amygdala had no effect on the animal's display performance. Each point on the curve represents an accumulation of ten trials.*

mating and breeding. It is of great evolutionary interest to discover that there exists a primate form such as the squirrel monkey which, like a number of submammalian species, uses the same form of display in both courtship and in the show of aggression in fending off intrusive males. Wickler (1966) has described so-called sentinel monkeys in troops of baboons and green monkeys in Africa which sit at lookout sites with their thighs spread and a display of partial erection while the troop feeds or takes a siesta. He regards this display as an "optical marker of boundaries," warning other monkeys not to intrude.

It is a long leap from monkeys to man. Do the comparative observations have any human relevance? In mythology the gods

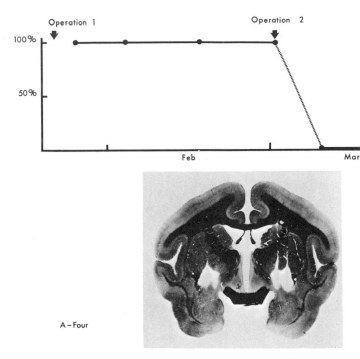

Coagulation of Globus Pallidus

Fig. 11. *The lesions shown above involve the ansa lenticularis, globus pallidus, and caudal part of the anterior commissure. After coagulation of these structures the monkey "A-Four" displayed in 100 percent of daily trials. When additional lesions were placed in the caudal part of the globus pallidus, there was no inclination to display.*

Pan, Priapus, Amon, Min, and others are all associated with fertility and often portrayed with an enlarged or erect phallus that is superstitiously endowed with the power of protection. In Asia Minor, for example, phallic images associated with Priapus were placed at vantage points for the protection of orchards.

In primitive cultures in different parts of the world the territorial aggressive implications of penile display are illustrated by houseguards—stone monuments showing an erect phallus—used to mark territorial boundaries. It is as though a visual, urogenital symbol is used as a substitute for the olfactory, urinary, territorial markings of macrosmatic mammals.

Gajdusek (1970), in an article on Stone Age man, has called attention to the parallel between the display behavior of squirrel monkeys and certain behavior of Melanesian tribes. "I have noted," he states,

quite similar presentation and display in both spontaneous and socially ritualized behavior in some New Guinea groups. It is similarly used to express both aggression and dominance, in the form of a distant greeting or appeasement, in obviously erotic dancing, and also as a spontaneous expression of anxiety, joy, or elation. This is particularly obvious among the Asmat and Auyu-related peoples of southern New Guinea. When frightened, excited, elated, or surprised, groups of Asmat men and boys spontaneously meet the precipitating event by a penile display dance, which involves much the same sequence as the presentation display of the squirrel monkey. This behavior is performed on the arrival of strange visitors, on the departure of strangers who have been received with friendship, or in response to excitement or anxiety-producing events, such as the burning of a house, victory in fighting, a severe thunderstorm, completion of a communal effort involving exertion. In more formalized ritual form, the vocalization, thigh spreading, genital grasping and rubbing, erection and pelvic thrusting behavior pattern has been introduced

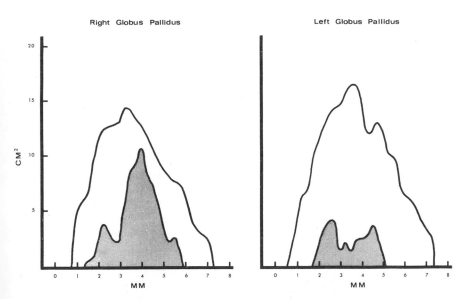

Fig. 12. *Planimetric measurements of destruction of the globus pallidus (shaded area) in the case described in Figure 11. The upper curve is a plot of the total areal measurements of the globus pallidus at millimeter levels in the frontal stereotaxic plane.*

into a traditional night dance of the Asmat and Auyu peoples, which at times may become even more overtly erotic and copulatory.

The males of these and surrounding groups on the coastal plain wear no genital covering at all. In the cultures further inland, however, the males have adopted a less active and more continuous genital display with the male attire consisting of a wide array of prominent penis coverings: nuts or shells, or braided sheaths or gourds; the beak of the hornbill has been used by many groups for this purpose. In most of the Highland cultures of western and central New Guinea, this phallocrypt has become an enormously elongated gourd. To the north of the central ranges, in the Sepik headwaters, the penile covering has been replaced by a baseball-sized spherical gourd, worn only over the distal part of the penis. The ritual dance of the Waina-Suwanda peoples leaves no ambiguity, explicitly emphasizing the display nature of the performance. Thus, for the purpose of the dance, the usual glans penis-covering gourd is replaced by a much larger and longer gourd, which throughout the dance is flipped from between the legs up against the abdominal wall by undulating movements of the thighs and pelvis.

We have, thus, a full complex of genital display performances which, at their extremes, are closely similar patterns to the display performance of the squirrel monkey. [pp. 58 & 59.]

In chapter 24 of Genesis, Abraham says to his eldest servant, "Put I pray thee, thy hand under my thigh [and] swear . . . that thou shall not take a wife unto my son of the daughters of the Canaanites." Thigh is used here euphemistically for the genitals. In his three contributions to the theory of sex Freud commented that the "child is above all shameless, and during its early years it evinces definite pleasure in displaying its body and especially its sexual organs" (1948, p. 52).

In the squirrel monkey, a display may be triggered by reflection of a single eye (MacLean 1964b). It is as though the eye and the penis acquire an equivalent meaning through generalization. In Italy, less than two hundred years ago, amulets showing an erect phallus are said to have been worn as a protection against the evil eye (Knight 1865). Some individuals, notably a number with a diagnosis of schizophrenia, are thrown into a panic if someone catches their eye, recalling that the word panic derives from the god Pan, who found amusement in terrifying "travelers" (i.e., strangers).

In conclusion, there arises a question that I have considered elsewhere: Is it possible that primitive man may have learned that by covering himself he reduced unpleasant social tensions arising from the archaic impulse to display and that this, rather than modesty, has led to the civilizing influence of clothing? (MacLean 1962).

REFERENCES

Andrews, R. J. The displays of the primates. In J. Buettner-Janusch (ed.), *Evolutionary and genetic biology of primates*, vol. 2. New York: Academic Press, 1964.

Broca, P. Anatomie comparée des circonvolutions cérébrales. Le grand lobe limbique et la scissure limbique dans la série des mammifères. *Revue Anthropologique (Paris)* 1878, 1(2): 385–498.

Dua, S., & MacLean, P. D. Localization for penile erection in medial frontal lobe. *American Journal of Physiology* 1964, 207: 1425–34.

Fisher, C., Gross, J., & Zuch, J. Cycle of penile erection synchronous with dreaming (REM) sleep. *Archives of General Psychiatry (Chicago)* 1965, 12: 29–45.

Freud, S. *Three contributions to the theory of sex.* A. A. Brill (trans.), Nervous and Mental Disease Monograph, New York, 1948.

Gajdusek, D. C. Physiological and psychological characteristics of Stone Age man. In *Engineering and Science* 1970, 33: 26–33 and 56–62. Symposium on Biological Bases of Human Behavior, California Institute of Technology, Pasadena, March 1970.

Howard, H. E. *An introduction to the study of bird behavior.* Cambridge: University Press, 1929.

Klüver, H., & Bucy, P. C. Preliminary analysis of functions of the temporal lobes in monkeys. *Archives of Neurology and Psychiatry (Chicago)* 1939, 42: 979–1000.

Knight, R. P. *A discourse on the worship of Priapus and its connexion with mystic theology of the ancients.* London, privately printed, 1865.

MacLean, P. D. Psychosomatic disease and the "visceral brain." Recent developments bearing on the Papez theory of emotion. *Psychosomatic Medicine (New York)* 1949, 11: 338–53.

──────. Some psychiatric implications of physiological studies on frontotemporal portion of limbic system (visceral brain). *Electroencephalography and Clinical Neurophysiology* 1952, 4: 407–18.

──────. Chemical and electrical stimulation of hippocampus in unrestrained animals. II. Behavioral findings. *AMA Archives of Neurology and Psychiatry* 1957, 78: 128–42.

──────. Contrasting functions of limbic and neocortical systems of the brain and their relevance to psychophysiological aspects of medicine. *American Journal of Medicine* 1958, 25: 611–26.

_____. New findings relevant to the evolution of psychosexual functions of the brain. *Journal of Nervous and Mental Disease* 1962, 135: 289–301.

_____. Man and his animal brains. *Modern Medicine* 1964, 32: 95–106.(a)

_____. Mirror display in the squirrel monkey, Saimiri sciureus. *Science* 1964, 146: 950–52.(b)

_____. The brain in relation to empathy and medical education. *Journal of Nervous and Mental Disease* 1967, 144: 374–82.

_____. Alternative neural pathways to violence. In L. Ng (ed.), *Alternatives to violence.* New York: Time-Life Books, 1968.

_____. The triune brain, emotion, and scientific bias. In F. O. Schmitt (ed.), *The neurosciences second study program.* New York: The Rockefeller University Press, 1970.

_____. A triune concept of the brain and behavior, Lecture I. Man's reptilian and limbic inheritance; Lecture II. Man's limbic brain and the psychoses; Lecture III. New trends in man's evolution, In T. Boag (ed.), *The Hincks memorial lectures.* Toronto: University of Toronto Press (in press).

MacLean, P. D., Denniston, R. H., & Dua, S. Further studies on cerebral representation of penile erection: caudal thalamus, midbrain, and pons. *Journal of Neurophysiology* 1963, 26: 273–93.

MacLean, P. D., Denniston, R. H., Dua, S., & Ploog, D. W. Hippocampal changes with brain stimulation eliciting penile erection. In *Physiologie de l'hippocampe.* Paris: Colloques Internationaux du Centre National de la Recherche Scientifique, 1962, 107: 491–510.

MacLean, P. D., Dua, S., & Denniston, R. H. Cerebral localization for scratching and seminal discharge. *Archives of Neurology (Chicago)* 1963, 9: 485–97.

MacLean, P. D., & Ploog, D. W. Cerebral representation of penile erection. *Journal of Neurophysiology* 1962, 25: 29–55.

Papez, J. W. A proposed mechanism of emotion. *Archives of Neurology and Psychiatry (Chicago)* 1937, 38: 725–43.

Penfield, W., & Jasper, H. *Epilepsy and the functional anatomy of the human brain.* Boston: Little, Brown, 1954.

Ploog, D., Hopf, S., & Winter, P. Ontogenese des Verhaltens von Totenkopf-Affen (Saimiri sciureus). *Psychologische Forschung (Berlin)* 1967, 31: 1–41.

Ploog, D. W., & MacLean, P. D. Display of penile erection in squirrel monkey (Saimiri sciureus). *Animal Behavior* 1963, 11: 32–39.

Wickler, Von W. Ursprung und biologische Deutung des Genitalpräsentierens männlicher Primaten. *Zeitschrift für Tierpsychologie* 1966, 23: 422–37.

part II

Maternalism and Women's Sexuality

chapter 5

Interrelationships between Sexual Responsiveness, Birth, and Breast Feeding*

Niles Newton†

There is a tendency in our society to place special emphasis on the types of female sexual behavior that are of particular pertinence to adult men. Thus women's responses in coitus are singled out for considerable attention while discussion and research on the psychophysiologic aspects of their other reproductive behavior tends to be muted. Full understanding of female sexuality, however, requires consideration of all their reproductive responses.

Males can form reproductive relationships only with females. Their adult reproductive behavior is limited to one act—coitus. Adult females, on the other hand, have at least three acts of interpersonal reproductive behavior—all three involving the participation of two human beings. These behavior patterns are (1) coitus, (2) parturition, (3) lactation.

*This review was supported in part by The John R. and Doris J. Haire Foundation.
†Niles Newton, Ph.D., Northwestern University Medical School, Chicago, Illinois.

Here we will consider the close interrelation of these three psychophysiologic functions. In practical terms, this implies that what occurs on the delivery table is very pertinent to what will transpire later in the marital bed and that mother-baby relationship without enjoyable lactation is in a somewhat similar psychophysiologic position as a marriage without enjoyable coitus.

Before discussing characteristics common to all three reproductive interpersonal acts, the similarities between coital behavior and birth behavior, and between coital behavior and lactation behavior will be discussed.

RELATION OF BIRTH BEHAVIOR TO COITAL ORGASM

The relation of birth behavior to coital behavior becomes apparent when accounts of uninhibited reproductive actions are reviewed. Some years ago in reading Read's observations of natural childbirth (1944, 1949, 1950a, 1950b) and Kinsey, Pomeroy, Martin, and Gebhard's detailed descriptions of orgasm behavior (1953) I was impressed by the similarity of the reactions manifested in both behaviors. Indeed, uninhibited, undrugged childbirth and sexual excitement are similar in the following characteristics:

> Breathing
> Vocalization
> Facial expression
> Uterine reactions
> Cervical reactions
> Abdominal muscle reactions
> Position
> Central nervous system reactions
> Strength and flexibility
> Sensory perception
> Emotional response

The Kinsey et al. data (1953) came from interviews, from scientifically trained persons observing human sexual activities, and from reports of physiologic experiments. The Read data came from his report of 516 consecutive labors published in *Lancet* (1949), as well as from his books (1944, 1950a, 1950b). He made every effort to keep women free from fear or disturbance in labor and thus uninhibited. Much of the birth data is also corroborated by films taken of women undergoing natural childbirths or, more recently, of women using a similar technique called psychoprophylaxis.

Since in this country it is the custom to move, strap down, and otherwise disturb even unmedicated women as they approach the birth climax, the behavior noted by Read is not so frequent nor so pronounced here.

My analysis (Newton 1955) of the Read (1944, 1949, 1950*a* 1950*b*) and Kinsey et al. (1953) data specifically showed these comparisons:

UNDISTURBED, UNDRUGGED CHILDBIRTH	SEXUAL EXCITEMENT
Breathing	
In the first stage of labor breathing becomes deeper during contractions.	During the early stages of sexual excitement, breathing becomes faster and deeper.
Second stage labor brings on very deep breaths with breath holding.	As orgasm approaches, breathing may sometimes be interrupted.
Vocalization	
There is a tendency to make noises, grunts in the second stage of labor.	There is also tendency to make gasping, sucking noises as orgasm approaches.
Facial expression	
During the second stage of labor, the face gets intense, a stressed look, which makes observers often assume the woman is suffering great pain. As birth climax approaches, the face looks like that of an athlete undergoing great strain.	As orgasm approaches, face gets what Kinsey et al. call a "tortured expression"—mouth open, glassy eyes, tense muscles. The face looks like that of an athlete under great physical strain.
Uterine reactions	
The upper segment of the uterus contracts rhythmically during labor.	The upper segment of the uterus contracts rhythmically during sexual excitement.
Cervical reactions	
Loosening of mucus plug from os of cervix is one of the standard signs of early labor.	In sexual excitement, cervical secretion may loosen mucus plug which ordinarily lies at os of cervix thus opening it for spermatozoa.

UNDISTURBED, UNDRUGGED CHILDBIRTH

SEXUAL EXCITEMENT

Abdominal muscle reactions
These contract periodically in second stage labor; a strong urge to bear down develops as delivery approaches.

During sexual excitement, abdominal muscles contract periodically.

Position
The usual position for delivery in our society is with the woman flat on her back with legs wide apart and bent.

The birth position is commonly used for coitus—a woman on her back with legs bent and wide apart.

Central nervous system reactions
Women tend to become uninhibited during parturition, particularly as the baby descends the birth canal. Veneers of conventional behavior disappear in the later stages of labor.

During coitus, inhibitions and psychic blockages are relieved and often eliminated.

Strength and flexibility
Delivery of the baby through the narrow passage calls for unusual strength and body expansion.

In sexual excitement unusual muscular strength develops. Many persons become capable of bending and distorting their bodies in ways they could not otherwise.

Sensory perception
In labor the vulva becomes anesthetic with full dilation so that the woman often must be told of the birth of the baby's head.

In coitus the whole body of the sexually aroused person becomes increasingly insensitive even to sharp blows and severe injury.

During undrugged labor, uninhibited by fear, there is a tendency to become insensitive to surroundings as delivery approaches. Amnesia develops.

As sexual orgasm approaches, loss of sensory perception is nearly complete—sometimes leading to moments of unconsciousness.

Suddenly, delivery complete, the woman becomes wide awake.

After sexual orgasm there is a sudden return of sensory acuity.

Emotional response
After the birth of the baby there is a flood of joyful emotion. Read describes it as "complete and careless ecstasy."

After coital orgasm there is often a strong feeling of well-being.

Another physiologic similarity was pointed out to me recently. While speaking at an Ob-Gyn Postgraduate Course at the American College of Surgeons 1970 Annual Clinical Meeting, I mentioned that it is possible for women to have a marked emotional reaction to birth. After the talk Dr. Evan Evans of Ogden, Utah, came up to me. He said he had noted in some of his patients marked clitoral engorgement which begins about the time the cervix is 8 or 9 cm dilated and lasts until about the time the episiotomy is sewed up. He has noticed this phenomenon especially since he has encouraged husbands to be in the delivery room. His patients deliver after having attended parents' classes. They receive paracervical and pudendal block, which is sufficient without other medication to carry them through the last part of labor.

Such observable clitoral engorgement has also been reported to occur in some women during sexual excitement by Masters and Johnson (1966). They reported that observable tumescence of the glans does not develop until sexual tensions have progressed well into the excitement phase of the sexual response cycle and it persists throughout the remainder of the sexual response cycle or for as long as any significant degree of sexual stimulation is maintained.

Masters and Johnson (1966) also noted that sexual excitement can occur during birth. They have reported on twelve women, who during the second stage of labor experienced "grossly intensified versions of the sensations identified with this first stage of subjective progression through orgasm [p. 136]." All of these women had delivered babies on at least one occasion without anesthesia or analgesia.

THE RELATION OF BREAST FEEDING BEHAVIOR TO COITAL ORGASM

The similarity between lactation and coital response is equally clearly defined. The survival of the human race, long before the concept of "duty" evolved, depended upon the satisfactions gained from the two voluntary acts of reproduction—coitus and breast feeding (Newton & Newton 1967). These had to be sufficiently pleasurable to ensure their frequent occurrence. Thus it is not surprising to find the following marked psychophysiologic similarities between lactation and coitus:

1. Uterine contractions occur both during suckling (Moir 1934; Newton & Newton 1950) and during sexual excitement (Kinsey et al. 1953; Masters & Johnson 1966).

2. Nipple erection occurs both during nursing and sexual excitement. Masters and Johnson (1966), studying nipple erection as part of sexual excitement, observed an increase of 0.5-1.0 cm in nipple length that was due to stimulation. Gunther (1955), in a study of nipple protractility of breast-feeding mothers (measured with suction), found that those whose total nipple protractility was 2.5 cm usually experienced successful breast feeding, whereas those with just 0.25 to 0.50 cm less protractility were notably less successful in establishing breast feeding.

3. Breast stroking and nipple stimulation occur both during breast feeding and in sexual foreplay. Under conditions of unrestricted, uninhibited sucking which characterize many traditional, historic, and preliterate human cultures, the young infant stimulates the breast many times during the day and may sleep near the approachable nipple at night, intermittently sucking throughout the sleeping hours (Mead & Newton 1967; Newton 1971). As the infant grows older he shows eager body responses to nursing. Rhythmic movements of hands, feet, fingers and toes may occur. The mother's breast may often be stroked by the infant's hand as he moves. Erection of the penis is common in male babies. After feeding there is often a relaxation that is characteristic of the conclusion of satisfactory sexual response (Newton & Newton 1967).

4. Emotions aroused by sexual contact and by breast-feeding contact both involve skin changes. Sexual excitement causes marked vascular changes in the skin, and breast feeding raises body temperature as measured in the submammary and mammary skin area. In fact, this is such a key phenomenon in lactation that the milk supply has been found to be significantly and highly correlated with rise in the mammary skin temperature during nursing (Abolins 1954).

5. Milk let-down or the milk-ejection reflex may be triggered not only by breast feeding but by sexual excitement. Masters and Johnson (1966) reported that in two out of three lactating women

observed under experimental conditions, milk was observed to run from both nipples simultaneously during and immediately subsequent to an orgasmic experience. The involuntary leakage was noted to occur during both coital and automanipulative activity. Campbell and Petersen (1953) have reported that the degree of milk ejection appears to be related to the degree of sexual response in coitus. Their major source of data was a woman with an inadequate nipple sphincter on her left breast, so that the milk-ejection reflex could be easily noticed. The observability of the milk depends not only on the triggering of the milk-ejection reflex but also on the action of the nipple sphincter which may hold back the flow.

6. The emotions experienced during sexual arousal and the emotions experienced during uninhibited, unrestricted breast feeding may be closely allied. Masters and Johnson's (1966) study group included 24 women who nursed their babies two months or more. The women reported sexual stimulation induced by suckling their infants—frequently to plateau tension levels and, on three occasions, to orgasm. Even in this relatively uninhibited study group, guilt feelings were expressed by six of the women when reporting sexual feelings related to nursing. It is possible that this type of hesitancy may have been a factor in Hytten, Yorston, and Thomson's (1958) report that none of 32 primigravidas who breast fed for three months or more found it physically or emotionally pleasurable. On the other hand, Newson and Newson (1962), using questions that probed beyond the conventional answers, found that 66 percent of the mothers who breast fed for two weeks or more actively enjoyed the experience, often describing feelings of tenderness and closeness engendered by the breast-feeding act.

7. An accepting attitude toward sexuality may be related to an accepting attitude toward breast feeding. Sears, Maccoby, and Levin (1957) found that mothers who had breast fed were significantly more tolerant of sexual matters such as masturbation and social sex play. Masters and Johnson (1966) noted that for the first three months after delivery, the highest level of sexual interest was reported by the nursing mothers. As a group, they reported interest in as rapid a return as possible to active coition with their husbands.

Feelings of aversion for the breast-feeding act appear to be related to dislike of nudity and sexuality. Newson and Newson (1962) after interviewing more than 700 English mothers, commented: "For many mothers, modesty and feeling of distaste form a major factor in their preference for the artificial methods [p. 1745]." Salber, Stitt, and Babbot (1959), in studying reasons given for not attempting to nurse, found that an emotional barrier was the most common reason given, expressed by 55.8 percent of women. "Women who had an emotional barrier to breast-feeding included those who were disgusted at the thought of feeding or who were extremely embarrased by the idea because of excessive modesty. Some could not explain their feelings but knew very strongly they did not want to breast feed [p. 311]."

The reason the sensuous nature of breast feeding is so seldom recognized in our society may be the same reason birth orgasm is so seldom seen. Current social patterns are very effective in inhibiting the psychophysical reciprocity of lactation. Mother and infant are usually separated except for brief contacts during their hospital stay. Rigorous rules about duration and timing of each sucking period have been invented and are enforced by persons who usually have never successfully breast fed even one baby. Probably most people in our society would be willing to concede that we would cause coital frigidity if we prescribed the act only at scheduled times and laid down rules concerning the exact number of minutes intromission should last. Mother-baby interactions can be similarly disturbed by similar types of rules.

SIMILARITIES BETWEEN ALL THREE REPRODUCTIVE INTERPERSONAL ACTS

We have been discussing the psychophysiological similarities between coital response and lactation and parturition responses. However, possibly far more important is the thread of similarity between all three aspects of the triad. Coitus, birth, and breast feeding have similar biologic roles, since all three involve reproductive relationships between two individuals. They may share the following three basic characteristics:

1. They are based in part on closely related neurohormonal reflexes.

2. They are sensitive to environmental stimuli, being easily inhibited in their early stages.

3. All three appear, under certain circumstances, to trigger caretaking behavior which is an essential and important part of mammalian reproduction.

Related Neurohormonal Reflexes

Although the physiology of the neurohormonal reflexes involved in coitus, parturition, and lactation is currently only fragmentarily understood, there is still considerable experimental evidence suggesting that similar physiologic processes may be involved. A classic experiment conducted by Debackere, Peeters, and Tuyttens (1961) in Ghent, Belgium, illustrates this interrelationship. These investigators joined the circulatory systems of pairs of sheep. Plastic tubes were used to connect the jugular vein of one animal with the jugular vein of the other. A ram was joined with a lactating ewe. The seminal vesicles and ampullae of the ram were massaged often to the point of emission.

After a minimum of 30 seconds there was often a sharp rise of pressure in the udder of the connected ewe, indicating that the milk-ejection mechanism had been triggered by the blood of the sexually stimulated ram. Two ewes were also joined together. The vagina of one member of the pair was repeatedly distended with a balloon. The stimulation of the vagina in the one ewe often caused signs of milk ejection to occur in the other ewe. It should be noted in this connection that vaginal dilation occurs normally in both coitus and parturition.

This experiment demonstrates the interrelatedness of sexual excitement, lactation, and birth on a neurohormonal level, in which oxytocic substances appear to be involved.

Inhibition through Environmental Disturbance

Another similarity in all three interpersonal reproductive acts is that they appear to be easily inhibited in their initial phases by environmental disturbances. There may be a sound biological reason why this is so.

Coitus, labor, and lactation leave the participants particularly vulnerable to outside dangers during the period reproductive action is taking place. Coitus involves a lessening of sensory acuity as orgasm approaches, making the participants less aware of environmental changes. Parturition is a time of maximal defenselessness for both female and young. The female with a fetus in her birth canal cannot move with normal efficiency. The newly emerged young are in a peak state of helplessness. During milk exchange the same type of vulnerability is also present. Mother and offspring, united in the nursing act, are not in an optimum position for fight or flight.

Survival, therefore, would be most likely to occur in those individuals and those species that are able to regulate reproductive acts so that they occur in relatively safe surroundings which elicit calm emotions. It is not surprising that folkways and cultural patterns have long recognized that coitus, parturition, and lactation proceed most smoothly when the surroundings are particularly sheltered or considered to be relatively safe.

Inhibition of Sexual Functioning

Coitus is usually patterned to proceed with minimal environmental disturbance. Even people of preliterate human societies of the type that accept extensive premarital and extramarital coitus usually still have a tendency to withdraw during the sexual act into the semi-isolation of the palm grove, the garden patch, or the shelter of darkness (Ford & Beach 1951). The effect of environmental factors in inhibiting sexual response in human beings is thoroughly recognized in the treatment techniques of Masters and Johnson (1970) for dealing with human sexual inadequacy in modern American society.

Environmental factors also influence the sexual performance of domestic animals. This has been particularly noted in the case of cattle, sheep, swine, horses, and dogs (Hafez 1962). Domestication involves a selective process fostering reproduction and genetic survival in individuals and species that do not easily become sexually inhibited under the disturbances of captivity. It is likely that sexual functioning is more inhibited by environmental disturbances in mammals not so selectively bred.

Inhibition of Milk Ejection

It has long been recognized that lactation is sensitive to environmental disturbance. Successful dairy farming depends upon the knowledge that a cow will not easily "let down" or eject her milk to a stranger, nor if she is milked in a strange barn. Even preliterate peoples have developed elaborate techniques for inducing the inhibited milk-ejection reflex to function (Amoroso & Jewell 1963).

Ely and Peterson (1941) experimentally studied the inhibition of milk let down. During milking, cats were placed on the backs of cows, and paper bags were blown up and burst to make loud noises. Under these conditions less milk was obtainable from the udder than usual. However, milk flow was restored to normal by the administration of pitocin, the natural form of the hormone oxytocin. Ely and Peterson (1941) postulated a neurohormonal mechanism regulated in part by central nervous system factors. The primary stimulus is sucking applied to the nipple, which triggers the discharge of oxytocin, from the posterior pituitary gland, that is carried to the breast in the blood. The oxytocin acts on the myoepithelial cells around the alveoli, causing them to contract, thus pushing out the milk into the larger ducts, where it is more easily available to the baby.

The psychologic importance of the milk-ejection reflex in human beings was first emphasized by Waller in his book, *Clinical Studies in Lactation*. He used case histories to illustrate the fact that milk ejection can be inhibited by embarrassment and can be conditioned so that it is set off by the mere thought of the baby far away.

Michael Newton and I (1948) experimentally inhibited the milk-ejection reflex in a mother through distractive techniques that did not appear to disturb the baby. These consisted of placing the mother's feet in ice water, painfully pulling her toes, and asking her the solution of mathematical problems, punishing mistakes with electric shocks.

Table 1 shows how the amount of milk obtained by the baby varied. On control days, when there was no disturbance, the baby obtained significantly more milk than when the mother was subjected to disturbance. The amount of milk rose to near normal, however, when oxytocin was injected to artificially set off the milk-ejection reflex.

The relation of the reflex as set off by natural stimuli to the overall availability of milk was studied experimentally (Newton &

Table 1. *Effect of maternal disturbance and oxytocin on the amount of milk obtained by the baby*

Maternal disturbance	Mean amount of milk obtained by infant during standardized feeding (gm)
No distractions—no injection	168
Distraction—saline injection	99
Distraction—oxytocin injection	153

Newton 1950). The baby was first allowed to nurse fully to set off the milk-ejection reflex. Then, the breasts were each pumped for five minutes. Finally, 3 units of oxytocin (Pitocin) were injected, and each breast was pumped again for five minutes. Mothers who subsequently breast fed successfully had all but 27 percent of their milk available to the baby or the breast pump, thus showing minimal inhibition of the milk-ejection reflex. However, mothers who were unsuccessful in their attempts to breast feed adequately showed marked milk-ejection inhibition. In their cases 47 percent of the milk in their breasts was not available to baby or breast pump until milk ejection was artifically triggered by the injection of oxytocin. The difference between the two groups was statistically significant ($p < .01$).

The milk-ejection reflex appears to be very sensitive to small differences in the oxytocin level, suggesting that minor psychosomatic changes may influence the degree to which the milk is available to the baby. Wiederman, Freund, and Stone (1963) found that the intravenous threshold dose of oxytocin needed for response was 0.25 to 10 mμ.

Inhibition of Fetus Ejection

The deleterious effect of fear and disturbance on labor has also long been recognized in a general way. Eastman and Hellman (1961) in their textbook have written of the harmful influence of fear on labor. Veterinary and animal behavior literature indicates recognition of the same phenomenon (Bleicher 1962; Freak 1962; Hafez 1962). In an effort to study these important clinical observations in a controlled manner, Foshee, Peeler, M. Newton, and I carried out a series of experiments on CFI-strain mice. Since "labor sitting" in mice proved to be tedious, we developed a method of getting a high proportion of "dated" pregnancies in one night of exposure (Newton & Newton 1968).

To test the inhibitory effects of environment on labor, we alternated pregnant mice at term between two different types of environment (Newton, Foshee, & Newton 1966a). One environment was a cage with a nesting box similar to that in which the mice had been housed since birth. The other environment was a small glass fish bowl imbued with the strange odor of cat urine. Mice that had all become pregnant during the same night were moved from the familiar cage to the glass bowl at regular one- and two-hour intervals. During each time period the number of mice in each type of environment was the same. Yet we found the delivery rate in the two environments was not the same. Significantly ($p < .01$) more first deliveries took place in the sheltered familiar cage. Only six first deliveries took place in the glass bowls with cat odor, as opposed to nineteen in the familiar cage with sheltered environment. Significant ($p < .05$) differences were also found in the total number of pups born in each environment; the familiar cage with shelter received the most pups (see Table 2).

We also studied the delay in time before the first delivery in mice, all of whom had become pregnant the same night (Newton, Peeler, Newton 1968). In this experiment (see Table 3), one group of mice was moved every two hours between two glass bowls to give them continuous disturbance. Another group was rotated be-

Table 2. *Relation of environment to number of mouse pups delivered*

	Number of pups born in familiar cage with shelter	Number of pups born in glass bowls with cat odor
Number of first-born pups	19	6
Total number of pups born	138	87

Table 3. *Effect of continuous disturbance on time of first delivery and pup mortality*

Group	Hours to first delivery		Total number pups found	
	Mean	Median	Dead	Alive
Familiar cage with nesting material	12.77	10.00	28	321
Glass bowl, no shelter	17.10	18.50	43	306

tween two familiar cages containing fluffy nesting material under which they usually hid. Those continuously moved between glass bowls with no shelter available delivered their first pups significantly ($p < .05$) later than those who had shelter continuously available. Environment not only influenced the time birth occurred but also was related to pup mortality: 54 percent more dead pups were found born to mice delivering in an environment where no shelter was available than among the controls. This difference was statistically significant ($p = .036$).

In two other experiments we studied the effect of brief, sudden change on the speed of labor (Newton, Foshee, & Newton 1966*b*) (see Table 4). Mice were systematically disturbed (and presumably frightened) by subjecting them to complete olfactory, kinesthetic, and visual change for one minute after the birth of their second pup. A laboratory assistant gently picked up the mouse and placed it in cupped hands, completely enclosing it for one minute. The control group was not handled. Two types of subjects were used. In Experiment A all the mice used had experienced only routine handling. Experiment B was identical to Experiment A except that all mice in both control and disturbed groups had been previously subjected to fifteen periods of systematic human handling which included hand-cupping. The undisturbed mice delivered their next pups in about 12 to 13 minutes, but the disturbed mice were markedly slower in delivering the next pup. Labor after disturbance was significantly slower ($p < .05$) in both Experiment A and Experiment B. In each experiment the disturbed mice took over eight minutes longer than the controls to produce the next pup, a slowing of labor by about 65 to 72 percent (see Table 4).

Based on these experiments, we (Newton *et al.* 1966*b*; Newton, Peeler, Newton 1968) have hypothesized a *fetus-ejection reflex* similar to the milk-ejection reflex hypothesized by Ely and Petersen (1941). This reflex is thought to be initially triggered by gentle stimulation of the lower genital tract at term, causing the release of oxytocic substances. These, in turn, act to cause uterine contractions of the slowly augmenting type. The fetus-ejection reflex, like the milk-ejection reflex, appears sensitive to cortical influence and can easily be inhibited. It is possible that the fetus-ejection reflex is as important to the management of normal labor as the milk-ejection reflex is to the management of successful lactation and dairy farming.

Triggering of Caretaking Behavior

Coitus, labor, and lactation are similar in yet one more respect. All three of them are related to caretaking behavior, an essential element in successful reproduction. All three are interpersonal, psychophysical acts that are psychologically intertwined with affectionate partnership formation and caretaking behavior. Coitus, labor, and lactation alone cannot secure successful reproduction— the caretaking behavior is an essential ingredient in the whole.

An overview of societies indicates that the most usual human pattern is that of males caring for women with whom they are

Table 4. *Effects of disturbance on labor speed*

Groups	Minutes between birth of second and third pups (Means)	Parturient mice involved (Number)
Experiment A:		
Controls	13.2	16
Disturbed	21.8	12
Experiment B:		
Controls	12.0	11
Disturbed	20.7	15

cohabiting (Mead & Newton 1967). Each society may channel this urge into different patterns of help but basically the male *homo sapiens* usually defends and protects his vulnerable child-bearing mate and often gives her considerable economic support.

Similarly, females who form satisfying mating relationships with men usually accompany the coital behavior with an urge to care for the man in various other ways—like cooking for him, making a home for him, and being emotionally committed to his well-being.

The intense emotions involved in orgasm are, in fact, a perfect model for operant conditioning. The pleasure male and female gain during coitus may tend to condition them to the other partner and to bind them in reproductive partnership so the children are more likely to have two adult individuals on the scene. *Operant conditioning, reinforced through coital pleasure, may be the biologic foundation upon which patterns of family life are built.*

Marriage and divorce statistics are in favor of this thesis. Paul Gebhard (1966) in a study on the relationship of the female orgasm rate to the quality of the marriage, suggests indeed that what clinicians have always suspected to be true is true. Unhappy marriages were characterized by a lower female orgasm rate. Clark and Wallen (1965) reported a similar finding. Decreasing coital responsiveness during the first five years tended to be associated with negative marriages whereas increasing sexual responsiveness during the first five years was associated with marriages positive in quality.

Finally, Rainwater (1966) reported a marked statistical association between enjoyment of sex and cooperative marriage relationships. A lower-class sample was used. In this group a high association was found between enjoyable sex and other shared activities. Sixty-four percent of white wives who shared other activities with their husbands reported great enjoyment and interest in sex. Only 18 percent of white wives who did not share their activities with their husbands reported similar sexual enjoyment. Similar, but less marked, results were found for the rest of the sample. More cooperative sharing behavior was accompanied by more enjoyment of sex by Negro wives, white husbands, and

Negro husbands, although in these cases the association was not quite as marked.

The relationship between birth and caretaking behavior does not appear to have been extensively studied in humans. The hypothesis that birth can be a maturing experience which tends to orient women toward more responsiveness is supported by Masters and Johnson (1966), who reported that women who have borne children may be more sexually responsive. They found that parous women tend to differ from nonparous women by being more erotic during early pregnancy.

Perhaps their major finding, however, concerns the differences between sex skin coloring of women who have borne children and those who have not (Masters & Johnson 1966). Nulliparous women in the plateau phase were found to have sex skin color changes in the labia minora that varied from pink to bright red. Women who had borne children, however, could go some degrees beyond this. Their color changes typically varied from bright red to deep wine color. The degree of color changes appears to be so closely correlated with pelvic and labial varicosity and other sexual reactions that Masters and Johnson state, "It is obvious that the sex skin (labia minora) provides satisfactory clinical evidence of the degree of sexual tension experienced by individual. . . . Generally, the more brilliant and definitive the color change, the more intense the individual's response to the particular means of sex stimulation [p. 42]."

The relationship between lactation and caretaking behavior has been more extensively studied. On the human statistical level, maternal interest and behavior and breast feeding have been reported to be correlated in the majority of studies investigating this point. However, since it has been shown that the personality and attitudes of the mother are related to her choosing to breast feed, controlled investigative methods are desirable. Peeler, Rawlins, and I (1968) undertook a study of this problem—on an experimental level in mice, and on a statistical level in human mothers. Since caretaking behavior is known to be related to preceding pregnancy, the duration of lactation, contact with the young, the age of the young, and previous experience and type of family grouping, all these factors were controlled in our study of mice.

Nulliparous mice of the CF1 strain were bred and permitted to raise a litter. On the day of weaning, while the maternal nipples were still developed, operations were performed under sodium pentobarbital anesthesia. Test mice had all ten nipples removed, and control mice were given a sham operation near each nipple. The mice were re-bred, using a modification of the Newton dated pregnancy technique. Test and control mice that delivered on the same day were placed in pairs in cages and given a litter of pups belonging to neither of them. Thus, each experimental cage contained one nippleless mouse that had just delivered a litter, one lactating mouse that had experienced a sham operation and had just delivered a litter, and a litter of newborn mice belonging to neither mother. The new mouse families were then left undisturbed for two days.

Both the nippleless mice and the mice that were feeding the pups on casual inspection acted very maternally toward the pups. Both mother mice lived in a nest together with the pups, cuddling them most of the time. It should be remembered that both of the mice had successfully raised litters before and therefore were experienced in mothering behavior. Routine tests of maternal behavior applied over the course of ten days, however, showed some differences. In the 14 tests, the lactating mice showed higher mean absolute maternal behavior scores in 13 tests and equal scores on one test. Retrieving tests showed no significant difference between test and control mice, but significant differences were found when barriers were placed between adoptive mother and young in an attempt to measure the strength of the maternal drive. Lactating mice tried significantly more frequently to burrow under a sieve to reach their pups, and significantly more frequently crossed a shock barrier to be with them (Table 5).

Human data, collected along with the mouse data, suggested a similar relationship. Totally lactating mothers were paired with nonlactating mothers. They were matched for education and parity. The lactating and nonlactating mothers showed one significant difference ($p < .01$) in the four behavior dimensions studied. Seventy-one percent of the nursing mothers and only twenty-six percent of the nonnursing mothers encouraged physical contact between themselves and their babies by sometimes or often having

Table 5. *Behavior of matched pairs of mice*

	Lactating members of pairs	Nonlactating members of pairs	Probabilities by Wilcoxon Matched Pairs Signed Rank Test
Rescue-Retrieving Test			
Mean no. pups carried day 5	4.7	2.5	
Mean no. pups carried day 6	4.3	2.7	
Scatter-Retrieving Test			
Mean no. pups carried test 1, day 7	4.6	3.3	
Mean no. pups carried test 2, day 7	3.9	3.9	
Burrowing Behavior—Sieve-Barrier Test			
Mean no. min. burrowing-day 3	4.1	0.5	< .01
Mean no. min. burrowing-day 4	3.8	0.4	< .01
Mean no. min. burrowing-day 9	4.1	0.9	
Mean no. min. burrowing-day 10	3.8	0.7	
Location in Cage-Sieve-Barrier Test			
Mean no. min. away from litter-day 3	45.4	48.4	
Mean no. min. away from litter-day 4	43.6	49.9	
Mean no. min. away from litter-day 9	44.0	46.3	
Mean no. min. away from litter-day 10	45.8	48.0	< .02
Shock-Barrier Test—Day 12			
Mean no. min. spent with pups	20.1	9.5	< .01
Mean no. times crossed toward pups	8.6	3.5	< .01

the baby in bed with them (Table 6). Lactation may influence maternal behavior in selective ways. Operant conditioning may be one factor involved.

CONCLUSION

In conclusion, we can say that women have a more varied heritage of sexual enjoyment than men. Their reproductive behavior repertoire involves three intense interpersonal reproductive acts. In any discussion concerning sexuality of women or their role in life, full account needs to be taken of the marked intercorrelations and interrelationships between coital response, parturition response,

Table 6. *Behavior of matched pairs of humans*

	Lactating members of pairs (%)	Nonlactating members of pairs (%)
Mother sometimes or often sleeps or rests in bed with baby	71	26
Mother definitely states baby not spanked	87	95
Mother holds baby ½ hour or more when not eating	57	62
Mother in different building from baby less than 3 hours daily	95	86

and lactation response. In the management of reproductive behavior, the underlying similarities of all three should be kept in mind. It is of biological and clinical significance that coitus, birth, and lactation appear to have a common neurohormonal base and share the tendency to be inhibited by environmental disturbance. All three appear, under some circumstances, to trigger caretaking behavior, which is an essential part of mammalian reproduction.

REFERENCES

Abolins, J. A. Das Stillen und die Temperatur der Brust. *Acta Obstetricia et Gynecologica Scandinavica* 1954, **33**: 60–68.

Amoroso, E. C., & Jewell, P. A. The exploitation of the milk ejection reflex by primitive peoples. *Occasional Paper No. 18 of the Royal Anthropological Institute* 1963, 126–36.

Bleicher, N. Behavior of the bitch during parturition. *Journal of the American Veterinary Medical Association* 1962, **140**: 1076–82.

Campbell, B., & Petersen, W. E. Milk let-down and orgasm in human female. *Human Biology* 1953, **25**: 165–68.

Clark, A., & Wallen, P. Women's sexual responsiveness and the duration and quality of their marriages. *American Journal of Sociology* 1965, **71**: 187–96.

Debackere, M., Peeters, G., & Tuyttens, N. Reflex release of an oxytocic hormone by stimulation of genital organs in male and female sheep studied by a cross-circulation technique. *Journal of Endocrinology* 1961, 22: 321–34.

Eastman, N. J., & Hellman, L. M. *Williams Obstetrics* (12th ed.), New York: Appleton, 1961.

Ely, F., & Peterson, W. E. Factors involved in the ejection of milk. *Journal of Dairy Science* 1941, 24: 211–23.

Ford, C. S., & Beach, F. A. *Patterns of sexual behavior.* New York: Harper & Row, 1951.

Freak, M. J. Abnormal conditions associated with pregnancy and parturition in the bitch. *Veterinary Record* 1962, 74: 1323–35.

Gebhard, P. H. Factors in marital orgasm. *Journal of Social Issues* 1966, 22: 88–95.

Gunther, M. Instinct and nursing couple. *Lancet* 1955, 1: 575–78.

Hafez, E. S. (ed.) *The behavior of domestic animals.* Baltimore: Williams & Wilkins, 1962.

Hytten, F. E., Yorston, J. E., & Thomson, A. M. Difficulties associated with breast feeding. *British Medical Journal* 1958, 1: 310–15.

Kinsey, A. B., Pomeroy, W. B., Martin, C. E., & Gebhard, P. H. *Sexual behavior in the human female.* Philadelphia: Saunders, 1953.

Masters, W. H., & Johnson, V. E. *Human sexual response.* Boston: Little, Brown, 1966.

———. *Human sexual inadequacy.* Boston: Little, Brown, 1970.

Mead, M., & Newton, N. Cultural patterning of perinatal behavior. In S. A. Richardson and A. F. Guttmacher (eds.), *Childbearing—its social and psychological aspects.* Baltimore: Williams & Wilkins, 1967.

Moir, C. Recording the contractions of the human pregnant and nonpregnant uterus. *Transactions of the Edinburgh Obstetrical Society* 1934, 54: 93–120.

Newson, L. J., & Newson, E. Breast feeding in decline. *British Medical Journal* 1962, 2: 1744–45.

Newton, M., & Newton, N. Let-down reflex in human lactation. *Journal of Pediatrics* 1948, 33: 698–704.

Newton, N. *Maternal emotions.* New York: Hoeber, 1955.

———. Psychologic differences between breast and bottle feeding. *American Journal of Clinical Nutrition* 1971, 24: 993–1004.

Newton, N., Foshee, D., & Newton, M. Parturient mice: effects of environment on labor. *Science* 1966, 151: 1560–61. (a)

———. Experimental inhibition of labor through environmental disturbance. *Obstetrics and Gynecology* 1966, 27: 371–77 (b)

Newton, N., & Newton, M. Relation of the let-down reflex to the ability to breast feed. *Pediatrics* 1950, 5: 726–33.

———. Psychologic aspects of lactation. *New England Journal of Medicine* 1967, 277: 1179–88.

———. A simple method of obtaining dated pregnancies and observable labors in experimental mice. *American Journal of Obstetrics and Gynecology* 1968, 100: 871–74.

Newton, N., Peeler, D., & Newton, M. Effect of disturbance on labor: an experiment using 100 mice with dated pregnancies. *American Journal of Obstetrics and Gynecology* 1968, 101: 1096–1102.

Newton, N., Peeler, D., & Rawlins, C. Effect of lactation on maternal behavior in mice with comparative data on humans. *Lying-in: The Journal of Reproductive Medicine* 1968, 1: 257–62.

Rainwater, L. Some aspects of lower class sexual behavior. *Journal of Social Issues* 1966, 22: 96–108.

Read, G. D. *Childbirth without fear*. New York: Harper & Brothers, 1944.

———. Observations on a series of labors with special reference to physiological delivery. *Lancet* 1949, 1: 721–26.

———. *The birth of a child*. New York: Vanguard, 1950. (a)

———. *Introduction to motherhood*. New York: Harper & Brothers, 1950. (b)

Salber, E. J., Stitt, P. G., & Babbott, J. G. Patterns of breast feeding in family health clinic. II. Duration of feeding and reasons for weaning. *New England Journal of Medicine*, 1959, 260: 310–15.

Sears, R. R., Maccoby, E. E., & Levin, H. *Patterns of child rearing*. Evanston: Row, Peterson, 1957.

Waller, H. *Clinical studies in lactation*. London: Heinemann, n.d.

Weiderman, J., Freund, M., & Stone, M. L. Human breast and uterus: comparison of sensitivity to oxytocin during gestation. *Obstetrics and Gynecology* 1963, 21: 272.

chapter 6

Maternalism in Fetal Hormonal and Related Syndromes

Anke A. Ehrhardt*

The influence of fetal hormones on sexual organs and on parts of the central nervous system, mediating aspects of sexual behavior in mammals, has been discussed extensively. The principle that has evolved, based on many animal experiments, seems to be: If androgen is present at the critical time of differentiation, the external genitalia become masculinized; if androgen is not present, or its action successfully blocked, the external genitalia are feminized. Equally, if androgen is present in sufficient amounts and at the critical time of CNS differentiation, sexual behavior will be masculinized after being primed with male hormones at puberty. If androgens are absent or blocked, the animal, after having been treated with female gonadal hormones at puberty, will behave sexually predominantly like a female.

*Anke A. Ehrhardt, Ph.D., Departments of Pediatrics and Psychiatry, Children's Hospital, State University of New York at Buffalo.

The principle is simple. However, findings from different laboratories have not always been consistent, partly due to premature generalizations from the behavior of one mammalian species to another, partly due to inaccuracies in reporting and comparing dosage and timing of hormonal treatment, and partly due to poor definition of the behavior under study.

Premature generalizations and ill-defined behavioral patterns have led to contradictions in the study of sexual behavior, and especially in the study of maternal behavior. The term "maternal behavior" itself is confusing, since in mammals it is not only the biologic mother who takes care of the young, although she is typically the one who is the most attentive to the offspring after having given birth to them. Males have also been observed to show many aspects of so-called maternal behavior. Thus, "parental behavior" was suggested as an alternative term (Lehrman 1961). Parental behavior, however, excludes other members of the group who often participate in the protection and care of the young, as has been observed in free-living langurs (Jay 1963) or baboons (DeVore 1963). As a way out, maternal behavior has been redefined as the behavior of the mother and her surrogates in the presence of the young (Rheingold 1963).

EFFECTS OF FETAL HORMONES ON MATERNAL BEHAVIOR IN ANIMALS

The female's behavior during parturition is usually centered on the various aspects of delivery and the products of birth—the fetuses, placenta, and birth fluids. Once born, the neonate's urgent need for food, warmth, and sheltering is typically matched by the most common aspects of maternal behavior—nest building, licking, nursing, and retrieving.

These basic components of maternal behavior appear in many species of mammals. However, the patterns, sequences, intensity, and frequency of responses to the young vary in characteristic ways from species to species, and sometimes even among different strains of one species (see review by Lehrman 1961).

The onset of those aspects of maternal behavior which the biologic mother typically expresses after parturition seems to be strongly influenced by hormonal changes before or at the time of parturition. It has been proposed for the rat (Rosenblatt 1970) and for the rabbit (Zarrow, Farooq, Denenberg, Sawin, & Ross 1963) that the onset of several aspects of maternal behavior is triggered by an altered ratio of progesterone and estrogen, with a decrease of progesterone levels and a subsequent increase of estrogen levels shortly before parturition. Prolactin and oxytocin, the two pituitary hormones that trigger lactation and uterine contractions, seem to be contributing, but not the only, responsible factors in the onset of all aspects of maternal behavior. While a combined treatment with progesterone, estrogen, and prolactin induced lactation in all nonpregnant female rabbits under study, only a few were observed to build a maternal nest, suggesting that lactation and maternal nest building are two separate events correlated in time but not with an entirely common mechanism (Zarrow et al. 1963). On the other hand, treatment with estradiol and progesterone at a critical ratio in which progesterone had to be terminated several days before estrogen, promptly triggered maternal nest building in all ovariectomized nonpregnant female rabbits under study, independent of lactation.

In an experiment by Obias (quoted by Rosenblatt 1970), female rats were hypophysectomized on the 13th day of pregnancy; pregnancy was maintained, probably because of placental secretion of luteotropic hormones. Many of these hypophysectomized rats had difficulty giving birth. However, the ones which survived exhibited nest building, crouching, and retrieving, and were, except for their failure to lactate, similar to intact mothers.

Not only hormones have an influence on maternal behavior. It can be strongly altered by external stimuli, in particular, by the presence of the young after birth, which seems to be largely responsible for the maintenance of maternal behavior.

The presence of small pups can be such a powerful stimulus that even male rats, if exposed long enough, have been observed to respond to the pups with crouching, licking, and retrieving responses, and, to a lesser extent, nest building. According to the pooled observations of various investigators (Lehrman 1961), laboratory male rats usually do not participate in the care of small pups. In the experiment by Rosenblatt (1967), male rats and females after parturition differed mainly in latency of onset of maternal behavior. It took male rats several days, generally at least five, of exposure to a new litter of small motherless pups before they responded to the young, while female rats show the same behavior components immediately after birth.

These studies clearly suggest that males, as well as females, have the capacity for maternal behavior in their repertoire. This was proven experimentally by Fisher (1956, 1966) when he induced nest building, retrieving, and grooming of the young in adult male rats by chemical stimulation with testosterone salt injected directly into various sites of the hypothalamus.

On the basis of the presented evidence, the question regarding fetal hormonal effects on those neural structures that may be involved in the expression of maternal behavior is not whether fetal androgens suppress maternal behavior all together. Rather, the question is whether fetal androgens alter the sensitivity to hormonal changes and external stimuli that trigger maternal behavior and, thus, whether fetal androgens change the intensity and frequency of the various responses to young offspring.

There are very few studies that have been explicitly designed as a study of fetal hormonal effects on maternal behavior. An example are the experiments by Anderson, Zarrow, and Denenberg (1970) on maternal behavior in the domestic rabbit. Two types of nest building were observed in the rabbit. In one type the nest was made of straw, paper, and similar materials available to the rabbit and occurred in both nonpregnant and pregnant rabbits under diverse conditions. The second type was a larger nest consisting of considerably more straw, excelsior or similar material, plus a new feature—loose hair that the doe plucked from her fur and deposited into the nest as lining and covering shortly before parturition. This type of nest is called a "maternal nest" and is normally seen only during pregnancy (Ross, Sawin, Zarrow, & Denenberg 1963). Maternal nest building could be induced with a treatment of progesterone and estradiol in ovariectomized female rabbits. The same treatment was totally inadequate to initiate any maternal nest building in the castrated male.

In a subsequent experiment, pregnant rabbits were treated with testosterone at different times of gestation and with different dosages. While testosterone had no apparent effect on the pregnant doe herself, her female offspring were born with masculinized genitalia. These fetally androgenized female rabbits were ovariectomized at adulthood and treated with progesterone and estrogen. The same hormonal treatment that triggered maternal nest building in 90 percent of the ovariectomized female controls induced maternal nest building in only 11 percent of the fetally androgenized females and in none of the male control group.

It appears that fetally androgenized female domestic rabbits are less sensitive than other female rabbits to the induction of one specific aspect of maternal behavior, namely, the building of the characteristic maternal nest. They resemble, in this aspect, the intact or castrated males.

The possibly organizing effect of fetal hormones on the nervous system is more subtle in primates than in rodents and in the rabbit. The sexual and maternal behavior of primates depends even more on environmental experiences and is less dependent on postnatal hormonal activation. Fetal androgens seem to lead to sex-specific behavior patterns established in childhood, long before pubertal hormones begin to act on the central nervous system. For instance, genetic female rhesus monkeys whose mothers had been injected with androgens during pregnancy were not only born with masculinized external genitalia but showed also childhood play behavior more similar to males than to normal females (Goy 1970).

It is known from field studies on langurs and baboons that interest in infants is sexually dimorphic in childhood social behavior patterns. While male juvenile langurs and baboons play almost exclusively with other male age-mates and pay only perfunctory attention to the infants of the group, the female juvenile spends much of her time with adult females, participating in taking care of the infants (Jay 1963; DeVore 1963).

MASCULINIZING AND NONMASCULINIZING FETAL HORMONAL
EXPOSURE IN HUMAN FEMALES:
CHILDHOOD REHEARSAL OF MATERNALISM

The categories for analysis of sex differences in maternal behavior in human beings, as well as the techniques for assessing them, are still largely a matter of empirical trial and error. As in other mammals, human females are the ones who typically have the major responsibility of taking care of infants after giving birth to them. At the same time, we know that human males, as other male mammals, are also capable of and often participate in caring for small children. In further analogy between animal-experimental and free-observational evidence, it does seem, however, that human females typically take a greater interest from early childhood on in the various aspects of care-taking behavior centered around babies. Social environmentalists tend to argue that all sex differences, including expression of maternal behavior, are due to social conditioning along the lines of the stereotyped sex roles expectations. On the basis of the presented evidence from animal studies, it is possible that fetal hormones may be one of the variables that interact with social conditioning. The comparison of human females who have been exposed to abnormal levels of fetal hormones with normal control or clinical contrast groups gives insight into possible effects of fetal hormones on maternal behavior.

Fetal androgenization chiefly occurs in two syndromes of human females, namely, in progestin-induced hermaphroditism and in the adrenogenital syndrome. In both groups the genetic female fetus is exposed to an excess of androgens. The result is masculinization of the external genitalia and unaffected, normal female internal organs. The masculinization of the external genitalia can vary from an enlarged clitoris to a normal-appearing penis and empty scrotum.

The progestin-induced condition occurred predominantly in the fifties as an untoward side-effect of treatment with progestinic drugs in mothers who had a history of habitual miscarriages. Post-natally, the affected child needs only surgical correction of the genitalia and no hormonal treatment.

The adrenogenital syndrome is transmitted as a recessive genetic trait. The source of androgenization is the individual's own hyperactive adrenal gland that begins producing too much of the adrenal's masculinizing hormone in utero and continues doing so after birth if not corrected with cortisone. The condition requires lifetime hormonal control with cortisone and early surgical feminization of the external genitalia.

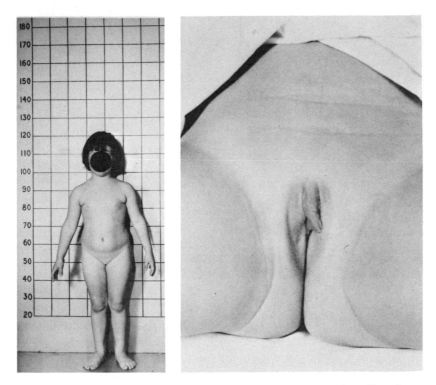

Fig. 1. *Progestin-induced hermaphroditism in a female showing clitoral enlargement.*

A third condition, Turner's syndrome, illustrates the other end of the spectrum—nonandrogenizing fetal hormonal exposure. Girls with this syndrome have streak gonads and, therefore, none of their own fetal gonadal hormones to influence fetal differentiation. The basic etiologic defect is genetic, typically, there is a missing sex chromosome so that the chromosome count is usually either 44 + XO or a mosaic of 44 + XO in some cells and 44 + XX in others.

In the study of prenatal hormonal influences on behavior in human females,* we evaluated ten girls with progestin-induced

*The studies of prenatal hormonal influences on certain aspects of postnatal behavior in human females were carried out at The Johns Hopkins Hospital in collabora-

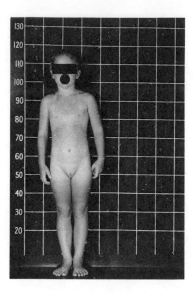

Fig. 2. *Adrenogenital syndrome in a female treated with cortisone since one year of age.*

hermaphroditism, fifteen girls with the early-treated adrenogenital syndrome, and fifteen girls with Turner's syndrome. Cortisone treatment for the adrenogenital syndrome has only been available since 1950. The progestinic drugs with masculinizing side effects were also mainly prescribed in the fifties. Consequently, the age of the patients ranged, at the time of study, between early childhood and teenage, with most of the children being in middle childhood and early teenage. The youngest girl was four and the oldest was sixteen years of age. Girls with Turner's syndrome fell into the same age range.

The patients were matched with normal control girls selected from Baltimore public schools on a one-to-one basis according to age, race, socioeconomic status of the family, and IQ. Thus, all together, we studied eighty children and their mothers with several sex-role preference tests and semistructured interviews. The interviews included items which have proven to be sexually dimorphic in large samples of normal boys and girls and concerned behavior

tion with John Money, and with the assistance of Ralph Epstein, Kathryn Evers, Nanci Greenberg, and Dan Masica who worked as students in the Psychohormonal Research Unit.

which could be clearly and operationally defined. The data based on those interviews were abstracted and tabulated according to coding scales that ranged from two- to five-point ratings. The agreement between mothers and daughters was generally high. Thus, the answers were pooled. Two people tabulated the data from the files independently. In the comparison of patient and control groups, dichotomous data were statistically tested with the McNemar Test for the Significance of Changes between Related Samples (Siegel 1956). Interview data given ratings on three-, four-, or five-point rating scales were tested with the Sign Test (Siegel 1956).

Table 1 summarizes the findings on marriage and maternalism and shows some striking differences between the groups with fetal masculinization and their control groups, respectively. There were significantly fewer girls with the adrenogenital syndrome who reported fantasies of becoming a bride. The girls with progestin-induced hermaphroditism did not differ from their controls with respect to wedding and marriage. In both groups with fetal masculinization, significantly more girls wanted to have a career and significantly fewer girls wanted to become a full-time

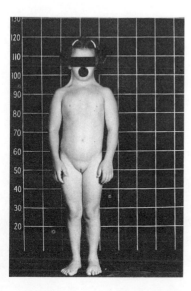

Fig. 3. *Turner's syndrome in a female with XO chromosome constitution.*

Table 1. *Marriage and maternalism*

	Results: Statistical Comparisons		
	PI vs C (N=10) (N=10)	AGS vs C (N=15) (N=15)	TS vs C (N=15) (N=15)
1. Wedding and marriage anticipation in play and daydreams	o	*	o
2. Priority of marriage vs. career	*	*	o
3. Daydreams and fantasies of pregnancy and motherhood	o	*	o
4. Toy preference (dolls vs. cars, guns, etc.)	*	*	o
5. Interest in infant care	o	***	o

Legend:
PI   = Progestin-induced hermaphroditism
AGS = Adrenogenital syndrome
TS   = Turner's syndrome
C   = Matched controls
o   = No significant difference
*   = $p \leq .05$
***   = $p \leq .001$

housewife and mother. Equally, there were significantly fewer girls in the group with the adrenogenital syndrome who stated that they had fantasies and daydreams about pregnancy and having children. Girls with progestin-induced hermaphroditism were no different from their controls in this regard.

There was a minimum of interest in doll play in both groups with a history of fetal masculinization. Most of them preferred or equally liked cars, guns, trucks, and other boys' toys. Girls with the adrenogenital syndrome differed, also, significantly in their interest in taking care of infants and participating in baby care of a younger sibling or a neighbor's child. More than half of the patient group stated they were totally indifferent to small infants, while only two girls in the control group reacted similarly.

Girls with Turner's syndrome did not differ in any aspect of maternal play from their controls. On the contrary, there was even a tendency to be more interested in small children and in becoming a mother (Ehrhardt, Greenberg, & Money 1970).

From the data presented, both groups with fetal masculinization appear to have less interest in several aspects of childhood rehearsal of the wife and mother role. The patients did not exclude the possibility of getting married and having children one day, but doll play and infant care were low on their priority list of interesting activities in play and in fantasies. Instead they preferred to be outdoors and to participate in active athletics. Many of them seemed to have a high level of physical energy expenditure and preferred to play with boys rather than with girls, if given the choice. Consequently, significantly more girls in each of the two groups with fetal masculinization were called and identified themselves as tomboys throughout all or most of their childhood. Their tomboyism did not include implications of homosexuality and future lesbianism, or a belief of having been assigned to the wrong sex. Equally, very few mothers were deeply concerned about their daughters' tomboyism. They rather considered it as a developmental peculiarity and felt that their daughters' interests and activities were still in the range of acceptable female behavior (Ehrhardt, Epstein, & Money 1968).

An interesting side finding was that in both groups with fetal androgenization significantly more IQs were at the superior level than arc expected in the normal population, suggesting that fetal androgens may have a favorable influence on postnatal intellectual development (Ehrhardt & Money 1967; Money & Lewis 1966). In this context, intelligence is a side track. However, it is important to emphasize that the low interest in maternalism cannot be attributed solely to high IQ, since patients and controls were matched on this criterion.

Certain aspects of gender identity differentiation as a female, particularly the interest in childhood rehearsal of aspects of the maternal role, may be modified by fetal androgens. Postnatal androgens are not relevant, since girls with progestin-induced hermaphroditism were no different hormonally after birth than other females; and girls with the adrenogenital syndrome, in our sample, were treated successfully with cortisone from early childhood on.

Of course, it remains to be seen how low interest in some aspects of maternalism in childhood will correlate with maternal behavior in adulthood. We have to wait until our patients are adults to ascertain their actual choice between career and motherhood and their efficiency in maternal care.

MASCULINIZING AND NONMASCULINIZING FETAL AND POSTNATAL HORMONAL EXPOSURE IN HUMAN FEMALES: ASPECTS OF ADULT MATERNAL BEHAVIOR

Genetic females with the adrenogenital syndrome who were born before cortisone treatment became available in 1950, were exposed to high levels of androgen before and after birth. These patients lived with the additional burden of postnatal virilization, including absence of pubertal changes, beard growth, low voice, and short stature because of rapid osseous development, until they were finally treated with cortisone.

In a study of 23 women with the late-treated adrenogenital syndrome, who ranged in age from 19 to 48 years at the time of their last psychological follow-up, we found that even strong tomboyism in childhood did not preclude marriage, childbearing, and family life in adulthood (Ehrhardt, Evers, & Money 1968). Presently, 12 women of the sample of 23 have gotten married, of whom 5 have given birth to at least one child. Consistent with the answers of the early-treated adrenogenital group in childhood, when asked how they would decide on the "ideal status" in their personal lives, a minority of them wanted to be a full-time wife with no outside job or career. Most of them were equally interested in a job, or even preferred a full-time career, and a few disliked the idea of marriage altogether. Eleven (52 percent) of the 21 for whom we had sufficient information concerning their attitude toward raising a family stated that having children usually did not enter their thoughts, dreams, or fantasies. We also found, in the files of 12 of these patients, information regarding the desire to hold and cuddle very small infants. Only 2 (17 percent) stated a positive and genuine desire to be affectionate with small infants,

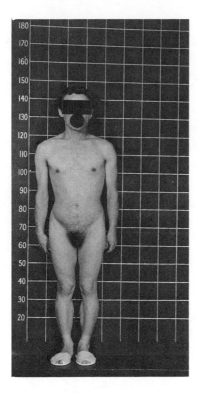

Fig. 4. *Adrenogenital syndrome in a female before treatment with cortisone at age twenty-three.*

while the other 10 were noncommittal and preferred children who were at least toddlers. Some of them stated that they did not dislike infants, but felt insecure and clumsy handling small babies.

These adult patients were quite different in their reactions to aspects of marriage and maternal behavior from a group of 10 adolescents and adults with the androgen insensitivity (testicular feminizing) syndrome. The latter patients are genetic males. However, they are born with completely female-appearing external genitalia, since the cells of their bodies are totally unable to respond to male sex hormones which are made in their typically undescended testes. They respond, instead, to the small amount of female sex hormones—estrogen—which is produced in the testes. Before birth the masculine internal development commences, but is not completed. It goes far enough to prevent female development. There are no ovaries and tubes and no uterus; consequently, there are no menstruation and fertility. Patients with an androgen insensitivity syndrome, like Turner's syndrome, illustrate the principle of nonandrogenizing fetal hormone exposure.

We found that these women had an entirely female gender identity (Money, Ehrhardt, & Masica 1968). In contrast to the women with the late-treated adrenogenital syndrome, the predominant goal of the majority was to become a full-time wife and have children by adoption. Four of them were married at the time of the study. All ten (100 percent) of them stated that the idea of raising a family frequently entered their thoughts, dreams, and fantasies. This is a significant difference from the group with the late-treated adrenogenital syndrome, in which the corresponding percentage was only 52 percent. Two of the married women had adopted two children each and made, according to their husbands' and their own statements, very good mothers. Six (60 percent) stated that they strongly desired to hold and cuddle a small infant. The corresponding percentage in the group with the late-treated adrenogenital syndrome was 17 percent.

The difference in adult maternal interests between the two groups is in agreement with their predominant childhood play pattern, respectively. While most women with the androgen insensitivity syndrome were very interested in doll play and infant care, the majority of women with the late-treated adrenogenital syndrome had shown the typical tomboyish pattern with little rehearsal of maternal behavior, as already described for the girls with progestin-induced hermaphroditism and the early-treated adrenogenital syndrome.

DISCUSSION

Our findings in human females with fetal androgenizing or nonandrogenizing hormonal exposure may be seen as a corroboration of the findings in lower mammals. Exposure to abnormally high levels of fetal androgens seems to be correlated with a low interest in some aspects of maternal behavior in genetic females, while absence or blockage of fetal androgens is correlated with a completely normal maternal response in females with one missing sex chromosome or in females with a male chromosome pattern.

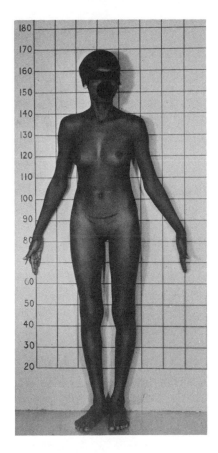

Fig. 5. *Androgen insensitivity (testicular feminizing) syndrome in a female with XY chromosome constitution.*

Nonetheless, one must be cautious not to attribute too much to fetal hormones. We know that gender identity differentiation in human beings, as in other primates, depends on the interaction of several factors in which social environmental experiences play a major, if not the most important, role.

The social conditioning in the patients with Turner's syndrome, or the androgen insensitivity syndrome, was completely toward a female gender identity, since the parents were always sure to raise a daughter. The influences exerted on the child from the parental environment were, therefore, exclusively feminine.

In the two groups with fetal masculinization, the parents' knowledge of their daughters' genital abnormality at birth may have influenced their reactions toward their daughters' behavior in different ways. Some parents may have accepted it; others may have attempted to discourage it. We found, however, no consistent difference in parental attitude toward their daughters' behavior between patient and control groups.

REFERENCES

Anderson, C. O., Zarrow, M. X., & Denenberg, V. H. Maternal behavior in the rabbit: Effect of androgen treatment during gestation upon the nest-building behavior of the mother and her offspring. *Hormones and Behavior* 1970, 1: 337-45.

DeVore, I. Mother-infant relations in free-ranging baboons. In H. L. Rheingold (ed.), *Maternal Behavior in Mammals.* New York: Wiley & Sons, 1963.

Ehrhardt, A. A., Epstein, R., & Money, J. Fetal androgens and female gender identity in the early-treated adrenogenital syndrome. *John Hopkins Medical Journal* 1968, 122: 160-67.

Ehrhardt, A. A., Evers, K., & Money, J. Influence of androgen and some aspects of sexually dimorphic behavior in women with the late-treated adrenogenital syndrome. *John Hopkins Medical Journal* 1968, 123: 115-22.

Ehrhardt, A. A., Greenberg, N., & Money, J. Female gender identity and absence of fetal gonadal hormones: Turner's syndrome. *John Hopkins Medical Journal* 1970, 126: 237-48.

Ehrhardt, A. A., & Money, J. Progestin-induced hermaphroditism: IQ and psychosexual identity in a study of ten girls. *Journal of Sex Research* 1967, 3: 83-100.

Fisher, A. E. Maternal and sexual behavior induced by intracranial chemical stimulation. *Science* 1956, 124: 228-29.

_____. Chemical and electrical stimulation of the brain in the male rat. In R. A. Gorski and R. E. Whalen (eds.), *The brain and gonadal function*, vol. III. *Brain and behavior.* Berkeley: University of California Press, 1966.

Goy, R. W. Experimental control of psychosexuality. *Philosophical Transactions of the Royal Society of London*, B 1970, 259: 149-62.

Jay, P. Mother-infant relations in langurs. In H. L. Rheingold (ed.), *Maternal behavior in mammals.* New York: Wiley & Sons, 1963.

Lehrman, D. S. Hormonal regulation of parental behavior in birds and infra-human mammals. In W. C. Young (ed.), *Sex and internal secretions.* Baltimore: Williams & Wilkins, 1961.

Money, J., Ehrhardt, A. A., & Masica, D. N. Fetal feminization induced by androgen insensitivity in the testicular feminizing syndrome: effect on marriage and maternalism. *John Hopkins Medical Journal* 1968, 123: 105-14.

Money, J., & Lewis, V. IQ, genetics, and accelerated growth: adrenogenital syndrome. *Bulletin of The John Hopkins Hospital* 1966, 118: 365-73.

Rheingold, H. L. *Maternal behavior in mammals.* New York: Wiley & Sons, 1963.

Rosenblatt, J. S. Nonhormonal basis of maternal behavior in the rat. *Science* 1967, 156: 1512-14.

_____. Views on the onset and maintenance of maternal behavior in the rat. In L. R. Aronson, E. Tobach, D. S. Lehrman, & J. S. Rosenblatt (eds.), *Development and evolution of behavior: essays in memory of T. C. Schneirla.* San Francisco: W. H. Freeman, 1970.

Ross, S., Sawin, P. B., Zarrow, M. X., & Denenberg, V. H. In H. L. Rheingold (ed.), *Maternal behavior in mammals.* New York: Wiley & Sons, 1963.

Siegel, S. *Nonparametric statistics for the behavioral sciences.* New York: McGraw-Hill, 1956.

Zarrow, M. X., Farooq, A., Denenberg, V. H., Sawin, P. B., & Ross, S. Maternal behaviour in the rabbit: endocrine control of maternal nest-building. *Journal of Reproduction and Fertility* 1963, 6: 375-83.

chapter 7

Women's Sexual Arousal*

Gunter Schmidt and Volkmar Sigusch†

There is rarely a discussion about male-female differences in sexual behavior in which the lesser capacity of women to be sexually aroused by external stimuli has not been emphasized. We are living in times when a constant decrease in sex differences encompassing many areas of sexuality can be observed, and the alleged greater appeal of pictorial and narrative stimuli to men is one of the few remaining arguments for the supposed hyposexuality of women. Therefore, woman's sexual arousal has become a central theme in the analysis of sex differences and gender roles in sexual behavior.

Kinsey and his coworkers (1953) gave evidence of considerable differences in the readiness of the average male and the average female to respond to pictorial and narrative stimuli. Until now

*Translated by Fred Klein, Switzerland.
†Institute für Sexualforschung, Hamburg, Germany.

their study was the most extensive work about sex differences with respect to psychosexual stimulation. They found that arousal from explicitly sexual stimuli was much rarer among women than among men.

The sex differences Kinsey observed were so impressive that their validity was never seriously discussed or questioned, even though it is very difficult to obtain valid results regarding sex differences in psychosexual arousability through retrospective reports, which Kinsey used, because of the impossibility of exactly defining and controlling stimuli. For example, the answer to the question, if one was never, seldom, or often sexually aroused through pictures of sexual action, would depend on what type of pictures one had seen and on how often one had the opportunity to see such pictures. Kinsey's results, therefore, possibly reflect sex differences in the degree and type of experience with pictorial or narrative stimuli, rather than sex differences in psychosexual arousability. This is to be expected, since women in our society have not often experienced these types of stimuli. Furthermore, pornography is directed primarily to the needs of men.

Perhaps the fact that Kinsey's findings were so strongly indicative is the reason that relatively little critical discussion of his findings on pictorial and narrative stimulation has arisen. Kinsey concluded that the male is conditioned by sexual experiences more frequently than the female. This finding accords with the observation that one of the most important control mechanisms of female sexuality is denial of the opportunities "to learn how to be sexual" (Simon & Gagnon 1969). The desexualization of the learning environment of women during childhood and adolescence could explain the lesser arousability of women described by Kinsey. The limitation of opportunities for sexual learning also characterizes the sexual situation of women today in the western industrial societies. Today, however, this limitation is probably not as prevalent as for the women Kinsey studied twenty to thirty years ago, the majority of whom were born between 1900 and 1930.

If we keep in mind that Kinsey, because of his method, might have at least overestimated the sex differences in sexual arousal, that his results reflect the situation of women 20 to 30 years ago, and that there has been a general decline in sex differences in sexual behavior, then it appears necessary to reexamine the Kinsey results on pictorial and narrative stimulation.

This is only possible through experimental studies in which the stimuli can be controlled and defined and in which different types of stimuli are used. We have performed such studies on a group of women, who may be considered *relatively* sexually emancipated, namely, young women born in the forties who have enjoyed higher education. For such a group, it would be possible to determine whether and to what extent Kinsey's results reflect cultural conditioning and not principally sex differences in the capacity to react sexually to sexual stimuli.

METHOD

In three studies on the effects of pictorial and narrative stimulation of both men and women, we investigated a total of 298 female and 298 male students from Hamburg University. Table 1 shows some background data of the subjects who volunteered to participate in the experiments. They were predominantly in their early twenties, single, and had experienced coitus. At least with

Table 1. *Some background data of the subjects*

Items	Males			Females		
	Study 1 (Slides) N=50	*Study 2* (Films, slide series) N=128	*Study 3* (Stories) N=120	*Study 1* (Slides) N=50	*Study 2* (Films, slide series) N=128	*Study 3* (Stories) N=120
Age (years)						
Range	19–27	20–29	19–30	19–27	19–28	19–31
Median	23.3	23.5	23.7	23.2	21.4	22.9
Marital status						
Single	96%	91%	88%	96%	98%	93%
Married	4%	9%	12%	4%	2%	7%
Coitus experience						
Yes	78%	74%	86%	74%	73%	75%
No	22%	26%	14%	26%	27%	25%

respect to age and marital status the sample can be viewed as fairly representative of the West German student population.

Different sets of stimuli were used in the three studies. They were as follows:

Study 1. Seventy-two black and white slides of sexual content, consisting of three parallel series of 24 pictures each, were used as stimuli. The slides showed seminudes and nudes of the opposite sex, necking, petting, coitus, and oral-genital activities. Each slide was shown for 20 seconds, with the exposition time of the whole set totaling 24 minutes. Fifty men and fifty women comprised the sample of this study.

Study 2. The stimuli consisted of color and black and white films and slide series of the following four themes: *Petting I*, with both partners undressing to their underwear and petting without reaching orgasm; *Petting II*, with both partners completely undressing, petting, and reaching orgasm through oral-genital stimulation; *Coitus I*, with manual-genital foreplay and face to face coitus; and *Coitus II*, with manual- and oral-genital foreplay and coitus in different positions.

Each of the themes was presented in color film, in black and white film, in color slide series, and in black and white slide series. Therefore, our material, produced especially for the experiments, consisted of a total of 16 stimulus sets. The black and white films were copies of the corresponding color films. The slides were taken by a time-sampling method during the film shooting. The exposition time for each film and slide series was 10 minutes. Each subject was shown only one set and each set was seen by a total of 8 males and 8 females. In this article we will present the combined results for the 16 stimulus sets, although the significance of stimulus-variables will not be analyzed. One hundred and twenty-eight men and 128 women took part in this study.

Study 3. Two stories involving the sexual experience of a young couple served as stimuli. Necking, petting (including oral-genital activities), coitus in various positions, and orgasm were described in detail. While the proceedings in both stories, which were written especially for this study, are similar, the stories differ in the degree of tenderness and romanticism expressed. The reading time for both stories was approximately 20 minutes.

As a stimulus each subject was given one of the two stories to read. All together 120 men and 120 women were tested, 60 of whom read one story and 60 read the other. We will present the combined results for both stories.

In all three studies the subjects were confronted with the stimuli in individual sessions. The experimenter left the examination room, so that the subjects were completely alone while they saw the films or read the stories. The experimenters were of the same sex as their subjects.

In the studies, the following data were gathered: 1. Background data; 2. subjective rating of the sexual arousal; 3. spontaneous emotional reactions to the psychosexual stimulation; 4. physiological-sexual reactions during the psychosexual stimulation; 5. emotional and autonomic reactions in the 24 hours after the psychosexual stimulation (compared with the previous 24 hours); 6. sexual behavior and reactions in the 24 hours after the psychosexual stimulation (as compared with the previous 24 hours).

All of the data was accumulated by means of questionnaires. The aforementioned data categories 2 and 3 were taken directly following the confrontation with the stimuli. Categories 1, 4, 5, and 6 were answered in a questionnaire which the subjects filled out 24 hours after viewing the films, or slides, or reading the stories. The anonymity of all answers was guaranteed to all the subjects.

A detailed description of the method of our experiments can be found in Sigusch et al. (1970) and Schmidt and Sigusch (1970).

EMOTIONAL RESPONSES TO PICTORIAL AND NARRATIVE STIMULATION

Ratings of Sexual Arousal

In studies 2 and 3, the subjects had to judge on a nine-point scale if and how strongly they were sexually aroused. These ratings were made directly after viewing the film or slide series or directly after reading the story.

Table 2 shows the mean arousal ratings of men and women for both studies. The ratings vary between the values 4.7 and 5.7, in

Table 2. *Ratings of sexual arousal (means, standard deviations) immediately after the psychosexual stimulation*

	Males				Females		
	M*	s	N		M*	s	N
Study 2							
(Films,							
slide series)	5.2	1.8	128		4.7	2.3	128
Study 3							
(Stories)	5.7	1.7	120		5.4	2.1	120

*Low value = low sexual arousal; high value = high sexual arousal.

Significance of the sex difference according to t-Test: $p = 0.05$ (Study 2); not significant (=ns, Study 3).

the category, "moderately stimulating." The means for the men in both studies are higher than for the women. Thus, the men describe themselves as being "sexually aroused" to a greater extent. These sex differences, however, are only slightly pronounced and statistically significant in only one study. Furthermore, they represent only average tendencies with great interindividual variability. The frequency distribution of the sexual arousal ratings show that 42 percent of the female film and slide viewers and 41 percent of the female story readers found their stimuli more arousing than the average (median) man.

Both the men and the women were somewhat more stimulated by the stories than by the films and the slides. However, because the stimuli are not directly comparable, because of their differential content and exposition time, no generalized conclusions should be drawn. We are not examining whether texts or films and slide series are sexually more stimulating, rather whether and to what degree sex differences are demonstrable in psychosexual stimulation for various stimuli.

Other Spontaneous Emotional Responses

Sexual arousal is obviously not the only emotional response generated by the viewing of the films or slides or by the reading of the stories. In order to measure other emotional changes we used a semantic differential which the subjects filled out before, as well as directly after, the exposure to the stimuli in studies 2 and 3.* The subjects were asked to describe their "present feelings" on this semantic differential. A comparison of the answers before and after the exposure to psychosexual stimuli provided us with information about the spontaneous emotional reactions to the films, slides, and stories.

Table 3 shows the results for men and women in both studies. There were significant changes under all 4 tested conditions (both sexes and both studies) for 8 of the 24 items. For five other items, it is possible to statistically demonstrate changes for three conditions in which the results for the fourth condition also point in the same direction; nevertheless, these do not reach the necessary level of statistical significance. Accordingly, the men and women described themselves after viewing the films or slides and after reading the stories, predominantly as (in this order): more excited, more innerly agitated, more aggressive, more bored, more emotional, wilder, more driven, more cheered up, more shocked, jumpier, more repelled, more numb, and more uninhibited. In addition, in both studies the men were significantly more impulsive, while the women were more irritated and disgusted after the psychosexual stimulation than before the confrontation with the stimuli.

These changes offer evidence that the viewing of films and slides with sexual themes, as well as the reading of sexual stories by men and women, lead to emotional activation and agitation, emotional instability, increases in emotional tensions, and, finally, to a lesser extent, to an emotional defense reaction (i.e. shocked, repelled, disgusted). However, one must keep in mind that these emotional changes are to be judged only in relation to the previous emotional profile, obtained under "normal" conditions. So that, for example, after the psychosexual stimulation the subjects felt themselves to be relatively more strongly repelled as compared to

---

*In study 2 the first semantic differential, together with the background data, was taken (in group sessions) a week before the showing of the films and slides. In study 3 the first semantic differential was taken (in individual sessions) directly before the reading of the stories. Despite these differences in method, remarkably corresponding results were achieved in both studies.

Table 3. Judgment of "present feelings" (means) on the semantic differential before and immediately after the psychosexual stimulation

Items	Males						Females					
	Study 2 N=128			Study 3 N=120			Study 2 N=128			Study 3 N=120		
	before	after	p*	before	after	p*	before	after	p*	before	after	p*
Gregarious–withdrawn	2.4	2.1	.01	2.4	2.1	ns	2.4	2.2	ns	2.3	2.3	ns
Concentrated–not concentrated	2.5	2.4	ns	3.0	2.5	.05	2.6	2.5	ns	2.5	2.5	ns
Unconcerned–shocked	3.0	3.4	.05	3.1	3.3	.05	3.0	3.7	.001	3.1	3.8	.001
Friendly–aggressive	2.3	2.9	.01	2.4	3.4	.001	2.7	3.4	.001	2.9	4.1	.001
Innerly agitated–innerly calm	4.9	4.1	.01	5.0	4.0	.001	4.3	3.7	.001	4.5	3.5	.001
Angered–amused	5.2	5.2	ns	5.0	5.5	.001	5.1	4.8	.01	4.7	4.8	ns
Cheered up–depressed	3.2	2.9	.001	3.1	2.7	.001	3.2	2.9	.05	3.5	2.8	.001
Composed–excited	2.7	3.9	.001	2.7	4.2	.001	2.9	4.5	.001	3.3	4.7	.001

124

Attracted–repelled	2.6	2.9	.05	2.5	2.9	ns	3.0	3.4	.05	2.6	3.7	.001
Passive–active	5.2	5.2	ns	5.3	5.1	.05	5.0	5.0	ns	5.3	5.3	ns
Numb–clear	6.0	5.9	ns	6.0	5.6	.001	5.9	5.4	.001	5.8	5.5	.05
Intolerant–tolerant	6.3	6.2	ns	6.4	6.3	ns	6.2	6.0	ns	6.1	5.8	ns
Impulsive–controlled	5.0	4.6	.05	5.0	4.3	.001	3.8	3.3	ns	3.7	3.4	ns
Relaxed–driven	2.8	3.1	ns	2.5	3.4	.001	3.4	3.8	.001	3.2	3.6	.05
High spirited–dejected	2.4	2.3	ns	2.4	2.3	ns	2.4	2.6	ns	2.6	2.6	ns
Inhibited–uninhibited	4.5	4.8	ns	4.6	4.9	.05	4.2	4.6	.05	4.2	4.6	.01
Jumpy–loose	4.7	4.4	ns	5.0	4.4	.05	4.4	3.7	.001	4.6	4.1	.05
Irritated–lazy	5.3	5.2	ns	5.3	5.2	ns	5.0	4.5	.001	4.9	4.5	.05
Quarrelsome–obliging	5.2	5.2	ns	5.4	5.2	.05	4.8	4.7	ns	5.1	4.5	.05
Sure–unsure	2.5	2.3	ns	2.3	2.3	ns	3.0	2.9	ns	2.6	2.6	ns
Interested–bored	1.7	2.3	.001	1.7	2.4	.001	1.9	2.3	.001	1.8	2.3	.001
Gentle–wild	3.0	3.4	.01	2.7	3.4	.001	3.5	4.0	.05	3.2	3.9	.001
Emotional–cool	4.0	3.5	.05	4.2	3.4	.001	3.4	2.9	.01	3.4	2.8	.001
Disgusted–pleased	5.0	5.0	ns	5.3	5.1	ns	4.9	4.4	.01	4.8	4.2	.05

*Significance of the differences between "before" and "after" according to Sign-Test.

before. But, on the average, they still chose the category "attracted" rather than "repelled."

Thus, the emotional reactions of men and women to pictorial and narrative stimulation are in principle quite similar. Possible differences with respect to sex in the degree of emotional changes (equal difference between the first and second semantic differential) were checked by analyses of variance (sex and time of filling out the semantic differential [before versus after the experiment]) for each item of the differential. For three items in study 2 and seven items in study 3 there were significant interactions between sex and time of completion, denoting different emotional changes for men and women. In study 2 the women were relatively more shocked, more irritated, and more disgusted than the men. Likewise, in study 3 the women were more shocked and more disgusted than the men. Moreover, they were more repelled and quarrelsome, while the men were relatively more amused, impulsive, and driven. Correspondingly, this data shows that women have a stronger tendency to react with avoidance and an emotional defense reaction to pictorial and narrative stimuli than men, who react with a greater emotional activation to the same stimuli (indicated, however, only in study 3).

The fact that not only sexual arousal but also avoidance responses to pictorial and narrative stimuli (by women more than men) are exhibited supports the presumption that ambivalent and conflicting reactions are registered to a psychosexual stimulation. We tried to investigate the incidence of ambivalent reactions and based our estimates on the responses to three open questions,* to which the subjects had to answer directly after the stimulation. Such answers in which sexual arousal *and* sexual avoidance (antipathy, rejection, aversion, disgust, fear) were clearly verbalized, were defined as "ambivalent."† Based on this rough and simple criterion it was found that upon viewing the films and slides

---

*The questions read as follows: 1. Describe, in a few sentences, your impressions and reactions while viewing the pictures or film (while reading the stories). 2. Which scenes were most stimulating for you and why? 3. Which scenes caused you to react negatively, and why?

†Avoidance responses in reaction to the appearance of persons or surroundings shown in the experiments or in reaction to the choice of words in or the style of the stories were not taken into account.

series, 40 percent of the women and 37 percent of the men, and upon reading the stories, 38 percent of the women and 26 percent of the men, clearly reacted ambivalently. Ambivalent reactions to psychosexual stimulation, thus, are rather frequent, if one considers that the above-mentioned figures are probably minimum estimates, because many subjects could not describe exactly their complex feelings in their answers to the open questions.

Emotional Responses in the Twenty-four Hours after the Stimulation

Using the ratings of sexual arousal, the semantic differential, and the open questions we were able to determine the emotional changes experienced during or immediately after the pictorial and narrative stimulation. Moreover, we were interested in the emotional reactions of the subjects in the 24 hours after the experiment.

On the questionnaire, which the subjects filled out 24 hours after the psychosexual stimulation, they had to judge whether they experienced changes with respect to their inner uneasiness, concentration ability, general activity, aggressiveness, sleep, and autonomic complaints in the 24 hours after the experiment as compared to the previous 24 hours.

These results are compiled in Table 4. The men show a significant increase in inner uneasiness and of general activity in both studies, although in one there was a significant decrease in concentration ability, as well as more restless sleep. For the women, with one exception, significant results are given for all 6 items in both studies. There was an increase of inner uneasiness, general activity, aggressiveness, and autonomic complaints, and a decrease in concentration ability, as well as a more restless sleep (only significant in study 2).

The emotional after-effects of pictorial and narrative stimulation appear to be somewhat greater for women than for men, the women exhibiting more significant changes. But this sex difference has not been statistically verified (cf. Table 4). It cannot be proven that the observed emotional changes experienced by the women on the day following the psychosexual stimulation (as compared to the previous day) were greater than by the men.

Table 4. *Emotional and autonomic reactions in the 24 hours after the psychosexual stimulation*

Items		Males				Females			
		Study 2 (Films, slide series) N=128		*Study 3* (Stories) N=120		*Study 2* (Films, slide series) N=128		*Study 3* (Stories) N=120	
		%	p*	%	p*	%	p*	%	p*
1. Inner uneasiness	increased	27	.001	26	.001	38	.001	32	.001
	decreased	6		6		2		11	
	no change	67		68		60		57	
2. Concentration ability	increased	4	.01	7	ns	9	.001	10	.05
	decreased	14		8		25		20	
	no change	82		84		66		70	
3. General activity	increased	18	.001	21	.01	23	.05	27	.01
	decreased	5		6		13		7	
	no change	77		73		64		66	
4. Aggressiveness	increased	15	ns	13	ns	23	.001	22	.01
	decreased	10		7		7		7	
	no change	75		81		70		71	
5. Sleep	more restless	9	ns	7	ns	18	.001	7	ns
	quieter	4		6		5		10	
	no change	87		87		77		82	
6. Autonomic complaints	increased	5	ns	8	.01	14	.001	13	.05
	decreased	1		1		2		5	
	no change	94		91		84		82	

*Significance of the difference between the first two categories (increased vs. decreased); according to chi-square (*the category "no change" has been omitted*):

Significance of the sex differences according to chi-square (*the category "no change" has been omitted*):
Study 2. All items not significant.
Study 3. All items not significant.

Thus we can register an emotional activation and instability in the 24 hours after the experiment (which also clearly resulted in a spontaneous emotional reaction during or directly following stimulus confrontation). However, it seems important to point out that although significant changes were registered, they were slight to moderate ones. The majority of subjects did not register emotional changes in the 24 hours after the experiment.

SEXUAL RESPONSES TO PICTORIAL AND NARRATIVE STIMULATION

Physiological-sexual Reactions during the Stimulation

In all three studies we asked the subjects whether they had experienced physiological-sexual reactions while viewing the films or slides or reading the stories. It is clear that such questions had to be limited to a few reactions which are easily and reliably perceived by the subject.

For the women in all three studies corresponding results were achieved in which the stimuli utilized brought about physiological-sexual reactions to approximately the same degree (Table 5). The women most often reported sensations in the genital area (65 to 80 percent). The second most frequent reaction observed (about 25 percent) was a vaginal lubrication. Sensations in the breasts were reported by only a small number of women (less than 10 percent). Extremely few, only 2 out of the 298 investigated females, reached an orgasm during the viewing or the reading of the stimuli.

For the men very similar results were obtained for all studies, irrespective of the type of stimuli (Table 5). The most frequently reported physiological-sexual reaction by the men was an erection. Roughly 80 to 90 percent had at least a slight or moderate erection; about 20 to 30 percent had a full erection. A preejaculatory emission (16 to 30 percent) was much less frequently experienced. As with the women, orgasms resulting from psychosexual stimulation among men were extremely seldom: only 8 out of all the 298 investigated male subjects had an ejaculation when viewing or reading the stimuli. With one exception, these were not sponta-

Table 5. *Physiological-sexual reactions during the psychosexual stimulation (in percentages)*

Males

	Study 1 (Slides) N=50	Study 2 (Films, slide series) N=128	Study 3 (Stories) N=120
Preejaculatory emission			
don't know	18	23	19
no	52	52	65
yes	30	25	16
Erection			
none	20	14	9
slight, moderate	58	55	66
full	22	31	25
Duration of erection			
none	not asked	14	9
to 2'		25	25
3'–5'		38	38
+ 6'		23	28
Ejaculation			
no	98	96	98
yes	2	4	2
Any reaction†			
no	20	13	9
yes	80	87	91

Females

	Study 1 (Slides) N=50	Study 2 (Films, slide series) N=128	Study 3 (Stories) N=120
Vaginal lubrication			
don't know	8	18	16
no	68	54	57
yes	24	28	28
Genital sensations*			
don't know	0	6	4
no	34	29	16
yes	66	65	80
Sensations in the breasts			
don't know	not asked	7	8
no		84	84
yes		9	8
Orgasm			
no	98	100	99
yes	2	0	1
Any reaction**			
no	30	28	17
yes	70	72	83

*Feelings of warmth, pulsations, "itching."
†Preejaculatory emission and/or erection and/or ejaculation.
**Vaginal lubrication and/or genital sensations and/or sensations in the breasts and/or orgasm.

neous ejaculations. They were produced by masturbation during the psychosexual stimulation.

The observed physiological-sexual reactions of men and women can hardly be compared in detail, since the anatomical substrates are different. However it is important to emphasize that in all three studies the greater majority of men (80-91 percent) as well as women (70-83 percent) experienced some sort of physiological-sexual reaction within themselves. These findings say nothing about the possible physiological reactions under the influence of pictorial and narrative stimulation, as we obtained only those reactions localized in the genital area which were so pronounced that they could be registered by the subjects themselves. Nevertheless, our results allow us to surmise that sexual differences in physiological sexual reactions to sexual stimuli—visual and written—are only slight.

Masturbatory Activity during the Stimulation

In studies 2 and 3 we asked the subjects whether they had stimulated their genitals during the viewing of the films or slides or during the reading of the stories. Moreover, we defined genital stimulation as manual touching of the genitals through the clothing or directly, interfemoral friction, or squeezing the genitals against objects. For both studies 18 percent of the women, and 21 percent of the men in study 2 and 17 percent of the men in study 3, indicated this type of masturbatory activity—for both sexes, a minority, though not a small one. Obviously, this activity was only transitory or not very intense genital stimulation, as very few men and women reached an orgasm. Sex differences appear to be slight and insignificant. Men and women have the same readiness to revert to masturbatory activities when they are sexually aroused through films, slides, or stories.

Sexual Behavior in the Twenty-four Hours after the Stimulation

On the day after the stimulation by slides, films, or stories the subjects were asked about the incidence and frequency of various sexual behavior and responses in the 24 hours before and the 24 hours after the stimulation. A comparison of the answers for the time preceding and following the experiment permits us to estimate if and to what extent pictorial and narrative stimulation encouraged sexual activity. Table 6 shows the results for the male and female subjects.

If the psychosexual stimulation had no influence on sexual behavior on the day following as compared with the preceding day, the same number of subjects would have indicated reduced or increased sexual activity. However, in the 24 hours after the psychosexual stimulation, more women reported increased as opposed to diminished masturbation, petting, and coitus activities, as well as an increased number of orgasms. This increase of activity is significant for masturbation and petting in one study and for coitus and total orgasm in two studies. A sexual stimulation through slides, films, and stories thus enhanced the women's desire for sexual activity. This activation of the sexual behavior, however, is only small to moderately pronounced. Some 85 to 90 percent of all the women reported masturbatory activity in the 24 hours after the stimulation to be unchanged or diminished as compared with the preceding day; almost 90 percent reported petting and coitus activity, and 80 percent the number of total orgasms as constant or reduced.*

The influence of pictorial and narrative stimulation on women is obviously greater in the scope of sexual fantasy and drive than in the area of sexual behavior. In the studies in which we asked appropriate questions, there was a significant increase in sexual fantasies, talk about sex, sexual tensions, and in desire for sexual activity on the day following the stimulation. There was also a relatively higher percentage with unchanged or reduced activities for these items (53 to 73 percent).

There were similar results for the men. In two of the studies there was a significant increase in masturbation and total orgasms in the 24 hours following the stimulation. An increase in petting activity in one study is significant, but a significant increase in coitus activity is not to be found in any of the studies. Neverthe-

*That does not mean that the increase in sexual activity by the remaining 10 to 20 percent can rest solely on the psychosexual stimulation, because surely without this stimulation a few of these subjects normal daily fluctuations in sexual behavior could result in an increase.

Table 6. Sexual behavior and sexual reactions in the 24 hours before and in the 24 hours after the psychosexual stimulation

Items		Males						Females					
		Study 1 (Slides) N=50		Study 2 (Films, slide series) N=128		Study 3 (Stories) N=120		Study 1 (Slides) N=50		Study 2 (Films, slide series) N=128		Study 3 (Stories) N=120	
		%	p*	%	p*	%	p*	%	p*	%	p*	%	p*
1. Masturbation	+	28	.01	30	.001	17	ns	14	ns	14	.01	11	ns
	−	6		11		14		4		4		6	
	=	66		59		68		82		82		83	
2. Petting	+	12	.05	5	ns	not asked		12	ns	9	.05	not asked	
	−	0		6				8		2			
	=	88		89				80		89			
3. Coitus	+	16	ns	15	ns	10	ns	12	ns	14	.05	19	.01
	−	4		9		12		6		5		5	
	=	80		76		78		82		81		76	
4. Total orgasms	+	34	.01	41	.001	32	ns	22	ns	22	.001	22	.01
	−	8		15		22		10		5		8	
	=	58		44		45		68		73		69	
5. Sexual phantasies†	+	not asked		33	.001	18	.001	not asked		35	.001	27	.001
	−			2		3				2		1	
	=			65		78				63		72	

133

Table 6. (Continued)

Items		Males						Females					
		Study 1 (Slides) N=50		Study 2 (Films, slide series) N=128		Study 3 (Stories) N=120		Study 1 (Slides) N=50		Study 2 (Films, slide series) N=128		Study 3 (Stories) N=120	
		%	p*	%	p*	%	p*	%	p*	%	p*	%	p*
6. *Talks about sex*	+	not asked		34	.05	37	.001	not asked		47	.001	42	.001
	−			18		9				14		8	
	=			48		54				39		49	
7. *Sexual tension*	+	40	.05	32	.05	27	ns	34	.05	35	.01	38	.01
	−	16		19		28		14		18		18	
	=	44		49		44		52		47		44	
8. *Wish for sexual activity*	+	not asked		41	.001	36	.05	not asked		46	.001	43	.001
	−			14		22				11		13	
	=			45		42				43		44	

+ In the 24 hours after the psychosexual stimulation > in the 24 hours before.
− In the 24 hours after the psychosexual stimulation < in the 24 hours before.
= No difference between the 24 hours before and the 24 hours after the psychosexual stimulation.
* Significance of the difference between the first two categories (+ vs −) according to Sign-Test.
† Phantasies during coitus, petting, or masturbation not included.

Significance of the sex differences according to chi-square (*the category = has been omitted*):
Study 1. ns: items 4, 7; too few cases: items 1, 2, 3.
Study 2. p = .05: item 2; ns: items 1, 3, 4, 6, 7, 8; too few cases: item 5.
Study 3. p = .01: item 3; p = .05: item 7; ns: items 1, 4, 6, 8; too few cases: item 5.

less, the men show a significant increase in sexual fantasies, talking about sex, sexual tensions, and a desire for sexual activity on the day after the experiment. All these changes—in sexual behavior, sexual fantasy, and sex drive—are only observed for a minority of the men. For the majority, sexual activity (59 to 95 percent), sexual fantasy and sex drive (59 to 72 percent) are unchanged or reduced on the day following the experiment.*

If one wishes to ascertain if the activation in the 24 hours after the pictorial and narrative stimulation is greater for the men or the women, it is necessary to compare the relationship of the increase (+) to the decrease (−) of both sexes for each item. We performed such a statistical analysis for each item and study. In study 1, there were none; in study 2, one, and in study 3, two sex differences in the increase/decrease rate.

In most cases, the results for men and women show similar changes. Where there were significant differences, the women show a greater change with reference to sexual activation (study 2: petting; study 3: coitus and sexual tensions). Significant differences resulted mainly in the study in which stories were used. Stories activated women more than men, while the sexual responses to films and slides on the day after the stimulation are more or less the same for men and women. As previously mentioned, this investigation is not meant to compare the effects of differential stimulus types. Nevertheless, it is apparent that the changes in the male sexual responses are slighter for stories than for films and slides. For the women a similar differentiation is not evident.

Fantasies during Masturbation and Coitus, and Coitus Techniques in the Twenty-four Hours after the Stimulation

In studies 2 and 3 we asked those subjects who masturbated or had coitus in the 24 hours after the stimulation about the influence of the stimuli on their masturbatory or coital behavior. As Table 7 shows, we were able to establish a distinct influence from pictorial and narrative stimulation on the masturbatory fantasies. Of those who masturbated on the day after the experiment, 44 to

*See footnote, page 10.

Table 7. *The influence of the psychosexual stimulation on phantasies and sexual techniques during masturbation and coitus in the 24 hours after the psychosexual stimulation (in percentages)*

Items	Males			Females		
	Study 1 (Slides)	*Study 2* (Films, slide series)	*Study 3* (Stories)	*Study 1* (Slides)	*Study 2* (Films, slide series)	*Study 3* (Stories)
Only subjects who masturbated in the 24 hours after the psychosexual stimulation						
1. Phantasies during masturbation about the stimuli						
no	35	32	56	33	57	69
yes	65	68	44	67	43	31
	N=17	N=50	N=32	N=9	N=23	N=16
Only subjects who had coitus in the 24 hours after the psychosexual stimulation						
2. Phantasies during coitus about the stimuli						
no	67	82	89	62	84	63
yes	33	18	11	38	16	37
	N=12	N=28	N=27	N=8	N=25	N=27

136

...seldom or never used techniques during

coitus foreplay

no	not asked	89	89	not asked	96	96
seldom used		11	7		0	4
never used		0	4		4	0
		N=28	N=27		N=25	N=27

4. Previously seldom or never used coitus positions

no	not asked	82	96	not asked	96	96
seldom used		14	0		0	4
never used		4	4		4	0
		N=28	N=27		N=25	N=27

Significance of the sex differences according to chi-sqare:
Study 1. Too few cases.
Study 2. p = .05: item 1; ns: item 2; too few cases: items 3, 4.
Study 3. p = .05: item 2; ns: item 1; too few cases: items 3, 4.

68 percent of the men and 31 to 43 percent of the women thought about the films, slides, or stories. In both studies the percentage for men is higher, whereby the sexual difference is significant in one study. It would thus seem that men are more ready than women to incorporate the stimuli into their masturbation fantasies.

The influence of the stimuli on coital fantasy was smaller, especially for the men. Of those subjects who had coitus on the day after the experiment, only 11 to 18 percent of the men and 16 to 37 percent of the women thought about the stimuli. Sex differences are nonexistent (study 2) or significantly more for the women (study 3). Sexual stories appear to have a greater effect on the women's coital fantasies than the men's.

Although the stimuli showed or described various coital techniques in detail, their influence on sexual techniques during coitus foreplay and during coitus itself was only slight for both sexes and in both studies. Only 0 to 4 percent of those subjects who had coitus on the day after the stimulation reported coitus positions or foreplay techniques they had never practiced before. Zero to 14 percent reactivated coitus techniques which they had previously only seldom used. Because of the small number of cases, it is not possible to arrive at any conclusion regarding the statistical significance of sex differences. The data, however, make it clear that men and women very rarely initiate new techniques or reactivate seldom practiced ones following pictorial or narrative stimulation.

WOMAN'S SEXUAL AROUSAL AND SOCIAL CHANGE OF SEXUALITY

According to our results, the pattern and intensity of reaction which was given in response to explicitly sexual stimuli were generally the same for men and women. On the average, stimulation using "hard core" sexual pictures, films, and stories led to a subjectively described "moderate" sexual excitation, whose physiological correlates were consciously registered by most of the men and women. In many cases, this sexual arousal induced through external stimuli led to an intensification of sexual activity for a short time. This sexual activation—only observed by a minority of the subjects—was limited almost always to sexual practices which were used regularly by these men and women. Sexual stimulation is integrated into the behavior pattern previously developed by the individual. The stimulation resulted, if at all, in reality adapted, but in no way in uninhibited or uncontrolled, sexual behavior.*

The nonsexual emotional reactions to pictorial and narrative stimulation among men and women are characterized by emotional activation, an increase in emotional instability, and, to a lesser extent, avoidance. Ambivalent and conflicting reactions to sexual arousal are not infrequently observed. These emotions appear spontaneously during confrontation with the stimuli, but they are also observed for a minority of the subjects on the day following the stimulation.

When significant sex differences are found, they represent exclusively minor shifts in the total pattern described. As such, the subjective stimulation ratings for women lie somewhat lower than for men. Women mobilize emotional defense reactions more often.[†] On the other hand, their readiness to satisfy externally induced arousal through sexual activity is obviously somewhat greater than for men, if the stimuli used are sexual stories.** However, these variations cannot divert attention from the fact that women can react to the same extent and in the same direction as men do to pictures, films, and stories with an explicitly sexual content. This holds true for the short-term effects of sexual stimuli, and for subjects who have never, or only seldom, seen such "hard core" material.

Our results were taken from a selected sample—a highly educated group of young, West German men and women. These students comprise a social group within the total society which in regard to sexual experience and attitude can be considered especially permissive. We do not rule out the possibility that in other

*This has also been verified by new Danish and American studies in which single coitus-experienced subjects, when it came to an activation of their behavior by sexual stimulation, masturbated, while married couples exhibited an increase in marital coitus (Kutschinsky 1970; Mann et al. 1970; Mosher 1970).

†On the role of guilt and anxiety in woman's psychosexual arousal see Mosher & Greenberg 1969.

**This result corresponds with those of a study by Jacobovits (1965) that women can be more stimulated through certain sexual stories than men.

social groups (higher age levels or lower social strata) sex differences in psychosexual arousability do still exist. But for purposes of theoretical discussion this is relatively unimportant. We are concerned here with the fact that the effect of pictorial and narrative stimulation, at least under definite social conditions, is as strongly and quite similarly structured for both women and men. This has been verified in studies of American and Danish students (Mosher 1970; Kutschinsky 1970) which yielded similar results.

Our results differ considerably from Kinsey's findings about extensive sex differences in the area of psychosexual arousability. We have already taken into account that the sex differences described by Kinsey could at least be partially due to the methodological shortcomings. However, in our opinion the discrepancy between his and more recent studies is probably an indication of cultural and historical changes. His findings cannot serve as evidence for a lesser capacity of women to become sexually aroused by pictorial and narrative stimuli. They reflect one aspect of the cultural desexualization of women in western societies, which 20 to 30 years ago, when Kinsey collected his data, was more extensive than today.

Indeed, we have seen in the last decades sexual behavior and attitudes toward sexuality among men and women continuously approaching each other. As far as the data collected permits us to make generalizations, this convergence process in the younger generation has progressed *relatively* the furthest in northwest European societies such as Sweden, Denmark, West Germany (cf., among others Christensen 1966, 1971; Giesse & Schmidt 1968; Zetterberg 1969; Israel et al. 1970; Sigusch & Schmidt 1970; Schmidt & Sigusch 1971). This convergence can also be observed in the United States though with a distinct time lag (Luckey & Nass 1969; Christensen & Gregg 1970; Christensen 1971).

For example, in the northwest European societies referred to, there is complete agreement in the younger generation that the overwhelming majority of men and women (90 percent and more) have permissive premarital standards. Abstinence or the traditional double standard are decidedly minority positions. Accordingly, the incidence of premarital coitus for men and women is equally high. Boys have their first coitus experience on an average only half a year earlier than girls. The tendency for partner mobility in all studies is still higher for men than for women, yet we can observe here a trend toward convergence. On one hand, men are not "promiscuous" to the degree which was a result of an extreme double standard. On the other hand, women now show a greater readiness for partner mobility than earlier. With respect to masturbation, however, the most definite sex differences still exist. Our last survey in West Germany on 600 16- and 17-year-old boys and girls (Sigusch & Schmidt 1970) allows us to observe a trend toward convergence, at least with regard to the age at which subjects had their first masturbation experience. Comparisons with earlier studies indicate the median age for first masturbation by women has dropped from 21 to 17 years within the last decade. The changes in female masturbatory behavior will perhaps become a central aspect in the theoretical discussions of sexual gender roles in the near future.

Christensen (1966, 1971) has illustrated the parallelism between the convergence of the male and female behavioral patterns and sexual liberalization. Because this liberalization in the sixties (comparable with that of the twenties) progressed relatively rapidly, the convergence has also accelerated (Luckey & Nass 1969; Bell & Chaskes 1970; Sigusch & Schmidt 1970; Christensen & Gregg 1970; Christensen 1971). This is true for the United States as well as for the northwest European societies. Nevertheless, there still exists the previously mentioned differences between the two culture areas: greater restriction and clearly more pronounced sex differences in the scope of sexuality in the United States.

It is hardly necessary to emphasize that the convergence process of male and female sexual behavior patterns has in no way come to an end nor among the younger northwest European generation has the sexual inequality of the sexes been abolished. With respect to sexual initiative there are only two predominant patterns: either the man takes the initiative most of the time, or both the man and the woman take the initiative to an equal degree. Women are almost never allowed to develop a greater sexual initiative. The woman is permitted only to exhibit sexual drive and develop sexual initiative in the same degree as the man, but not in a greater degree. Here, quite traditional sexual gender roles still exist, although they are milder, subtler, and more masked. They will only be dissolved if the gender roles lose their rigid dichotomy to an even greater extent than at present.

Nevertheless, it seems useful to view our results on woman's sexual arousal in connection with the convergence process described briefly above. The greater ability of young women today, as compared with those Kinsey studied, to be stimulated by explicitly sexual stimuli—slides, movies or stories—is obviously only one symptom or one result of a long and still incompleted process of the resexualization of women.

Analyzing these processes demands an understanding of sexual and social changes in the position of women in western industrial societies. This is not the function of this paper. However, we may predict that the process of convergence will continue and that many sex differences in sexual behavior which are still propagated today will vanish. They will, as has the thesis of reduced female arousability, be unmasked as an example of sexual prejudice.

REFERENCES

Bell, R. R. & Chaskes, J. B. Premarital sexual experience among coeds, 1958 and 1968. *J. Marr. Fam.* 1970, 32: 81–84.

Christensen, H. T. Scandinavian and American sex norms: some comparisons with sociological implications. *J. Soc. Iss.* 1966, 22, no. 2: 60–75.

———. Sexualverhalten und Moral. Eine kulturvergleichende Untersuchung. Reinbek: Rowohlt, 1971.

Christensen, H. T. & Gregg, C. F. Changing sex norms in America and Scandinavia. *J. Marr. Fam.* 1970, 32: 616–27.

Giese, H., & Schmidt, G. Studenten-Sexualität. Verhalten und Einstellung. Reinbek: Rowohlt, 1968.

Israel, J., Gustavsson, N., Eliasson, R.-M., & Lindberg, G. Sexuelle Verhaltensformen, der schwedischen Großstadtjugend. In: M.-B. Bergströmwalan (Ed.), *Modellfall Skandinavien? Sexualität und Sexualpolitik in Dänemark und Schweden.* Reinbek: Rowohlt, 1970.

Jakobovits, L. A. Evaluational reactions to erotic literature. *Psychol. Rep.* 1965, 16: 985–94.

Kinsey, A. C., Pomeroy, W. B., Martin, C. E., & Gebhard, P. H. *Sexual behavior in the human female.* Philadelphia and London: Saunders, 1953.

Kutschinsky, B. The effect of pornography—an experiment on perception, attitudes, and behavior. *Technical reports of the commission on obscenity and pornography*, vol. 8. Washington, D.C.: U.S. Government Printing Office, 1970. (Acc. to *The report of the commission on obscenity and pornography*. New York: Random House, 1970.)

Luckey, E. B., & Nass, G. D. A comparison of sexual attitudes and behavior in an international sample. *J. Marr. Fam.* 1969, 31: 364–79.

Mann, J., Sidman, J. & Starr, S. Effects of erotic films on sexual behaviors of married couples. *Technical reports of the commission on obscenity and pornography.* vol. 8. Washington, D.C.: U.S. Government Printing Office, 1970. (Acc. to *The report of the commission on obscenity and pornography*. New York: Random House, 1970.)

Mosher, D. L.: Psychological reactions to pornographic films. *Technical reports of the commission on obscenity and pornography*, vol. 8. Washington, D.C.: U.S. Government Printing Office, 1970. (Acc. to *The report of the commission on obscenity and pornography*. New York: Random House, 1970.)

Mosher, D. L., & Greenberg, I. Females' affective responses to reading erotic literature. *J. Consult. Clin. Psychol.* 1969, 33: 472–77.

Schmidt, G., & Sigusch, V. Sex differences in responses to psychosexual stimulation by films and slides. *J. Sex Res.* 1970, 6: 268–83.

_____. Arbeiter-Sexualität. Eine empirische Untersuchung an jungen Industriearbeitern. Neuwied: Luchterhand, 1971 (in press).

Sigusch, V., & Schmidt, G. Schüler-Sexualität. Dokumentation der Ergebnisse einer Untersuchung an 16– und 17 jährigen Schülern und Schülerinnen. Hamburg, 1970 (mimeographed).

Sigusch, V., Schmidt, G., Reinfeld, A., & Wiedemann-Sutor, I. Psychosexual stimulation: sex differences. *J. Sex Res.* 1970, 6: 10–24.

Simon, W., & Gagnon, J. H. On psychosexual development. In Goslin, D. A. (ed.), *Handbook of socialization theory and research*. Chicago: Rand McNally, 1969.

Zetterberg, H. L.: Om sexuallivet i Sverige. Stockholm: Statens offentliga utredningar, 1969.

chapter 8

Maternalism, Sexuality, and the New Feminism

Alice S. Rossi*

The task of an "overview" discussant is never a simple one, but I think in the present case there are very special factors which make my task particularly complex. For one, the three panel participants have themselves given "overview" papers: each panelist has done an excellent job of summarizing a decade or more of research of their own and others in their particular specialties. I have had the pleasure of reading many of their basic research papers and am frank to admit the reading was not always easy going for a non-medically trained sociologist. This taps a second difficulty: I am asked to review research in areas outside my own professional specialty in the sociology of the family. Third, I am asked to add a new ingredient not present in the three review papers: how the new feminism relates to the research areas under review and what

*Alice S. Rossi, Ph.D., Goucher College, Towson, Maryland.

the possible future changes in women's sexuality and maternalism may be, under the impact of the feminist renascence. Since I am also a participant in the feminist movement, I have the further difficulty of balancing the perspective of a family sociologist and that of a feminist. As I am sure you will sense in the course of my remarks, this is not always an easy or congenial combination.

What I shall do is to sketch something of the thrust of the new feminism in the United States, a necessary preliminary on the probably valid assumption that few in this audience are intimately linked with this particular social movement. From this background sketch I shall discuss in a more theoretical way the characteristics of women attracted to and involved in the movement, largely based on my own work on women college graduates. Finally, I shall discuss several of the findings and interpretations of our panelists to illustrate the application of a sociological and of a feminist perspective to research on sexuality and maternalism.

FEMINISM IN THE UNITED STATES

The first important characteristic to note about the feminist movement in the United States is its cyclical nature. While there have been men and women in almost every period of American history who wrote critically about the position of women and espoused a vision of more desirable relations between the sexes, there has been an overall ebb and flow to feminist history—periods of heightened activity in the form of political action and publication, followed by periods of demise in feminist analysis and politics. The first publicly visible feminist agitation had its inception in 1848 in Seneca Falls, New York, when Elizabeth Cady Stanton and her friends drew up their Declaration of Sentiments and held the first women's rights conference in American history (Lerner 1970; O'Neill 1969). Feminist activity spread quickly during the middle decades of the nineteenth century, stimulated in part by the gathering strength of the abolitionist movement, as women applied the abolitionist's analysis of the position of the slave to their own position as women. There were several minor waves of quiescence and activity in the women's rights movement from the late 1860s until the passage of the suffrage amendment in 1920.

Then the depression, war, a long period of economic affluence and social traditionalism intervened before feminism became a lively national issue again in the mid-1960s.

The first formal sign of the new feminism was probably the establishment of the Kennedy Commission on the Status of Women, prompted not by a feminist impulse but by the post-Sputnik concern for fuller utilization of womanpower as a resource to meet national professional and technical needs. The impact of the commission's work, however, was to spark a mood of rising expectations among numerous women who worked with the national commission, and later the state commissions, and who were encouraged to believe that the nation was finally going to do something to improve the economic and legal status of women. By the spring of 1966 many felt the legislative and executive branches of government were dragging their feet and that the women's efforts and rising expectations would be dashed by a reluctant Congress. In the fall of 1966 a small group of women gathered in Washington to found the National Organization for Women (NOW). From that tiny group of less than one hundred women, we have grown in four years to a major feminist organization of several thousand members and one hundred chapters across the country. In the first year or so, NOW viewed itself as a kind of NAACP for women, dedicated to a partnership of the sexes but with a particularly strong emphasis on the economic, legal, and political rights of women. We were willing to work within the present economic-political system and to cooperate with men, though often feeling keen resentment toward them. NOW has been attacked by more radical feminist groups for being an "elitist" or a "move over boys" type of feminism, but, in point of fact, a great deal of its efforts have gone into the quiet but difficult work of legal defense of women who have experienced job discrimination, most often working class women holding down factory jobs. NOW has been, I suspect, more effective in reaching and defending the rights of poor working women in the United States than its critics, who talk about the rights of poor women but have done very little as yet for or with them.

Outside New York, NOW has not had the degree of national media coverage that the more radical women's liberation groups have had in the past year or so (Rossi 1970). There is little shock value for the media to exploit in sustained efforts at legal redress compared to flamboyant tactics or a substantive focus on more emotionally charged areas of life. An "ogle men" campaign in the streets gets media coverage more readily than testimony before a senate committee.

There are more basic differences, however, between the women's rights and the women's liberation sectors of the new feminist movement. There were few women *under* thirty years of age among the founders of NOW in 1966; there were few women *over* thirty years of age among the women's liberation groups which began to form in 1967. Both sectors have become more heterogeneous in age composition since 1966, but style and structure were laid down by the earliest members. NOW is a more highly structured organization with a focus to its selection of issues on which to influence opinion or seek passage of a legislative bill. In keeping with the style of the younger generation, women's liberation groups have been more radical, more diffuse, and highly personal, particularly in the early stages of group formation. Their style is symbolized by the small "consciousness-raising" group, which typically begins with discussion of the key issues facing individual women in their personal lives: relations with family, lover, husband, boss; problems of personal identity and self-worth; life goals or barriers to their pursuit (Micossi 1970). A successful group is one that moves on from personal "rap" sessions to institutional analysis, political ideology, and action, a shift that occurs only when group members come to believe the problems they had viewed as personal or neurotic hang-ups are shared by many women and are more properly viewed as the products of inadequacies of institutional arrangements in the society. Since the groups obviously pre-select themselves, an important question for future research and historical analysis will be the extent to which the problems such group members find they share in common are really shared in common with a significant proportion of American women who have not come anywhere close to joining liberation groups. Proposals for institutional change are designed to affect a significantly large proportion of community members. Whether new facilities such as communal housing, abortion centers, and child care centers would be used by women who have not undergone the consciousness-raising experience of women's liberation groups, is an open question.

To catch the flavor of the difference between a women's rights group like NOW and a radical feminist group like "The Feminists" in New York, let me use their own words. NOW had dedicated itself to the goal of "true equality for all women in America in fully equal partnership with men." A typical resolution in the marriage and family area is phrased as follows: "Marriage should be an equal partnership with shared economic and household responsibility and shared care of the children. . . .the economic responsibility for the family should be shared proportionately according to income if both partners work outside the home. . .if only one partner works outside the home, half the income should by law belong to the other partner (NOW 1970)." By contrast, The Feminists' policy statement characterizes the group as "a political organization to annihilate sex roles," and states one requirement for membership in the following terms (Firestone & Koedt 1970):

(a) Because THE FEMINISTS considers the institution of marriage inherently inequitable, both in its formal (legal) and informal (social) aspects, and

(b) Because we consider this institution a primary formalization of the persecution of women, and

(c) Because we consider the rejection of this institution both in theory *and in practice* a primary mark of the radical feminist, WE HAVE A MEMBERSHIP QUOTA: THAT NO MORE THAN ONE THIRD OF OUR MEMBERSHIP CAN BE PARTICIPANTS IN EITHER A FORMAL (WITH LEGAL CONTRACT) OR INFORMAL (E. G., LIVING WITH A MAN) INSTANCE OF THE INSTITUTION OF MARRIAGE. August 8, 1969 (pp. 116–17) (emphasis in original document).

This should not be taken to mean that all women's liberation groups reject marriage or hate men. There is diversity among the groups and each group undergoes changes during its growth. I think it is an understandable reflection of the group experience they have undergone that there is a stage at which a great deal of anger is directed toward men. One of the most striking experiences a woman has in affiliating with any feminist group is the novelty of experiencing sex solidarity. It is interesting sociologically to examine our social structure for examples of socially permissible solidary ties among women. They are few and far between outside the circle of kin. Human survival and the need for high fertility to counteract high mortality may well have pressed to minimize intra-sex relationships outside the family. In American society, women's friendships have been often superficial and difficult because women have been socially and sexually competitive with each other. It is also rare outside the family setting to find social situations in which women are in the majority and men the minority. I have seldom seen more awkward and uncomfortable men nor more solidary women than on occasions when a man happened by while a women's liberation group was in session. Whether a brother, husband, or lover, one could feel a bristling atmosphere in the room as the women closed ranks momentarily against a familiar, but suddenly alien, male intruder. Several recent researchers attempting to study women active in the women's liberation movement have noted the high level of anger the women report and occasionally display toward men. But it must be understood that the review of the social psychological process of cultural conditioning such women have undergone in such a group is a powerful experience. To come to believe at the age of twenty-two that all your life you have been subtly molded into roles that bind and restrict your autonomy and independence carries a powerful emotional charge.

Any group that achieves a noncompetitive, empathic atmosphere also becomes a magnet that repeatedly draws members back to it for social acceptance and emotional gratification. As contemporary societies come to grips with the need to reverse social sanctions which encourage high fertility, I would predict that cultural patterns which restrict access between adults of the same sex will decline. If intimacy and social support needs are met in same-sex relationships and this occurs on a large enough scale, we might then find a decline in the proportion of the population who marry or have children, and an increase in homosexuality. From last summer's Gay Liberation march in New York streets to yesterday's radical feminist newspaper, it is apparent how widespread and alive the issue of homosexuality has become among circles of educated young people. The rapidity of change within the feminist movement can be illustrated by the fact that three years ago some women withdrew from membership in NOW over an abortion-repeal resolution, while at this year's convention members struggled over a lesbian-support resolution. As in all political movements, the more radical sector is a critical source and pressure for change in the mainstream organizations.

One must be cautious in drawing even tentative generalizations concerning a movement that is undergoing rapid change, but to date there is one point on which almost all sectors of the feminist movement agree: a rejection of any physiological, as opposed to a culturally conditioned, basis to sex differences. This view is the result of concern that any evidence of physiological influences will be taken as grounds for the perpetuation of sex inequalities in family, political, and occupational roles. A recent, highly publicized example was the intense reaction of feminist groups to Dr. Berman's public statements concerning the emotional correlates of menstrual periodicity.

Many of my feminist friends consider me close to a traitor to the cause to hold the view that there is still too much research to be done in the interstices between the biological and social sciences to hold a rigid position against neurohormonal influences on human behavior that may differentiate between the sexes as well as within sex. Very few articulate feminist spokeswomen have familiarized themselves with research on human periodicity or the psychophysiological similarities Niles Newton traces across the reproductive triad of childbirth, lactation, and coitus. I think, however, that this limitation to the feminist view reflects its short, four-year history. The individual and group discovery of how cultural conditioning affects American women has a concomitant, a tendency to believe that what women are like is what men have wanted them to be and therefore cannot be desirable. When a woman first realizes she has been trained to repress perfectly natural aggressive responses, she will first take pleasure in releasing such feelings when situations trigger them, before she can face the possibility that the cooperative, nurturant qualities traditionally associated with her sex may be more valuable in a better vision of a better world than the competitive, hostile qualities traditionally associated with the male sex.

HORMONE BALANCE AND SOCIAL BEHAVIOR

With some hesitation, I now plan to attempt a rather wide-ranging extrapolation from the rigorous research of Anke Ehrhardt and John Money (1967; Ehrhardt et al. 1968a, b; Money et al. 1968), by proposing a direction someone will hopefully take from the results of their research on fetal hormone balance impact on subsequent personality and social behavior. I assume most medically trained men and women, like those of us in the behavioral sciences, are interested in research on extreme cases outside the normal range for the light they shed on the normal range and not merely for diagnosis and treatment of abnormality. Ehrhardt (in press) has summarized the wide range of fetal hormone balance and its social correlates from the late adrenogenital syndrome, in which an excess of androgen triggers masculinization of genetic females, to testicular feminization, in which androgen insensitivity triggers feminization of genetic males.

Of particular sociological interest are the different social characteristics associated with either an excess of, or a cellular insensitivity to androgen. A genetic female with high exposure to androgens has a profile of high energy expenditure in childhood through tomboyish and sports activities, reduced interest in care-taking of the very young, and greater interest in work away from the home, while a genetic male insensitive to androgen outdoes control females in doll play, fantasy about having children, and preference for early stages of child development. These findings raise the possibility that somewhat similar hormonal factors might be responsible not only for some social differences that differentiate between normal males and females but, of even greater interest to me, that they might account for part of the observed variations *within* sex.

Such research in the interstice between biology and sociology could be enormously illuminating in the area of the family and occupational roles of men and women and to variation among women in the balance between their family and career interests and in their position vis-à-vis the feminist movement. Let me sketch briefly the design and results of some research I have conducted, link it to current political demands of feminist groups, and then suggest a possible connection to the research findings of Ehrhardt and Money on the social behavior correlates of hormonal balance.

SELF-SELECTED PIONEERS

The cyclical nature of the feminist movement means there have been a series of pioneer cohorts and only isolated instances of second-generation feminists, women reared as feminists by feminist mothers. Pioneer cohorts—whether political dissenters, revolutionaries, 1910 suffragists, or new feminists in 1970—are, by definition, social deviants from the conventional, norm-accepting mainstream of a population. A study of the first-generation pioneers of a social movement, therefore, is a study of social deviance. I am not using deviance in a pejorative sense, but to refer to social marginality and departure from the modal cultural expectations of a given time and place in history.

To describe deviant patterns always implies a standard of mainstream modality. To do this in the instance of young educated women in the 1960s, I shall first sketch a modal profile based on the results of my work on the family and career expectations of some 15,000 women college graduates (Rossi 1965). Their characteristics are similar to the implicit standard for comparison against which Ehrhardt described the extreme variants in the fetal hormone cases. The modal college graduate woman comes from a suburban home with a successful professional or business father and a homemaker mother, has done well in college academically and socially, and reports a high level of heterosexual dating stretching back to early high school years. She marries, about a year after college graduation, a man of similar or greater educational attainment, only slightly older than herself and of similar religion and life-style preferences. Looking ahead, she envisages a life centered around a suburban home, a family of three or four children, a diverse social and leisure life, and a possible return to employment when her children are well along in school. She will work in such fields as social work, library science, teaching, or in a secretarial job. She expects a happy marriage like that of her parents and wants to take primary responsibility for home maintenance and the care of her children.

None of the above characteristics are typical of the women college graduates who showed very high levels of career commitment, a choice of a predominantly masculine profession, or a feminist orientation and desire to work for women's rights organizations. Each of these three more deviant patterns are found among less than 10 percent of the sample. Women who identify themselves as eager to work for women's rights, like those headed for careers in law or a doctorate in history, are more apt to show the following family role expectations: they want very small families; are willing to delegate home maintenance and child care to hired help; do not particularly enjoy domesticity; see themselves as dominant, agnostic, unconventional, and competitive women with high levels of energy and managerial ability; and reject close contact with their own or their parents-in-law as emotionally important to them. By their mid-twenties, many are either still unmarried or tend to be somewhat less happy in marriage than their more conventional women classmates.

This study shows that a feminist perspective or commitment to work for women's rights is often associated with prominent career interests and a nontraditional, truncated commitment to family roles. Deviance in one area of life is related to deviance in other areas as well.

More important to the research was the question of what produced this inverse relationship between career or feminist commitment and family role commitment. One could argue that career committed women were making pragmatic adjustments of their family role expectations in anticipation of the complex and demanding career choices they had made. If there were a purposeful reduction to the family commitment, then one should theoretically expect no empirical relationship between current family expectations and any measure of early development of family life experience. But the data showed such pragmatic readjustment to be the exception rather than the rule. Any element of discord in the family of origin—an unhappy parental marriage, dominant

working mothers, unsuccessful breadwinner fathers, friction between mother and daughter—were all found to be related to low
family-role commitment on the part of the daughters in their mid-
twenties. Often they had a low involvement in heterosexual relations in high school or college.

In a sociological survey using a very large sample one cannot
hope to answer more subtle psychodynamic questions nor do
more than suggest underlying physiological factors that may be
associated with the social role and life-goal data available for analysis. Yet in reading the papers by Ehrhardt, I found myself thinking of the possibility that beneath the sociological data on current
and future plans might be not only the psychological factors related to the quality of early family relationships, but also the
physiological variables. *Role deviance among women requires a
profile of high physical energy and psychological toughness.* Could
these qualities in turn be triggered by a more-than-usual hormonal
balance tipped to androgen excess outside the modal range of
female variation? If the menarche triggers greater estrogen output,
could the late maturers among my deviant types have had a longer
moratorium from more traditional feminine concerns? Does a
drop in age in the menarche over the past fifty years mean a
shrunken moratorium at a critical stage of female development?
What influences do hormonal balance and age of menarche have
on sex differences in cognitive and achievement performance
which have been observed to widen during the later elementary
and junior high school ages? One thinks of Ehrhardt's observation
that IQ levels were particularly high among her adrenogenital
syndrome cases. Does excess androgen trigger an elevation of
physical energy and provide increased motivation for performance
in cognitive as well as athletic areas?

Also of particular relevance to an understanding and interpretation of the new feminism is the striking similarity between the
Ehrhardt–Money profile of excess androgen cases and the areas of
sexuality and maternalism the feminists have concentrated on.
Feminists of all political stripes have been united in their insistence on the right of women to control their own bodies, have been
sharply critical of masculine assumptions concerning female sexuality, and, hence, have demanded safe contraceptives and abortion repeal, less sexual swaggering from men, and free child care

facilities in universities and places of employment. In other words, there is a firm rejection on the part of feminists of any but a wanted pregnancy, a call for an altered view of sexuality, and institutional help in discharging care-taking responsibility.

In light of the youthfulness of women's liberation members, it is understandable that their focus has been on the reproductive issues that are of key salience at their stage of life—sexuality, contraception, and the concern for unwanted pregnancies. It is less clear why the same groups, often composed of largely unmarried women, are equally firm in the demand for free child care facilities. I believe this is only, in part, out of concern for their married group members who do have young children or an anticipation of their own future needs. There is also an element of psychological distancing from intimate relations with the very young and an element of ambivalence toward pregnancy and childbirth. Family roles are far more affected by a constricted ability to cope with intimacy and body contact than impersonal work roles are. Minimal contact with an emotionally impoverished father may spare a child some degree of psychological harm, and the father can achieve a sense of self-esteem by his adequate performance in impersonal occupational settings. The constraints of conventional maternal roles in American society, however, have meant that similarly emotionally impoverished mothers have had maximal impact on their young and no arena in which their esteem could be heightened by demonstrating impersonal competencies of a job-skill variety.

None of the questions I have posed find definitive answers in the medical or sociological research literature. It is embarrassing to realize how narrow and unimaginative the research has been in family sociology on parental roles. We do not know how much variation there is in a normal population with respect to the stage of child development parents enjoy most or least, nor what accounts for variations among adults in such preferences. This information could also serve as a standard against which to assess Ehrhardt's findings and to gauge variation among college graduates. The clinical literature is full of the consequences of poor mothering, but provides little help in specifying the components of good mothering. In our society an individual takes vocational tests to spot interests and aptitudes, has a wide range of choice in the selection of jobs, and considerable freedom to change jobs or career fields. But men and women have had little freedom of choice where parenthood is concerned and little help to arrange child care to maximize close association with children at an age the parent is most comfortable with or minimize association at ages the parents are least comfortable with. Nor can we have ex-children as we can have ex-jobs, at least not legally, though psychiatrists can clearly attest to the psychological pattern of ex-children.

Social institutions should accommodate a variety of styles of mothering, which they clearly do not at the present time. It is my hope that a new generation of research workers, working together to study maternalism, will fill the gaps in our knowledge of the now grey areas between the body and the social person.

SEXUALITY AND FEMINISM

In Niles Newton's review (in press) of the literature on the female reproductive role, she makes the interesting point that our society mutes the childbirth and lactation phases, preferring to heighten the emphasis on the sexual phase of the female reproductive role. She comes rather close to a feminist perspective in further noting that the special focus on women's sexual response may reflect that this aspect of the reproductive triad is of particular pertinence to adult men. In an ironic way, contemporary feminists reveal themselves as perfect, though rebellious, products of the same society, for they too have focused far more on sexuality than on maternalism, and certainly not on the childbirth or lactation components of maternalism.

Having recently read a good deal of current feminist literature on female sexuality, I have a distinct impression that many feminists are swinging as far to a one-sided view of female sexuality as Freud and his psychoanalytic descendents did to theirs.* The radical feminists have siezed upon the physiological findings of Mas-

*Apart from the direction illustrated in the text, it is also apparent that many feminists are buying the narrow health concerns of the medical profession in concentrating on the physiological side effects of the pill. There should be more concentrated attention paid by researchers and feminists to the differential impact of various types of contraceptives upon mood, periodicity, and alterations in erotic response.

ters and Johnson not only as a refutation of the Freudian concept of vaginal orgasm, but have done them one better. One reads the claim that this research proves the "chauvinist myth of the vaginal orgasm," but what is now substituted is a view that female orgasm is explicitly and narrowly a clitoral orgasm. Thus, one reads that clitoral foreplay is a concept created for male purposes and one which works to the disadvantage of women; as soon as the woman is aroused the man changes to vaginal stimulation, leaving her both aroused and unsatisfied (Firestone & Koedt 1970). Men fear they will become sexually expendable if the clitoris is substituted for the vagina as the center of pleasure for women because "vaginal penetration does not necessarily stimulate an orgasm in women since the clitoris is located externally and higher up (p. 41)." It will come as no surprise to read the conclusion that, based upon anatomical data, lesbian sexuality could make an excellent case for the extinction of the male organ. One of my recent correspondents wrote a lengthy argument to the effect that women will shortly have no need to seek intelligent mates because they will soon be able to use frozen semen from high IQ men and can therefore advocate a vasectomized society. Western societies have long been burdened by a polarity between "Eve" and "Mary": sex with the bad temptress, procreation with the good woman. But we have paid no attention to the corresponding distinction between an "Adam" and a "Joseph." Yet this correspondent seemed to be hinting at such a dissociation between the men with whom a woman enjoys sex and the man in absentia who fathers her child— a feminist's immaculate conception, perhaps?

Exclusive focus on clitoral orgasm is no advance over an exclusive focus on vaginal orgasm, and the pendulum of feminist thought will no doubt swing back to a steadier course in short order. At the same time, I must also confess to a sense of malicious pleasure shared with the radical feminists when I think of all the women during the past thirty years who have been encouraged by authors and therapists to consider themselves shamefully inadequate because they could not achieve a "mature vaginal orgasm." The feminists clearly do have a point that vaginal penetration may be a maximizing condition for impregnation but is not a requirement for the erotic orgasmic satisfaction of a woman; in this they are supported by the work of Masters and Johnson. It should also be noted, however, that the physiological confinement of the Masters and Johnson research, like American gymnastic "how to" sex manuals, does not offer much help to those trying to understand the contributions of cultural and emotional components to sexual enjoyment. Nor have feminists or sex educators yet paid much attention to hormonal influence upon sexual behavior.

Research by Sopchak, Sutherland, and Waxenberg is highly suggestive and important in this connection. Waxenberg (1969) has found that a woman in whom adrenalectomy has been combined with ovariectomy, involving the loss of her major source of androgens, subsequently shows an impairment of the purely erotic component of sexuality but no impairment of the affectionate, anaclitic component. This is an important reminder that the affectionate component of sexuality is not physiologically dependent upon the erotic component. Using exogenous sex hormones, Sopchak and Sutherland (1960) have shown that it is androgens which provide the hormonal basis for the erotic component of female sexuality, since estrogen therapy had no effect on sexual desire but androgen therapy heightened female libido.

Is it too much of a speculative leap to suggest connections between this body of hormonal research and the physiological substratum underlying the social characteristics of the androgen-excess syndrome cases in the work of Ehrhardt and Money and perhaps the social and political characteristics of the deviant college graduates in my work as well? If androgens work by increasing vascularization of the vulval area, sensitizing the clitoris, and stimulating metabolism to effect an increase in general well-being and therefore increased libido, could we have here indirect evidence of hormonal influence that contributes to variation in the balance of erotic versus affectionate components in female sexuality? Could heightened androgen production coupled with emotional tension in the family of origin lead to an adult woman with a very high level of physical and intellectual energy and of erotic sexuality, but a less-than-normal capacity for intimacy or attraction to care-taking responsibilities? Further, Paige and Bardwick have investigated the effect of oral contraceptives on cyclic mood changes associated with menstruation and found not only that the mean levels of hostility are highest premenstrually and lowest at ovulation but also that women on combination pills remained at a higher level of hostility throughout the cycle than was shown premenstrually by non-pill or sequential pill-taking women, presumably demonstrating the influence of the steady dosage of progestin through the menstrual cycle (Bardwick 1968; Ivey & Bardwick 1968; Paige 1969; Bardwick 1971).* Whatever the merit of this line of speculation, and its implicit research hypotheses, it is clear that to translate such ideas into a research design requires the development of less expensive and less tedious techniques for typing the level and balance of sex hormones of each individual than presently exist.

SEX DIFFERENCES IN PSYCHOSEXUAL STIMULATION IMPACT

There are two sets of comments, one methodological and one substantive, that I would like to develop in connection with the interesting experimental studies of Schmidt and Sigusch on psychosexual stimulation (Sigusch et al. 1970; Schmidt et al. 1969; Schmidt & Sigusch 1970). One of the more interesting things about their work is that the results conflict with those of Kinsey (1948, 1953). Kinsey found that men exceeded women in being sexually aroused by isolated stimuli, such as naked persons of the opposite sex or pictures of sexual scenes, while women were aroused almost as often as men by continuous stimuli, such as moving pictures or literary material. Schmidt and Sigusch find only minor sex differences in sexual response to visual stimuli (both sexes report genital reactions), stronger responses from women in spontaneous emotional expression and lability during the experiment, and somewhat stronger female responses in emotional lability and sex activation during the twenty-four hours following the experiment.

The authors suggest that these differences may be due to two things. First, the Kinsey data did not stem from experiments but from questionnaires and were, therefore, dependent on recall over

*Gaer Luce, *Biological rhythms in psychiatry and medicine*, U.S. Department of Health, Education and Welfare, National Institute of Mental Health, PHS Pub. No. 2088, 1970.

a long time period. They further suggest that as western societies carry a great deal more sexual stimuli designed to appeal to men than to women, men remain saturated with such stimuli and, therefore, report higher levels of response to visual stimuli than women. A second explanation they offer is that sexual arousability is a function of the sexual emancipation of women and that social change is being reflected in the comparison between the Kinsey and the Schmidt research findings. With a decline in the double sex standard, women are freed from their former desexualization and as a result, now report greater sexual responsiveness than in the 1940s.

I question these explanations for several reasons. There is an assumption that self-reports in both studies are equally frank reports on sexual arousal. But precisely because the whole societal atmosphere is now so much more open where sexual matters are concerned, their results may reflect not a change in women's actual responsiveness, but a change in their willingness to *report* on sexual arousal. Second, and perhaps more interesting for future trends, we are clearly a long way from any final state of a liberated sexuality in western societies. Premarital sex has clearly become more prevalent and represents a trend that will no doubt continue in the future. As Schmidt and Sigusch show, German data indicate greater readiness among women for partner variety in premarital sex than earlier studies reported.

American patterns on premarital sex, however, are more apt to be confined to coitus between men and women who later marry. A recent publication reports that half the Yale undergraduates had yet to experience coitus (Feller et al. 1970). In a very recent national sample of 8,000 freshmen and junior undergraduates on American campuses, 50 percent of the male, and 32 percent of the female unmarried students had experienced sexual intercourse, with a greater increase in sexual experience between freshmen and junior year for men than for women (Rossi & Groves 1970). The same study, however, showed that only 26 percent of the undergraduates took the view that sexual relations were appropriate "only when married." In contrast to these American data, Schmidt reports a range from 73 percent to 85 percent of the Hamburg student samples who had experienced coitus.

While cross-cultural data do indeed suggest greater restrictions and more pronounced sex differences in sexuality in the United States than in western European countries (particularly Sweden, Denmark, and West Germany), I suspect it is still the case in Europe as in the United States that men cannot accept a woman as a sex instructor or initiator nearly so frequently as women accept men as sex instructors or initiators. Schmidt and Sigusch, themselves, suggest a limitation to their interpretation, for they report a negative correlation of −38 between arousal ratings and favorable feeling ratings in the responses of men and women to films and still pictures. Perhaps one element in this negative correlation is an attitude that the *display* of coitus, while sexually arousing, is inappropriate and a violation of privacy. Nevertheless, I would assume that under societal circumstances of a full sexual liberation there would be a positive correlation between arousal ratings and favorable-feeling ratings, and I would take their results as an indication that there is still much change ahead to correct the desexualizing or distorted sexual components of social conditioning.

Putting this idea together with the results of Schmidt and Sigusch suggests an interesting possibility for sexual behavior and responsiveness in the future. If we accept the view that we are still far from having lost the double standard in sexual behavior, yet find little by way of sex difference in degree of response to psychosexual stimuli in 1970, is it possible that a more liberated sexual atmosphere in the future might find women *exceeding* men in responsiveness to such stimuli? The physiological potential seems to be there, as witness the finding of Masters and Johnson that women have a greater physiological capacity than men for orgasmic response. We have tended to see the prevalence of erotic stimuli in our culture as a reflection of male dominance. Indeed, this has been at the heart of much feminist criticism about the display of women as sex objects. It is just possible that in the future another interpretation could be placed on this—that such stimuli serve the function of artificially stoking male sexual interest. This is analogous to the rather different interpretations that can be placed on the historic development of patriarchal family systems. Did they develop because the dominant sex wished to impose upon the weaker sex and keep the woman in a submissive second-sex position, or did they develop as a masculine status compensation for the woman's biological ability to bear children and, hence, the fertility essential to sustain an agricultural society? So, too, does the fact that older men are the primary consumers of pornographic literature mean older males are more sexual than younger men or does it mean that such men require extra stimulation to increase their libidinal level and response?

There is one other aspect of the analysis of Schmidt and Sigusch that I found particularly suggestive. The authors report that men find nudes and semi-nudes more sexually stimulating than women do, while women judge romantic content pictures more favorably and as sexually stimulating. In one paper they suggest moving pictures and literary material "must be assumed to be more romantic than sexual in nature." I think there are reasons for this to which the male researchers may not be sensitive. As long as men are generally the initiators and directors of the sexual scene, isolated visual stimuli will be sufficient to effect male arousal but insufficient for a woman because little about her potential erotic experience can be gauged from most still pictures. A continuous stimulus like a film or a novel has the advantage for a woman of providing a variety of cues to the likely attentiveness of a male to her sexual preferences. The gymnastic "quickie" act of rapid coital thrusting which figures in American films and novels tells something about male directors and novelists and may gratify the average man's sexual fantasies, but it leaves many women sexually cold—particularly if they reject a rhesus monkey type of sex partner. Research has frequently suggested that sexual response is very subject to environmental distraction; so too visual sexual stimuli may have within them negative or distracting qualities that turn off the very arousal value that Schmidt and Sigusch are trying to study. I would suggest, only half facetiously, that they have a highly sexed feminist view their film and picture stimuli and report the elements she finds positive and negative in impact upon her arousal response; then compare these with the responses of a more traditional woman. It may also be possible for the researchers to test my suggestions with their present data. In the papers they have produced so far, data on films and still pictures have not been analyzed separately; nor have the two sets of brief stories *with* and *without* what they call "romantic content" been reported separately. Such internal comparative analysis might illuminate the components of sex differences discussed above.

Further, to label nude scenes of coitus as sexual but scenes that do not expose the genitals as "romantic" may be to reveal a phallic fallacy to which male researchers are particularly prone. What is called a "romantic" scene may be sexual in stimulation to a woman because it says something about the quality of the sexual experience she could expect to follow it, and not because women are more dependent upon the affectionate dimension of sexuality than the erotic one.

The second set of questions the papers of Schmidt and Sigusch stimulate concerns methodological points—in particular the basic ratings used to measure response to the visual material. Let me make my point by indirection first. In the American film, *Five Easy Pieces*, there is a sex scene in which the male lead engages in a whirling dervish series of gyrations around a bedroom, flings his partner to the bed, and seconds later sits up with a post-coital display of an athletic T-shirt labeled Triumph. I would recommend the use of this film sequence to Schmidt and Sigusch and make a prediction concerning sex differences in arousal response: a great many more men than women would report high arousal ratings, and a significant proportion of the women would report unfavorable feeling ratings.

There is a methodological point here, for this sex difference and its meaning could only be demonstrated if the rating scales were revised. You will recall that the arousal scale is a seven-point scale ranging from "high arousal" to "no arousal" and the feelings scale is a seven-point scale ranging from "high favorable" to "high unfavorable" feelings. In their present form, the only way my hypothesis about a response to the *Five Easy Pieces* film sequence could be indicated would be by the finding that a higher proportion of women than men report "no arousal" and "high unfavorable" feeling ratings. Women who reject the Tarzan sex partner would be grouped with women insensitive or resistant to sex stimulation under any circumstances. Even a combined usage of the two rating scales does not, therefore, permit testing out important dimensions of response to the psychosexual stimuli provided in the experiments.

There is one other assumption in the arousal rating that I question: genital sensations are necessarily sexual in emotional connotation. Perhaps this is true for men, but many women experience clitoral engorgement in situations of stress and tension without sexual stimuli or association. For example, friends report clitoral sensation while taking important college examinations, and research and observation indicate this may also occur during childbirth. Indeed Newton reports such an observation from an obstetrician in her paper at this symposium. The physiological manifestation may *appear* sexual, but the emotions associated with it are not.

A key and consistent element in my comments on the work of Schmidt and Sigusch is the complex blend of positive and negative components in the stimuli themselves. It might be desirable to try to isolate this by breaking the favorable-unfavorable rating scale into two separate scales. Confronted with a complex stimulus, many men and women could well report high ratings on both a favorable-feelings scale and an unfavorable-feelings scale, or low on both, or disparate combinations. There is empirical and theoretical precedence for such a treatment. When Norman Bradburn (1969; Bradburn & Caplovitz 1965) tried to investigate happiness based on self-ratings on degree of psychological well-being, he found that high ratings were not necessarily produced by the absence of worry and strain and the presence of good experiences and feelings, but of a *balance* between the two independently rated dimensions: high happiness ratings were found when positive experiences exceeded negative experiences. The same balance theory could be applied in the area of responses to psychosexual stimulation. Some suggestion that this would be a fruitful line of analysis is found in their own experimental data on semantic differential responses: students report post-exposure responses, indicating both increased pleasurable excitement and attraction, and increased negative responses of irritation, anger, and repulsion.

MATERNALISM AND SEXUALITY

It has always been a source of intellectual pleasure to read Niles Newton's work, nowhere more so than in her recent papers which bring together the threads of the varied research she and others have conducted on the physiological similarities among childbirth, lactation, and sexuality (Newton 1955, 1963, 1970, in press; Newton & Newton 1967; Newton et al. 1968). I would like to start with her discussion of the cultural variation in these elements in reproductive roles as a jumping-off point for a discussion of the disassociation in American society between maternalism and sexuality. She notes that the greater stress on the sexual phase of female reproductive roles in American society is in sharp contrast to the relaxed and unrestricted manner in which birth and breast feeding are handled in many other cultures. Non-western societies which show an easy, natural pattern of maternalism are also characterized by an indulgence and acceptance of the sexual component of maternalism which western societies deny to maternal behavior.

The sexual aspect of the mother-child relationship has certainly figured in psychoanalytic theory, though more often within a triad that keeps the father firmly in the picture. The cultural repression of sexuality in any form in western maternal child relations is underlined by the contrast provided by even a slight exposure to ethnographic literature. It is difficult to imagine an American mother engaging in labial, clitoral, or penile stimulation of her infant without guilt or social condemnation, but this is an accepted and expected pattern in many societies in which maternalism is closely linked to sexuality.

In societies in which childbirth and lactation are handled in a relaxed and open manner, mothers are also permitted and encouraged to take sexual pleasure in their infants. This pleasure may be enhanced by the frequently associated pattern of prolonged post-childbirth sexual abstinence in many such societies. Social anthropologists have tended to view such sexual abstinence as serving a child-spacing function and assuring the adequate nurturing of one child before the onset of a second pregnancy, and medical research supports the view that breast feeding is a natural, if unreliable, form of birth control.

But an awareness of the intimate connection between genital stimulation and lactation suggests that such sexual abstinence may strengthen the bond between mother and child by permitting sensual gratification in maternity, which our society officially denies to mothers. The more conventional a woman the greater may be the conflict in her mind about the sexual aspect of nursing her child. We even complicate the whole situation for a nursing mother by leaving ambiguous the medical specialty to which the breast belongs—anything requiring mechanical repair is apparently the domain of obstetrics, while its functional output in the form of milk supply is the concern of pediatrics. Yet a culturally permissible association of sexuality with lactation may stimulate maternal milk supply, as suggested by Campbell and Petersen's finding of a positive correlation between the amount of milk ejection and degree of sexual arousal (1953). Presumably therefore, societies which do not disassociate sexuality from maternalism may have mothers who easily produce large quantities of milk. Though stimulation by sucking increases milk flow, the American woman who resumes sexual activity about six weeks post delivery may worry about the adequacy of her milk supply and psychologically fear that milk loss during sex play and coitus is robbing her infant of adequate nutrition. Though the objective facts may contradict such an outcome, nursing mothers may experience a psychological conflict between spouse and child, sex and maternity, that may have a negative impact on both roles (Newton & Newton, 1967). There may be a legitimate basis for a western analyst to argue that there is a gap between an infant's absolute need for mothering and a woman's relative need to mother (Benedek 1959); but a woman in many primitive societies may satisfy both sexual and care-taking desires through the nursing of her young, with the result that she experiences less of a need imbalance between herself and the infant than western women and their bottle-fed babies do.

I am suggesting that Christian theology and its associated male-dominant family and political systems have imposed a wedge between maternalism and female sexuality. We define maternity in culturally narrow ways, clearly differentiating it from sexuality, and requiring that women deny the evidence of their senses by repressing the component of sexuality in the maternal role. I suspect that the more male dominance characterizes a western society the greater is the disassociation between sexuality and maternalism. It is to men's sexual advantage to restrict women's sexual gratification to heterosexual coitus, though the price for the woman and a child may be a less psychologically and physically rewarding relationship. Cultural insistence that the breast is more a sexual than a maternal object—currently more acceptable publicly in a sexual display than in a maternal display of nursing—may be accepted by women who then refuse to try nursing their infants or discontinue it upon discovering that it involves a physiological blend of the sexual and the maternal.

American women have also not received much assistance from the medical or social sciences. How many American women approach pregnancy with any advance knowledge that nursing a baby will entail sexual stimulation of her genitalia? At most she is apt to know that lactation triggers uterine contractions which facilitate the postchildbirth recovery of the uterus, and if she is fortunate enough to have a physician and a personal network of family and friends with positive views toward nursing, she may herself view nursing as the best means to provide her infant with a cheap, easily available, well-balanced source of nutrition. But has she knowledge of the sexual pleasure, vaginal lubrication, or clitoral sensation that may accompany breastfeeding? No. A conspiracy of silence robs her of such advance knowledge. Many women have told me that they never extrapolated the connection between breast stimulation in sexual foreplay and genital response to the nursing situation, with its more prolonged and frequent breast stimulation.

Of course, as Niles Newton's research papers amply illustrate, such knowledge does exist, but it has not yet found its way into sex education or child-rearing literature and certainly not into the sociological literature on the family. Family sociologists, in my observation, have been not only predominantly male, but all too often puritanical, conventional, and uncomfortable with their own body functions, as well as those of women. I am told this is not infrequent among male obstetricians and gynecologists as well. We know that lactation, like parturition, is restricted and made more difficult and painful by fear and anxiety, by unfamiliar surroundings, and by distraction. Though we might well have gotten along without such knowledge, we even know that plunging a nursing mother's feet into ice water, painfully pulling her toes, and administering an electric shock when she does not respond quickly enough in giving a solution to a mathematical problem, reduces her milk flow (Newton & Newton 1948, 1967). We also know from the work of Mead and Newton (1967; Newton 1970) that labor is remarkably short and painless in a society with relaxed sexual attitudes, like that of the South American Siriono where birth is an easy, public event controlled by the mother herself, but that it is a prolonged, painful process among the Cuna in Panama who prevent young girls from learning about either coitus or childbirth until the final stages of the marriage ceremony. Not surprisingly, pregnancy and birth are viewed by the Cuna as a secret fearful time of anxiety and pain.

Teaching family and sex to undergraduate American women, I have the distinct impression that our society is closer to the uptight Cuna than to the relaxed Siriono. Most Americans when questioned about the use of a rocking chair by nursing mothers will stress its lulling and comforting impact on the infant. Far fewer are aware that the rhythmic motion of the chair enhances the sensual pleasure of the nursing mother as well. Yet rhythmic movement has often been experienced as sensually stimulating to women, as witness the use by nineteenth- and early twentieth-century factory owners of supervisors whose job was to watch for sexual responses among women workers operating foot-treadle sewing machines.

It does not seem to matter which dependent variable medical and clinical researchers have concentrated on as a major focus of research on female reproductive roles; there is now cumulative evidence of the interrelatedness of the components of female reproductive experience. Good sexual adjustment, positive enjoyment of pregnancy, low profiles of nausea during pregnancy, easier and shorter labor, desire for and success at breast feeding, preference for a natural or minimal-drug childbirth, all seem to form a coherent syndrome. And what of the personality and role profile of women with these characteristics? They can scarcely be traditional, submissive women, for it takes a high level of assertiveness and unconventionality for an American woman to experience natural childbirth, success at nursing, or gratification in sex. Men, her parents, the nursing, medical and psychiatric professions have all stood as barriers rather than supporting aides in her search.

Such women have also not yet emerged in the ranks of the feminist movement. New feminists have not voiced criticism of the cultural and medical restraints on maternalism. The present generational cohort of feminists are young in chronological age, in ideology, and in their social movement. The older feminists like myself had their children in the 1950s and either gave in to medical prejudices or fought as I did to have the experiences they wanted against the views of doctors, parents, and most friends.

Thus far the health and medical professions have been the target of political pressure and ideological criticism from the new feminists on the issues of safe contraceptives, abortion law repeal, and the theories about female sexuality. I predict, and indeed hope that this paper will stimulate a shift of the target to the obstetrical field, not merely for surgical help to remove an unwanted pregnancy, but with the demand for the right to actively enjoy pregnancy and control the childbirth experience. I would put some hard questions to the medical and nursing professions: How dare you strap us down on a delivery room table? How dare you claim you "deliver" us when you cheat us of the knowledge and the experience of actively giving birth to our own child? Why are we moved from a relatively cozy setting at the end of the first stage of labor to a blindingly lit delivery room, cut off from our supportive men, while you try to anaesthetize us in second-stage labor just when we have reached the point where we can do something? Newton's tracing of the similarities between childbirth and sexuality suggest to this woman feminist and sociologist that physicians sense this linkage, treat women in childbirth as they have in sex, and thus cheat women of a full, controlling role in the childbirth experiences. The whole paraphernalia of medicine—anaesthesia, the abyss below the delivery table—serve the function of retaining the dominant status of the attending physician, and thus prevent women from seeing that a physician is her "aide" in giving birth, and not her lordly "deliverer."

CONCLUSION

One feminist wrote (Goldman 1970): "Woman's development, her freedom, her independence, must come from and through herself. . . . by asserting herself as a personality and not as a sex commodity; by refusing the right to anyone over her body; by refusing to be a servant to God, the state, society, the husband, the family. . . .by freeing herself from the fear of public opinion and public condemnation . . . . Only that will set woman free (p. 63)."

This was not written this year or last, but sixty five years ago by a feminist and an anarchist, Emma Goldman. It is a message more attuned to the new feminism in the United States today than it was to her suffragist contemporaries at the turn of the century, and it is being heard more today than in her own time. As a consequence of this change, I have great confidence that the current stage of the feminist movement in the United States has greater potential for human liberation than at any previous stage in its history.

REFERENCES

Bardwick, J. M. Summary of symposium on physiological contributions to the personality development of women. Presented at the American Psychological Association, San Francisco, August 1968 (mimeographed).

————. The psychology of women. New York: Harper & Row, 1971.

Benedek, T. Parenthood as a developmental phase. Journal of American Psychoanalytic Association 1959, 7(8): 387–417.

Bradburn, N. M., & Caplovitz, D. Reports on happiness. Chicago: Aldine, 1965.

Bradburn, N. M. The structure of psychological well-being. Chicago: Aldine, 1969.

Campbell, B., & Petersen, W. E. Milk let-down and orgasm in human females. Human Biology 1953, 25: 165–68.

Ehrhardt, A. A. & Money, J. Progestin-induced hermaphroditism: IQ and psychosexual identity in a study of ten girls. Journal of Sex Research 1967, 3(1): 83–100.

Ehrhardt, A. A., Epstein, R., & Money, J. Fetal androgens and female gender identity in the early-treated androgenital syndrome. Johns Hopkins Medical Journal 1968, 122: 160–67. (a)

Ehrhardt, A. A., Evers, K., & Money, J. Influence of androgen and some aspects of sexually dimorphic behavior in women with the late-treated androgenital syndrome. Johns Hopkins Medical Journal 1968, 123(3): 115–22. (b)

Ehrhardt, A. A. Maternalism in fetal hormonal and related syndromes. In J. Zubin and J. Money (eds.), Contemporary sexual behavior. Baltimore: The Johns Hopkins University Press, 1972, pp. 99–115.

Feller, R., Fox, E., & Schwartz, P. *The student guide to sex on campus*. New York: New American Library, 1970.

Firestone, S., & Koedt, A. (eds.) *Notes from the second year: major writings of the radical feminists*. New York: Radical Feminism, 1970.

Goldman, E. *The traffic in women and other essays on feminism*. New York: Times Change Press, 1970, pp. 51-63.

Ivey, M. E., & Bardwick, J. M. Patterns of affective fluctuation in the menstrual cycle. *Psychosomatic Medicine* 1968, 30(3): 336-45.

Kinsey, A. C., Pomeroy, W. B., & Martin, C. E. *Sexual behavior in the human male*. Philadelphia: W. B. Saunders, 1948.

Kinsey, A. C., Pomeroy, W. B., Martin, C. E., & Gebhard, P. H. *Sexual behavior in the human female*. Philadelphia: W. B. Saunders, 1953.

Lerner, G. The feminists: a second look. *Columbia Forum*, Fall, 1970, 24-30.

Mead, M., & Newton, N. Cultural patterning of perinatal behavior. In S. A. Richardson & A. F. Guttmacher (eds.), *Childbearing: its social and psychological aspects*. Baltimore: Williams and Wilkins, 1967, pp. 142-244.

Micossi, A. Conversion to women's liberation. *Trans-Action* 1970, 8(1/2): 82-90.

Money, J., Ehrhardt, A. A., & Masica, D. M. Fetal feminization induced by androgen insensitivity in the testicular feminizing syndrome: effect on marriage and maternalism. *Johns Hopkins Medical Journal* 1968, 123(3): 105-14.

National Organization for Women. Action resolutions passed by members at the Fourth Annual Conference, March 20-22, 1970 (mimeographed).

Newton, N. *Maternal emotions*. New York: Paul B. Hoeber, 1955.

———. Emotions of pregnancy. *General Obstetrics and Gynecology* 1963, 6(3): 639-67.

———. Interrelationships between sexual responsiveness, birth, and breast feeding. In J. Zubin and J. Money (eds.), *Contemporary sexual behavior*. Baltimore: The Johns Hopkins University Press, 1972, pp. 77-98.

Newton, N., & Newton, M. Let down reflex in human lactation. *Journal of Pediatrics* 1948, 3: 698-704.

———. Psychologic aspects of lactation. *New England Journal of Medicine* 1967, 277: 4-12.

———. The effect of psychological environment on childbirth: combined cross-cultural and experimental approach. *Journal of Cross-Cultural Psychology* 1970, 1(1): 85-90.

Newton, N., Peeler, D., & Newton, M. Effect of disturbance on labor. *American Journal of Obstetrics and Gynecology* 1968, 101(8): 1096-1102.

O'Neill, W. *Everyone was brave*. New York: Quadrangle, 1969.

Paige, K. E. *The effects of contraceptive on affective fluctuations associated with the menstrual cycle*. Ph.D. dissertation, University of Michigan, 1969.

Rossi, A. S. Barriers to the career choice of engineering, medicine, or science among American women. In J. A. Mattfield & C. G. van Aken (eds.), *Women and the scientific professions*. Boston: M.I.T. Press, 1965.

———. Women—terms of liberation. *Dissent*, November-December 1970: 531-41.

Rossi, P. H., & Groves, W. E. Study of life styles and campus communities. Baltimore, 1970 (unpublished press release).

Schmidt, G., Sigusch, V., & Meyberg, U. Psychosexual stimulation in men: emotional reactions, changes of sex behavior and measures of conservative attitudes. *Journal of Sex Research* 1969, 5(3): 199-217.

Schmidt, G., & Sigusch, V. Psychosexual stimulation by films and slides: a further report on sex differences. *Journal of Sex Research* 1970, 6: 268-83.

———. Women's sexual arousal. In J. Zubin and J. Money (eds.), *Contemporary sexual behavior*. Baltimore: The Johns Hopkins University Press, 1972, pp. 117-43.

Sigusch, V., Schmidt, G., Reinfeld, A., & Wiedemann-Sutor, I. Psychosexual stimulation: sex differences. *Journal of Sex Research* 1970, 6(1): 10-24.

Sopchak, A. L., & Sutherland, A. M. Psychological impact of cancer and its treatment, VII: exogenous sex hormones and their relation to life-long adaptations in women with metastatic cancer of the breast. *Cancer* 1960, 5: 857-72.

Waxenberg, S. E. Psychotherapeutic and dynamic implications of recent research on female sexual functioning. In G. D. Goldman & D. S. Milman (eds.), *Modern woman: her psychology and sexuality*. Springfield, Illinois: Charles C Thomas, 1969, pp. 3-24.

chapter 9

The New
Black Feminism:
A Minority Report

Julia Mayo*

The focus of the new feminism—sexual equality—fails to appeal to black women because it is based on the faulty premise that the common denominator is sex. In the present social revolution, sex is but one factor in a multivariant equation. Whereas it may be true that the female sex represents a minority status, it does not represent a group of anything. Social change can be effected by a group that is identifiable by a collective response to its minority status and by a group that is cohesive and viable (Kinney 1971). Unfortunately, minority groups too often are identified and dealt with, not by what unites them but by what separates them. What prevents the formation of a solidified group of women is, among other things, color.

A major complaint of white women has been against the Madison Avenue concept of feminism. Women's liberation groups have

*Julia Mayo, D.S.W., St. Vincent's Hospital and Medical Center, New York, N.Y.

been protesting and effecting some changes in the advertising media because they found women as women exploited for commercialism. But, consider the insult added to injury to black women by some of the hair coloring advertisements, such as one in which a blond huskily inquires, "Don't you wish you were one, too?" The inclusion of black comedians in TV commercials for sun tan lotions and the recent addition of hair product ads for blacks are belated but welcome and significant attempts to recognize that there are those in the viewing audience who may not fit the prevailing American standard of what constitutes beauty. If you color a woman black, do you have a black woman? No, the color black goes deeper than the skin. It penetrates and permeates the soul and psyche and what emerges is a black feminine mystique. Therein lies a partial answer to why the new feminism does not appeal to the masses of black women.

Although Shirley Chilsolm and a few other black women tend to side with some aspirations of the women's lib movement, the majority of black women essentially view the new feminism as a dialogue between white women and white men with any benefit to black women accruing solely as a side effect (King 1971). The fact of the matter is that, albeit on the bottom of the power base, white women are still within the power structure of the "establishment."

For the black woman the problem is simultaneously simple and complex. If the issue is male chauvinism, the problem is simple for, however misunderstood or misused, the term implies male superiority and excessive use of an ascribed prerogative. The black male chauvinist outside of his own immediate domain is a relative rarity. How can one be against someone whose ascribed prerogative within the accepted system is virtually nonexistent?

According to Pasamanick (1969) "mechanization and new methods have made the Negro superfluous in the rural South, condemning him to slow starvation or refugee status in the North." Commenting on the apparently expendable position of latter-day Negroes in the United States, he caustically states: "The Iron Mountain mentality of brutal repression of demands for a decent life has been endemic in American Society since its inception. The Indian, the Negro, the alien have served in the past, and racism has been its base."

Even the most recent and most favorable labor statistics fail to alter substantially the basic fact of Pasamanick's indictment. Herman Miller, director of Census Population Studies, commenting on the results of the 1970 census, reported to the *New York Times* (Rosenthal 1971) that whereas "the income of young black Northern couples with children rose dramatically in the nineteen-sixties, for a larger number of black families, headed by only a mother, the decade ended the way it began, in deep poverty." The proportion of black families headed by women has increased to a level three times that of whites. Despite findings that families headed by women in both races are often as stable as those with both parents present, an increasing number of female-based black families are falling into poverty. George Wiley, director of the National Welfare Rights Organization states: "The failure to be able to provide for your family when that's what society expects of you is an assault on your manhood so it's a natural reaction when things get too tough to bug out." In a report on family stability, Farley and Hermalin (1971) point out that the "majority of both blacks and whites are in statuses indicative of family stability and that contrary to the images which are sometimes portrayed, most black families are husband-wife families and the majority of black children live with both parents." The conclusions of the latest census analysis show black families in the South now have an income of 57 percent of average white income while black families in the North went from 71 to 73 percent of average white income. The income level for all black families over the last decade rose from a pitiful 51 to 61 percent of average white income.

A NEW HISTORICAL VIEW

It is not the intention of this discussion to document the history of the Negro (some prefer the term, black) in this country, nor of the status of black women in this country. Rather focus will be on certain omissions, points of emphasis, and differential interpretation.

The power structure of this country has decreed that, in general, the status of black women is relevant only to the status of black men, not to other women. For black women to engage actively in the current sex battle would make them much like hard-hearted Hanna who in the ballad "poured water on a drowning man." It would be a cruel joke on the average black man to demand from him that which he is not yet able to give. White feminism conveniently forgets this, if, indeed, it was ever remembered. Sociologists, psychologists, and sundry others have conducted numerous studies exclusively dealing with some specified aspect of Negro family life. For generations they not only spoke for blacks but in place of, to, at, and against, but seldom with blacks. Inevitably, however, these studies have shown repeatedly that when blacks and whites are matched comparably with respect to socioeconomic status, outcome with respect to achievements, values, goals, stability, aspiration, attitudes, and spheres of influence is likewise comparable. The gradations of power continue to be monitored by social class. Thus similarities between middle-class blacks and middle-class whites are far greater than similarities among blacks in general or among whites in general. This is fine so far as it goes. The problem is that while the majority of whites are middle class, the majority of blacks fall below middle socioeconomic status and a substantial number constitute a poverty base. Heiskanen (1971) in a review of sociological studies over the past decade, which revealed "a ratio of studies of middle class groups to lower class groups nearly six to one," scores "the whole hearted endorsement of the cultural homogenization theme and the rejection of diversity as a conceptual alternative."

The contemporary view, as espoused by Moynihan (U.S. Department of Labor 1965) and Pettigrew (1964), focuses on breakdown in the Negro family and in the female-based matriarchal family structure. Female heads of households, absent fathers, and all the attendant social and economic ills are all too familiar facts. Too often, however, right answers are accompanied by wrong reasons. Breakdown of the Negro family implies it was at one time together. The wonder is, in face of deliberately systematized policies to prevent stabilization, that any family emerged at all. Liebow (1967) maintains that the post-slavery era which decreed a legacy of matriarchy, poverty, and lower-class status has resulted in the exclusion of the black male from the mainstream of the American economy, and, because of either his inability or unwillingness to assume responsibility for his family, he has become entrapped in a "culture of poverty." The Moynihan solution, which would attack the problem of poverty and the matriarchal structure, has been tried and found wanting. This approach alone cannot be successful because it does not touch on the fundamental issue of the powerlessness of the lower-class black male to protect his family according to the value system of the larger society in which he lives (Grier & Cobbs 1968). The cogent observation of De Tocqueville, on life in America more than 100 years ago, on the powerlessness of Negroes to exercise their legal rights because the "will of the white majority" opposes them, holds in many instances just as true today. Anecdotes by De Tocqueville graphically illustrating the "tyranny of the majority and the concurrance of the courts" are pointedly set forth by Eberts and Witton (1970). Rights, legal or otherwise, will not be enforced where the dominant group does not wish to enforce them. Poverty, per se, can be solved. Other minority and immigrant groups have successfully risen above it (Glazer 1963). A matriarchy, per se, is not a deterrent to family stability—e.g., Jewish family structure and to some extent Italian family life. What then is the difference with the black family? It is simply that no other minority group has been programmed for failure by a legally sanctioned and legally enforced system to deprive the black male of what symbolizes his maleness, namely, his role, not of provider but of protector. From what source can the black male seek, not in theory but in practice, redress of any wrong done to him or his family, unless the white majority consents to such redress. On whom can the black male depend to enforce his right to protect his family when the enforcers themselves join against him? Power to the people means one of two things: power to join the "establishment" or power to change it. This power all other groups have acquired. This power the black is just beginning to get, the greatest impetus stemming from the civil rights act of 1964 and the more recent legal services program of the Office of Economic Opportunity.

AN ERA OF POLARIZATION

There is much truth in the adage that if one wants to keep his friends he should avoid discussions of sex, religion, and politics.

The adage is equally applicable to the topics of race and age. Lines have been drawn not only between groups on these issues, but, of late, polarization has occurred within groups. Former alliances based on tradition have given way to new alliances based on peer groupings and common values. Hence, we can find within a single family polarization of attitudes and values on any number of issues; youth vs. age, homosexual vs. heterosexual, peace vs. war, middle class vs. lower class, separatism vs. integration.

Most white Americans live by the Boy Scout motto, "Be Prepared." They are future-oriented, as any progressive surviving civilization must be. Blacks have been accused of being concerned with only the present, of being childlike in their inability to delay gratification. It is easy for those who have, to exhort those who have not to wait. Man may not live by bread alone, but he cannot live very long without it. Blacks also know that delayed gratification can be a euphemism for being put off and put down. Too many blacks have seen a generation born and buried on delayed gratification. Given the present white standard and the past black norm a future of continued second-class citizenship for blacks is assured. So long as the single standard of "white only" prevails, equality within the female sex, much less between the sexes, cannot be achieved. The new feminism demands freedom for women to make choices about their own lives. Some of the demands that white women are making include: (1) equal pay for equal work and proportional representation in all types of work; (2) maternity leave with no loss of seniority; (3) legal and medical protection from unwanted pregnancies; (4) adequate, economical child care facilities for working mothers; (5) access to all public places; (6) freedom from sexual exploitation; (7) escape from suburbia, kitchen gadgets, baby sitting, and bras.

These seem for the most part to be logical, reasonable demands to which any fair-minded person would readily accede, for in the main they constitute the right to self-determination. Now, try them for a moment on the black woman to see how they fit.

Equal pay for equal work and proportional representation: This means the right to compete with black men for the few jobs of janitor, custodian, stock clerk, sanitation engineer, and similar lower-class jobs. A moot point in the argument of relative factors

contributing to instability in black families has been the traditionally favored position of the black female in getting and keeping better-paying jobs.

Legal and medical protection for unwanted pregnancies: The
system never actively enforced abortion laws where blacks were
concerned—a common attitude being that blacks never had unwanted pregnancies. The concern of black women is legal and
medical protection for the wanted pregnancies.

Adequate, economical child care facilities for working
mothers: Black women, poor black women, have always made up
the majority of the female labor force. Now that middle-class and
affluent white mothers are joining the labor force in rapidly increasing numbers, day care facilities are viewed as necessary and
positive adjuncts to family life, rather than as temporary shelters
for neglected, dependent children whose parents allegedly had
little interest in and less time for them. Many a black mother, who
for years has had no alternative but to accept whatever day care
arrangements she could make, would gladly exchange day care
facilities for an adequate plan that would enable her to remain in
her own home providing care for her own children.

Access to all public places: The law has never objected to
black women going any place black men went, including public
toilets, where signs in the past not uncommonly read, "white ladies," "white men," and "colored."

Freedom from sexual exploitations: Despite Benjamin Frank-
lin's sage observation that after dark all women look alike, no
white man has ever been lynched for raping a black woman. In
fact, sexual exploitation of the black female was an expected right
of slave owners, who valued their slaves as much for breeding
potential as for work. Nor has the practice of wet-nursing white
babies by black nannies been so long abandoned as not to be
remembered by the present generation.

Freedom from suburbia, kitchen gadgets, babysitting, and
bras: Most black women dream of the day they can escape the
rat-infested, treeless, cement jungle for a blade of grass and the
fresh air of the suburbs. In a world of the common kitchen, where
one schemes for ways to use the stove first, concern about gadgets
is a cruel mockery. And as for taking off the bra, for many a black

women it has been only recently she has been able to afford to put one on. Since most black women either have themselves, or know someone who has done baby sitting for a living, it is an achievement and a status symbol to be able to remain at home and care for one's own children. In some respects much of what is causing agitation and concern to middle-class white women may be considered as stemming indirectly from the advanced liberation of the black woman. The present generation of black women is no longer available for exploitation by anyone, black or white, male or female. In effect, black women have said clean your own house, feed and raise your own children, make the bed your own man lies in, and, moreover, take the pats on the rear and lewd glances as generations of black women have had to do. That vast pool of exploited black women who make it possible for the fairer sex to become ladies is vanishing. Ironically, for years the black woman has been free to do all of the things the white woman is now demanding just as the black woman is trying so hard to give them up. And give them up she must if there is ever to be any masculinity for the black male.

THE BLACK FEMININE MYSTIQUE

Black women, today, recognize that without liberation for the black male there can be no real freedom for anyone. There is no place in the present day scheme of things for black Delilas. And black women are determined to give birth to no more "raisins in the sun." The liberation the black woman seeks is from the oppression which results from the color black, for it is the image of blackness to which she responds and which ties her to the black male. White male dominance rigidly pursues the preservation and stability of the family according to the white ideal only. In no other country has a shrine to "momism" been erected as in America. For some the black norm has found personal and cultural reinforcement in the myth that family stability is an attribute and prerogative of whites only and that the black matriarchy, like the biblical Ham, was to be a perpetual negative legacy. Purged at last of the fatal poison of self-hatred, most blacks have rejected the myth along with the legacy. Janus faced, the black mystique contains a duality that compels the black woman to share the scepter of power with the black male, while yet retaining for herself her own unique individuality. The transitional period during which black men experience and learn the feel and effective use of power and its accompanying responsibility is a grave one, and one in which the role of the black woman will bear significantly on the full realization of black masculinity.

In a relationship in which they have never been peers, black women find it difficult to sympathize, much less empathize, with white women, for inwardly many have often harbored feelings of being better as women all the while they had to wear the saffronia cloak. The clenched fist and erect arm of the black power symbol in Freudian dynamics is more powerfully evocative as a symbol of black masculinity and sexuality than as a symbol of black opposition. But blacks must not only escape from the ghetto but from ghetto psychology as well. The sword of the new feminism is double edged. To win rights based solely on sex may well mean a Pyrrhic victory; of getting more freedom in ways the black woman in the ghetto does not want, namely, more female-based households, more farmed-out children, more higher paying lower-class jobs. For many poor black women the well-known blues song, "My Man—He's Gone Again" may well have to be rewritten "My Man—He's Gone for Good." The price of equality between the black sexes has been one blacks could ill afford. The psychological thrust of the saw, he who puts the bread on the table and guards the door has the right and dignity of ultimate decision, has not been misunderstood by the black female. Lower-class black women are tired of being forced to make decisions. They are tired of the exclusive right of self-determination and long for the right of shared destiny and mutual participation in family matters. For many in the ghetto it's the family that pays together that stays together. As past generations of black women have subtly taught their sons to renounce their manhood to save their lives, present day generations are overtly teaching their sons to assert their manhood to save the race. Significantly, it was the new black feminine mystique that gave impetus to the civil rights movement by the refusal of a black woman to get out of her seat on a bus, thereby launching the now historic Montgomery, Alabama, bus boycott. It was only when black women got off their feet that black men began to stand on theirs.

The dramatically poignant painting by Norman Rockwell on a (circa) 1955 cover of the *Saturday Evening Post* of the little black girl in starched stiff dress flanked by federal marshalls escorting her to a desegregated school in the face of a hostile crowd of white adults is pathetically reminiscent of leading a lamb to the slaughter. It depicts, however, the desperate sacrifice that black parents have been willing to make to attempt to become part of the American mainstream. Blacks of all classes have been made painfully aware that no number of scientific degrees, no amount of talent or genius, courage, morality, beauty, or money entitles them to first-class citizenship. As the late Malcolm X scathingly reminded a black academician critical of his views, that he, a professor no less than an ignorant sharecropper, was to the whites just another nigger. White America responds to what it sees and for blacks, it sees not a person but a color, a color to which it has been specifically conditioned to react in a predetermined way. The effect on blacks has been to make them increasingly aware that since the path of individual achievement is meaningless, the only effective way to achieve cultural assimilation is to follow some of the strategies of immigrant groups. Numerous ethnic groups have entered the American mainstream while still retaining and cherishing those cultural attributes that identify them as a specific ethnic group.

The black ethos has emerged from a recognition that "denial of difference is as little helpful as the assertion that the existence presents an unbridgeable gulf between the races (Jahoda 1961)." Survival of the black in this country has depended upon his ability to accurately interpret his environment. And that interpretation has always been predicated on recognition of the day-to-day reality of difference in matters black and white. The recent separatism advocated by black radicals may not be defensible or even sensible on any number of grounds. However, it is readily understandable psychologically. The goal of getting it together is ego identity for the black, first as an individual wherein he can come by "an accrued confidence in his ability to maintain an inner sameness and continuity that will be matched by the sameness and continuity of one's meaning for others (Jahoda 1961)." Heretofore, the boundary between what has been inner and what has been outer has been so fluid and contradictory as to prevent crystallization and cohesiveness of a uniquely black ethos. In the never ending cycle of *sein und werden* blacks are discovering the tremendous potential of being uniquely black.

Involved in this struggle to become, to be somebody, are black women no less than black men. The primary source of satisfaction that a black woman seeks and needs in being a woman lies within and must be first experienced, shared, and gratified within her own ethos, before she is able to move beyond it. So long as it is the female who bears the offspring, sex-role imprinting, with its attendant psychological effects, will take precedence over and survive any major attempts to equate the sexes (Kinney, 1971). So long as black women have black sons they will remain skeptical of an alliance with women to achieve a dubious equality which guarantees less than full manhood for him for whom she has labored and given birth. For the black woman, maternalism, sexuality, and the new feminism come full circle back to the black male.

REFERENCES

Eberts, P. R., & Witton, R. A. Recall from anecdote: Alexis De Tocqueville and the morphogenesis of American. *Amer. Soc. Review* 1970, 35: 1081-97.

Farley, R., & Hermalin, A. Family stability: a comparison of trends between blacks and white. *Amer. Soc. Review*. 1971, 36: 1-7.

Glazer, N., & Moynihan, D. *Beyond the melting pot.* Cambridge, Mass.: M.I.T. Press, 1963.

Grier, W., & Cobbs, P. *Black rage.* New York: Basic Books, 1968.

Heiskanen, V. S. The myth of the middle class family in American family sociology. *The Amer. Soc.* 1971, 6: 14-18.

Jahoda, M. Race relations and mental health. Belgium: UNESCO, 1961, 44 pp.

King, H. The black woman and women's lib. *Ebony Magazine* February, 1971, pp. 68-75.

Kinney, C. Reflections on the 1969 resolutions of the women's caucus. *The Amer. Soc.* 1971, 6: 19-22.

Liebow, E. *Tally's corner.* Boston: Little, Brown, 1967.

Pasamanick, B. A tract for the time: some sociobiologic aspects of science, race and racism and their implications. In Zubin, J., and Shagass, C. (eds.), *Neurobiological aspects of psychopathology.* New York: Grune & Stratton, 1969, pp. 223–33.

Pettigrew, T. *A Profile of the negro american.* Princeton: D. Van Nostrand, 1964.

Rosenthal, J. Census data shows blacks still poor. Census finds rise in negro families headed by women. *New York Times.* Feb. 11; Feb. 26, 1971, p. 1.

U.S. Dept. of Labor: *The negro family: the case for national action.* Washington, D.C.: Government Printing Office, 1965.

part III

Integration of
Clinical and
Behavioral Approaches

chapter 10

Human Sexual Autonomy as an Evolutionary Attainment, Anticipating Proceptive Sex Choice and Idiodynamic Bisexuality *

Saul Rosenzweig †

When in the course of human events a "sexual revolution" is ostensibly occurring, the critical spectator is impelled to re-examine it in the light of its antecedents. The phrase is then seen to denote a phase of Western cultural history appearing against the broad background of mammalian evolution. For in telescopic perspective, 20th-century, post-Freudian man is the latest variant of *Homo sapiens*, a sexually dimorphic mammal. To provide such a

*Copyright © 1973 by Saul Rosenzweig.

†Saul Rosenzweig, Ph.D., Departments of Psychology and Psychiatry, Washington University, St. Louis, Missouri.

To my friend Willard M. Allen, former Chairman of the Department of Obstetrics and Gynecology, Washington University School of Medicine, I gratefully dedicate this paper. During its gestation it was my good fortune to have him, the codiscoverer and christener of progesterone, as my socratic midwife.

perspective is the initial aim of this treatise. Its further objective is to depict the continuous and relentless increase of human sexual autonomy in the course of evolution. The contemporary sexual revolution thus becomes genetically and dynamically intelligible, and its potential impact for the individual human being comes into focus.

THE EVOLUTION OF MAMMALIAN MATING BEHAVIOR

In the present survey, mammals are considered in three groups: subprimate, primate (which comprise the monkeys, lemurs, and apes), and hominid, i.e., *Homo sapiens.*

First to be noted are the controlling conditions of mating behavior as shown in Figure 1. The dominant regulatory mechanism proceeds from estrus in the subprimate, such as dog, cat, guinea pig, to menstruation, which, in the strict sense, is found for the first time in the higher primates (Asdell 1946, p. 23; Corner 1947, pp. 69–70; Hardin 1970, pp. 59–60; Zuckerman 1932). Menstruation continues in hominid females with the important addition of complex psychosomatic, primarily cognitive, determinants (Aronson 1959, p. 99). In man, both female and male, these latter aspects, summarized here under the term encephaliza-

CONTROLLING CONDITIONS OF MAMMALIAN MATING BEHAVIOR			
	DOMINANT REGULATORY MECHANISM	TEMPORAL AVAILABILITY OF FEMALE	PREVAILING HEGEMONY
I. SUBPRIMATE	Estrus	Periodic	Heteronomous (External)
II. PRIMATE	Menstruation	Periodic or Continuous	Autonomic (Internal)
III. HOMINID	Encephalization	Continuous	Autonomous

Figure 1

tion, include the advanced use of language and symbolic thought. Fantasy and learning play a decisive role. Culture represents an institutionalization of these higher human capacities and, in turn, culture enters into the regulation of mating and of sexual behavior in general.

From the standpoint of duration, mating behavior varies at each of the three mammalian levels; in subprimates it is usually "seasonal," i.e., periodic or limited to narrowly defined days, sometimes even hours, when ovulation is occurring and impregnation is most assured. Only at such periods is the female sexually receptive (Asdell 1946). Nonhuman primates represent an intermediate condition. In free-ranging specimens, especially among the monkeys, breeding is seasonal, but most baboons and higher apes, including gorillas and chimpanzees, mate throughout the year (Lancaster & Lee 1965). Nevertheless, even these higher primates have been noted to show fairly definite preferences for mating at the fertile phase of the menstrual cycle (Zuckerman 1930, p. 749). In the hominid, mating behavior is no longer periodic but continuous (Ford & Beach 1951; Huxley 1923). In a sense, the male gains more than the female in this advance, i.e., in rutting mammals the male responds automatically to the female in heat, but in the higher primates, and particularly in humans, the male may invite the mating act, though a mutual decision is ordinarily involved.

Along with these changes the prevailing source of control moves from heteronomy to autonomy. In subprimates, exogenous factors are vital in complementing an endogenous rhythm; conditions of light, temperature and rainfall determine the onset of estrus (Amoroso & Marshall 1960; Marler & Hamilton 1966). In primates and in hominids, control of mating is partly autonomic, i.e., under the direction of the hormones supplied by the gonads via the pituitary gland, and partly in response to cognitive determinants mediated by the hypothalamus and the neocortex (Ford & Beach 1951; Young 1961, passim). The shift toward the cognitive has been demonstrated by experimental ablation of cortical tissue in animals (Beach 1947, 1958, 1964). Results indicate that in subprimate mammals, in which the beginning of cortical control can already be observed, the male is more affected than the female by such ablation. The differential finding is not surprising since the hormonal control of the sexual cycle both in estrus and in menstruation in the first instance concerns the female rather than the male. As an expression of the prevailing cortical control, learning begins to be important for mating behavior. An example is afforded by primates raised in isolation, without opportunity to learn by experimenting with peers. Such animals fail at maturity in performing copulation (Harlow & Harlow 1965, pp. 328f.). The same determining effect of learning is, of course, quite familiar to the clinician who deals with human sexual problems such as male impotence and male homosexuality, both of which are known to be often a result of particular conditioning experiences (Johnson 1968; Masters & Johnson 1970; Schrenck-Notzing 1892). It is not, however, to be inferred that the hormones have nothing to do with sexual behavior in humans since hormones do govern the development of secondary sex characters and have been demonstrated to determine relative strength of drive. But the organization of sexual patterns is now generally held to be largely a matter of cognitive factors controlled by the cortex and related to learning, both individual and cultural. "Autonomous," as expressed in Figure 1, is intended to convey this comparative emancipation of hominid mating behavior from heteronomous or external control and from internal, hormonal dominance (Young 1961, passim).

Gains in autonomy, as just traced and as will be further described below, are not an unmixed blessing. Here as elsewhere freedom demands guidance, not just morally but biologically; for augmented autonomy, unless met by other capacities, may produce confusion. Automaticity has its built-in response mechanisms; autonomy demands responsibility—the ability to respond adaptively. The above cited example of psychic male impotence illustrates this negative potential of increased autonomy, but the potential for maladjustment is far broader. By some theorists modern neuroticism has been attributed in large measure to the over-encephalization of sexuality (Freud 1898, 1908; Galt 1947).

THE EVOLUTION OF MAMMALIAN SEXUAL AUTONOMY

Next to be considered are the stages of mammalian sexual autonomy that extend beyond mating as shown in Figure 2. Outstand-

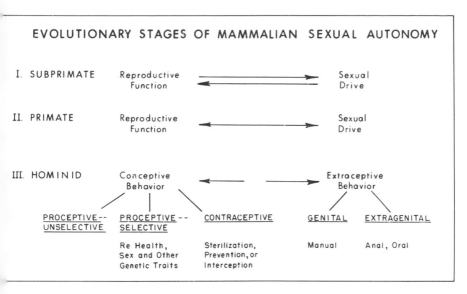

Figure 2

ing here is the gradual separation of the sexual drive from the reproductive function. In subprimates, sexual drive is for the most part limited to the time of estrus, and estrus coincides with ovulation; barring accident, copulation entails conception and propagation. In the higher, nonhuman primates (apes) which menstruate, sexual drive begins to separate from reproduction. Copulation may occur throughout the month but exogenous influences prevail in most monkeys. Finally, in humans, sexual activity as such becomes independent of reproduction though, of course, reproduction when it occurs involves sexual activity (Ford & Beach 1951, passim).

It is paradoxically striking that, as contrasted with estrus in the subprimate female, some human females who exhibit preferences for coitus at particular stages of the menstrual cycle tend to elect the immediate premenstrual days, and these days belong to the so-called safe period. In other women, however, there is, as in lower animals, an intensification of sexual drive at the time of ovulation (Ford & Beach 1951, pp. 205–213; Hampson & Hampson 1961; Rosenzweig 1943).

With the emancipation of sexual drive from reproduction a further increment of human sexual autonomy appears: the deliberate control of conception is ushered in together with a choice among various sexual behavior modalities with no reproductive consequences. A need exists for a consistent conceptual language to express these developments. On the model of the terms *conception, conceptus,* and *contraceptive,* the words "proceptive" and "extraceptive" are here introduced. Similarly, "extragenital" is suggested to supplement *genital.* The term *proceptive*, referring to planned conception with a positive goal, is preferred to *eugenic* because it more specifically points to personal preferences instead of social regulation intended to improve racial stock. In like manner, "interception" and "interceptive"* are superior to *abortion* and *abortifacient*, both because they attenuate emotional connotations and because they fit precisely into the consistent language schema of human sexual reproduction employed here. *Extraceptive* refers to sexual behavior outside the conceptive or reproductive function. *Extragenital* means extraceptive behavior which involves bodily areas other than the genitals (oral, anal) and is superior to the Freudian term *pregenital* because, as will be shown later, Freud's designation entails a teleological espousal of "genital primacy" as if it represented a developmental law of nature. The general implication in all the above terminology is that any behavior to be classified as sexual must involve orgasm, actual or potential.

As regards conceptive behavior, a threefold choice exists: "proceptive–unselective" refers to the ordinary situation in which coitus occurs with no special plan or precaution. "Proceptive–selective" refers to coitus accompanied by an option for offspring with particular characteristics, e.g., healthy rather than defective, male or female. Contraceptive methods are obviously those that prevent conception through some form of permanent sterilization, through preventive devices used at the moment of coitus, or by interception of the conceptus.

*The term "interceptive" is owed to Naqvi and Warren (1971) whose paper came to the writer's attention after the present manuscript had been sent to the editors. That their neologism agrees so exactly with those that had been proposed in the present paragraph confirms the current need for this new terminology.

The control of conception, though long practiced sporadically, began in a systematic sense only about a century and a half ago (Himes 1963). Building on the analysis of population by Malthus (1798) toward the end of the eighteenth century, Place (1822) and others went on, in the early part of the nineteenth, to recommend the control of population by contraceptive devices.* This birth control movement culminated in the oral contraceptive pill which came into general use in 1960 (Drill 1966), a practice estimated to have been employed by about 10,000,000 American women by 1971. The current literature includes suggestions for a male contraceptive pill, a once-a-month female pill, and a pill taken by the woman immediately after coitus (Swyer 1967). In addition to temporary measures, the more permanent intrauterine device (IUD) and the methods of sterilization by tubal ligation in the female and vasectomy in the male are being widely adopted (Hardin 1970).

Induced abortion has become prevalent worldwide during the past decade (Grisez 1970; Hall 1970). By 1971 it had been legalized, with variations, in seventeen states of the U.S.A. Segments of the population are strongly opposed to it, but the trend appears to be unabated. As recently as October 1970 the U.S. Supreme Court ruled a Wisconsin anti-abortion law unconstitutional.

Contraception in the interest of population control on a social scale has enlisted the support of philanthropic groups, national governments, and the United Nations. The aim is to contain the population explosion by limiting family size within the bounds of adequate food supply, medical care, and educational and employment opportunities. To date such social engineering has been implemented by offering contraceptive information and devices to individuals on a voluntary basis, but it has been found that ignorance, apathy, and indolence in seeking such help or in applying it have largely defeated the objectives (Ehrlich & Ehrlich 1970;

---

*It is noteworthy that the American utopian John Humphrey Noyes, who founded the Oneida Community, based an essential part of his scheme upon the proposition that in the past, human sexual activity had been mistakenly confounded with reproduction. He was a pioneer in birth control (by *coitus reservatus*) and in 1869 instituted the first organized experiment in human eugenics (called by him "stirpiculture"). In his early prospectus (Noyes 1849) he stated: "... as propagation will [in the social order of the future] become a science, so amative intercourse will become one of the 'fine arts.' "

Parkes 1966, pp. 145–57; 170–81). Efforts to improve the effectiveness of these programs energetically continue through new research approaches and better social planning. But the sense of critical urgency has inspired occasional discussions of the right to conceive or bear children—a right until now universally acknowledged for married couples. Those who stress the social as well as the individual responsibility involved in procreation speculate that a time may arrive when governmentally imposed birth control may become desirable, or even mandatory, despite the distasteful features entailed. One such suggestion proposes an as yet undefined "infertility diet" for all mature citizens which could be neutralized by an antidote obtainable only upon the issue of a pregnancy license. In the immediate future the imposition of such a regimen is unlikely, for even if it were to gain social approval the dietetic formula is still conjectural (Goldzieher 1965; Swyer 1967; Wolstenholme 1963, pp. 103f., 274f.).

While contraceptive methods intended to prevent or interrupt pregnancy are strongly entrenched, the proceptive (eugenic) phase of human sexual autonomy is still largely speculative or experimental. In the latter half of the nineteenth century Francis Galton (1908; see also Pearson 1914–30), stimulated by the theory of evolution, which was promulgated by his cousin Charles Darwin, undertook a study of individual differences geared to race improvement. Such planned improvement by breeding he christened "eugenics." In animal husbandry these procedures have long been employed and have undergone considerable experimentation. To multiply the breeding advantages of genetically superior bulls, artificial insemination has for years been practiced by cattle raisers. A complementary method known as "artificial inovulation" has been successfully employed though it is still essentially experimental (Taylor 1968, pp. 31f.). By this procedure ova extracted from one animal are implanted in another where they develop to parturition. Since vastly more eggs are available than ripen and are impregnated by the natural means, this method makes it theoretically possible to multiply the breeding potential of a superior female just as artificial insemination can multiply the potential of the male. Moreover, fertilized eggs have been transported to distant lands where they have been implanted in and brought to term by a "foster mother" (Hunter, Bishop, Adams, & Rowson 1962). Quite recently the technique reached a new level of efficiency (Kiewit 1971). Though applicable to humans, artificial inovulation has not yet been reported for them.

On the other hand, artificial insemination in cases of human male infertility or impotence is fairly common. It has been roughly estimated that 5,000 to 10,000 instances occur in the United States annually (Leach 1970, pp. 71-84). Suggestions for its proceptive use have frequently been made. One modification has recourse to the freezing and storage of sperm for deployment at some future time (Hoagland 1943; Parkes 1966, pp. 262-75). Szilard (1961, pp. 87-102) in 1948 composed a satiric piece of science fiction, based partly on this innovation, which projected the condition of modern technological society by a century. But in our own time a more immediate use has been found for the delayed action of sperm. Semen banks for frozen deposits are already doing business in New York City, Minneapolis, and elsewhere. While home collection is customary, at least one institution maintains an ejaculatorium where, with various kinds of erotic assistance, the semen may be conveniently produced by depositors. Many clients are men who are planning to have a vasectomy but, knowing that reversal of the operation is not guaranteed, wish to take out insurance against a future change of mind. If all their present children should die accidentally or, if for any other reason, they should want to procreate, the "frozen assets" can be withdrawn for deployment. Some would-be fathers whose semen at any one ejaculation has proved insufficient for a fertile result plan on accumulating enough sperm to raise the count to an effective level (*Time*, 1972).

The phenomenal progress in molecular biology, especially the discovery of the genetic code in DNA, has inspired both hopes and fears for even more radical engineering of human reproduction. In prospect are not merely the obviously desirable elimination of inherited disease and defect but the selective guidance of evolution according to preestablished, positive criteria (Muller 1960; Taylor 1968, pp. 158f.; Wolstenholme 1963, pp. 247f. by Muller).

PROCEPTIVE CHOICE OF NEONATE SEX

A striking instance of the progression from the speculative to the practicable in proceptive human reproduction is the impending choice by parents of the sex of their offspring (Leach 1970, pp. 89-94; Parkes 1966, pp. 158-69; Taylor 1968, pp. 39-43). From earliest recorded history, dating back to Egyptian papyri, parents have been eager to have advance information and, if possible, power to control the sex of progeny (Abdul-Karim & Iliya 1961; Blakely 1937; Cederqvist & Fuchs 1970). Folklore is replete with bizarre formulas for accomplishing these objectives. In recent years science has begun to provide reliable procedures for attaining them, and it is predictable that a new epoch of human history in which family planning will move from a chiefly negative or contra-ceptive to a positive or proceptive modality is imminent. Not only the size of the family but the sex of the children, their birth order and spacing will then come under parental autonomy. At the out-set, such choice will probably involve only individual instances, e.g., a family with several successive children of identical sex will decide to have a child of the opposite sex or else have no more. But in due course total family design will be planned. In terms of human sexual autonomy, a momentous step forward will have been made when man supplants nature in deciding the sex design of his family.

There are three radically simple but practicably still remote possibilities that will be mentioned but not further considered here: (1) clonal reproduction by cellular surgery in which the nucleus of a body cell is combined with the cytoplasm of an egg cell (the nucleus of which has been eliminated) to replicate the sex, and all other genetic characteristics, of the body-cell donor; (2) *in vitro* fertilization ("test-tube babies") with gestation to a point at which sex assay can be reliably made, followed by im-plantation of the accepted embryo in a receptive uterus; (3) chem-ical intervention during very early pregnancy, when decisive sexual differentiation has not yet occurred in the embryo, so that a po-tential female becomes a male or vice versa (Gurdon & Uehlinger 1966; Lederberg 1966; Neumann & Elger 1966; Taylor 1968, pp. 22-43). A generation hence some such procedure as one of the foregoing may actually be employed, but discussion will here be focused on already existing and practicable techniques.

The background for the immediately available method of proceptive sex choice is found in two medical departures of the past ten to fifteen years: (1) In order to interrupt further gestation of offspring with sex-linked hereditary diseases, procedures have been developed for prenatal sex ascertainment as early as the 12th to 15th week of fetal life. Through amniocentesis (by which a portion of the amniotic fluid is aspirated) and sex chromatin analysis of the fetal tissue contained in the extract, the sex of the conceptus can now be predicted with high reliability (Fuchs & Cederqvist 1970; Nadler 1968a, 1968b, 1969; Serr, Sachs, & Danon 1955). In the most advanced development of this procedure the amniotic fluid is drawn off transvaginally, rather than transabdominally, and it does not have to be replaced with other fluid as formerly was the practice. The transvaginal method is considered to be easier and safer, and it can be carried out for reliable sex determination somewhat sooner than the transabdominal, i.e., as early as the 12th to 14th week of pregnancy (Papp, Gardó, Herpay, & Árvay 1970). (2) During the same decade abortion induced on request has become widely prevalent (Callahan 1970; Grisez 1970; Hall 1970; Hardin 1970; Noonan 1970). Foreign countries, e.g., Hungary and Japan, took the lead, but in the last few years more and more states of the U.S.A. have modified their laws in this direction. For instance, the present law of New York State permits abortion through the 24th week of pregnancy upon application by the mother. Concurrently, procedures for inducing abortion at the various stages of gestation have been progressively perfected. Notable among these is vacuum aspiration (or suction) which can be employed for the termination of pregnancy through the first trimester (Vojta 1967). It can be carried out in a matter of minutes and, if performed by a skilled operator, is considered to be almost completely without risk. With abortions being performed in ever increasing numbers, simpler and safer methods continue to be devised. As of this writing, either the very simple vacuum aspiration or dilation-and-curettage methods, which require as little as five to fifteen minutes by the obstetrician and a few hours to one night in the hospital by the patient, can be used during the 12th to 14th week of gestation, a date by which prenatal sex determination can be reliably made. The more complicated saline induction procedure, employed after the 16th week of pregnancy, is not required for proceptive sex choice as outlined above.

The foregoing developments, while not yet applied for the parental control of a normal offspring's sex, will undoubtedly soon be so utilized. Theoretically there is nothing to interdict such application now in those parts of the world, including states of the U.S.A., where abortion on request is lawful. An obstetrician could be asked by a pregnant woman to perform an amniocentesis and sex chromatin assay just before the end of the third month of gestation in order to ascertain the health and sex characteristics of the fetus. (The physician could have no legitimate objection if he had the necessary experience and technical assistance.) If the sex of the embryo proved not to be the one desired by her (and her husband), she could, on her own initiative, proceed to obtain an abortion. Obviously these steps could be taken at present only by a well-informed individual with sufficient funds to defray the expenses. But in due course these limitations are destined to recede as lay information increases and as the technical facilities become simplified, more readily available, and less expensive.*

But the above method suffers from an obvious disadvantage in being retrospective. It postpones the ascertainment of sex and any further decisive action until after fetal differentiation has occurred. There is, to be sure, the mitigating circumstance that the odds for parents to get what they want are 50–50 (the random sex ratio in the general population being estimated as 105 males to 100 females); a reversal of the choice made by nature would thus be needed in only half the cases. Nevertheless, it would clearly be preferable for the parental choice to precede rather than to follow fetal sex differentiation if such an option were practicable.

One path to such a prearrangement of sex has been experimentally pursued for some time. It relies upon the fact that the sex of the offspring is the contribution of the father alone: spermatozoa with X chromosomes produce females while those with Y chromosomes are responsible for males. On this basis research has been conducted to separate X from Y sperm in

*See note on page 230.

samples of semen from rabbits and livestock by techniques of sedimentation, centrifugation, and electrophoresis (Bhattacharya 1964; Schilling 1966; Sevinç 1968). These separations have been validated by using the products in artificial insemination. The results, though promising, have not thus far been replicable. Authorities, however, predict that in the near future a reliable technique of separation will be developed (Cederqvist & Fuchs 1970, p. 164). If the procedure could then be extended to human sperm, the X or Y variety could be selectively used with women. In this context artificial insemination would have the advantage of utilizing the husband's own sperm. Moreover, it would be resorted to by a marital pair only on those rare occasions on which a specific sex choice was required. Other offspring would be male or female as chance decreed, with contraception being employed in usual sex relations.

Like the three techniques mentioned at the outset, though belonging much less to the "brave new world," the capacity to assort sperm still lies in the future. Instead there is at hand a less complete and somewhat controversial method that, while depending upon the fact that sperm are of two types, does not require their *in vitro* separation. Based on the assumption that X or gynosperm are favored in the race to fertilization by an acid environment and that Y or androsperm by an alkaline one, this procedure attempts to favor the one or the other type by selective coitus. Specifications are alternatively offered for the male and for the female (Shettles 1961, 1970). Preliminary results, though encouraging, are far from definitive because the observations were not made under rigorous experimental conditions. For present purposes, however, the details of the method or exact degree of its efficacy are irrelevant. What is significant is the proposal for selective intercourse, by whatever specifications are later shown to be valid, as a way of biasing the balance during coitus toward androsperms or gynosperms. Though in and for itself such a practice would not assure sex choice, it might contribute some leverage in the desired direction. If so, it would constitute a first step in an eventual prospective method of sex choice to replace the retrospective one described above as presently available.

A second ingredient of such an eventual procedure is found in some recent research which substitutes for amniocentesis a blood test demanding much less of the patient. On the basis that the amniotic sac is not, after all, impervious, this method assesses very small samples of fetal tissue that have penetrated through the amnion into the blood stream. Though the technique involves some as yet laborious and incompletely proved measures of X and Y fetal constituents, it holds out promise for a simplified method of fetal sexing (Schröder & de la Chapelle 1972; Walknowska, Conte, & Grumbach 1969). Again, the details are less important than the direction indicated for a second step in an eventual method of sex choice which is uncomplicated and permits early and easy detection of fetal sex.*

Finally, it is anticipated that to replace the far more cumbersome and expensive practices of obstetrical abortion an effective and safe, perhaps self-administered, interceptive medication will be produced in the near future (Embrey 1970; Karim & Filshic 1970; Leach 1970, pp. 44–46; Naqvi & Warren 1971).

Taken in combination these three steps may be visualized as the ultimate procedure of choice: selective coitus, XY blood or other readily accessible chemical test, and an optionally used interceptive. By such a procedure, whatever its finally proven details, parental choice of neonate sex would become fairly simple and straightforward and would involve practically no more obstetrical intervention than now occurs with the permanent contraceptives and the supervision of normal pregnancy.†

The expected demographic effects of proceptive sex choice are necessarily conjectural. Some observers predict that parental choice would not materially affect the sex ratio in the population (Parkes 1968, p. 168). Others foresee some initial effort by individuals or by societies to reverse the almost universal preponderance of females over males (Cederqvist & Fuchs 1970, p. 172). Some expect more complex effects and point to possibly serious imbalance that can be avoided only by an early confrontation of the issue. One could then be prepared in advance for any necessary

---

*Simpler even than a blood test is a preliminarily announced saliva test making use of a marketable wafer (Pre–Na–Tell) which will allegedly enable the expectant mother to predict the sex of the fetus five months before birth (*St. Louis Post–Dispatch*, April 23, 1972, p. 9E, col. 1).

†If one were to use FASCOI for the immediately available "fetal appraisal via sex chromatin with optional interception," the acronym SXYI (pronounced sĕxi) might serve for the three-step eventual method: "selective coitus, XY chemical test, interceptive as needed."

social regulation which it would be much more difficult to impose after sex choice is being widely exercised (Leach 1970, pp. 93-94).

Some attempt has been made empirically to explore the relationships between preferred sex of offspring and present family size (Fawcett 1970; Freedman, Freedman, & Whelpton 1960; Pohlman 1967; Pohlman & Pohlman 1969; Rainwater 1965). Pohlman and Pohlman (1969, p. 71), for example, have concluded on the basis of such evidence as now exists that the size of a family is often larger than would be the case if "birth planning" could encompass not only the number of offspring but their sex as well. They have further stressed that absence of sex choice increases the incidence of unwanted or rejected children, many of whom belong to the "wrong sex" category (ibid., pp. 186, 209, 442). It is thus probable that sex choice would automatically reduce the absolute size of the family—a desirable social result—and that it might eliminate some present psychological problems in parent-sibling and sibling-sibling relationships. The obvious corollary cannot, however, be overlooked; when family planning includes the sex of offspring new psychological problems will arise between parents intent upon making a decision and in social groups expressing a preference for one or the other of the sexes. In a preliminary questionnaire survey of a university student population, Markle and Nam (1971) have pointed up this latter issue. The entire problem of sibling status (Sutton–Smith & Rosenberg 1970) will also assume quite new proportions and our present very limited knowledge of this topic will need to be reexamined and rigorously pursued.

One must agree with Leach (1970) that "There are few biomedical areas where calm, widespread public discussion is more urgently needed. . ." (p. 94). It would lend weight to such discussion if systematic investigation were carried out on latent attitudes toward this new phase of human sexual autonomy.

STAGES OF SEXUAL EMANCIPATION IN RECENT HUMAN HISTORY

Turning now to extraceptive behavior, one may first recall that as late as the Victorian era sex was formally regarded as intended not for recreation but for procreation (Acton 1857; Taylor 1954, pp. 209-10). Women were not uncommonly expected to submit to coitus, not to enjoy it, and to bring forth children in natural pain, the legacy of Eve. Hence the use of anesthetics to ease labor was seriously questioned on religious grounds until Queen Victoria herself supported the vanguard by being delivered of a son, in 1853, while she was under chloroform (Keys 1963, p. 35; Pearsall 1969, p. 202). In fact, sexual behavior was from time immemorial indulged in for pleasure by man, and such behavior included not only the conceptive but the extraceptive and extragenital as well.

But it was not until the turn of the nineteenth century that extraceptive sexuality acquired a scientific status as part of normal human behavior. For this advance the observations of Havelock Ellis (1936; see also Ellis & Symonds 1896) and of Sigmund Freud (1905) were largely responsible. Just as the credit for a systematic grasp of population control goes to Malthus (1798) and to Place (1822), Freud was the most influential modern authority in making human extragenital behavior a subject for scientific consideration. Freud enlarged the concept of sexual libido. Following a prior systematic outline of erogenous zones, derived from the study of hysteria (Chambard 1881), he described infantile sexuality in a series of autoerotic stages aligned with these zones—oral, anal, phallic. He regarded these stages as forerunners of mature genital sexuality—"genital primacy"—adapted to reproduction. Hence he called them "pregenital." As already noted, this hallmark of Freud's theory has a teleological tendency—a tendency shared by the Judeo-Christian religious and legal tradition. Freud's highly conservative, even reactionary, sexual views led him to regard excessive early masturbation as a threat to full potency in marriage (Freud 1908, 1912); homosexuality he could tolerate but never endorse (Wortis 1963); women he characterized as suffering from penis envy in unconscious recognition of their inferiority, and he insisted upon the vaginal orgasm as a necessary step beyond the clitoral type if the female is to become a mature wife and mother (Freud 1933, Lecture 33). He himself did not, at least consciously, recognize the strong influence of tradition on his thought; instead he posited a recapitulative, evolutionary basis for the stages of the libido in man's ontogeny—a basis not supported by current scientific opinion. It is on these grounds that in the present formulation the term *extragenital* or, more generally, *extraceptive* is used to describe the sex play of childhood and the cognate sexual activity of adults. These terms and the related formulations imply no preconceived notions as to developmental stages or eventual reproductive functioning.

Freud was a pioneer with reservations (perhaps one should say "ambivalence") despite the fact that he was a pioneer. In this regard he resembled his predecessor the Rev. T. R. Malthus (1798, 1803), pioneer of the presently called "population explosion," who opposed strictly artificial control of procreation. In the first presentation of his thesis concerning population control, he relied upon the checks of Nature—famine, vice, war, and pestilence, which happen remarkably to correlate with the four horsemen of St. John's Apocalypse. Only in his second edition, five years later, did he allow for moral restraint (chastity or abstinence), but still without permitting mechanical aids of any kind (McCleary 1953, pp. 83f.). Again, Malthus's successor Darwin, despite his bold formulation of natural selection, wavered inconsistently and rather obsessively between this theory and a more moralistic or teleological (Lamarckian) position, as Darlington (1960) has convincingly shown.

Such vagaries aside, the last two centuries of Western history have witnessed a gradual emancipation of thought with respect to human sexual behavior which may be roughly represented in four cumulative phases, as shown in Figure 3. The first was characterized by the expectation that libido would be expressed only at the genital area and only with a procreative or conceptive goal. This orientation is still the conventional, lower-class view of sex in marriage (Rainwater 1971). Then, largely as a result of "Malthusian" thought, genital sexuality with an extraceptive (contraceptive) end became sanctioned in ever widening circles. Birth control by any potentially effective method was accepted as both individually moral and socially desirable. Next, as a consequence of Freud's observations, it was recognized that conceptive behavior has certain natural extragenital avenues of outlet. Normal sexual intercourse is not limited to the directly reproductive organs. Libido is not limited to the genital organs alone. But Freud, as

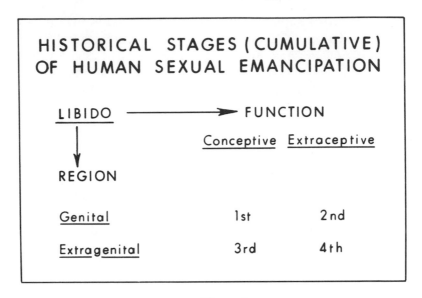

Figure 3

above noted, was never able to accept the full implications of his extragenital orientation. Psychoanalytic therapy as conducted by him had as one of its chief goals the attainment of genital primacy in both male and female patients. While he could connive at oral genital and homosexual practices, he was never able to accept or to endorse the complete divorce of reproductive function from sexual behavior. For him such behavior had of necessity to recognize and to honor procreation as its "natural" end. Finally, on the basis chiefly of Kinsey's surveys (1948, 1953), it was realized, and begins now gradually to be accepted, that sexual behavior may be both extraceptive in function and extragenital in outlet. Sexual behavior is no longer necessarily tied to procreation, let alone marriage, or to the genital areas. Mouth, anus and other extragenital zones may figure partially or exclusively in acceptable sexual activity, without any reproductive intent. Moreover, such behavior may, in a consenting subculture, involve a variety of partners (Smith & Smith, in press). This fourth phase implies a radical reorientation regarding the so-called sexual perversions and, indeed, regarding the role of all sexual expression in human existence. The further development of this phase requires much more extensive knowledge as to consequences than is now available, and it will demand social changes through education, legislation, and other sources of sanction. Its ultimate realization is, however, inevitable if the trends of long-range mammalian evolution and of recent social history here sketched have been correctly grasped.

The broader historical grounds for the foregoing generalizations have already been cited. It is appropriate next to examine the evidence for the specific forms of extraceptive behavior. The data indicate that nonreproductive sex play and variety in coital positions first appear explicitly and recurrently at the primate level (Beach 1958, pp. 130, 139). Prepubertal sex play is found among primate peers. The ventral posture in coitus, as contrasted with rear entry in subprimate mammals, emerges in primates (Campbell 1967, p. 258), and at least one authority (Schultz 1969, p. 183) has pointed out the "amazing variety" of mating postures among the great apes (see also Bourne 1971, Chapter 11). As regards homosexuality, scientific observers, who since about 1910 have attempted sporadically to gather data on this matter, have arrived at conflicting conclusions. Those with more psychoanalytic orientation (Hamilton 1914; Kempf 1917) do not hesitate to ascribe homosexuality to primates, but others maintain that as a fixed sexual pattern it is not found among monkeys and apes (Harlow & Harlow 1965, p. 323; Morris & Morris 1966, p. 187).

As for man, genital extraceptive behavior, namely masturbation, has in recent years acquired a wide emancipation. In a survey of attitudes toward this practice in the Occident, as reflected in authoritative writings in the past two centuries, Spitz (1952) credits psychoanalysis with being chiefly responsible for this liberalization. But one must here distinguish between psychoanalysis and Freud himself. In any event, the exorcism of the demons previously thought to preside over masturbation is now so complete that Pomeroy (1968), a former collaborator of Kinsey, in his manual on sex education for boys encourages masturbation, where the inclination exists, as a helpful preparation for later heterosexual proficiency.

In this context belongs the increasing social tolerance of obscenity and pornography, as attested by the recent Report of a

Federal Commission (Lockhart 1970). Though more circumscribed, a liberalization of attitudes toward sex perversions is also
observable. A marked difference in the openness of discussion of
the topic is, at any rate, demonstrable. The change is epitomized
in the following paradigm: in 1844 Kaan published the first modern *Psychopathia Sexualis*; it was written completely in Latin. The
more famous Krafft-Ebing published the first edition of his *Psychopathia Sexualis* in 1886, written in German but with Latin passages at the more graphic points. The same half-and-half solution
was adopted in the first English translation of that work, published in 1893. Finally, in 1965 two independent and simultaneous all-English translations of this classic made their appearance.
The Latin escape hatch, no longer needed, was effectually closed.

Homosexuality, though still generally deprecated, has gained a
considerable measure of acceptance. In 1967 such behavior between consenting adults (twenty-one years or over) in private was
legalized in England and Wales; by 1971 two states of the U.S.A.,
Illinois and Connecticut, had laws of this nature and there were
indications that others might follow suit in the near future (Hyde
1970; Wolfenden Report 1957). Such legislation makes specific
provision for the protection of minors and prohibits homosexual
behavior in public places, but these specifications merely parallel
those in effect for heterosexual behavior.* A law prohibiting oral-
genital behavior, a common practice among homosexuals but prev-

---

*Considerable confusion exists in the public mind and even in the minds of some
professionals as to the scope of homosexuality. Many of the world's eminent men have
been characterized as homosexual though the correct designation should have been, for
want of a better term, bisexual. Not a few of these individuals have been married and
have produced offspring despite their homosexual proclivities and practices—tendencies
that may have preceded or followed the marriage. The fact is that in the general male
population the homosexual and heterosexual roles are not mutually exclusive. On the
basis of his extensive data, Kinsey (1948, pp. 636–59) stated: "Since only 50 per cent of
the population is exclusively heterosexual throughout its adult life and since only 5 per
cent of the population is exclusively homosexual throughout its life, it appears that
nearly half (46%) of the population engages in both heterosexual and homosexual activities, or reacts to persons of both sexes, in the course of their adult lives" (p. 656). The
biological and psychological characteristics of those persons who have the dual potential
in greater degree or in greater readiness for expression are as yet undetermined. However,
it may be anticipated that in ascertaining these characteristics, provision will have to be
made to distinguish conceptually between the epicene, in whom the masculine and
feminine potentials neutralize each other, and the bisexual, in whom these traits are
mutually enriching.

alent also in heterosexual couples, was adjudged unconstitutional by a federal district court in Texas (Buchanan v. Batchelor, 308 Fed. Supp.—D.C.N.D. Tex., 1970). It should, however, be noted that the ruling was made not in order to sanction such practices specifically but on the basis that the First Amendment to the Constitution was violated by the statute through its "overbreadth" in that "it reaches the private, consensual acts of married couples. . . . entitled to an injunction against future enforcement of the act (pp. 729f.)."

In conceptual terms erotic deviations such as homosexuality can no longer be classified as immoral or unholy on the ground of being nonreproductive and, hence, contrary to nature. By that criterion, in these days of widely practiced contraception, the vast majority of regularly occurring marital coitus would have to be called "perverse." It appears not improbable that more permissive attitudes toward variety in sexual expression will increase in a society attuned to the perils of the population explosion rather than to the divine behest, "Be fruitful and multiply."

Though a multiplicity of factors is doubtless responsible for the increasing emancipation above sketched, it is worthy of particular note that economic forces are probably among the most influential. Greater tolerance toward contraception, and even abortion, and toward homosexuality and other deviations from conceptive sexuality may owe as much to social policy based on economics as to any advance in human enlightenment. For most of these extraceptive and extragenital practices contribute, directly or indirectly, to population control, a highly desirable objective in modern civilization. If, moreover, warfare should at long last be abolished as a way of solving international differences, one of the chief Malthusian checks to overpopulation would be eliminated and the need for other controls, accentuated. It is clear that in the long-range view increasing sexual emancipation is essential to any widespread improvement in the quality of human life.

AUTONOMY IN HUMAN PSYCHOSEXUAL ROLES

The third sector of human sexual autonomy is found in ontogenetic development. Concern for the autonomy of the individual in matters of education, health, and welfare generally has been a consistent motif in the United States during the past century and is epitomized in the progressive extension of the franchise. In the year 1870 the 15th Amendment to the Constitution which enfranchised the blacks became law; 1920 saw the ratification of the 18th Amendment on the enfranchisement of women; in 1970 an enactment by Congress for the first time extended the franchise to youth at age eighteen in federal elections, and in the ensuing year the 26th Amendment broadened this right to all elections. Though franchise means only the right to vote, the striking advance in this civic function implies some liberalization of other elective functions including the sexual. The "sexual revolution" had been in the making during all the preceding century though the label itself apparently dates back only to about 1929, when it appeared in a collective volume entitled *Sex and Civilization* (Schmalhausen 1929).

In the bio-evolutionary perspective (Ploss 1884; Briffault 1927), the problem of women's rights and the historical movement for sex equality become intelligible at this point. Because of her procreative fertility the human female has in many primitive cultures been exalted as the Great Mother goddess, e.g., Diana with the innumerable breasts; but in the civilized patriarchal household she became the wife who not only bore and suckled the children but was expected to accede to the male libidinally as well.* In the course of recent occidental history a countervailing remedy has been sought by some exceptional women and men. In this movement it is the advances of biology, medicine, and government that have been exploited. A clear recognition of the separa-

---

*What produced this evolution? Some speculations imply that the hive life of the *Aphis* may have afforded the male hominid an aversive model: in this bee society the queen is the mother, the other females, the workers who produce the honey; but the male has become either a momentary fecundator, who literally dies for love (even as Aphrodite is born out of the ocean froth which symbolizes the semen and blood of the severed genital of Uranus), or as a drone is driven from the hive to perish. Against such a prototype the human male saw fit to protect himself: he rebelled and took control of the system as priest, paterfamilias, and pimp. The female might be religiously revered as a Virgin, but in the home she was expected to deliver and rear offspring; and in both the home and the brothel she was intended to provide libidinal satisfaction to the male. Not surprisingly some sensitive males, the neurotics, have shown an uneasy awareness of this precarious social arrangement. Hence their "castration anxiety," as labeled by Freud.

tion of the reproductive function from the sex drive and of the consequences that can be made to flow from it by rational control have been stressed. Mother rites, expressing an apotheosis of fertility, have yielded to the rights of the mother to birth control and even to abortion on demand; and the wife, aligning herself with male workers, has refused to remain a captive in a male-dominated household. Instead she has sought education and a professional career, property rights equal to her husband's, and political enfranchisement as a means to both these ends (Mill & Mill 1851, 1869, 1951; Morgan 1970). *Pari passu* the libidinal services of women as prostitutes has been combatted by the champions of women's rights. Both the mistress, who catered for an exorbitant price to the sexual appetites of the affluent male, and the wench, who was demeaned to produce pleasure and/or wealth for males at competitive prices, were deplored as social evils. These conditions, it was maintained, must give way to an acknowledged equality of the sexes. Women began openly to demand appreciation as persons who are partners and companions in all biological, economic, and political arrangements and who have an autonomous voice in the engineering of these goals. And that voice has become truly articulate as these demands have begun to be formulated not merely as protests but as an assertion of the masculine and feminine gender (psychological) roles, both in women and in men, as predominant over the male and female sex (biological) functions (Millett 1970). The position is increasingly tenable because these biological functions are being subjected, at a phenomenal rate of acceleration, to biomedical control which already exceeds anything that the pioneers of sex equality a century ago could have envisaged in their wildest fantasies of rebellion.*

In the extension of human sexual autonomy to ontogenetic development, the emancipation of the masculine and feminine

---

*It is of more than passing interest that one unsung prophetess of this movement is Breuer's patient "Anna O" (Breuer & Freud 1895) who as Bertha Pappenheim (1899; see also Edinger 1968) devoted her post-morbid life to social work for the care and education of children born out of wedlock, for the redemption of sexually wayward girls, and for the extermination of the white slave traffic. Freud, as a paradoxical pioneer, learned from Breuer and from this case history; but he was incapable of learning from the recovered patient who, therefore, regarded Freudian psychoanalysis as "a two-edged sword" wielded by the founder with regressive ambivalence.

roles from the conceptive function as such stands out. The artificiality of the concepts *masculine* and *feminine* considered purely in biological terms has been repeatedly noted during the past generation. Kinsey (1941) in his first published paper on human sexuality posited a continuum, as contrasted with a dichotomy, of masculinity-femininity. He included this concept and developed it into a heterosexual-homosexual rating scale in his epoch-making book (Kinsey, Pomeroy, & Martin 1948, pp. 636–39). Earlier, in a 1939 Phi Beta Kappa address, he had provided the general background for this approach when he chose the theme "Individuals" and attacked general science for ignoring the inconvenient but patent diversity in all living species (Christenson 1971, pp. 3–9). Margaret Mead (1949) in the same decade stressed the cultural modeling of the sex roles. Shortly thereafter Ford and Beach (1951) extended this awareness in *Patterns of Sexual Behavior*. Beginning in the 1950s, Money, Hampson, and Hampson (1955) brought new, empirically based insights to the problem of sex roles in their studies of hermaphroditism. These anomalies, viewed as "experiments of nature," led to the definition of masculinity and femininity in a several-step, sequential paradigm. Five prenatal sex criteria—chromosomal, gonadal, hormonal, internal genital and external genital—were described in conjunction with the postnatal sex of assignment and rearing and the emergent gender identity of the individual. From clinical research it was concluded that the ultimate sex role of the patient depended mainly not on the biological criteria, but on the two last social and psychological factors which, incidentally, appeared to be almost irreversibly fixed by age two (Money 1965, 1969, 1971). These results are consonant with other findings, already mentioned, on the crucial importance of learning and cortical control in human sexual response.

It is important to recognize the emphasis placed in Money's observations on the principle of what may here be termed "developmental disjunction." Noting that the concepts of heredity and environment must now yield to a concept of genetic and environmental interaction at critical periods, he formulates a sequence of developmental differentiations at every stage of which a choice is made and error is possible (Money 1972). At conception this choice is determined by whether the *chromosomal* complement to the female's X will be a sperm with X or Y. In the former case a female, in the latter, a male will begin embryonic life. After the chromosomal choice, *gonadal* differentiation follows at about the sixth week through a choice between testis or ovary from a common *Anlage*. In the XX embryo the rind of the undifferentiated gonad proliferates to form an ovary and the core becomes vestigial; in the XY, the core proliferates and the rind vestigiates. The next criterion (and double phase) is *hormonal*: it asserts itself at the fetal period to determine the formation of the genital ducts and, again, at puberty to control masculine or feminine maturation. In the earlier period, at the differentiation of the *internal genitalia*, the principle of vestigiation is once more exemplified. A choice is made between the Mullerian (female) or the Wolffian (male) duct, both present at the start. The latter can develop, at the expense of the former, only if the proper hormonal additive from the already developed fetal gonad is available, and that gonad must be a testis. In the presence of ovary alone (or of no gonads at all), the female duct will be formed.* The next step concerns the *external genitalia* which emerge at about the tenth week. Here the principle of disjunction is one not of the residual vestige but of an option between homologues from the same *Anlagen*. The genital tubercle will become either the penis or the clitoris; the genital folds, either the foreskin and the wrap-around of the penis (including the penile urethra) or the hood of the clitoris and the labia minora; the genital swelling develops into the scrotum or the labia majora. The later steps occur postpartum. In keeping with what is observable at birth, physician and parents assign a sex to the child—boy or girl; the *sex of rearing* is then usually consonant with this assignment, but in ambiguous cases conflict in the rearing and

*As Money (1972, p. 567) puts it, "There is no doubt about it that nature's first disposition is to make a female." These words conceivably veil a cryptomnesia from Shakespeare who, after extolling "the master-mistress of [his] passion," displayed his ever-astonishing prescience by concluding Sonnet XX as follows:

And for a woman wert thou first created;
Till Nature, as she wrought thee, fell a-doting,
And by addition me of thee defeated,
By adding one thing to my purpose nothing.
  But since she prick'd thee out for women's pleasure,
  Mine be thy love, and thy love's use their treasure.

in the evolving sexual role of the child may result. The *core gender identity*, a psychological emergent, follows the principle of the early embryonic stages, i.e., with both masculine and feminine potentials at the start; but at this stage, with a critical period at around twenty months postnatally, a choice is made not with vestigiation but with dissociation of the unselected alternative. Money stresses a correlation with linguistic attainment since the child's command of gender words will be crucial in determining what he assigns sexually to others and to himself. The attainment of language at about age two thus establishes a critical period for gender identity. After that period a reversal is hazardous to undertake since it is practically impossible to accomplish and the attempt may result merely in serious conflict and confusion of the sexual role. But Money here leaves open the fate of both bilingualism and bisexuality. Though the child may and usually does learn the sexual language of the boy or of the girl, as applied to himself, and dissociates the alternative—learning to be a boy is at the same time learning not to be a girl, and vice versa—the alternative is not destroyed. It remains latent in the personality as a possible form of sexual communication. To what extent the bipotentiality can develop without confusion and even with a broadened range of expression has never been scientifically studied in terms of the foregoing sequence of differentiations. It remains to inquire, theoretically and then empirically, whether, as with bilingual individuals, command of more than one sexual language is feasible. To posit the question is not necessarily to opt for bisexual behavior in the literal sense, but, as will appear presently, an important general question is thus raised regarding the masculine and feminine attributes of personality that are collateral with but not necessarily expressed in sexual acts as such (Rosenberg & Sutton-Smith 1972).

On the foregoing basis the paradigm now to be presented may be considered an extrapolation of Money's observations to normal and mature personality development. It is assumed that the masculine and feminine psychosexual roles are plastic. The emergence of these roles from three distinguishable gender modules is postulated: "ambisexual," "disexual," and "amphisexual."

The infant is bipotentially masculine and feminine, i.e., ambisexual or neutral as to sex role. Freud's designation "polymorphus perverse" was undoubtedly an intuitive recognition of the same point but, as already noted, he abandoned, or at least debased, the insight by propounding a theory of *pregenital* libido stages. Biologically the sex play of young primates and of human infants demonstrates the ambisexual gender module, and from this matrix, shaped by social influences, the human masculine and feminine roles develop through maturational learning.

The gender modules are not conceived as regular stages of development. The rule here is like the answer given by a modern scenario director to the question whether every film has a beginning, a middle, and an end: "Yes, but not necessarily in that order." Nevertheless, in Western cultures—and in some others—tradition favors and tends to impose an order: the disexual module supervenes upon the ambisexual at puberty and demands an inhibition of the feminine by the masculine or, reciprocally, the masculine by the feminine in the interest of progenitive performance. The perpetuation of the race and of the culture group is thus to be assured. But a continuum rather than a dichotomy is involved; disexuality is achieved by individuals in varying degrees, and some of them indefinitely retain a high degree of plasticity in sex role (Diamond 1968, p. 439).

The third or amphisexual module involves a relaxation of the distinction between masculine and feminine, followed by an integration of both, at psychological maturity. Even the physical masculinization of the female and the feminization of the male after the reproductive peak portends such a change. The male is now freer to accept some of his previously rejected femininity, and the female can deal similarly with her masculinity. While this module is most fully exemplified in the creative worker, whether in science, art, industry, or other occupation, it is probably in parenthood that it is most commonly experienced. The disexual module brings a new organism into the world. The nurturing role, so essential to the development of all mammalian progeny (Lehrmann 1962; Rheingold 1963), affords opportunity for creating through amphisexual love and care the most precious of man's cultural products—the child who will continue the process of human life. But other modes of creation are also important for the individual and for society. It is for this reason that the various modules of psychosexuality need now to be fully investigated by scientific methods.

To the limited extent that the transition from the ambisexual to the disexual and the amphisexual can be regarded as an orderly progression, the concepts of the eminent biologist Coghill (Herrick 1949) seem to apply. The fact that Coghill carried his interpretation from the study of embryogenesis in *Amblystoma* (where he made his earliest direct observations) to human motivation and personality renders this reference the more germane. He observed and repeatedly confirmed that undifferentiated action of the whole animal when first stimulated is followed in the course of growth by differentiated partial responses and, finally, by an integration of the partial patterns within the total pattern of the organism. In this developmental process the more or less autonomous partial patterns are not added together but combine in an organized fashion whereby the dominant whole supersedes the separate parts in accomplishing adaptation more completely. Coghill saw in this sequence a justification for viewing the organism as moving toward increasing autonomy, and he speculated that wholesome personality development follows a similar trend. In a sense, the above developmental account of the gender modules may be regarded as an extension of this general interpretation of biological growth.*

At this point one must revert to the biological significance of sexual reproduction itself in order to appreciate the derivation of the above formulation of psychosexual genesis from biological genetics. In sexual reproduction, as contrasted with parthenogenesis (with females alone reproducing only females) or the various forms of asexual propagation, every individual obtains a set of chromosomes from each of two parents, and this mixture is passed

---

*In a more primitive form of theory, the mythology of ancient Greece, the schema of the gender modules receives an allegorical and intuitive type of support. When, in the legend, Oedipus was confronted at the gates of Thebes by the Sphinx who asked him what creature it is that goes on four feet in the morning, on two at noon, and on three in the afternoon, he solved the riddle by correctly answering "Man." However, crawling as an infant on all fours, then walking upright on two legs, and finally using a cane provides a solution only at the manifest level, as a first approximation. At the latent level the solution may lie in the alleged progression of the gender modules: M ± F (ambisexual); M vs. F or F vs. M (disexual); M X F (amphisexual). The key role of the prophet Tiresias throughout the play *Oedipus the King* (Sophocles, 1885 translation) tends to support this interpretation. In the course of his life history, which was presumably well

on in further permutations to offspring. Thus through the generations there is a continuous recombination of genetic material. In this process the number of genes is so vast that no two individuals of a sexually reproducing population are exactly alike at birth. It is one of life's "miracles" that every organism has a unique combination of genes which is not apt to recur even in a population of quadrillions. The uniqueness of the individual is thus a direct result of sexual reproduction and, since this system is encountered at the highest levels of evolution only, one may infer that nature's way is to create biological diversity through sexual reproduction. Lower species may propagate more rapidly and on a larger scale but at the expense of evolutionary adaptability—a fact which to some biologists implies the ultimate extinction of such species.

Dobzhansky (1962) and Mayr (1963, pp. 648 f.) have stressed the uniqueness of each individual's genetic constitution. Haldane (1949, pp. 409-10) has underscored genetic diversity as congenial to a democratic social order. Genetic differences are, however, no longer conceived to be absolutes since they are molded by environmental interaction, except for extreme cases of defects which yield only so much to experience. More obvious even than genetic diversity is the uniqueness of each individual's response to his particular environment. Out of the interplay of the unique genetic constitution and the unique experiential milieu creatively emerges the idioverse, the population of past and potential events which is the personality. In idiodynamic and biopsychological terms the human personality is man's prime creation (Rosenzweig 1958).

For man's maximum autonomy obviously lies in his creative capacity. In what ways the gender modules enter into the creation of a personality and its various productions constitutes one of the most intriguing of the unsolved problems of science. It is not unlikely that each of the modules carries its own creative potential. But how, or how much, sexual fulfillment and/or frustration contribute to creativity, whatever the dominant module, still remains to be discovered.

---

known to the Greek audience, Tiresias had undergone a remarkable succession of sexual metamorphoses that led to his uncanny wisdom (Ovid, 1963 translation, p. 67). Sophocles may have regarded this history as having peculiarly prepared the eventual seer for his part in the drama of Oedipus.

SUMMARY AND CONCLUSION

Mammalian evolution, up to and including *homo sapiens* in the twentieth century, reveals a continuous enhancement of sexual autonomy.

The sexual drive of subprimate mammals is rigidly limited to the time of estrus or heat which is, in turn, controlled by external, largely climatic, factors. Coital activity occurs only during ovulation, i.e., at maximal fertility. A degree of autonomy first appears (phylogenetically) when estrus in subprimates is succeeded by menstruation in primates. Mating behavior is now no longer an almost automatic, compulsive response by the male to the female in heat; copulation may occur at any time during the female sexual cycle. A degree of emancipation from the hormones in both male and female next appears as the brain becomes increasingly involved in the patterning and release of sexual response. Encephalization, through learning and other experience, largely supplants both heteronomous control (by light, temperature, humidity) and hormonal control.

An even larger increment of autonomy is introduced by the gradual separation of the sexual drive from the reproductive function—a separation which becomes practically complete at the hominid level. Sexual behavior now is optionally independent of conception, and this gain in autonomy is compounded in both the reproductive and nonreproductive forms of sexuality. A wide range of options emerges, conceptively and extraceptively. Reproduction can be prevented and, within limits, guided; and a variety of genital and extragenital practices appear.

An imminent advance in conceptive autonomy lies in the methods now available that make it possible to choose the sex of offspring. The fetal assay of sex chromosomes, by sex chromatin analysis, with optional interception (abortion) can now be put to such application by informed parents. Eventually proceptive choice of neonate sex will probably be much simplified to comprise selective coitus (by procedures intended to favor X- or Y-spermatozoa), followed at early pregnancy by an XY blood or other chemical test, and by recourse to an interceptive (abortifacient) suppository or pill as needed. A new epoch of sexual autonomy is thus at hand. While the choice of the sex of offspring will at first perhaps affect only a single instance in a family, total family design may be expected to supervene and to include the number of children, the sex of each, their birth order, and spacing. Complex psychodynamic and social implications may be anticipated from such a regimen. It is not too early to consider what they may be and to provide for dealing with them.

In the last two centuries of Western history a progression of opinion monitoring a systematic advance in human sexual emancipation is observable as follows: (1) the limitation of sexual (genital) behavior to the conceptive function; (2) the acceptance of genital intercourse with an extraceptive (contraceptive) end; (3) the recognition of extragenital behavior as a natural part of conceptive sexuality; (4) increasing tolerance of extraceptive behavior extragenitally expressed.

The final aspect of autonomy is ontogenetic. Sexual reproduction in its very essence appears to be nature's way of increasing biological diversity. The continuous recombination of chromosomes from two parents practically assures the genetic uniqueness of every individual at birth. This uniqueness is further compounded by ontogenetic experience, not only by the vast diversity of environmental contributions but by the recombination within the individual of the gender modules which appear to derive from biosexuality. It is in this last recombination that the ultimate in human sexual autonomy is implicit. The potential lies in the plasticity of the gender modules (ambisexual, disexual, and amphisexual) from which the masculine and feminine roles emerge in various patterns. When these patterns are attuned to the genetic and experiential uniqueness of the individual, they contribute to the complete idiodynamic development of the person. Psychosexual autonomy as an evolutionary attainment thus approaches its culmination.

REFERENCES

Abdul-Karim, R., & Iliya, F. Antepartal diagnosis of sex. *Journal Medical Libanais* 1961, 14: 410–15.

Acton, W. *The functions and disorders of the reproductive organs.* London: Churchill, 1857.

Allen, W. M. Progesterone: how did the name originate? *Southern Medical Journal* 1970, 63: 1151–55.

Amoroso, E. C., & Marshall, F. H. A. External factors in sexual periodicity. In A. S. Parkes (ed.), *Marshall's physiology of reproduction* (3rd ed.) vol. I, part 2. London: Longmans, 1960, pp. 707–831.

Aronson, L. R. Hormones and reproductive behavior: some phylogenetic considerations. In A. Gorbman (ed.), *Comparative endocrinology.* New York: Wiley, 1959, pp. 98–120.

Asdell, S. A. *Patterns of mammalian reproduction.* Ithaca, N.Y.: Comstock, 1946.

Barnes, A. C. Fetal indications for therapeutic abortion. In A. C. DeGraff and W. P. Creger (eds.), *Annual Review of Medicine* 1971, 22: 133–44.

Beach, F. A. Evolutionary changes in the physiological control of mating behavior in mammals. *Psychological Review* 1947, 54: 297–315.

––––––. *Hormones and behavior.* New York: Hoeber, 1948.

––––––. Neural and chemical regulation of behavior. In H. F. Harlow and C. N. Woolsey (eds.), *Biological and biochemical bases of behavior.* Madison, Wis.: University of Wisconsin Press, 1958, pp. 263–84.

––––––. Biological bases for reproductive behavior. In W. Etkin (ed.), *Social behavior and organization among vertebrates.* Chicago: University of Chicago Press, 1964, pp. 117–42.

––––––. (ed.) *Sex and behavior.* New York: Wiley, 1965.

Bhattacharya, B. C. Pre-arranging the sex of offspring. *New Scientist* 1964 (Oct. 15, No. 413): 151–52.

Bingham, H. C. Sex development in apes. *Comparative Psychology Monographs* 1928, 5: 1–161.

Blakely, S. B. The diagnosis of the sex of the human fetus in utero. *American Journal of Obstetrics and Gynecology* 1937, 34: 322–35.

Bourne, G. H. *The ape people.* New York: Putnam, 1971.

Brecher, E. M. *The sex researchers.* Boston: Little, Brown, 1969.

Briffault, R. *The mothers: a study of the origins of sentiments and institutions.* New York: Macmillan, 1927, 3 vols.

Callahan, D. *Abortion: law, choice and morality.* London: Macmillan, 1970.

Campbell, B. G. *Human evolution.* Chicago: Aldine, 1967.

Cederqvist, L. L., & Fuchs, F. Antenatal sex determination: a historical review. *Clinical Obstetrics & Gynecology* 1970, 13: 159–77.

Chambard, E. *Du somnambulisme en général: nature, analogies, signification nosologique et étiologie, avec huit observations du somnambulisme hystérique.* Paris: Doin, 1881.

Christenson, C. V. *Kinsey: a biography.* Bloomington, Ind.: Indiana University Press, 1971.

Corner, G. W. *The hormones in human reproduction.* Princeton, N.J.: Princeton University Press, 1947.

———. *Attaining manhood* (2nd ed.). New York: Harper, 1952.

Cowie, V. Amniocentesis: a means of pre-natal diagnosis of conditions associated with severe mental subnormality. *British Journal of Psychiatry* 1971, **118**: 83–86.

Darlington, C. D. *Darwin's place in history.* Oxford: Blackwell, 1960.

DeVore, I. (ed.) *Primate behavior.* New York: Holt, Rinehart & Winston, 1965.

Diamond, M. (ed.) *Perspectives in reproduction and sexual behavior.* Bloomington, Ind.: Indiana University Press, 1968.

Dickinson, R. L. *Control of conception.* Baltimore: Williams & Wilkins, 1931.

———. *Human sex anatomy* (2nd ed.). Baltimore: Williams & Wilkins, 1949.

Dobzhansky, T. *Mankind evolving.* New Haven: Yale University Press, 1962.

Drill, V. A. *Oral contraceptives.* New York: McGraw–Hill, 1966.

Edinger, D. *Bertha Pappenheim: Freud's Anna O.* Highland Park: Ill.: Congregation Solel, 1968.

Ellis, H. The doctrine of erogenic zones. In *Studies in the psychology of sex,* vol. III. New York: Random House, 1936, pp. 111–20. (Originally published 1920.)

———. *Studies in the psychology of sex,* vols. I–IV. New York: Random House, 1936.

———. *Psychology of sex* (rev. ed.). New York: Emerson, 1938.

Ellis, H., & Symonds, J. A. *Das Konträre Geschlechtsgefühl,* Leipzig: Wigand, 1896.

Embrey, M. P. Induction of abortion by prostaglandins E_1 and E_2. *British Medical Journal* 1970, **2**: 258–60.

Erlich, P. R., & Erlich, A. H. *Population, resources, and environment.* San Francisco: W. H. Freeman, 1970.

Etzioni, A. Sex control, science, and society. *Science* 1968, **161**: 1107–12.

Fawcett, J. T. *Psychology and population: behavioral research issues in fertility and family planning.* New York: Population Council, 1970.

Ford, C. S., & Beach, F. A. *Patterns of sexual behavior.* New York: Harper, 1951.

Freedman, D. S., Freedman, R., & Whelpton, P. K. Size of family and preference for children of each sex. *American Journal of Sociology* 1960, **66**: 141–46.

Freud, S. Sexuality in the aetiology of the neuroses (Eng. trans.). *Standard edition of the complete psychological works*, vol. III. London: Hogarth, 1962, pp. 261–85. (Originally published in German 1898.)

_____. Three contributions to the theory of sexuality (Eng. trans.). *Standard edition of the complete psychological works*, vol. VII. London: Hogarth, 1954, pp. 123–245. (Original German edition 1905.)

_____. Civilized sexual morality and modern nervous sickness (Eng. trans.). *Standard edition of the complete psychological works*, vol. IX. London: Hogarth, 1959, pp. 177–204. (Originally published in German 1908.)

_____. Contributions to a discussion on masturbation (Eng. trans.). *Standard edition of the complete psychological works*, vol. XII. London: Hogarth, 1958, pp. 239–54. (Original German edition 1912.)

_____. Civilization and its discontents (Eng. trans.). *Standard edition of the complete psychological works*, vol. XXI. London: Hogarth, 1961, pp. 57–145. (Original German edition 1930.)

_____. Femininity. Lecture XXXIII of New Introductory Lectures on Psycho-Analysis (Eng. trans.). *Standard edition of the complete psychological works*, vol. XXII. London: Hogarth, 1964, pp. 112–35. (Original German edition 1933.)

Fuchs, F., & Cederqvist, L. L. Recent advances in antenatal diagnosis by amniotic fluid analysis. *Clinical Obstetrics & Gynecology* 1970, **13**: 178–201.

Galt, W. E. Sex behavior in primates. *Annals of the New York Academy of Sciences* 1947, **47**: 617–30.

Galton, F. *Memories of my life*. London: Methuen, 1908.

Gardner, R. L., & Edwards, R. G. Control of the sex ratio at full term in the rabbit by transferring sexed blastocysts. *Nature* 1968, **218**: 346–48.

Gebhard, P. H., Pomeroy, W. B., Martin, C. E., & Christenson, C. V. *Pregnancy, birth and abortion*. New York: Hoeber, 1958.

Goldzieher, J. W. Future approaches to conception control. *Pacific Medicine and Surgery* 1965, **73**: 69–73 and 78.

Grisez, G. G. *Abortion: the myths, the realities, and the arguments*. New York: Corpus Books, 1970.

Group for the Advancement of Psychiatry, Committee on Psychiatry and Law. *The right to abortion; a psychiatric view*. New York: Scribner, 1970.

Gurdon, J. B., & Uehlinger, V. "Fertile" intestine nuclei. *Nature* 1966, **210**: 1240–41.

Haldane, J. B. S. Human evolution: past and future. In G. L. Jepsen, E. Mayr, and G. G. Simpson (eds.), *Genetics, paleontology and evolution*. Princeton, N.J.: Princeton University Press, 1949, pp. 405-18.

Hall, R. E. (ed.) *Abortion in a changing world*. New York: Columbia University Press, 1970, 2 vols.

Hamilton, G. V. A study of sexual tendencies in monkeys and baboons. *Journal of Animal Behavior* 1914, 4: 295-318.

Hampson, J. L., & Hampson, J. G. The ontogenesis of sexual behavior in man. In W. C. Young (ed.), *Sex and internal secretions* (3rd ed.), vol. II. Baltimore: Williams & Wilkins, 1961, pp. 1401-32.

Hardin, G. *Birth control*. New York: Pegasus, 1970.

Harlow, H. F., & Harlow, M. K. The affectional systems. In A. M. Schrier, H. F. Harlow, and F. Stollnitz (eds.), *Behavior of nonhuman primates*, vol. II. New York: Academic Press, 1965, pp. 287-334.

Himes, N. E. *Medical history of contraception*. New York: Gamut, 1963.

Hirschfeld, M. *Sexual pathology* (Eng. trans.). Newark, N.J.: Julian Press, 1932. (Original German edition, 3 vols., 1917-20.)

Hunter, G. L., Bishop, G. P., Adams, C. E., & Rowson, L. E. Successful long-distance aerial transportation of fertilized sheep ova. *Journal of Reproduction and Fertility* 1962, 3: 33-40.

Huxley, J. Sex biology and sex psychology. In *Essays of a biologist*. New York: Knopf, 1923, pp. 131-73.

Hyde, H. M. *The love that dared not speak its name*. Boston: Little, Brown, 1970.

Johnson, J. *Disorders of sexual potency in the male*. Oxford: Pergamon, 1968.

Kaan, H. *Psychopathia sexualis*. Leipzig: Vos, 1844 (in Latin).

Karim, S. M. M., & Filshic, G. M. Use of prostaglandin E_2 for therapeutic abortion. *British Medical Journal* 1970, 3: 198-200.

Kaufman, J. J., & Borgeson, G. *Man and sex: a practical manual of sexual knowledge*. New York: Simon & Schuster, 1961.

Kempf, E. J. The social and sexual behavior of infra-human primates with some comparable facts in human behavior. *Psychoanalytic Review* 1917, 4: 127-54.

_____. The origin and evolution of bisexual differentiation. *Journal of Genetic Psychology* 1947, 71: 85-136.

Keys, T. E. *The history of surgical anesthesia*. New York: Dover, 1963.

Kiewit, F. Embryo transplant in cattle may revolutionize breeding. *Kansas City Star*, 1971 (reported in *Biomedical News*, Washington, D.C., September 1971).

Kinsey, A. C. Criteria for a hormonal explanation of the homosexual. *Journal of Clinical Endocrinology* 1941, 1: 424–28.

Kinsey, A. C., Pomeroy, W. B., & Martin, C. E. *Sexual behavior in the human male*. Philadelphia: Saunders, 1948.

Kinsey, A. C., Pomeroy, W. B., Martin, C. E., & Gebhard, P. H. Concepts of normality and abnormality in sexual behavior. In P. H. Hoch and J. Zubin (eds.), *Psychosexual development in health and disease*. New York: Grune & Stratton, 1949, pp. 11–32.

———. *Sexual behavior in the human female*. Philadelphia: Saunders, 1953.

Kinsey, A. C., Pomeroy, W. B., Gebhard, P. H., Martin, C. E., Field, A. W., & Short, J. D. *Report of the Institute for Sex Research, Indiana University, Bloomington, Indiana, June 30, 1955*. Bloomington, Ind.: Institute for Sex Research, 1955.

Kiser, C. V. (ed.) *Research in family planning*. Princeton, N.J.: Princeton University Press, 1962.

Krafft-Ebing, R. von. *Psychopathia sexualis, mit besonderer Berücksichtigung der conträre Sexualempfindung*. Stuttgart: Enke, 1886 (in German with Latin passages).

———. *Psychopathia sexualis, with special reference to contrary sexual instincts*. Eng. trans. of the 7th German edition (German 1892). Philadelphia: Davis, 1893.

———. *Psychopathia sexualis; a medico-forensic study*. Introduction by Ernest van den Haag. Translation from the Latin by H. E. Wedeck. First unexpurgated edition in English. New York: Putnam, 1965.

———. *Psychopathia sexualis, with especial reference to the antipathic sexual instinct; a medico-forensic study*. Translated from the 12th German edition. Introduction by F. S. Klaf. Foreword by D. Blain. New York: Stein & Day, 1965.

Lancaster, J. B., & Lee, R. B. The annual reproductive cycle in monkeys and apes. In I. DeVore (ed.), *Primate behavior*. New York: Holt, Rinehart & Winston, 1965, pp. 486–513.

Leach, G. *The biocrats*. New York: McGraw–Hill, 1970.

Lederberg, J. Experimental genetics and human evolution. *Bulletin of the Atomic Scientists* 1966, 22: Oct., 4–11.

Lehrman, D. S. Hormonal regulation of parental behavior in birds and infra-human mammals. In W. C. Young (ed.), *Sex and internal secretions* (3rd ed.), vol. II. Baltimore: Williams & Wilkins, 1961, pp. 1268–1382.

———. Interaction of hormonal and experiential influences on development of behavior. In E. L. Bliss (ed.), *Roots of behavior*. New York: Hoeber, 1962, pp. 142–56.

Lockhart, W. B. (ed.) *The report of the commission on obscenity and pornography*. Washington, D.C.: U.S. Government Printing Office, 1970.

MacLean, P. D. New findings relevant to the evolution of psychosexual functions of the brain. *Journal of Nervous and Mental Disease* 1962, 135: 289-301.

_____. Man and his animal brains. *Modern Medicine* 1964, 102: 95-106.

Malthus, T. R. *An essay on the principle of population, or a view of its past and present effects on human happiness*. New York: Ward, Lock, 1890 (originally published 1798, 2nd ed. 1803).

Markle, G. E., & Nam, C. B. Sex predetermination: its impact on fertility. *Social Biology* 1971, 18: 73-83.

Marler, P., & Hamilton, W. J. *Mechanisms of animal behavior*. New York: Wiley, 1966.

Marshall, D. S., & Suggs, R. C. (eds.) *Human sexual behavior: variations in the ethnographic spectrum*. New York: Basic Books, 1971.

Masters, W. H., & Johnson, V. E. *Human sexual response*. Boston: Little, Brown, 1966.

_____. *Human sexual inadequacy*. Boston: Little, Brown, 1970.

Mayr, E. *Animal species and evolution*. Cambridge: Harvard University Press, 1963.

McCleary, G. F. *The Malthusian population theory*. London: Faber & Faber, 1953.

McKusick, V. A. *Human genetics* (2nd ed.). Englewood Cliffs, N.J.: Prentice-Hall, 1969.

Mead, M. *Male and female*. New York: Morrow, 1949.

Medawar, P. B. *The future of man*. New York: Basic Books, 1959.

Meyer, R. The male pill? In D. Charles (ed.), *Progress in conception control*. Philadelphia: Lippincott, 1967, pp. 92-95.

Mill, J. S., & Mill, H. T. *Essays on sex equality*. (Edited with an Introductory Essay by A. S. Rossi.) Chicago: University of Chicago Press, 1970 (originally published as separate papers 1851, 1869, and 1951).

Miller, G. S. The primate basis of human sexual behavior. *Quarterly Review of Biology* 1931, 6: 379-410.

Millet, K. *Sexual politics*. Garden City, N.Y.: Doubleday, 1970.

Money, J. (ed.) *Sex Research: new developments*. New York: Holt, Rinehart & Winston, 1965.

_____. *Sex errors of the body: dilemmas, education, counseling*. Baltimore: The Johns Hopkins Press, 1968.

_____. Sex reassignment as related to hermaphroditism and transsexualism. In R. Green and J. Money (eds.), *Transsexualism and sex reassignment*. Baltimore: The Johns Hopkins Press, 1969, pp. 91–113.

_____. Sexually dimorphic behavior, normal and abnormal. In N. Kretchmer and D.N. Walcher (eds), *Environmental influences on genetic expression: biological and behavioral aspects of sexual differentiation*. Fogarty International Center Proceedings No. 2. Washington, D.C.: U.S. Government Printing Office, 1971, pp. 201–12.

_____. Determinants of human sexual identity and behavior. In C. J. Sager, & H. S. Kaplan (eds.), *Progress in group and family therapy*. New York: Brunner/Mazel, 1972, pp. 564–86.

Money, J., Hampson, J. G., & Hampson, J. L. An examination of some basic sexual concepts: the evidence of human hermaphroditism. *Bulletin of the Johns Hopkins Hospital* 1955, 97: 301–19.

Moore, K. L. (ed.) *The sex chromatin*. Philadelphia: Saunders, 1966.

Morgan, R. (ed.) *Sisterhood is powerful*. New York: Random House, 1970.

Morris, D. (ed.) *Primate ethology*. Chicago: Aldine, 1967.

Morris, R., & Morris, D. *Men and apes*. London: Hutchinson, 1966.

Muller, H. J. The guidance of human evolution. In S. Tax (ed.), *Evolution after Darwin. The evolution of man*, vol. II. Chicago: University of Chicago Press, 1960, pp. 423–62.

Nadler, H. L. Antenatal detection of hereditary disorders. *Pediatrics* 1968, 42: 912–18. (a)

_____. Cultivated human fetal cells derived from amniotic fluid. *Journal of Pediatrics* 1968, 72: 576–77. (b)

_____. Prenatal detection of genetic defects. *Journal of Pediatrics* 1969, 74: 132–43.

Naqvi, R. H., & Warren, J. C. Interceptives: drugs interrupting pregnancy after implantation. *Steroids* 1971, 18: 731–39.

Neumann, F., & Elger, W. Permanent changes in gonadal function and sexual behaviour as a result of early feminization of male rats by treatment with an antiandrogenic steroid. *Endokrinologie* 1966, 50: 209–25.

Noonan, J. T. (ed.) *The morality of abortion*. Cambridge: Harvard University Press, 1970.

Noyes, J. H. *The Bible argument: defining the role of the sexes in the kingdom of heaven*. Reprinted from the First Annual Report of the Oneida Association, 1849. Oneida, New York: Oneida Reserve, 1849.

Ovid (Publius Ovidius Naso). *Metamorphoses*. Translated by R. Humphries. Bloomington: Indiana University Press, 1963.

Papp, Z., Gardó, S., Herpay, G., & Árvay, A. Prenatal sex determination by amniocentesis. *Obstetrics and Gynecology* 1970, 36: 429–32.

Pappenheim, B. (P. Berthold, pseudonym). *Frauenrecht: Schauspiel in drei Aufzügen.* Dresden und Leipzig, 1899.

Parkes, A. S. *Sex, science and society.* London: Oriel, 1966.

Pearsall, R. *The worm in the bud: the world of Victorian sexuality.* New York: Macmillan, 1969.

Pearson, K. *The life, letters and labours of Francis Galton.* Cambridge: Cambridge University Press, 1914–30, 4 vols.

Pincus, G. Fertilization in mammals. *Scientific American* 1951, **184**: 44–47.

———. *The control of fertility.* New York: Academic Press, 1965.

Place, F. *Illustrations and proofs of the principle of population.* (New edition by N. E. Himes.) New York: Augustus M. Kelley, 1967 (originally published 1822).

Ploss, H. H., Bartels, M., & Bartels, P. *Woman; an historical, gynaecological and anthropological compendium.* (Edited by E. J. Dingwall.) London: Heinemann, 1935, 3 vols. (original edition in German, by Ploss alone, in 2 volumes, 1884).

Pohlman, E. Some effects of being able to control sex of offspring. *Eugenics Quarterly* 1967, **14**: 274–81.

Pohlman, E., & Pohlman, J. M. *The psychology of birth planning.* Cambridge, Mass.: Schenkman, 1969.

Pomeroy, W. B. *Boys and sex.* New York: Delacorte, 1968.

———. *Girls and sex.* New York: Delacorte, 1969.

Rainwater, L. *And the poor get children: sex, contraception, and family planning in the working class.* Chicago: Quadrangle Books, 1960.

———. *Family design: marital sexuality, family size, and contraception.* Chicago: Aldine, 1965.

———. Marital sexuality in four "cultures of poverty." In D. S. Marshall and R. C. Suggs (eds.), *Human sexual behavior.* New York: Basic Books, 1971, pp. 187–205.

Rheingold, H. L. (ed.) *Maternal behavior in mammals.* New York: Wiley, 1963.

Rosenberg, B. G., & Sutton-Smith, B. *Sex and identity.* New York: Holt, Rinehart & Winston, 1972.

Rosenzweig, L., & Rosenzweig, S. Notes on Alfred C. Kinsey's pre-sexual scientific work and the transition. *Journal of the History of the Behavioral Sciences* 1969, **5**: 173–81.

Rosenzweig, S. The photoscope as an objective device for evaluating sexual interest. *Psychosomatic Medicine* 1942, **4**: 150–58.

———. Psychology of the menstrual cycle. *Journal of Clinical Endocrinology* 1943, **3**: 296–300.

_____. The place of the individual and of idiodynamics in psychology: a dialogue. *Journal of Individual Psychology* 1958, 14: 3-20.

Rosenzweig, S., & Freedman, H. A "blind test" of sex-hormone potency in schizophrenic patients. *Psychosomatic Medicine* 1942, 4: 159-65.

Schilling, E. Experiments in sedimentation and centrifugation of bull spermatozoa and the sex ratio of born calves. *Journal of Reproduction and Fertility* 1966, 11: 469-72.

Schmalhausen, S. D. The sexual revolution. In V. F. Calverton and S. D. Schmalhausen (eds.), *Sex and civilization.* New York: Macaulay, 1929, pp. 349-436.

Schmalhausen, S. D., & Calverton, V. F. (eds.) *Woman's coming of age: a symposium.* New York: Liveright, 1931.

Schrenck-Notzing, A. von. *The use of hypnosis in psychopathia sexualis.* New York: Julian Press, 1956. (Copyright 1895. Original German Edition 1892.)

Schröder, J., & de la Chapelle, A. Fetal lymphocytes in the maternal blood. *Blood* 1972, 39: 153-62.

Schultz, A. H. *The life of primates.* New York: Universe Books, 1969.

Serr, D. M., Sachs, L., & Danon, M. The diagnosis of sex before birth using cells from the amniotic fluid (a preliminary report). *Bulletin Research Council of Israel* 1955, 5B: 137-38.

Sevinç, A. Experiments on sex control by electrophoretic separation of spermatozoa in the rabbit. *Journal of Reproduction and Fertility* 1968, 16: 7-14.

Sheps, M. C., & Ridley, J. C. (eds.) *Public health and population change.* Pittsburgh, Pa.: University of Pittsburgh Press, 1965.

Shettles, L. B. Conception and birth sex ratios. *Obstetrics and Gynecology* 1961, 18: 122-30.

_____. Factors influencing sex ratios. *International Journal of Gynaecology and Obstetrics* 1970, 8: 643-47.

SIECUS (Sex Information and Education Council of the United States) *Sexuality and man.* New York: Scribner, 1970.

Sloane, R. B. (ed.) *Abortion: changing views and practice.* New York: Grune & Stratton, 1971.

Smith, J. R., & Smith, L. G. (eds.) *Co-marital sex: recent studies of sexual alternatives in marriage,* in press.

Sophocles. *Oedipus the king.* Translated into English verse by E. D. A. Morshead. London: Macmillan, 1885.

Spitz, R. A. Authority and masturbation; some remarks on a bibliographical investigation. *Psychoanalytic Quarterly* 1952, 21: 490-527.

Sutton-Smith, B., & Rosenberg, B. G. *The sibling*. New York: Holt, Rinehart & Winston, 1970.

Swyer, G. I. M. Fertility control: achievements and prospects. *Journal of Reproduction and Fertility* 1967, 14: 295–307.

Szilard, L. *The voice of the dolphins and other stories*. New York: Simon & Schuster, 1961.

Taussig, F. J. *Abortion: spontaneous and induced*. St. Louis: Mosby, 1936.

Taylor, G. R. *Sex in history*. New York: Vanguard, 1954.

———. *The biological time-bomb*. London: Thames & Hudson, 1968.

Time. Frozen assets. January 3, 1972, p. 52.

Vojta, M. A critical view of vacuum aspiration: a new method for the termination of pregnancy. *Obstetrics and Gynecology* 1967, 30: 28–34.

Walker, K. M. *Sexual behaviour: creative and destructive*. London: Kimber, 1966.

Walknowska, J., Conte, F. A., & Grumbach, M. M. Practical and theoretical implications of fetal/maternal lymphocyte transfer. *Lancet* 1969 (1): 1119–22.

Weiler, H. Sex ratio and birth control. *American Journal of Sociology* 1959, 65: 298–99.

Williams, G. *The sanctity of life and the criminal law*. New York: Knopf, 1957.

Winick, C. *The new people: desexualization in American life*. New York: Pegasus, 1968.

Winston, S. Birth control and the sex-ratio at birth. *American Journal of Sociology* 1932, 38: 225–31.

Wolfenden Report. *Report of the committee on homosexual offenses and prostitution* (auth. Amer. ed.). New York: Stein & Day, 1963 (originally published in England 1957).

Wolstenholme, G. (ed.) *Man and his future*. Boston: Little, Brown, 1963.

Wortis, J. *Fragments of an analysis with Freud*. New York: Charter Books, 1963.

Young, W. C. Patterning of sexual behavior. In E. L. Bliss (ed.), *Roots of behavior*. New York: Harper, 1962, pp. 115–22.

———. (ed.) *Sex and internal secretions* (3rd ed.). Baltimore: Williams & Wilkins, 1961, 2 vols. (1st ed. by E. Allen, 1932; 2nd ed. by E. Allen, C. H. Danforth, and E. A. Doisy, 1939).

Zuckerman, S. The menstrual cycle of primates. *Proceedings of Zoological Society of London* 1930: 691–754.

———. *The social life of monkeys and apes*. New York: Harcourt, Brace, 1932.

NOTE TO DISCUSSION ON PAGE 200

The entire problem of induced abortion—from the standpoint of the law and of the psychological impact upon medical personnel and patients—is presently obscured by failure to recognize the distinction between early abortion, during the first 14–15 weeks of pregnancy, and late abortion. Not only are methods for the former simpler and safer to use, but the experience for the mother and for operating personnel is totally different from what it becomes later. In late abortions, the labor of parturition is actually induced by the use of hypertonic solutions. The fetus is apt to be "quick" and the idea of "mini-murder" is thus readily available for those who, quite rightly, are concerned about the sanctity of life. Early abortion differs in that the embryo is not yet quick; it is hardly more than a seedling which is to be mechanically uprooted, and not by the action of the mother, but by an outside operator. The procedure is the next thing to contraception, i.e., it resembles the insertion of an IUD or the fitting of a cervical diaphragm. If this crucial distinction were made clear to the public and were used as the basis for the legalization of abortion, this expedient might well spell the difference between success and failure. A limit would then need to be set at fifteen weeks for abortion on demand, with late abortions restricted to strictly therapeutic necessity; but such a provision would be justifiable. In the immediate context this distinction is crucial, since, as pointed out above, prenatal sex determination can now be reliably made by the fifteenth week; parental choice of neonate sex is hence feasible and compatible with early abortion.

chapter 11

Fact and Myth:
The Work of
The Commission on
Obscenity and
Pornography*

Morris A. Lipton†

"Congress, in Public Law 90–100, found the traffic in obscenity and pornography to be 'a matter of national concern.' The Federal Government was deemed to have a 'responsibility to investigate the gravity of this situation and to determine whether such materials are harmful to the public, and particularly to minors, and whether more effective methods should be devised to control the transmission of such materials.' To this end, the Congress established an advisory commission whose purpose was 'after a thorough study which shall include a study of the causal relationship of such materials to antisocial behavior, to recommend advisable,

*All quotations, illustrations and tables in the text are reprinted from *The Report of the Commission on Obscenity and Pornography*. Washington, D.C.: U.S. Government Printing Office, September, 1970.

†Morris A. Lipton, Ph.D., M.D., professor and chairman, Department of Psychiatry, University of North Carolina School of Medicine, Chapel Hill.

appropriate, effective, and constitutional means to deal effectively with such traffic in obscenity and pornography.'

"Congress assigned four specific tasks:

" ' (1) with the aid of leading constitutional law authorities, to analyze the laws pertaining to the control of obscenity and pornography; and to evaluate and recommend definitions of obscenity and pornography;

" ' (2) to ascertain the methods employed in the distribution of obscene and pornographic materials and to explore the nature and volume of traffic in such materials;

" ' (3) to study the effect of obscenity and pornography upon the public, and particularly minors, and its relationship to crime and other antisocial behavior; and

" ' (4) to recommend such legislative, administrative, or other advisable and appropriate action as the Commission deems necessary to regulate effectively the flow of such traffic, without in any way interfering with constitutional rights.'

"Public Law 90–100 became law in October, 1967, and the President appointed members to the Commission in January, 1968 (p. 1)."

The task given to the Commission, then, was to obtain facts, draw conclusions, and offer recommendations to the Congress. Implicit in this mandate was the assumption that the task was subject to scientific inquiry and that the data obtained would permit reasoned and reasonable conclusions. It may be said immediately that not all of the Commissioners and certainly not all of the public agree with this assumption. To some it is a matter of religious faith that explicit sexual materials are offensive and that their availability will lead to moral decay. No type or amount of evidence would be sufficient to alter these a priori conclusions. And since the Commission did not generally substantiate these subjective impressions, its findings and, retrospectively, its existence, have been deemed unacceptable.

To the Commissioners and the staff who felt that the subject was appropriate for scientific inquiry, the challenge was formidable and the achievements not entirely satisfactory. Usually, academicians have the leisure to acquire data at their own pace and to draw conclusions when these data are fully satisfactory. For the

Commission a deadline had to be met. Scientists do not as a matter of course have either the responsibility or the opportunity to translate their conclusions into recommendations which would influence national policy. The Commission had both, almost as a foregone conclusion. Finally, underlying the apparently lucid questions asked of the Commission by the Congress were the deeper and more complex issues of the sanctity of the First Amendment, the right of free enterprise, and the individual's freedom to read and view material of his choice. On the other hand was the issue of legal controls of the manufacture and sale of materials which might do harm or be offensive to the community.

Rather than summarizing the entire Commission's *Report*, I will devote myself to a brief sketch of the work of the Commission, its strategy, some of the facts which it generated, and some of the myths which it tried to dispel. Some of these myths existed before the Commission began its work, and some have been generated by the present administration and other critics since its completion. The work and conclusions of the Commission—a 369-page majority report, 255 pages of minority opinion and individual statements, and the almost 10,000 pages of supporting material derived from the 62 research contracts sponsored by the Commission is available in at least three editions: a $1.65 paperback, the official government publication selling for $5.50, and a hardback edition published by Random House. The technical documents are, or shortly will be, available from the Government Archives and it is likely that most of this material will appear in scientific journals.

First, in speaking about "facts" one must understand the term in a variety of ways. In some cases it may be equated with actual data, in other cases, with conclusions derived from these data. In the latter, it should be clear at the outset that very little of the data generated by the Commission's research have the certainty of the speed of light or even of the theory of evolution. Both the data and the conclusions have the types of limitations inherent within the social and behavioral sciences and are also limited by the time that was available for inquiry. They are approximations to truth with sufficient probability to warrant, in our view, the conclusions which we reached and the recommendations which we forwarded to the Congress. Here, then, are some dichotomies of fact and myth.

It is a myth that the membership of the Commission was appointed for political reasons and that it was academically oriented. The original Commissioners were appointed by President Johnson, and certainly almost everyone would agree that it was a nonpolitical, sound, and perhaps even distinguished, Commission. The individuals selected were experienced in the relevant sociological and technical areas—violence, the mass media, law enforcement, theology, growth and personality development, and the legal issues involved in censorship. Two were national leaders of antiobscenity organizations. The chairman, Dean William Lockhart of the University of Minnesota Law School, is a recognized authority on constitutional law and has written extensively on the First Amendment. By profession, six Commissioners were lawyers, two of whom were judges and one the attorney general of California. Three were sociologists, three were theologians, two were psychiatrists, one was a college teacher, one was a university librarian, and the remainder were in the publishing or broadcasting industries. It is a fact that only two of the original Commissioners had known political affiliations. One was the Democratic attorney general of California, and the other was the Republican ex-senator from New York, Kenneth Keating. After appointing Senator Keating as ambassador to India, President Nixon replaced him with Charles Keating, a practicing lawyer and head of the largest anti-obscenity organization in the United States—Citizens for Decent Literature. The political affiliations of the other Commissioners were not known even among themselves.

With the exception of Charles Keating, the Nixon administration appointee, who refused to work with the Commission and blanketly repudiated the entire report, thereby voting against all of its recommendations, it is untrue that the Commission as a whole agreed on nothing. The majority report and recommendations were based on at least a two-thirds majority of all the Commissioners. In addition, there was complete agreement on three items. The first was that hard-core pornography is personally distasteful. Second, it was felt that additional research was needed to confirm or deny, and certainly to refine, our conclusions. Third, it was agreed that members of the pornography industry were clever and motivated almost exclusively by financial gain. As an example, one edition of the Commission report, priced at $12.50, contains about 200 "obscene" photographs. There can be little doubt as to why they are included and why the book sells at so high a price. Yet the fact that they are printed in an official government report may well allow them to pass the Supreme Court test of obscenity, as defined in 1957 in the now-famous Roth case. In this decision, for the first time, the Supreme Court clearly stated that obscenity and pornography were not protected by the Constitution. However, in the same decision, it set up three criteria which must define such materials. First, that the dominant theme of the material as a whole appeals to a prurient interest in sex. Second, that the material is patently offensive because it affronts contemporary community standards relating to the representation of sexual matters, and third, that the material is utterly without redeeming social value. Strictly speaking, a scholarly document sponsored by the Congress and paid for by the citizenry should pass these tests even if it is made into a travesty by the illustrations.

A definition of obscenity based upon the above criteria is profoundly vague. Probably it represents the recognition by the justices that an absolute and static definition of obscenity is impossible. (The Commission also failed to achieve such a definition, and the Commission report uses the term "explicitly sexual material," in referring to its recommendations.) This definition of obscenity has created a labyrinth of legal and sociological confusion. To illustrate briefly, what is the community whose standards are offended? Is it a district, a county, a city, a state or the nation? If a small rural town in a large cosmopolitan state is offended by a bookseller or movie, is the material illegal for that town but legal in the adjoining city which is not offended? And who is to judge what the community's standards really are—the police chief, an elected board of censors, designated experts, a jury or a local judge? Does *Lady Chatterley's Lover* as a whole appeal solely to the prurient interest, and what of the bawdy cartoons or paintings of renowned artists. *What* is utterly without redeeming social value? Even the most perverse books, admittedly designed primarily for prurient interest, keep writers, photographers and printers employed.

The problem is further complicated by the cleverness of the businessmen in the pornography industry. Their motivations are clearly to make money. They recognize that this demands novelty, and so there has been a constant testing and pushing of the limits. Over the past forty years there has been an insidious evolution from the girl in lingerie, to the bare buttocks, to the nippleless breast, to the nippled breast, to the hairless crotch, to the hairy crotch, to the so-called "split beaver" or gaping crotch. The photography of heterosexual and homosexual intercourse has similarly evolved. Many court cases have been lost and later won as community standards have changed and as court decisions have liberalized. The process is still going on, and no one can predict whether it will continue, stop, or even reverse itself.

In 1969 the problem of the control of the distribution of obscenity and its lack of protection by the First and Fourteenth Amendments again came under the scrutiny of the Supreme Court in the case of Stanley vs. Georgia. In its decision the Court ruled that the private individual has a right, protected by the First and Fourteenth Amendments, to read or observe what he pleases—the right to satisfy his intellectual and emotional needs in the privacy of his home, even if the material is obscene and entirely without social value. In addition, the Court held that the government has no legitimate interest in protecting the individual's mind from the effects of obscenity and that governmental control of the moral content of a person's thoughts is wholly inconsistent with the philosophy of the First Amendment. Obviously, this makes the problem of control even more difficult.

To carry out its work, the Commission organized itself into four panels, entitled Traffic and Distribution, Effects, Legal Issues, and Positive Approaches. Each of these panels employed a full-time staff and had fiscal resources for the gathering of data and preparation of reports.

The Traffic and Distribution Panel found it a myth that the purveyors of pornography are highly organized into a gigantic, criminally controlled industry. The data reveal that it is a disorganized, chaotic industry made up largely of small businessmen who usually take high financial and legal risks for relatively small profits. A few of the most successful, obviously, do very well. The best estimate is that the entire industry of books, magazines, and specifically sexual movies grosses less than $500 million yearly. While hardly negligible, this figure is much smaller than had been anticipated, and is of course only a tiny fraction of the total book, magazine, and movie industry. A few typical estimates are that X-rated movies represent about 6.5 percent of the movie industry and exploitation and art films about 9 percent more. The mail-order business grosses $13 million annually, under-the-counter materials about $5-10 million, and "Adults Only" books and magazines about $80 million. The typical user is male, middle-aged, and middle class. This may be because of the great disparity between the low intrinsic value of the merchandise and its highly inflated price tag. The industry is growing, but it is not possible to predict how large, or how long, this growth will continue. After the relaxation of controls in Denmark, for example, the industry initially grew very quickly, but is now almost wholly dependent upon export and tourism. Whether a tapering-off can safely be predicted in the United States, with its greater sociological and geographical complexity, is difficult to say.

The work of the Effects Panel and the facts and myths it exposed should be of the greatest interest to behavioral scientists. Congress had given a mandate to make recommendations "after a thorough study which shall include a study of the causal relationship of such material to antisocial behavior." To fulfill this mandate, the Panel used several research strategies:

1. The existing literature was reviewed with respect to the occurrence of both data and opinions.

2. A national survey was conducted in order to discover attitudes and exposure of the U.S. population to pornography. This was a particularly important study because it attempted to determine the degree to which both adults and adolescents had actually been exposed, as well as their opinions about the effects of this exposure upon themselves and others.

3. Direct experiments were undertaken to assess the effects of exposure to pornography upon selected experimental subjects.

4. Retrospective studies on sexual deviants and criminals were performed to determine whether their exposure patterns were different from those of matched populations without histories of sexual deviancy.

5. A similar logic was employed to compare sex crimes and delinquency with estimates of the availability of erotic materials in Denmark and the United States.

The results of the literature survey showed much opinion and very little data. For example. " ' . . . eroticism frees the imaginations not only of children but of the child that is in the hearts of all men, leading them to go much further than they would go on their own. Inflamed fantasy leads to inflamed action (Kubie 1967: 69)' (p. 143)." " 'The publication and distribution of salacious materials is a peculiarly vicious evil; the destruction of moral character caused by it among young people cannot be overestimated. The circulation of periodicals containing such materials plays an important part in the development of crime among youth of our country (Hoover 1956: 211)' (p. 145)." Psychiatrists who have voiced their subjective views on the harmful effects of erotica include Max Levin, Natalie Shainess, Ernest van den Haag, and, most recently, Sheldon and Eleanor Glueck. On the other hand, one finds such statements as, " ' . . . people who read salacious literature are less likely to become sexual offenders than those who do not, for the reason that such reading often neutralizes what aberrant sexual interests they may have (Karpman 1954: 274)' (p. 147)." Other psychiatrists and experts in behavior have made similar statements.

The national survey, which cost about $250,000 and included interviews with 2,486 adults and 700 young persons aged 15 to 20 (representing completion rates of 70 and 90 percent respectively) randomly selected as a national probability sample, was the largest single piece of research undertaken. Methodologically, the survey was unique because trained interviewers spent at least one hour with each respondent.

In Figure 1 it is apparent that the public is not greatly concerned about the ubiquity of erotic materials. Only 2 percent of the population consider the problem to be among the three most significant social issues of the day. However, many of these people

Figure 1

Spontaneously Mentioned National Problems

(Question: "Would you please tell me what you think are the two or three most serious problems facing the country today?")

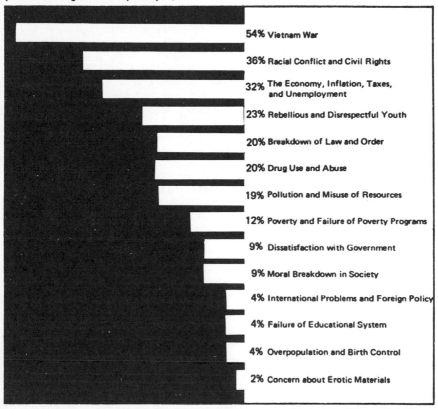

54% Vietnam War

36% Racial Conflict and Civil Rights

32% The Economy, Inflation, Taxes, and Unemployment

23% Rebellious and Disrespectful Youth

20% Breakdown of Law and Order

20% Drug Use and Abuse

19% Pollution and Misuse of Resources

12% Poverty and Failure of Poverty Programs

9% Dissatisfaction with Government

9% Moral Breakdown in Society

4% International Problems and Foreign Policy

4% Failure of Educational System

4% Overpopulation and Birth Control

2% Concern about Erotic Materials

Note — Adapted from Abelson, H., Cohen, R., Heaton, E., & Slider, C. Public attitudes toward and experience with erotic materials. *Technical reports of the Commission on Obscenity and Pornography*. Vol. 6.

are organized into publicity and action groups which are very vocal and have attracted some prominent and powerful individuals. Figure 1 also illustrates one of the problems inherent in research of this type. Retrospectively, more unequivocal results would have been obtained if the survey had asked people to rank order the ten most important social issues of the day. If so, it is possible, though very unlikely, that many of the people would have included pornography among these. However, the questionnaire was not structured that way because of inadequate time for complete consideration of the interpretations of possible outcomes.

Related to this issue is the myth that the public has a consensus of opinion regarding the effects of erotica. Table 1 shows that no more than two-thirds of the respondents agreed on anything, and opinions about the evil erotica does are matched by those about its good effects. For example, 50 percent of those surveyed

Table 1

Presumed Effects of Erotica: All Adults

[Question: "On this card are some opinions about the effects of looking at or reading sexual materials. As I read the letter of each one please tell me if you think sexual materials do or do not have these effects." (Q. 55; multiple responses]

	Has that effect: (N = 2486)		
Presumed Effects	Yes	No	Not Sure, No answer
Sexual materials excite people sexually	67%	17%	16%
Sexual materials provide information about sex	61%	27%	12%
Sexual materials lead to a breakdown of morals	56%	30%	14%
Sexual materials lead people to commit rape	49%	29%	22%
Sexual materials provide entertainment	48%	46%	6%
Sexual materials improve sex relations of some married couples	47%	32%	22%
Sexual materials make people bored with sexual materials	44%	35%	21%
Sexual materials lead people to lose respect for women	43%	41%	16%
Sexual materials make men want to do new things with their wives	41%	28%	32%
Sexual materials make people sex crazy	37%	45%	18%
Sexual materials provide an outlet for bottled up impulses	34%	46%	20%
Sexual materials give relief to people who have sex problems	27%	46%	26%

Note — Adapted from Abelson. H., Cohen, R., Heaton, E., & Slider, C. Public attitudes toward and experience with erotic materials. *Technical reports of the Commission on Obscenity and Pornography.* Vol. 6.

Table 2

Presumed Effects: Respondents' Own Experience and
Their Perceptions of the Experiences of Others

Presumed socially desirable effects:	% who say "yes, has effect"	(N=2486) Effect on respondent	On someone known personally	On no one known
Provide information about sex	61%	24%	15%	22%
Provide entertainment	48%	18%	16%	17%
Improve sex relations of some married couples	47%	10%	14%	23%
Provide an outlet for bottled up impulses	34%	3%	5%	21%
Give relief to people who have sex problems	27%	2%	7%	17%
Presumed effects not clearly socially approved nor disapproved:				
Excite people sexually	67%	15%	22%	32%
Make people bored with sexual materials	44%	20%	7%	18%
Make men want to do new things with their wives	41%	7%	13%	20%
Presumed socially undesirable effects:				
Lead to a breakdown of morals	56%	1%	13%	38%
Lead people to commit rape	49%	*	9%	37%
Lead people to loose respect for women	43%	5%	11%	26%
Make people sex crazy	37%	*	9%	27%

(Partial Table)

* Less than .5%

Note — Adapted from Abelson, H., Cohen, R., Heaton, E., & Slider, C. Public attitudes toward and experience with erotic materials. *Technical reports of the Commission on Obscenity and Pornography.* Vol. 6.

feel pornography leads to a breakdown of morals and an increase in rape, and a similar number feel that it offers entertainment and information.

It is a fact, as shown in Table 2, that people who think erotica is harmful feel that these deleterious effects apply more to others, while they themselves are personally benefited. However, these data are suspect in some details. For example, 49 percent of the people surveyed believe exposure to pornography leads to rape. Of these, 9 percent said they know someone personally on whom it had this effect. If this were true we would have a figure for the occurrence of rape many times higher than it in fact is. One suspects that they were referring to newspaper headlines and locally familiar names and faces. Breaking down the data into demographic characteristics, those who found little harm in pornography tended to have seen more of it and to be in general younger, better educated, and more "liberal." Finally, in contrast to a 1968 Gallup poll which showed 85 percent favoring controls, our data revealed that "although substantial proportions of the population endorse some form of restriction on the availability of erotic materials, nearly half (44%) qualify their response in terms of knowledge about the effects of such materials (p. 157)." Thus, 51 percent would sanction its availability if they were convinced that it was not harmful, while 79 percent would oppose availability if it were demonstrated to be harmful. At the polar position, 35 percent would oppose it even if it were shown not to be harmful, and 7 percent would favor it even if it were shown to be harmful. The majority of the people, however, clearly think that the regulations for the control of such materials should be determined by the results of studies on effect.

The national survey collected the opinions of the "average man." Opinions of "experts" were also obtained by survey. Table

Table 3

Juvenile Workers' Opinions About Erotic Books

[Question: "Do you think that reading obscene books plays a significant role in causing juvenile delinquency? "]

Respondents	N=1,188	% Yes	% No	Don't know; no response
Police Chiefs	389	57.6	31.4	11.0
Professionals[1]	799	12.4	77.1	10.5

[1]This group consisted of professional workers in child guidance, psychiatry, psychology, sociology, and social work.

Note — Adapted from Berninghausen, D. K., & Faunce, R. W. Some opinions on the relationship between obscene books and juvenile delinquency. 1965, unpublished.

Table 4

Psychologists' and Psychiatrists' Opinions
About the Effects of Pornography

[Question: "In your professional experience have you
encountered any cases where it appeared that pornography was a
causal factor in other antisocial behavior as defined above? "]

N = 3,423

Yes, convinced:	7.4%
Yes, suspected:	9.4%
No such cases:	80.0%
Not ascertained:	3.2%

[Question: "Persons exposed to pornography are more likely to
engage in antisocial sexual acts than persons not exposed? "]

Strongly agree:	1.1%
Agree:	12.9%
Disagree:	56.4%
Strongly disagree:	27.3%

Note — Adapted from Lipkin, M., & Carns, D. E. Poll of mental health professions.
Cited in the University of Chicago Division of the Biological Sciences and
the Pritzker School of Medicine *Reports*, Winter 1970, *20*, (1).

3 shows that law enforcement officers generally feel obscenity
plays a significant role in delinquency, while professionals dealing
with the treatment of behavior disorders feel otherwise. In a poll
of psychiatrists and psychologists (Table 4) made by the University of Chicago group, there is again only a small minority who
feel that exposure yields antisocial effects. Table 5 shows that sex
educators also feel that exposure to explicit sexual material does
little, if any, harm.

An example of the Effects Panel's second research strategy—
that of studying the effects of direct exposure on the immediate
and subsequent behavior of selected individuals—was the experiment conducted at the University of North Carolina with twenty-
three young men. Normal males, both married and unmarried,
were paid $100 to sit, comfortably and in private, in a room for
ninety minutes a day, five days a week for 3 weeks. The subjects
were seniors or graduate students of varied religious and political

Table 5

Opinions of Sex Educators
About Erotic Materials

[Question: "What, in your experience, are the likely consequences of adolescents' exposure to explicit sexual material? " (multiple response)]

Possible Effects	%	N
Sexual excitement	62	208
Provides status	53	176
Harmless outlet	42	140
Provides information	39	130
Little influence	21	69
Preoccupation	19	63
Undesirable sexual behavior	10	33
Lose respect for women	5	18
Moral breakdown	5	16
Boredom	4	13
Other		20

Note — Adapted from Wilson, W. C., & Jacobs, S, Survey of sex educators and counselors. *Technical Reports of the Commission on Obscenity and Pornography.* Vol. 10.

persuasions. In the room was a movie projector and a four-drawer file which contained an almost limitless quantity of pornography. In the top drawer were hardcore pornographic movies. The second drawer contained pornographic stills, the third pornographic novels, and the fourth a potpourri of *Life, Reader's Digest, National Geographic*, popular novels, etc. The subjects were free to do as they pleased, except that they were not allowed to read textbooks or to do homework, and they were required to list their activities on a prepared check-list at ten-minute intervals. They were required to urinate privately immediately before and after the experiment so that urinary prostatic acid phosphatase secretion might be measured as an index of stimulation. To avoid prostatic leakage, they were asked to put on a condom before each session and to drop the condom and its contents into the urinary bottle at the end of the ninety-minute period. Measures of interest, arousal, and/or satiation were made. Two indices were used. The first was how much time the students spent looking at each specific type of materials. The second was a biological indicator of arousal—the prostatic acid phosphatase measure.

Figure 2 shows the rapid diminution of time spent with the pornographic material. Movies were initially the most popular, and interest in them was lost most rapidly, to be replaced somewhat by books. Figure 3 shows the biological equivalent—again rapid loss of interest and evident satiation. Satiation was, however, never complete. Pornography does not become utterly bland, and the subjects were aroused by it and never fully sated—at least in the time period reported.

Figure 2

Satiation of Interest in Sexual Material
(Percent time spent looking at, or reading in each category and total)

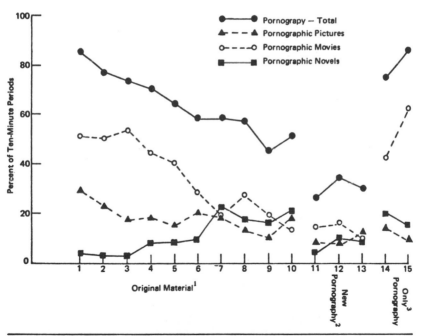

Note — Adapted from Howard, J. L., Reifler, C. B., & Liptzin, M. B. Effects of exposure to pornography. *Technical reports of the Commission on Obscenity and Pornography.* Vol. 8.

[1] "Original material" consisted of both erotic photographs, books, and films and nonerotic books.
[2] "New pornography" indicates that additional erotic material was made available.
[3] "Pornography only" indicates nonerotic material not available.

Figure 3

Satiation of Sexual Arousal
(Daily mean levels of urinary acid phosphatase activity)

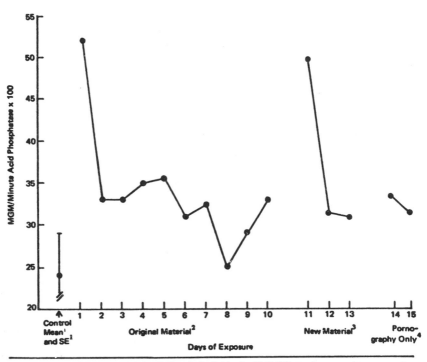

Note — Adapted from Howard, J. L., Reifler, C. B., & Liptzin, M. B. Effects of exposure to pornography. *Technical reports of the Commission on Obscenity and Pornography.* Vol. 8.

[1] Baseline values were obtained from specimens obtained during four successive days prior to the 90-minute sessions.
[2] "Original material" consisted of both erotic photographs, books, and films and nonerotic books.
[3] "New pornography" indicates that additional material was made available.
[4] "Pornography only" indicates nonerotic material was not available.

What of other effects? Two are worth noting. First, psychological tests before and after the experiment showed absolutely no change in MMPI profiles, mood, etc. Furthermore, the subjects reported no change in their sex behavior, except for slightly more variation in sexual technique and more conversation about sex.

At the conclusion of the experiment, this group of subjects could be considered experts who had seen more pornography in two weeks than most individuals would view in a lifetime. It is worth noting, therefore, that their attitudes about pornography either did not change or became more "liberal." Most of those who initially favored strict controls later felt the materials were probably harmless to adults. Those who initially opposed all censorship later tended to favor juvenile legislation. Many of the subjects felt it was extremely disproportionate for the Congress to spend $2,000,000 on an issue of so little social importance. In follow-up interviews on an incomplete sample a year later no detrimental effects were noted. It is probably not safe to generalize that the same results would have been obtained with younger or older people, with couples or groups, or with people who had different levels of education or intelligence. But the absence of any harm indicated by this study shows the feasibility of this type of research, and more types of subjects in different circumstances should be tested.

A few similar experiments have been done. In a study conducted at Stanford, married couples were exposed to pornography together. The effects, noted in Table 6 were an increase in conversation and fantasy about sex. A summary of studies conducted in the United States and abroad is shown in Table 7. There was a slight increase in coital frequency in the twenty-four hours after

Table 6

Frequency[1] of Conversation About Sex 24 Hours
Before and After Exposure to Erotic Film

	Males (N=187)	Females (N=176)	Total
Increased frequency	20%[2]	25%[2]	23%[2]
Decreased frequency	7%	6%	6%
Unchanged	73%	69%	71%

[1]Seven males and seven females did not report.
[2]Significant ($p < .001$) by sign test comparing number increasing with number decreasing.

Note — Adapted from Mosher, D. L. Psychological reactions to pornographic films. *Technical reports of the Commission on Obscenity and Pornography.* Vol.8.

Table 7

Coital Frequency 24 Hours Before
and After Exposure to Sex Stimuli

Population	N	No change	Decreased	Increased	
Married Danish males, 22-34[1] (Kutschinsky, 1970a)	42	71%	2%	26%	No
Married Danish females, 22-34[1] (Kutschinsky, 1970a)	28	68%	0	32%	test
Single German males, 19-27[2] (Sigusch, et al., 1970)	50	80%	4%	16%	(NS)
Single German females, 19-27[2] (Sigusch, et al., 1970)	50	82%	6%	12%	(NS)
Single German males, 19-27[2] (Schmidt and Sigusch, in press)	128	76%	9%	15%	(NS)
Single German females, 19-27[2] (Schmidt and Sigusch, in press)	128	81%	5%	14%	(.001)
Single German Males, 19-29[2] (Schmidt, et. al., 1969)	99	71%	11%	17%	(NS)
Single Canadian males, 18-25[2] (Amoroso, et al., 1970)	60	77.6%	10.3%	12.1%	(NS)
Single American males, 18-20[2] (Mosher, 1970a)	194	91%	4%	2%	(NS)
Single American females, 18-20[2] (Mosher, 1970a)	183	95%	2%	3%	(NS
Single American males, 18-30[2] (Davis and Braucht, 1970a)	121	82%	11%	7%	(NS
Married American males, 30-59 (Mann, et al., 1970)	48	---	---	36%	(.01
Married American females, 30-64 (Mann, et al., 1970)	32	---	---	28%3	(.01

[1]Subjects included some unmarried but coitally experienced persons.
[2]Subjects included both coitally experienced and inexperienced persons.
[3]Percent increase of experimental over control Ss. Additional tests found that mean sexual activity leve on film viewing nights exceeded those for the rest of the four-week period at high levels of significance for males (T=5.31,=48, p<.001) and females (T=4.19,=48,p<.001).

exposure, but always with the usual sex partner. If no partner was available there was a slight increase in masturbation.

The third strategy employed retrospective techniques. It is interesting that several studies of this type showed an inverse correlation between early exposure to pornography and later sexual deviance or crime. Figure 4, from the study conducted at UCLA, shows that 80 percent of normal adults questioned have had adolescent exposure to erotica. These figures agree with those obtained in the national survey. The percentage of those exposed to erotica is significantly lower for sex deviants and sex offenders. In terms of recent exposure the figures are somewhat similar except for homosexuals (Figure 5). The data are perhaps more strikingly seen when reported in numbers (Table 8), and they show that in the sample reported sex deviants and offenders have had significantly less than normal adolescent exposure to erotica. Finally, comparing the exposure of nonsexual delinquent and nondelinquent groups, Table 9 shows that there are no significant differences in exposure to erotica. Increased exposure is not at all characteristic of the delinquent or the sexual offender; if anything, decreased exposure is.

The last strategy compared the rise in availability of explicit sexual materials with rises in sexual crimes and deviancy. There is little doubt that crime in the United States is increasing (Figure 6). However, rape is not increasing as rapidly as homicide, robbery, larceny, or auto theft. Furthermore, arrests for sex offenses are not more than 2 percent of all arrests. Since the availability of erotica has increased much more rapidly than the increase in crime

Figure 4

Percent Reporting Adolescent Exposure to Photographic Depictions of Coitus

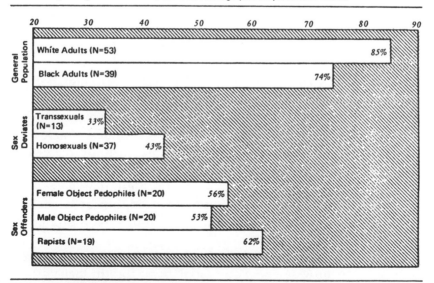

Note — Adapted from Goldstein, M. J., Kant, H. S., Judd, L. L., Rice, C. J., & Green, R. Exposure to pornography and sexual behavior in deviant and normal groups. *Technical reports of the Commission on Obscenity and Pornography.* Vol. 7.

Figure 5

Percent Reporting Recent Exposure to Photographic Depictions of Coitus

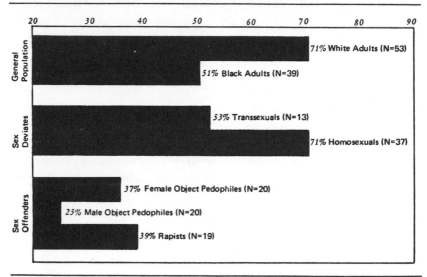

Note — Adapted from Goldstein, M. J., Kant, H. S., Judd, L. L., Rice, C. J., & Green, R. Exposure to pornography and sexual behavior in deviant and normal groups. *Technical reports of the Commission on Obscenity and Pornography.* Vol. 7.

rate, a causal relationship must be doubted, even though it cannot be disproved.

The Danish experience is valuable for study, even though their population is more homogenous than that of the United States (Tables 10 and 11). In Denmark erotic material was removed from the obscenity statute in June 1967. Total sex crimes, which had been relatively stable from 1958 to 1966, began to decrease—by 25 percent in 1967, 13 percent in 1968, and 30.5 percent in 1969. Homosexuality, exhibitionism, and child molestation decreased most. Rape and attempted rape also decreased, but by a smaller margin. Denmark also showed satiation—most of what is produced is exported or sold to tourists.

In summary, the findings of the Effects Panel were that research to date provides no substantial basis for the belief that erotic materials constitute a primary or significant cause of the development of character defects or that they operate as a significant determinative factor in causing delinquency in the young or crime among adults. Obviously none of these data should be taken as ultimate truths. Yet it is remarkable that all data pointed in the same direction. It is likely that most of the Commissioners attempted to approach the problem as a panel of jurists would approach an accused person—that sexually explicit or pornographic materials were innocent until proven guilty. They failed to find evidence of such guilt. Pornography is a nuisance to most people, entertainment and education to some, and evil to very few. It is as likely to do good as harm, it is quickly satiating, and it is not, in the view of those people questioned, among the most important social issues of the day. Morality, good taste, and appropriate sexual behavior cannot be legislated, but they can be instilled and developed through factual knowledge concerning sexual matters, combined with emotional and social guidance of high quality for both adults and adolescents. In fact, a greatly expanded program in sex education was one of the strongest recom-

Table 8

Frequencies of Exposure Among Sex Offenders, Sexual Deviants and Non-Offender Adults Reporting Adolescent Exposure to Photographic Depictions of Coitus

(Figures in Percentages)

| Population | Number of Photographs Seen | | |
	None	1 to 10	11 or more
White non-offenders (N=53)	15%	28%	57%
Black non-offenders (N=39)	26	23	51
Rapists (N=19)	38	38	24
Male object pedophiles (N=20)	47	24	29
Female object pedophiles (N=20)	44	17	39
Homosexuals (N=37)	57	14	29
Transsexuals (N=13)	67	8	25

Note — Adapted from Goldstein, M. J., Kant, H. S., Judd, L. L., Rice, C. J. & Green, R. Exposure to pornography and sexual behavior in deviant and normal groups. *Technical reports of the Commission on Obscenity and Pornography*. Vol. 7.

Table 9

Extent of Exposure Among Delinquent and Nondelinquent Youth[1]

Population	Erotic[2] Books	Erotic[2] Pictures
Incarcerated delinquents, 17-20 years (Propper, 1970)	77%	84%
National sample males, 18-20 years, living in parents' home (Abelson, et al., 1970)	68%	63%
National sample males, 21-29 years (Abelson, et al., 1970)	82%	81%
National sample college students 17-24 years (Berger, Simon & Gagnon, 1970a)	88%	95%
Urban working class high school students (juniors and seniors) (Elias, 1970)	95%	81%
Urban working class adolescents, 13-18 years (Berger, Simon & Gagnon, 1970b)	79%	77%
Los Angeles working class white males reporting on their adolescent experience (Goldstein, et al., 1970)	80%	85%
Los Angeles Black "Ghetto" males reporting on their adolescent experience (Goldstein, et al., 1970)	81%	78%

[1] "Extent" refers to the proportion of a given population reporting any experience with erotic material.
[2] Refers to depictions of heterosexual intercourse.

mendations of the Commission, one that has unfortunately been ignored by the sensationalists who focus on the recommendations concerning less legislation for adults.

The last myth is that the Commission report is a Magna Carta for pornographers. The report has been blanketly repudiated by the President and the Senate. The facts are that while two-thirds of the Commissioners agreed to recommend the removal of all existing federal and state legislation prohibiting access to pornography by consenting adults, there were other, and perhaps more important, adjunctive recommendations. Legislation was recom-

Figure 6

Percentage Change in Number of Adult Arrests for, and Known Cases of
Index Offenses, 1960-1969

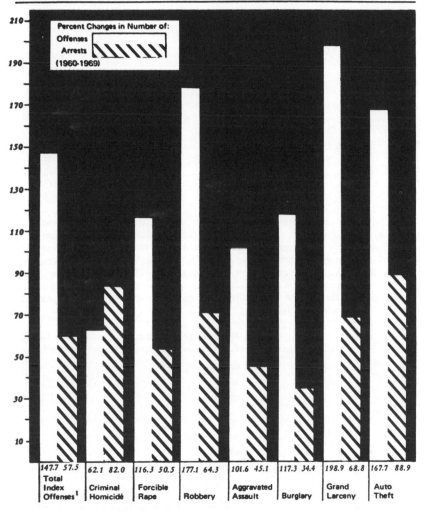

Note — Adapted from Federal Bureau of Investigation, United States Department of Justice. *Uniform crime
reports* — 1969. *Washington, D. C.: U. S. Government Printing Office, 1970, pp. 57, 110.*

1. The seven offenses included in the FBI's crime index are: criminal homicide, forcible rape, aggra-
vated assault, robbery, burglary, grand larceny, and auto theft.

Table 10

Total Sex Crimes Reported to the Police in Copenhagen, Denmark: 1958-1969

Year	Total Crimes[1]	Percent increase or decrease over previous year
1958	982	-0-
1959	1,018	+3.66
1960	899	-11.69
1961	1,000	+11.23
1962	749	-25.10
1963	895	-19.49
1964	732	-18.21
1965	762	-4.10
1966	783	-2.75
1967	591	-24.52
1968	515	-12.86
1969	358	-30.48

[1] Total reported sex crimes, 1958-1969 = 9284. These include: rape and attempted rape, coitus with minors, "indecent interference short of rape" with both minor girls and adult women, exhibitionism, peeping (voyeurism), homosexual offenses and verbal indecency. The original investigator omitted from his analysis, and without explanation, the "quasi-sex offenses" of bigamy, incest, livings off the earnings of a prostitute, inducing to prostitution, propositioning, and obscenity offenses (the latter eliminated by repeal of prohibitions against the dissemination of sexual materials).

Note — Adapted from Ben—Veniste, R. Pornography and sex crime — the Danish experience. *Technical reports of the Commission on Obscenity and Pornography.* Vol. 7.

mended to protect juveniles, not because the material was shown to be harmful but rather because it was found in the survey that parents wished such protection and because it was agreed that parents had the right to control the exposure of their children to all types of stimuli, including sexual stimuli. The Commission recommended statutes to protect adults who might find such material offensive, such as restrictions on public display and unsolicited mailing. A statute designed to protect the retailer who might sell or exhibit materials when he was unaware of the content was recommended. The Commission felt that removal of obscenity judgments from jurisdiction by federal courts and the Supreme Court might open a Pandora's box regarding political and religious "obscenities" that would threaten the First Amendment. The Commission recommended continued research to test the data which they generated and the conclusions which they drew from these data. Finally, the Commission recommended that there be sex education and community involvement with these issues because it concluded that age-appropriate education, rather than legal restriction, was the clearest route to diminished sexual crimes and healthier sexual and moral attitudes.

Some loud and important voices have been heard objecting to the conclusions and recommendations of the Commission. It is perhaps worth speculating about the nature of the criticism of the Commission report. Terms like "marshmallow heads," or "morally bankrupt," used to describe the members of the Commission, can

Table 11

Number and Percent Change in Sex Crimes Reported to Copenhagen Police, by Offense Category, 1958-1969

Offense Category	1958	1969	Percent Change
Heterosexual offenses	846	330	-61.0
Rape (including attempts)	52	27	-48.1
Intercourse on threat of violence or by fraud, etc.	11	8	-37.5
Unlawful interference short of rape with adult women	100	52	-48.0
Unlawful interference short of rape with minor girls	249	87	-65.1
Coitus with minors	30	19	-57.9
Exhibitionism	264	104	-60.6
Peeping	87	20	-77.0
Verbal indecency	53	13	-32.5
Homosexual offenses	128	28	-78.1

Note - Adapted from Ben-Veniste, R. Pornography and sex crime - the Danish experience. *Technical reports of the Commission on Obscenity and Pornography.* Vol. 7.

hardly be called criticism, but are rather invectives. The motives of those who use them undoutedly range from moral insult and indignation to political cynicism. The more serious criticisms, such as those offered in one of the minority reports, are of three types. There are moral absolutists, for whom the areas of concern are not only pornography but also the structure of the family, premarital sex, divorce, abortion, and even contraception. Questions of morality are not open for debate or scientific inquiry for they are matters of faith. Such a position must be respected, even if it is not accepted, for it is consistent and based upon the deepest religious convictions. There are also those who doubt the evidence. Some find it contrary to their personal or professional experience. Some begin with the posture that explicit sexual materials must be considered guilty until proven innocent. Such a position is based upon the judgment that in the sexual area any change from traditional and historical values is suspect. Such proof of total innocence is almost impossible to achieve—for anything. Finally, it is interesting to note a polarization of opinion around the rights of free speech and the right to bear arms, or, between sex and violence. In Denmark and the Scandinavian countries sexual permissiveness is high, but violence in sports and even in moving pictures and on television is strictly controlled. In this country those who most vigorously oppose gun control usually favor rigorous censorship of sexual materials and vice versa. Although these positions are frequently defended on constitutional grounds, there seem to be very few who are consistent in either defending or wishing to modify both the First and Second Amendments.

The Commission recognized that this country faces major problems in the areas of promiscuity, illegitimacy, venereal disease, sexual deviancy, and sexual crimes, but to attribute these to pornography and to pretend that they would be resolved if pornography were eliminated would be a disservice to the people of the United States. Such problems and their solution demand a mobilization of varied resources and multiple efforts, not a "displacement" or a dependence upon simplistic and naive reasons for their existence. The Commission hoped that their work would have some influence in extending the range of inquiry required for the solution of these problems. At the very least it has initiated a literature and established reputability in this area of sex research, and hopefully it will have some influence on the judicial and legislative processes concerned with pornography. Hopefully, the Commission Report will bring about a clearer understanding of both the facts and the myths surrounding the implications or lack of implications—legal, social, psychological, and economic—of the existence of explicit sexual materials in all cultures, and particularly in our own. The Commission concluded that an attitude of scientific inquiry brought to bear on the issue of pornography would most effectively lead to an understanding of its dimensions and functions, and thus to its effective national control.

chapter 12

Scientific Models
for Sexual Behavior
from the Clinician's
Point of View

Fritz A. Freyhan*

John F. Kennedy's "Ich bin ein Berliner" evoked an enthusiastic response which made history. When I declare that I have been a Berliner it is for the very different purpose of establishing my credentials for participation in this symposium. During the years when I went to school and studied medicine, Berlin was a city of great sexual freedom. Nudity, prostitution, pornography were highly visible. Literature, stage, cabaret, and the entertainment world featured sex, whether in earnest pursuit of social reform or for pleasure. Pornography of sorts was easily available on many newstands. Prostitutes accosted men openly from early afternoon to early morning hours, not only in side streets but in some of the shopping center areas and theater districts as well. Male prostitutes

*Fritz A. Freyhan, M.D., St. Vincent's Hospital and New York University, New York, N.Y.

dressed as alluring women were no rarity in the streets and performed in well-advertised night clubs. I cannot recall any storm in the news media about Berlin being depraved except in the press of the Right.

When I completed medical school the time had come to find a willing professor with an interesting topic for my doctoral thesis. This was in 1936 and I planned to leave for the United States as soon as I had obtained my medical degree. The only topic offered to me was in the field of venereal disease, investigating infertility as a complication of bilateral gonorrheal epididymitis. I took up quarters in the Rudolf Virschow Krankenhaus situated in the workers' district of Berlin, an area suffering from poor housing, overpopulation, and unemployment. My study required a follow-up of all those patients who had been treated for the indicated gonorrheal complications. After contacting patients through the mail, I had to do physical examinations of scrotum and testicles to discover scars and then examine their ejaculate under the microscope for the presence or absence of spermatozoa. The professor had not told me how to obtain the ejaculate, leaving such technical matters to me and a very able and knowledgeable male attendant. One obvious fringe benefit of this otherwise unexciting study was a realistic lesson about the intricacies and varieties of adult male masturbation patterns. Moreover, my exposure to the sexual activities of the enormous out-patient population—I served as an assistant during the slack hours of my study—educated me in the sexual behavior which caused such a stir when presented by Kinsey in his monumental survey. Of greatest importance, Berlin had become the site of the famous Institute of Sexual Science directed by Dr. Magnus Hirschfeld (1940) who had also established a Medical Society for Sexual Science and set up the first German marriage consultation bureau, which became a model for similar institutions in many other countries. Between the years of 1921 and 1932 the Institute of Sexual Science sponsored five international congresses for sexual reform which were held in Berlin. These meetings were organized by the World League for Sexual Reform. They dealt with the ever acute problems of abortion, homosexuality, and the myriad of other psychosexual problems.

Since I developed a special interest in psychiatry while still in medical school, I attended all elective seminars dealing with psychotherapy and psychoanalysis. I can say without reservation that I was privileged to have professors of outstanding accomplishments. Yet I cannot think of any subject which aroused in me such suspicion of scientific confusion as the material dogmatically taught to explain human sexual behavior. My sense of criticism grew after I began training as a psychiatrist in the United States. There seemed to be no relationship between the theory of normal and abnormal sexual behavior and the sexual facts of life, whether recorded historically or observable in existing contemporary societies. The forces of prejudice, morality, opinion, and pseudo scientism accounted for amazing contradictions in theory and worst of all in clinical practice.

The past decades have witnessed an increase in sexual research and this meeting reflects our growing awareness of the need for supplying facts and evidence rather than fiction and assumptions. A retrospective view proves, however, that this is not a simple matter of progression. We are still very far from approaching the Golden Age of Science. Ideology, dogma, and sometimes plain stupidity posing as scientific attitudes still impede the development of valid knowledge and its clinical and social application. In this respect we see a paradoxical situation in the disparity between governmental control of therapeutic drugs as compared with other therapeutic approaches. The public, today classified in public health as the consumer, benefits to a growing degree from stringent regulations which not only screen dangerous drugs but require proof of a drug's clinical effectiveness. Imagine for a moment that similar laws were applied to the treatment of human sexual health and dysfunction. The American Psychopathological Association has traditionally assumed the role of scientific conscience and watch dog when selecting a topic for the annual meeting (Freyhan 1970). The topic for this year reaffirms this aspiration and expresses our hope to contribute a cross-section of contemporary knowledge on sexual behavior.

MEDICAL ATTITUDES AND SCIENTIFIC MODELS

What have been some major attitudes and models of investigation which have influenced knowledge and manipulation of human sexual behavior? Generally, observers, physicians, and investigators proceeded from naturalistic, moralistic, and empirical positions. Preferences in basic attitudes and themes can be traced throughout history. A few examples will provide a proper perspective for an overview.

Sexual activity was regarded as a treatment for melancholia and other mental illness during various periods in the past. Constantine the African, in the Middle Ages, recommended coitus as effective tranquilization (Starobinski 1962). He reasoned that bad-tempered animals were known to become calm and docile after mating. A far more substantial use of sex as a treatment was introduced by two famous psychiatrists: Vincenzo Chiarugi (Starobinski 1962) in Italy and Johann Christian Reil (Starobinski 1962) in Germany, both pioneers of modern psychiatry in the eighteenth century. They thought of the sexual act as the most powerful and enjoyable physical sensation of which patients should not be deprived. While Chiarugi encouraged sexual activity for the mentally ill, Reil went further and thought it therapeutic to employ prostitutes for the satisfaction and improvement of hospitalized male patients. Only reluctantly did he exclude female patients because of the social problems of pregnancy. In theory, he thought that not only the sexual act but also pregnancy could have a therapeutic effect for the female patient's state of mind.

The use of infibulation by the medical profession throws quite another perspective on past attitudes toward sex. Infibulation refers to a variety of methods which make coitus impossible. For male infibulation, mechanical devices such as rings around the tip of the penis were used which interfered with erection and ejaculation. This practice originated in pre-Christian cultures. It was used for reasons of public modesty in the Greek civilization which permitted athletes to perform naked as long as the tip of the penis was covered. It also served as a forerunner of population control. Physicians in the eighteenth century, however, endorsed infibulation to prevent masturbation, which was then regarded not only as immoral but a cause of insanity. According to Schwarz's (1970) historical study of infibulation: "The height of the infibulation mania was reached towards the end of the 19th century when the solitary vice as it was called was more severely condemned than ever before. Under the cloak of scientific enlightenment and rational detachment, physicians the world over had fallen victims to the emotional appeal of Victorianism. To tolerate masturbation in the patient had become worse than performing an illegal abortion (pp. 964–94)." Infibulation was still recommended in the United States by Shannon (1920) in a treatise on the laws of sex life and eugenics.

Let us move from past attitudes to modern scientific models. Kinsey (1948), in reviewing the literature available when he began his extensive investigations found human sexuality "one of the most poorly explored fields in biology, psychology, or sociology (p. 21)." In giving credit to Ellis, Freud, Krafft-Ebing, and many others, he commented: "None of the authors of the older studies in spite of their keen insight into the meanings of certain things, ever had any precise or even approximate knowledge of what average people do sexually (p. 21)." He gave credit to Hirschfeld for his attempt at a systematic survey by obtaining histories of persons who visited his Sex Institute at Berlin, some as patients, others as visitors. In this manner Hirschfeld accumulated over 10,000 questionnaires covering multiple areas of sexual behavior. While they were inadequate by modern standards of sampling techniques, it was a beginning in standardizing techniques of fact-finding.

The discovery of infantile psychosexuality by Sigmund Freud has been acclaimed as a revolution which profoundly changed and influenced scientific and cultural understanding of human sexual behavior. What was Freud's model for obtaining clinical material? Most of you may be familiar with the photograph contained in Ernest Jones's (1955) "The Life and Work of Sigmund Freud." It shows Freud's famous consultation room in Vienna with its pillow and blanket covered sofa, many pictures and antiquities. Freud sat behind the sofa avoiding facial confrontation with his patients. Emphasis was placed on recollection of the past, the recovery of childhood memories on which the theory of infantile sexuality was built. The following comment by Freud (1943) illuminates his method of gathering data: "Quite often we do not succeed in bringing the patient to recollect what has been repressed. Instead of that, if the analysis is carried out correctly, we produce in him an assured conviction of the truth of the construction which achieves the same therapeutic result as a recaptured memory (p. 358)."

Chodoff (1966) in his recent critique of Freud's theory of infantile sexuality advances the opinion that an objective and un-biased assessment of the scientific validity of Freud's work on infantile sexuality has been lacking. According to Chodoff, Freud's theory "met with a reaction so uncritically rejecting on the part of the medical profession, and so unreservedly accepting on the part of his followers, that the atmosphere was not at all favorable for the kind of careful, painstaking, and objective exami-nation that so revolutionary a theory deserved (pp. 507–17)." Let us focus on a key statement by Freud (1938) concerning the transformation of puberty. Freud recognized the importance of the clitoris for masturbation. If, in his own words, "one wishes to understand how the little girl becomes a woman, he must follow the further destinies of the clitoris excitation. Puberty, which brings to the boy a great advance of libido, distinguishes itself in the girl by a new wave of repressions, which especially concern the clitoris sexuality (pp. 613–14)." Thus, he continues: "If the woman finally submits to the sexual act, the clitoris becomes stim-ulated and its role is to conduct the excitement to the adjacent genital parts; it acts here like a chip of pinewood which is utilized to set fire to the harder wood. It often takes some time before this transference is accomplished and during this transition the young wife remains anesthetic. This anesthesia may become permanent if the clitoric zone refuses to give up its excitability; a condition brought on by profuse sexual activities in infantile life (pp. 613–14)." Perhaps nothing in Kinsey's books aroused initially as much resistance and criticism as his reported evidence that such a transfer from "clitoral response into vaginal response" would in fact be a biological impossibility.

Freud's (1938) recognition of erogenous zones is curiously handicapped by adherence to his theory of infantile sexuality. In his discussion of the forepleasure mechanism he states: "In con-trast to the end pleasure or pleasure of gratification of the sexual act, we can probably designate the first as forepleasure. The fore-pleasure is thus the same as that which could already be furnished by the infantile sexual instinct, albeit on a reduced scale; while the end pleasure is new and is probably associated with conditions which first appear at puberty (pp. 606–07)." He warned that the mechanism through which the forepleasure is expressed presents an obvious danger to the attainment of the sexual aim.

May I emphasize that it is not my intention to engage in a general criticism of Freud's theories on sex but to examine the investigative model on which he based his dicta. It may be significant that Freud's own sexual experience appears to have been unusually limited. According to Ernest Jones (1955): "Freud was quite peculiarly monogomous. Of few men can it be said that they go through the whole of life without being erotically moved in any serious fashion by any woman beyond the one and only one. Yet this really seems to have been true of Freud since we must consider the momentary excitement over Gisella Fluss at the age of sixteen to have been an intense fantasy rather than a personal attraction. Such men are fortunate indeed if all goes well with the great choice, as happened to Freud, but whether they are to be regarded as representing the true normality of males is a question that only social or psychological anthropology can answer. Freud's deviation from the average in this respect as well as his pronounced mental bisexuality may well have influenced his theoretical views to some extent, a possibility to be borne in mind when assessing them (pp. 421–22)."

The question of personal sexual experience is of course a highly delicate one. Although many behavioral scientists have utilized their reactions in self-experimentations with various psychoactive drugs for understanding normal and abnormal behavior, there is as yet no trend on the part of investigators to use personal sexual experiences for scientific insight. A possible change in this direction may have been started by the British scientist who measured the effects of sexual activity on beard growth (Anon. 1970). Having to spend periods of several weeks on a remote island in comparative isolation, he devised a method for measuring his beard growth in relation to resumption of sexual activity when leaving the island. Even the presence of female company in the absence of intercourse caused an increase in beard growth. Moreover, he reported: "perhaps the most interesting feature of these changes was the way the increase in beard growth anticipated the resumption of sexual relationships (pp. 869–70)." Though remaining anonymous for obvious reasons, the editor of *Nature* vouched for the integrity of the investigator's scientific method. Personal observations have convinced me from adolescence through adult life that sex behavior cannot be understood in terms of a stimulus-response approach. Rather, there is evidence that desire, expectation, and fantasy influence physical systems resulting in complex changes of homeostatic balances.

Kinsey's model introduces for the first time new investigative parameters. In comparing different models, we must make some allowances for the Zeitgeist, but keep in mind that sexual behavior is independent of cultural fashions insofar as phylogenetically determined factors are concerned. Freud's model was clinically and theoretically naïve because it depended entirely on reported childhood experience totally ontogenetic in character. But I hasten to add that it is to his historical credit to have developed a new conception of the psychology of sexual behavior which alerted the world of science to the importance of sexuality. His dilemma arose from the confusion of models which did not distinguish between explaining sexual behavior and interpreting its meaning.

It remained for Kinsey to develop a model based on the facts of what average people do sexually. As a taxonomist he was primarily concerned with the measurement of variation in series of individuals which represent the species. But the fact-finding survey does not explain the real contribution of Kinsey's work. In his interpretation of sexual data he achieved a previously unknown degree of behavioral integration of ontogeny and phylogeny. In terms of ontogeny, Kinsey's main emphasis focuses on the influence of class and culture in the development of sexual behavior of socially identifiable groups. As a biologist he drew on his extensive knowledge of evolution of sexual behavior from subhuman to human species. Consider the arbitrary manner in which Freud divided sexual activities into forepleasure and end pleasure. Kinsey (1948) stressed that it is a mistake to think of the genitalia as the only "sex organs" and a considerable error to consider a stimulation or response which involves other areas as biologically abnormal, unnatural, contrary to nature, or perverse. As he puts it:

"Mouth, breast, anal or other stimulants involve the same nervous system, namely the whole nervous system which is involved in a genital response, and the arousal and orgasms which are effected by stimulation of the other areas involves the same physiology (as far as we yet understand them) which is involved in arousal and orgasm effected through the stimulation of the genital areas. That this is not generally understood he attributed to the considerable taboo in our culture, on all non-genital sexual activity. The lower mammals, unrestricted by social convention, know and utilize oral and anal stimulations as well as genital (pp. 573-74)."

The confusion between scientific models which explain behavior as opposed to those which interpret its meaning can be demonstrated by the misunderstanding of the significance of sexual positions. Few professional people are aware that the most common variant position for sexual intercourse is the one with the female above. This position was nearly universal in ancient Greece and Rome. Kinsey (1948) pointed out that it is shown in the oldest known depiction of human coitus dating between 3200 and 3000 B.C. Yet according to some popular psychodynamic interpretations this position made the female masculine and the male effeminate, if not actually showing him to be homosexual by his acceptance of it.

Kinsey's explanation of homosexual behavior has been particularly controversial. Although his scale of bisexuality ranging from fully heterosexual to solely homosexual behavior has in recent years found widespread acceptance, we are today once more at a stage of professional prejudice which finds expression in the appointment of committees and task forces to combat homosexuality by pronouncing it an illness. In the absence of valid knowledge and scientific consensus we can still profit from the following formulation by Kinsey (1948): "It would encourage clearer thinking on these matters if persons were not characterized as heterosexual or homosexual, but as individuals who have had certain amounts of heterosexual experience and certain amounts of homosexual experience. Instead of using these terms as substantives which stand for persons or adjectives to describe persons they may better be used to describe the nature of the overt sexual relations, or of the stimuli to which an individual erotically responds

(p. 617)." Based on Kinsey's findings that about 50 percent of the population had had at least one if not several episodes of homosexual activity during their life span, we can hardly afford a scientific pronouncement which characterizes psychosexual reactions between individuals of the same sex as rare and therefore abnormal or unnatural, thus constituting evidence of neurosis or personality disorders. This is not to deny that there are many individuals whose homosexual behavior reflects psychopathology of one type or another requiring psychiatric treatment.

If Kinsey had reason to be irritated by some unscientific pronouncements in the psychiatric literature, psychiatrists and other behavioral scientists had grounds to criticize his occasional overdependence on analogies between human and subhuman sexual behavior. This is well illustrated by Kinsey's interpretation of premature ejaculation. Kinsey (1948) suggests that the quick response of the typical male may be most unsatisfactory to a wife who is inhibited or natively low in response, as many wives are. Rejecting the idea that the male who responds quickly in a sexual situation is neurotic or otherwise abnormal, he refers to basic mammalian behavior and points out that in many species of mammals the male ejaculates almost instantly upon intromission. This led him to the conclusion that it would be difficult "to find another situation in which an individual who was quick and intense in his responses was labeled anything but superior (p. 580)" and that in most instances this describes exactly the rapidly ejaculating male, however inconvenient this quality may be from the standpoint of the wife in the relationship. In taking this position, Kinsey appears unaware that sexual activity involves communication and personal interaction without which it would in essence be reduced to two solo performances.

However, Kinsey's model introduced a comprehensiveness which set a high standard for scientific investigations of sexual behavior. We did not have to wait for *The Sensuous Woman* by 'J' (1969) to be informed that oral, anal, and other sexual acts are, as they always have been, vital ingredients of sensuous sexuality. But tempted as some may well be to dismiss the *Sensuous Woman* by 'J' as a frivolous ambition to make the best seller list, the book is not without merit. Critical women, patients and nonpatients, have told me that the book has helped them more than so-called authentic manuals, because of its matter-of-fact approach and reassuring tolerance of the range of normal activities. What we can learn from this is the basic insight that for most humans sexual behavior without appropriate sensuality is inadequate. Most of the scientific books, even though directed at the widest possible reading public, drown the essential facts of sensuality in the antiseptic language of technical detachment.

The most recent advance in model development is the work of Masters and Johnson, who will deliver the Paul Hoch Award Lecture at this meeting. Their most important innovation is the laboratory, in which sexual response phenomena can be investigated and recorded. Sexual responses involve anatomical structures and physiological systems. Functional variation and variability in relation to individual characteristics, age, and many other conditions have never before been objectively investigated on such a scale of significance. The strangest aspect of this model is not its existence but the lateness of its introduction. At a time when medical science includes heart transplantation and other daring procedures which have been hailed as milestones of progress, it seems anachronistic to advocate, rationalize, or worst of all, defend the laboratory model. Only perfectionists or obstructionists insist that one single model can do justice to all the parameters worthy of investigation. The path of progress includes addition, innovation, and then synthesis and integration of separately collected facets of knowledge.

Kinsey expanded our knowledge immensely by questioning what average people do sexually. But like clinicians he had to depend on what people say they do. The laboratory model advances knowledge to what men and women actually do sexually, permitting objective examinations and measurement. The work of Masters and Johnson (1966, 1970) has thus far provided important and previously not available data on the following: (1) physiological and psychological response phenomena during sexual activities, (2) alterations of these phenomena in the aging population, and (3) therapeutic modifications of varieties of sexual dysfunction based on psychophysiological information of sexual response patterns.

It takes much courage, integrity, and discipline to do research on actual sexual activity. But the merits of the model depend not on these human qualities of the investigators but on methodology and its suitability for duplication and comparative studies. This will require time and patience. But enough data of high credibility have been reported to justify the most serious consideration, particularly by clinicians. Neither analytic psychotherapy, behavior treatment, or any therapeutic approach, whatever its theoretical foundation, can survive unless it moves with the evidence of contemporary research. Many critics forget that regardless of the final validation of the psychophysiological data by Masters and Johnson, their data are not opposed by investigations of comparable scientific methodology. Much passionate criticism reflects distortions arising from careless reading of the authors' precise formulations of the research population, procedures, results, and implications. This applies particularly to the first volume, *Human Sexual Responses*."

I have some questions on the second volume. I find its title, *Human Sexual Inadequacy*, too broad, since the content is narrowed to what the authors call the marital-unit. Furthermore, the outline of the history does not cover the spectrum of overt activities and mental attitudes on which Kinsey placed such emphasis in terms of naturalness. Unless I am mistaken, there is no reference to oral eroticism. Van der Velde (1926) considered the "genital kiss" not only "absolutely unobjectionable" but "particularly calculated to overcome frigidity and fear in hitherto inexperienced women." While Masters and Johnson stress touch, vision, olfaction, and audition, their therapeutic format would seem to bypass the role of mouth and genitalia. The significance of oral sexual response lead Kinsey (1953) to comment: "It is not surprising that the two areas of the body which are most sensitive erotically, namely the mouth and genitalia, should frequently be brought into direct contact (p. 588)." Also not mentioned are other varieties of sexual activity which in 5,000 years of pornographic art were shown as natural practices in many cultures and may therefore be potentially therapeutic under specific circumstances.

I suspect that institutionalization, necessary for the survival of the Foundation, may have artificially limited the range of exploration and therapeutic format. What is a most impressive advance is Masters and Johnson's concept of and technique for desensitization of performance anxiety. This achievement should prove of considerable consequence for clinical methods of treatment.

Many psychiatrists will be rightfully dissatisfied with any model which neglects factors of psychological motivation and the dynamic aspects of partner relationships. Yet in concluding this overview, I find with regret how relatively few advances have been made by psychiatrists. But strangely, a very large number of psychiatrists were extremely critical, if not frankly hostile, in reaction to Kinsey's and Masters and Johnson's work. When in 1948 one very eminent psychoanalyst criticized Kinsey's work without giving due credit, I wrote an "Open Letter to the Editor" which was published in the same journal as rebuttal (Freyhan, 1948). Since what I said in 1948 regrettably still seems relevant today, I take the liberty of quoting the following passages from that letter: "Psychiatrists often indulge in autistic thinking and forget that they are in danger of intellectualistic isolation. We should not forget for a moment that many key analytic concepts, believed to be of universal psychologic or psychopathologic validity, were conceived and formulated during investigation of an incredibly small case material which was highly selective with regard to psychological, social, economic, and racial qualities." I continued: "One does not have to agree with either Dr. Kinsey's work as a whole or all of his critical statements concerning psychiatry but one must credit him with a spirit of objectivity and integrity free from superficiality or maliciousness." And in addressing myself to the charge that Kinsey had not given due consideration to psychological factors, I replied that we should not overlook "that psychiatrists, in spite of all claims to the contrary, lack biologic orientation and remain continuously preoccupied with psychodynamic concepts."

As far as the situation today is concerned, I doubt that we will make firm advances in understanding sexuality in terms of normality and pathology before we integrate models of investigation in the direction of an anthropological approach. Such an approach must bridge the gap between individual organism, psychosocial life style, and species behavior. Also, it must in some orderly fashion distinguish between biological and experiential determinants of sexual behavior. The crux of such a matrix was so concisely expressed by Alfred Grotjahn (1923) who said: "zwischen dem Menschen und der Natur steht die Kultur (p. 2)." Translated, but sounding less succinct, this means "Between men and nature stands culture."

REFERENCES

Anon. Effects of sexual activity on beard growth in man. *Nature* 226: 869–70. 1970,

Chodoff, P. A critique of Freud's theory of infantile sexuality. *Amer. J. Psychiat.* 1966, 123(5): 507–17.

Freud, S. *The basic writings of Sigmund Freud.* New York: Random House, The Modern Library, 1938.

———. Constructions in analysis (1938). In *Collected papers*, vol. 5. London: Hogarth Press, 1943.

Freyhan, F. A. An open letter to the editor, correspondence. *Psychosomatic Medicine* 1948, 10(5): 295.

———. The psychopathologist—what man of science? *Comprehensive Psychiatry* 1970, 2(5): 391–402.

Grotjahn, A. *Soziale Pathologie.* 3 Anfl. Berlin: J. Springer, 1923.

Hirschfeld, M. *Sexual pathology.* New York: Emerson Books, 1940.

'J'. *The sensuous woman.* New York: Lyle Stuart, 1969.

Jones, E. *The life and work of Sigmund Freud*, vol. 2. New York: Basic Books, 1955.

Kinsey, A. C. *Sexual behavior in the human male.* Philadelphia: W. B. Saunders Company, 1948.

———. *Sexual behavior in the human female.* Philadelphia: W. B. Saunders, 1953.

Masters, W. H., and Johnson, V. E. *Human sexual response.* Boston: Little, Brown, 1966.

———. *Human sexual inadequacy.* Boston: Little, Brown, 1970.

Schwarz, G. S. Infibulation, population control, and the medical profession. *Bulletin of the N.Y. Academy of Medicine* 1970, 46(11): 964–94.

Shannon, T. W. *Nature's secrets revealed: Scientific knowledge of the laws of sex life and heredity or eugenics.* Marietta, Ohio, Mullikin, 1920.

Starobinski, J. History of the treatment of melancholy from the earliest times to 1900. *Documenta Geigy Acta Psychosomatica* 1962, 4, 36-37; 60.

Van der Velde, Th. H. *Ideal marriage.* New York: Random House, 1926.

William Masters and Virginia Johnson

William Masters and Virginia Johnson Paul H. Hoch Award Lecturers, 1971

Introduction

It is obvious that Dr. Masters and Mrs. Johnson and their co-workers have made an extraordinarily significant and important contribution to knowledge and treatment in an area of human experience about which much has been written but of which little was objective until the report of their research and treatment program was published. In spite of all the criticism and negative feedback with which they have had to contend, they have made monumental contributions to the knowledge of sexual physiology and psychology. When people ask me what I think of the scientific merit of Masters and Johnson's work, I always answer that it would not matter if everything they have said were contradicted in the future, for nothing will ever change the fact that they have taken the risk and succeeded in establishing for all scientists the right to conduct research on human sexual behavior, even when it involves observing couples copulating. Their assertion of the right to academic freedom is of the same magnitude of achievement as that of Vesalius, who asserted against the church the right to dissect the human corpse.

Criticisms have been varied, but unfortunately there have been many examples of unwarranted and inappropriate derogation. Some of our misguided psychiatric friends have criticized their work, called it dehumanizing, and insisted that Masters and Johnson have not sufficiently considered the appropriate emotional factors involved in this aspect of human interaction. I suggest that such persons speak from an encyclopedia of ignorance. Many of the comments which they have made indicate a lack of familiarity with both the work being done at the Foundation and the books and articles which describe the work of the Foundation. One has only to observe the patients' change of attitude to know that their work is anything but dehumanizing. I have seen a marital couple appear for treatment hardly speaking to each other and leave two weeks later acting like honeymooners, with an entirely different outlook on life. Marmor wisely gauges their method when he suggests that the Masters and Johnson technique is "midway between a behavioral and psychodynamic approach." It is clear to me from observing their work with patients that they are, indeed, knowledgeable about the psychodynamic factors involved in marital interactions. The Foundation studies are in an area of human interaction so involved with emotion that it is difficult to develop an unprejudiced point of view. Nevertheless, as a result of their research, many of both old and current myths with regard to sexual function have been proven false.

In addition to the two major books, *Human Sexual Response* and *Human Sexual Inadequacy* authored by Dr. Masters and Mrs. Johnson, Dr. Masters by himself and with Mrs. Johnson has developed an extensive bibliography of scientific papers. These books have received a favorable reception by the professional groups concerned with sexual behavior, and the contribution made by these authors is significant.

It is our good fortune that Dr. Masters and Mrs. Johnson have been chosen to receive the Hoch Award and that they will describe some of their work to us this evening. Dr. Masters is a physician and educator who graduated from the Lawrenceville, New Jersey,

High School, received a Bachelor of Science degree from Hamilton College, and his medical degree from the University of Rochester in 1943. He was an intern and resident in obstetrics and gynecology at St. Louis Maternity Hospital and Barnes Hospital. He became a member of the faculty of the Washington University School of Medicine in 1947 and has continued as a member of that faculty to the present time. He is a member of numerous scientific organizations and the recipient of many honors.

His co-worker and associate director of the Foundation, Mrs. Virginia Johnson, has a background in psychology and music. She was with the St. Louis Daily Record from 1947 to 1950, when she was appointed to the Washington University School of Medicine as a research instructor; later she became a research associate of the Reproductive Biology Research Foundation. She is on the Board of Directors of the Family and Children's Service of greater St. Louis, a fellow of the Society for the Scientific Study of Sex, and a member of the Board of Directors of SIECUS.

It is a very special privilege to present to you Mrs. Virginia Johnson and Dr. William Masters.

RAYMOND W. WAGGONER, M. D.
University of Michigan School of Medicine

chapter 13

Current Status of the
Research Programs

William H. Masters and Virginia E. Johnson*

An investigation of human sexual function was initiated in 1954 under the auspices of Washington University School of Medicine. This program has continued since 1964 as an important segment of the total research supported by the Reproductive Biology Research Foundation. Three major aspects of human sexual response have been foci of investigation. In chronologic order these research ventures have included various aspects of sexual physiology, variants in the treatment of sexual dysfunction, and a combined laboratory and clinical evaluation of homosexual response patterns. Established Foundation policy requires that at least a decade be devoted to each area of human sexual functioning under investigation before reporting work in progress to the scientific community.

*The Reproductive Biology Research Foundation, St. Louis, Missouri.

Although a number of papers were published prior to the 1966 release of the first textual report to the scientific community, these preliminary publications frequently were incomplete and in some areas inadequate. Primarily they were presented as evidence of investigative objectivity, and, secondarily, they provided supportive evidence of research productivity for funding requirements. *Human Sexual Response* is a review of an eleven-year pursuit of laboratory attempts to define the physiologic components of human sexual functioning. Although a number of sexual fallacies and misconceptions were brought to scientific attention, the report remains incomplete. For example, the discussion of cardiorespiratory physiology is a superficial evaluation, evidencing little investigative depth.

In the early years, the work in sexual physiology was handicapped by problems of funding and concerns for protecting the anonymity of the subject population. Work was slowed frequently and even interrupted occasionally as funds ran out and/or as security techniques required revision. The primary objective was to eliminate, as far as possible, the influence of the artificiality of the laboratory environment upon the subject's levels of sexual response. A perpetual administrative problem was created by continuous attempts of the blatantly curious to penetrate the protective security established for those men and women who cooperated to provide laboratory evidence of the basic physiologic principles of human sexual function. Protection of subject anonymity always has been and always will be a total commitment of the Foundation's professional staff. At least two, perhaps three, years of research time could have been salvaged had the work been conducted with greater financial support and any significant evidence of maturity in either public or professional curiosity.

Credit must be given for the tremendous cooperation provided by those who worked with borrowed, rented, and usually secondhand equipment to design, produce, and activate acceptable physiologic recording techniques. Although certainly simplistic in character, these techniques ultimately enabled the staff to evaluate data assembled from prior publications by other sources and to record previously undeveloped material for scientific scrutiny.

In January 1959 the second aspect of the Foundation's research program relating to human sexual response was initiated.

This clinical component of the research design was designated "the rapid treatment of human sexual dysfunction." Based upon preliminary experimentation, a controlled clinical study was initiated which sought to integrate physiologic fact and psychosocial structure. This concept requires that therapists regard the interrelation of the psychologic and biologic systems as an operational necessity. The fundamental tenets of this clinical research were formulated in 1958, prior to establishing an eleven-year period of statistical control. Since objective evaluation of treatment techniques depends upon appreciation of the precepts involved, they will be presented in some detail.

First: Each partner in a marriage handicapped by some form of sexual inadequacy is considered to be responsibly (accountably) involved both in the physical functioning and the psychosocial aspects of the marital relationship. Therefore, both members of the distressed marital unit must be seen in therapy and, equally important, must voluntarily participate in the educative process that is the basis of the Foundation's treatment of sexual dysfunction. The marital relationship always is the primary target of therapeutic attention. Individual requirements, preferences, and goals are given consideration within the context of this relationship.

Second: It is believed that there are specific advantages inherent in the use of dual-sex teams in the treatment of marital units contending with symptoms of sexual dysfunction. Although team members' responsibilities are too numerous to detail here, the primary purpose for the use of a male-female team is to provide full and fair clinical representation for both members of a marital unit undergoing treatment. It is the female therapist's clinical obligation to help the wife define and express herself, to give support as she evaluates her position in the ongoing therapy process, and to interpret material of female orientation. It follows that the male therapist has a similar responsibility for the husband.

Third: The process of education within the course of therapy is dependent upon daily review of the patients' participation in a learning opportunity which has been provided when the marital pair "tries on" ideas and modes of interaction conceptualized for and with them during discussion sessions. The daily review is derived from the patients' account of their own attitudes and activities developing from the previous day's discussion. In this manner the marital pair explores the appropriateness and reliability of combinations of verbal and nonverbal, sexual and nonsexual communication in producing mutually desired feelings and attitudes. They subsequently may accept or reject any particular experience and its means of attainment as it does or does not support their mutual values and goals.

The content of any daily session may include an account of patient experience, discussion of related feelings and attitudes, as well as co-therapists' presentation of new information, correction of misinformation, and suggestions for altering patterns of behavior which have been defined as unsatisfactory by husband and/or wife. Repetition is employed frequently to achieve understanding and familiarity with effective patterns of interaction. Both exploration and experimentation are carried out by the marital partners under protective rules of conduct and, if necessary, intervention of the co-therapists. The therapy team imposes three rules of conduct upon the involved husband and wife to help achieve this protective environment.

1. Communication between the marital pair shall be an exchange based on self-interpretation and must never be allowed to impute feeling, meaning, or intent by one partner to the other.

2. Anger or frustation developing from a breakdown in communication between the marital partners shall be held in abeyance, to be described and dealt with in the next day's therapy session.

3. Those actions and ideas elected as appropriate and effective by either partner shall be introduced for the enhancement of both, but never at the expense of valued requirements of the other.

Fourth: This mode of psychotherapy presumes that human sexual functioning, like that of other animals, must be considered a natural process. It is not only unnecessary, it is impossible to "teach" the human male to achieve erection, the female to lubricate, the male to ejaculate, or the female to experience orgasm. The basic principle that must be accepted by patient and co-therapist alike is that physical expression of sexual tension is a natural function. From this platform of general agreement, therapeutic techniques can be activated which are designed to contribute to progressive removal of psychosocial blocks inhibiting sexual response. Possibly the key to professional and public acceptance of the concept of sexual response as a natural physical expression lies in appreciation of the fact that sexual function has a unique facility when compared to other physiologic responses of the human body. Sexual function so responds to psychosocial control that activity can be delayed indefinitely or even denied for a lifetime. No other basic physiologic process of the human body permits such a degree of inhibition without predictable impairment of body function.

Fifth: It is virtually impossible to establish treatment success with consistency when statistically evaluating a psychotherapeutic procedure. This is particularly true when the process requires the element of self-evaluation. Treatment failure is considered far easier to ascertain, although measurement of contributing factors may not be conclusive. Therefore, treatment statistics have been and will continue to be reported relative to goal failure rather than goal attainment.

Sixth: Regardless of the severity of the presenting clinical distress, symptom reversal during an acute phase of therapy is relatively unimportant, unless the newly created, supporting patterns of communication and interaction are sufficiently appreciated and maintained by the marital pair to sustain symptom reversal after termination of treatment. If a therapeutic procedure is not to be judged a failure, the patient must evidence a trend of continued or progressive improvement after termination of therapy, regardless of the techniques employed and/or the duration of the acute phase of therapeutic support. Therefore, the concept of a routine five-year follow-up of patients is applied to those marital units not identified as therapeutic failures during treatment for sexual dysfunction. Although the results would be of extreme investigative importance, rapid treatment failures are not followed in order to encourage every husband and wife whose problems have not been resolved by Foundation personnel to approach other means of psychotherapeutic support.

The Foundation's second report, again reflecting eleven years of research commitment, was published in 1970. Hopefully, this report will give value to precepts involved in the use of dual-sex teams in the treatment of sexual dysfunction. The results obtained must be generally supported by similarly constituted dual-sex teams working in different geographic areas before scientific security in concept and procedure can be established. Of theoretical import is the intriguing possibility of using dual-sex team techniques in the treatment of yet other forms of psychopathology. The technique's inherent facility as an educative format only underscores the possibility of other applications of the method, since practically all forms of psychotherapy are, in large measure, educative processes.

Concomitant with first attempts at expansion of the professional staff during the last three years, the efficacy of this program of psychotherapy has been lowered significantly. There has been a significant reduction in effectiveness of the treatment of impotence and a major increase in failure to resolve problems of non-orgasmic return. These decreases in treatment efficacy have resulted in a rigorous evaluation of the general therapeutic approach and of specific inadequacies in concept and technique of selection, training, and modes of evaluation of professional interaction for members of the professional staff. As a result of this self-evaluation conducted by the entire staff, some basic distractions to or inadequacies of staff function and of the psychodynamics of dual-sex team therapy have been demonstrated.

Four extraneous influences have contributed in large measure to the increased treatment failure rate. Hopefully, these factors have been resolved through reduction or elimination of their dominance in staff-time commitment. Excessive staff-time consumption has developed from:

1) Problems inherent in the selection and training of additions to the Foundation's professional staff. In view of clinical demand for treatment, staff expansion was long overdue before that level of financial security necessary for such expansion became available. In addition, the severely overloaded permanent staff was constantly distracted by extraneous demands. Training requirements also further diluted staff commitment to patient care. Specific training techniques had to be developed and were, at best, far from adequate in those first years. All of these factors contributed to reduction in therapeutic efficacy. Successful expansion of the permanent staff has gone a long way toward resolving these problems.

2) Major efforts to provide definitive sex information for public and professional consumption. The Foundation will have essentially withdrawn from this field by the end of 1971. Maturity achieved by such organizations as The Sex Information and Education Council of the United States (SIECUS) and the Center for the Study of Sex Education in Medicine has obviated responsibility in this area. In the future, staff-time committed to the dissemination of information will be strictly controlled. It is the Foundation's fundamental responsibility to provide definitive sex information through effective research. Widespread dissemination of this information must be assigned to other organizations specifically designed for this purpose.

3) Massive demand for treatment which overwhelmed somewhat frantic attempts of Foundation personnel to achieve selective balance and led to serious overscheduling at patient intake. Corrective measures have been taken and staff reaction has been entirely positive.

4) In brief, the Foundation's professional staff has been spread entirely too thin during the rapid-growth period. Such overcommitment of time and effort will not recur. The professional staff has achieved approximately 75 percent of its projected size. In the future, anticipated growth will occur at a slower, relatively nondemanding pace.

But there is no desire to overemphasize the negative in this discussion. There have been many positive returns in the past two years. Two of the three dual-sex teams trained to date are members of the Foundation's professional staff. The multiplicity of talents and disciplines these professionals possess argues well for improved therapeutic results in the future.

In January of 1971 the Foundation's long-anticipated postgraduate training program became a reality. Difficulties and inadequacies that were evident in prior training experience have underscored a number of principles vital to the new educative program: (1) Dual-sex trainee units must be closely integrated with the professional staff of the Foundation. The training period was designated as one month but this time commitment was altered as experience accrued. (2) Postgraduate training opportunity currently is being restricted to men and women with significant clinical experience. (3) One member of each trainee team must be a physician. Behavioral science orientation is highly desired as a credential for the other team member. (4) During the first year, postgraduate training will proceed at a deliberately slowed pace. This pace will enable the professional staff to analyze and revise these procedures as indicated. Accrued training experience will underscore what material and therapeutic techniques to emphasize, and in what manner, at what pace, and in what depth pertinent information should be made available.

Selection of the theoretically best qualified candidates for training will be carefully controlled by the review of professional credentials, investigation of referral sources, and personal interviews. While a background of academic commitment will be of major importance, there also will be a reflection of private practice interest in trainee team appointment. Geographic distribution of trainee teams will be a consideration but not a decisive factor in selection.

A fundamental truism has emerged from years of working in the psychosocially charged area of human sexual response. It applies to all disciplines without reservation. As a primary requisite for effective participation in programs oriented to human sexual behavior, basic scientists and clinical investigators concentrating on problems of sexual function or dysfunction must have achieved comfort with both their sexual identity and their sexual functioning. It is difficult enough for investigators or clinicians to maintain objectivity in this field without the additional handicap of a sex-related insecurity. Therefore, during the personal interviews required before applicants can be accepted for training, all trainees are being evaluated not only in regard to professional competence, but with relation to their concerns and degrees of comfort with sexual material.

Trainee teams must realize that six months to a year of clinical experience usually will be required before individual team members can expect to achieve real security in their professional interaction. The first year's clinical commitment should be held at a slow pace in order to encourage mutually intensive self-evaluation for team members.

Each trainee team will be followed closely after termination of training in St. Louis. There will be a scheduled visit to the trainee team by the Foundation's training personnel approximately six months after termination of the formal training period. Therapeutic techniques, knowledge of and demonstrated facility in use of pertinent clinical and laboratory material, general clinical expertise, team member interaction, and patient records and results will be evaluated by teaching professionals. Only subsequent to a positive report of such an on-the-screen evaluation, will the Foundation formally identify the trainee team as having successfully completed the training program.

It is inevitable that members of the Foundation's professional staff will achieve a greater return from the newly constituted postgraduate training program than that afforded the trainees. Security with a subject is best developed when one is required to organize and present the material with sufficient clarity to make a positive contribution to a teaching program.

Since July 1970, Dr. Raymond W. Waggoner and Dr. Emily H. Mudd have been associated with the Foundation on a part-time basis. In addition to their commitment as senior consultants to the Foundation's professional staff, they will concentrate their talents on the postgraduate training program. They have accepted responsibility for selection of candidates and supervision of training procedures. The value of this team of senior consultants to Foundation personnel and to candidates in training is immeasurable.

A number of functional and psychosocial problems inherent in the practice of dual-sex team therapy have emerged over the past decade. At this point in time it seems appropriate to pinpoint some of these problems in professional adjustments for those who currently are or in the future anticipate employing this manner of therapeutic approach.

1) Experience suggests that the most consistently recurring problem is the arbitrary tendency of the male professional to assume control of therapy at any given time, or for the female therapy partner to engender such male dominance by failing to accept her share of responsibility in the course of therapy. This observation has remained constant for each of the four teams trained to date. Every male-female team must be continuously careful to negate those cultural influences that tend to engender imposition of male dominance as a prerogative in personal or pro-

fessional interaction. If the male therapist exercises dominance as a privilege, he may commit the professional faux pas of attempting to describe or interpret for the wife of the sexually dysfunctional couple those details of sexual reaction that are particularly female in orientation. Examples of this type of therapeutic misfortune are provided by instances of a male therapist's attempt to verbalize the wife's subjective appreciation of sexual stimulation, the psychologic components of her approach to sexual interchange, or her objective or subjective appreciation of an orgasmic experience.

Obviously, it is equally erroneous for the female therapist to attempt any similar interpretive takeover of the husband's subjective or objective appreciation of sexual response.

2) Another problem arises when the female therapist attempts to interpret feminine accounts of sexual response and psychosocial interaction from a masculine-oriented point of view. While this pattern of interaction remains somewhat enigmatic, many women who involve themselves in formal training in the interest of professional status undergo some degree of psychic reorientation. They respond with an essentially masculine input as a means to overcome the unfair competitive detours placed upon them in our culture. Psychosocial trauma sustained during professional adolescence may show through the maturity of professional experience during professional attempts to interpret or react to a sexually distressed woman. Needless to say, a masculine clinical approach displayed by a female therapist is disconcerting or even traumatic to the female patient. The wife might fear that she does not have a female interpreter or true representation. As euphemistically described by Foundation personnel, she comes to the conclusion that she does not have a "friend in court." Such a conclusion, of course, is totally contrary to that intended by the dual-sex team concept.

3) A problem possibly unique to the Foundation's professional staff is the necessity for developing a common language for clinical interchange. This stimulating problem of professional interaction probably has emerged from inadequate exposure to or appreciation of those professional disciplines in which a staff member has not received training. As currently constituted, each member of the full-time, clinical staff represents in fact or in part at least two

different professional disciplines. Yet, no single discipline has more than one representative. It is apparent that there are tremendous advantages in having a variety of professional disciplines available to any treatment program. Each staff member must assume the responsibility for achieving some degree of familiarity with those multiple alternative disciplines to which he has not had sufficient prior exposure before a common language can be established to describe finite nuances of patient reaction. For example, the significance of psychotherapeutic terminology might not be appreciated in totality by a professional trained as a pediatrician or an obstetrician. Similarly, the full portent of the multiple physiologic facets of human sexual response is hard to absorb by those trained in the behavioral disciplines.

Experience has made it apparent that the language of personnel communication must be that of the clinically trained psychotherapist. It must be used in combination with an in-depth appreciation of the physiology of sexual response which, in turn, must become familiar not only to those with nonmedical professional orientation but also to many of those formally trained in medical fields.

4) Yet another problem area to emerge in the last few years has been the obvious failure of the referring authority (usually medical) to associate superficial complaints of physical sexual dysfunction with a depth of underlying psychosocial trauma. In contradistinction, and equally delimiting in concept, is the categorical assignment of underlying psychopathology to all individuals complaining of sexual dysfunction. In many instances, clinical complaints of sexual dysfunction do represent the underlying existence of major degrees of psychopathology, but probably an equal or greater number of patients experience severe sexual inadequacy without evidencing symptoms of accompanying severe psychopathology.

5) As stated previously, it is vital that psychotherapists dealing directly with clinical symptoms of sexual distress react from a sense of confidence and comfort in their own sexuality and sexual functioning. There is a tendency for a sexually insecure therapist to lose objectivity when dealing with a sexually distressed patient, particularly one of the opposite sex. Any failure to maintain per-

spective has grave potential for undermining the effectiveness of the professional's therapeutic approach to the patient's complaint of sexual inadequacy.

6) Problems of transference or a tendency toward countertransference have been observed, despite the protective screen inherent in the technique of dual-sex representation in therapeutic counsel. When sexual dysfunction is the presenting complaint, there is a tendency for both male and female patients to attempt identification with the authority of the opposite sex. Although professionals are presumed sensitized to this tendency, there have been times when patient transference was encouraged, or at least not discouraged, by a member of the Foundation's professional staff. An occasional inclination toward countertransference has been identified during the daily case evaluation sessions which are conducted by Foundation personnel. In no sense is the Foundation impugning the effectiveness of controlled transference as a psychotherapeutic technique, but it must be emphasized that such a technique has no place in the rapid treatment of sexual dysfunction.

7) When warring strangers (usually identified by such terms as husband and wife) are referred to the Foundation for treatment of sexual dysfunction, every effort is made to reconstitute their interpersonal relationships by catalyzing constructive communication. Identifiable, shared goals and common denominators of motivation provide the initial material for catalytic affect. Again and again the positive aspects of the unit's personal interactions must be emphasized if security in communication is to be established or restored. In the brief period of two weeks, both the husband's or wife's conscious or unconscious attempts at identification, each with the other, must be catalyzed successfully if there is to be a positive therapeutic return.

8) The basic value systems of both the husband and the wife must be defined in depth sufficient to implement therapeutic effort successfully. A superficial scanning of the husband's or wife's set of personal values, including their sexual value systems can indeed destroy therapeutic effectiveness. Superficiality of interrogation inevitably results in inadequate professional representation of the same-sex patient. The same-sex therapist must come to

appreciate the patient's attitudinal approach to the psychosexual influences of our culture. Problems arise when a professional does not develop a history which adequately reflects patient values or life style, and, under pressure to meet demands of the therapy, imposes an interpretation based upon his or her own limited personal experience. With sufficient authoritative identification of the patient's individual value systems and of the context in which they function, it is far easier to keep the Foundation's educative program focused on those things truly desired by the individual rather than those possibly imposed by the therapist's own value system.

9) There may be a tendency toward professional rigidity in assignment of highly structured roles to sexually dysfunctional husbands and wives. Therapists must remain constantly aware that they are dealing with two different personalities, two sets of values, and two individual expectations which have not been fully negotiated. Certainly they must anticipate the possibility of divergent concepts of life style developed from different experiential backgrounds. It must be kept in mind that a wide range of information is required to define common denominators from which to establish a secure foundation for patient interaction.

10) Patient screening has been and remains a serious problem. There is no place for the acute psychotic or the borderline psychoneurotic in the Foundation's treatment program, unless the patient is referred, with spouse, after adequate preparation and returned immediately to post-treatment control by a competent psychotherapist. Foundation screening techniques must be improved to eliminate the referral of such seriously involved patients without such protection. For that matter, the screening techniques must be improved in other aspects as well. Currently this problem is being studied extensively by Foundation personnel.

There is a third area of research interest that has involved the Foundation's professional staff. Since 1963 the laboratory and clinical response patterns of the homosexual male and female have been an integral part of a broad pattern of research in human sexual response. In large measure, those physiologic aspects of human homosexual functioning comparable to heterosexual response patterning have been recorded. Recently treatment programs have been constituted, but to date five-year follow-up data are not available. Patient intake has been restricted in order that in-depth evaluation of treatment procedure and patient reaction may be conducted during and immediately following the therapy commitment.

Treatment of homosexual dysfunction has been approached from three directions: (1) homosexuals desiring to convert or revert to some degree of heterosexual response patterning; (2) sexually dysfunctional men expressing a desire for return of sexual effectiveness in a response oriented to homophile patterning; and (3) nonorgasmic women seeking the privilege of fully responsive sexual experience in a homophile relationship.

Material returned from the Foundation's homosexual research programs will not be made available until the mid-seventies at the earliest. It is unrealistic to further dilute a massive literature already overburdened with unsupported theories of homophile responsivity. We know so little and there is so much to be done in this area of human sexual function.

Finally, a brief look to the future is in order. The decade of the seventies will find the Foundation's research commitments continuing to expand in both clinical and pre-clinical areas. From a clinical point of view, there is yet another step to anticipate in the Foundation's approach to the concerns of sexual function and dysfunction. When approaching an essentially unexplored clinical problem, researchers usually follow the well-ordered pattern of moving first to the laboratory, where every effort is made to provide, through basic science determinants, material pertinent to resolution of the clinical problem. As a second step, therapeutic suggestions and factual material developed in the laboratory are then applied to resolve the clinical concern. In the essentially unexplored area of human sexual function these first two steps have been taken in the last sixteen years. In normal progression, the inevitable third step of preventing distress looms invitingly large. As a clinical research commitment, the next decade will be devoted to devising ways and means for prevention of sexual dysfunction. Obviously, every professional discipline available to the Foundation will be employed in this clinical venture.

The goal of the basic science program is to establish a neurophysiology laboratory comparable in quality to the Foundation's biochemical research area. There is little need to support here the necessity for such a facility. In brief, we know a great deal of the neurophysiology of cardiorespiratory function, so the quality of medical care in this area increases each year. We are reasonably well informed in the neurophysiology of bowel and bladder function, and, as a result, the quality of related patient protection continues demonstrably upward. Obviously, we know little of the neurophysiology of human sexual function, particularly at the extracranial level, and the quality of our patient care in this area reflects this ignorance. In no sense will devotion to this research concentration carry the implication that all of the answers to human sexual dysfunction will be found in a neurophysiology laboratory. What is implied is the belief that approaches to treatment of sexual inadequacy will be positively influenced by productive research in this area. Inevitably, clinical approaches based on a firm, basic science foundation reflect this security in progressively elevated levels of patient protection.

There is so much to learn of the multiple facets of human sexual behavior. In the last few years legitimate investigation in this area has not only been acknowledged as professionally challenging but as socially acceptable. A massive, multidisciplined effort to interpret this last, essentially unexplored frontier of human function is long overdue.

part IV

The Brain and
Therapeutic Strategy
in Sex-behavioral
Pathology

chapter 14

The Relationship
of Altered Brain
States to Sexual
Psychopathology

Arthur W. Epstein*

Accumulating clinical evidence demonstrates a relationship between human sexual behavior and brain mechanisms, particularly those involving the limbic system and its connections. The role of this system in disorders of potency, drive, and behavior toward the sexual object is well documented. However, attempts to correlate sexual behavior with brain mechanisms cannot rest on anatomic localization alone but rather on the workings of the brain itself.

Mind is the manager of muscle (Sherrington 1937) and in a basic sense the study of sexual behavior toward an object must involve the organism's control of action. In terms of the brain's organization of motor activity, the basic patterns are two, namely, approach and avoidance. Denny Brown (1962) has described the unmasking of the basic approach and avoiding reactions as a result

*Arthur W. Epstein, M.D., Tulane University School of Medicine, New Orleans, Louisiana.

of their release from higher control by pathologic processes affecting the brain. These reactions not only appear in pathological states but are normally present in the fetus and the neonate. Twitchell (1969) has most recently studied the elementary avoiding and grasping (the prototype for approach) reactions in the neonate and notes that avoiding is dominant to grasping in terms of first appearance.

Avoiding and approach reactions are essential for the organism's adaptation to the environment. Objects eliciting pain are to be avoided; those eliciting pleasure approached. What is the approach behavior of the human neonate to an object? The mouth is used directly or the hand grasps the object placing it in the mouth. The object is taken into the body or, in another parlance, incorporated. The infantile organism employs mouth and hand for approach and incorporated behavior; the genitalia have not as yet reached a sufficient degree of functional maturity. These early approach reactions become associated with an affect. The affect, driving the organism toward approach of an object, has a pleasurable feeling. Human cerebral function seems so organized that an object encountered external to the organism may appear internally in the form of an image; the image becomes equivalent to the external object, and in this sense it too may be approached.

As all objects are probably not approached, it is assumed that a predilection exists in some—that is, certain objects have a greater capacity to evoke approach mechanisms. Objects of this type may have certain sensory characteristics of phylogenetic import or may be encountered at crucial periods of ontogenetic development (imprinting). Objects encountered in the early years of mental development would seem highly important in influencing sexual behavior.

In the young organism, then, we are considering a behavior chain which involves on the sensory side an early object and its properties and on the motor side an early motor pattern of approach; accompanying is an early affect which powers the organism toward contact with the object and often its incorporation. A chain of this type is related to the "active reflex" of Knoll (1969), the cerebral representation of which may be called an "active focus." The brain loci of such an active focus are probably widespread, but the affective component and perhaps the orienting responses to the object may be located in the limbic system.

As the brain matures, this "active focus," with its action patterns and affects related to early objects, becomes inhibited or modified. However, the focus may be released from inhibition by varied factors, including pathological processes affecting the brain. The release may be caused by impairment of inhibitory centers or overexcitation of the tissue containing the active focus. The overexcitation may have its roots in early life; perhaps the original affect and motor patterns associated with approach to the stimulating object were originally encoded in an altered brain milieu stemming from metabolic or other etiologic dysfunction. Such an overly excitable focus may never be subordinated by the usual inhibitory mechanisms. It is in this framework of brain dynamics, albeit speculatively proposed, that alterations in sexual behavior will be considered—keeping in mind the shortcomings of this approach, namely, incomplete present knowledge of brain function and the danger of confusing psychodynamic and neurophysiologic levels of integration. Sexual deviations, from the point of view of brain pathophysiology, may be viewed as release phenomena; not only may approach behavior be released but also the sexual affective force.

FETISHISM

The sexual deviation now called fetishism represents an extreme release of approach behavior toward an object, for the fetishist remains bound to the object by an intense affect. The object destined to become the fetish gains primacy early in life. Why does the young organism become fascinated with the object and after the initial period of approach desire repetitive approach? The future fetish object may have certain qualities of phylogenetic significance which evoke approach mechanisms, as is suggested, for example, by the observation of sexual arousal in two nonhuman primates by a boot (Epstein 1969); the nature of these hypothetical qualities is as yet unknown but may include shininess, texture, shape, pattern, or smell. On the other hand, the intrinsic qualities of the object alone may be less important than its association with another human to whom approach is desired (mother). In either case, it is likely that the object must be perceived at a critical period in ontogenetic (more specifically brain) development.

A fascination with given objects may occur in any infant or child, but in only a few do the objects become fetishes. In these instances a failure in cerebral integration is postulated: a primary effect on mechanisms ordinarily producing inhibition and/or over-excitability of the active focus (the neural area subserving the behavioral chain of the evoking object, approach behavior, and associated affect), or some combination of both. The presence of such a released focus may be inferred by the association of fetish-istic behavior with epilepsy or other neurological disorders. I have studied thirteen cases of fetishism or fetishism-transvestism, of which nine have abnormal electroencephalograms (shown in Fig-ure 1), two frank seizures, and five clinical evidence of brain dis-ease. Often the seizure-type, other clinical features, or the electro-encephalographic abnormality tend to implicate the temporal area of the brain (Epstein 1960, 1961, 1969). Krafft-Ebing (1931), Mitchell et al. (1954), Hunter et al. (1963) and Kolarsky et al. (1967) also report the occurrence of epilepsy in fetishists.

The tendency of the focus to become dominant, that is to become self-sustaining and recruit additional neural areas, is illus-trated by the case of Mitchell et al. (1954). In this instance, the patient "for as long as he could remember" had experienced pleas-ure when looking at a safety pin (the safety pin was a true fetish). Additional neural areas were joined to the active focus, for be-tween the ages of eight and eleven the sense of pleasure was fol-lowed by a "blank period." In his twenties the patient was ob-served to be "glassy eyed" after staring at the pin; he would make a humming noise and sucking movements with his lips, followed by a brief period of immobility. By age thirty-one the immobility was followed by automatisms and confusion; during some periods of confusion, presumably postictal, the patient would dress himself in his wife's clothing. Seizures only occurred when the safety pin served as a direct stimulus or as a mental image. A left anterior temporal lobectomy, necessarily including the uncus and anterior part of the hippocampus, was eventually done which abolished the fetishism. Pathological examination of the resected specimen re-

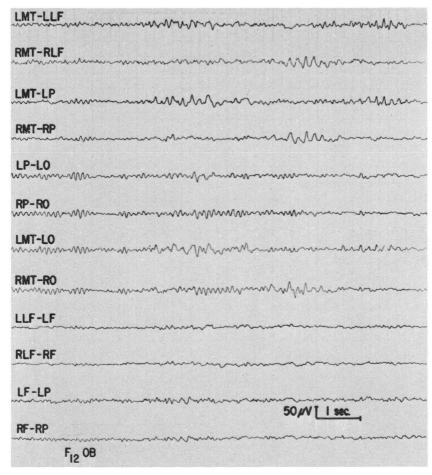

Fig. 1. *Electroencephalogram of a long-term hair fetishist, without clinical epilepsy, showing bilateral mid-temporal (LMT and RMT) slow (theta) bursts.*

vealed a gliotic process. Fetishism was also abolished by left anterior temporal lobectomy in the patient of Hunter et al., in which case gliosis was also present.

Analysis of the case of Mitchell et al. indicates that the active focus (cerebral representation of the fetish complex) has hyperexcitable or epileptogenic qualities; it also has the capacity to recruit other neural areas as is evidenced by the subsequent alterations in consciousness and motor acts (automatisms). The safety pin, and it alone, precipitated a seizure. From the point of view of clinical neurology, this is an example of reflex epilepsy. A similar example, precipitated by the fetish object, occurred in a shoe-fetishist described by Krafft-Ebing (1931). In short, the fetish object has the capacity to activate the specific neural tissue of the active focus to the epileptic level of excitability. But this reflex type of response to the fetish object is a characteristic of all fetishists, and in all instances, is probably related to clinical phenomena which may or may not be overt.

The fetishistic active focus is enduring—in one patient persisting for sixty years (Epstein 1969), in the Mitchell case for thirty years. Fetishism tends to begin in early life and persist; however, in some instances it may be first released in adolescence (Epstein 1961; Entwistle & Sim 1961) or later life (Davies & Morgenstern (1960) by seizures or other brain disease. In the adult fetishist the relationship to the fetish object may be understood as a release of an approach automatism toward a specific object. The fetishist must approach the object, often in inappropriate circumstances. When contact is gained the object may be placed in the mouth, rubbed over the body, stroked with the hand, or touched with the penis; all of these behaviors are a form of incorporation. The penis is now a mature effector organ, and ejaculation may occur on the object. The internal representation of the fetish object is also approached; this image is contacted for varied purposes, but particularly as an aid to ejaculation. The image may appear involuntarily, both in dreams and in the waking state; this intrusiveness of the image may have painful qualities.

TRANSVESTISM

In those instances when the object toward which approach automatisms are released are articles of feminine clothing, the organism's consummatory behavior may consist of putting the clothes on his body. This represents a fusion with or an incorporation of the object via the body surface. The objects clearly represent the female, and, therefore, in the simplest sense, transvestism represents a wish to join with or become a female. Perhaps one should emphasize the joining rather than the becoming, since the latter is more properly a form of transsexualism.

The active focus of transvestism subserves a behavioral system in which the individual approaches the objects and fuses them to his body, gaining consummation (reduction of the powering affect) through this fusion. This active focus may be excited as part of an abnormal brain discharge. Davies and Morgenstern (1960) describe an individual whose transvestism did not appear until middle life and then only after the development of temporal lobe epilepsy; this patient had an impulse to put on women's clothes during seizures themselves, which also included epigastric and jaw sensations. Walinder (1965) describes a man who developed transvestism at age twenty-three, five years after a cerebral concussion. Although seizure-free, his electroencephalogram was abnormal. The need to transvest was significantly improved with anticonvulsant medication, returning in full force when the medication was discontinued; the response of the transvestism to medication again suggests its relationship to abnormal brain discharge. Davies and Morgenstern report other cases of transvestism with temporal lobe dysfunction, including one with an astrocytoma in the right uncal region; this patient also had temporal lobe seizures. Temporal electroencephalographic abnormalities in other individuals with transvestitic behavior have also been found (Epstein 1961; Walinder 1965).

The transvestite must approach the desired object. He incorporates the object, thus satisfying his symbolic need. The power of the mechanism tends to make utilization of chronologically later methods of approach to the object, namely penile insertion and ejaculation, paler in comparison. Again, one may postulate a dominant focus favoring the appearance of an early approach automatism over later more fragile and differentiated modes.

TRANSSEXUALISM

Transsexualism, a problem of gender identity, would not appear subject to analysis as an active focus or approach automatism unless one could consider that gender identity is the result of repeated processes of incorporation of environmental figures.

Further, if certain aspects of maleness and femaleness are reflections of innate neural patterns, this neural substrate is subject to alteration by pathology.

Clark (1915) reported an example of effemination of behavior in a man with temporal lobe seizures. Effemination of behavior also occurred in the temporal lobe epileptic of Davies and Morgenstern. Blumer (1969) reviewed the electroencephalograms of fifteen transsexuals and considered only two clearly abnormal; however, he encountered three transsexuals with epilepsy, but whose seizures did not apparently have clear temporal lobe components. In short, the available data relating transsexualism to brain dysfunction is quite preliminary.

HOMOSEXUALITY

Homosexuality is a complex syndrome with many subtypes. Are there neural mechanisms which drive the male to the female and the female to the male? One would suspect that there are heterosexual orienting systems which are phylogenetically determined in the service of species survival. Olfaction, for example (Bieber 1960), may provide a basis for movement toward the heterosexual object. Although homosexuality is a varied disorder, the basic impairment is the failure to develop an approach reaction toward an individual of the opposite sex. This may be related to a dysfunction of neural mechanisms which in the ordinary course of ontogenetic development would subserve expression of such approach reactions in response to the appropriate stimulus; at present there are no recorded neurological cases to substantiate the hypothesis, although Kolarsky et al. (1967) report homosexuality as occurring in their cases of male sex deviation associated with early temporal lobe damage.

The adult male homosexual has a strong approach reaction to the penis as an object. The penis is often taken in the body via the mouth. The approach reaction to the penis may be based on very early experiences; the penis may be placed in the same category as other objects, such as the nipple toward which approach behavior was directed in earliest life. It is possible that there may not have developed adequate inhibition of this early approach behavior; in any event, mechanisms guiding the organism toward objects other than the category of nipple or penis are not available. Another factor which may give the penis primacy as an object is that described by MacLean (1962) in his discussion of penile display as a manifestation of dominance-submission behavior in the squirrel monkey. Human homosexuality has also been linked to dependency drives with a need to gain power from another male (Ovesey 1954). Penile display and the need to take in the penis of a fancied powerful male may represent in the human a phylogenetically based automatism which may be subserved by a neural mechanism. Again there is no clinical neurological data to substantiate this hypothesis.

In pedophilic homosexuality, the adult organism approaches an object or an image which is linked to the past. The individual must automatically approach this object which in the past evoked affect. It would seem that this early object was of sufficient power to create and maintain an active focus still operative in adult life. Roeder and Müller (1969) report relief of pedophilic homosexuality in three individuals after stereotaxic placement of a unilateral lesion in the nucleus ventromedialis (Cajal) of the hypothalamus. After this procedure one individual became unable to indulge in previously stimulating erotic fantasies; this is a clear reduction of approach behavior toward the desired object or a diminution in the strength of the active focus.

EXHIBITIONISM

In exhibitionism, the object evoking compulsive penile display is a person (female). The sight of the penis may produce varied emotional responses in the object, such as astonishment, fear, or interest. The exhibitionist is often interested in the emotional response of the object and feels empathy with the object in terms of the fancied response to the displayed penis. Rather than incorporating the object, the exhibitionistic chain of action involves an aggressive type of approach automatism toward the object.

Hooshmand and Brawley (1969) describe a man who displayed exhibitionistic behavior for one year. At least one episode occurred in a confused state and an electroencephalogram revealed a left temporal abnormality; use of anticonvulsant therapy diminished the exhibitionistic behavior. In a patient with a bilateral temporal electroencephalographic abnormality, I personally observed that the sound of a ringing bell was experienced as a seizure component. An identical sound occasionally was heard when the patient felt the need to display his penis. In both of these cases, compulsive genital display occurs as part of a seizure discharge and activation of this focus is thus a component of abnormal discharge in the temporal area.

The behavioral chain known as exhibitionism involves penile display toward the object rather than use of hand or mouth for incorporative purposes. Therefore, this approach automatism toward the object appears to represent a chronologically later ontogenetic mechanism. The action of penile display may have phylogenetic significance in terms of species survival—that is, penile display has adaptive value in terms of exciting the intended sexual partner and the displayer himself. Sexual affective responses of both participants may thus be enhanced. Penile display is often encountered in the childhood of the male, but it is usually later inhibited by the prevailing mores. In some instances, however, such as in the cases cited, this inhibition is overcome due to the existence of an overactive focus. It is of interest that genital display may occur as part of a temporal lobe seizure, but the more complex (or ontogenetically more mature) motor patterns of coital activity are not reported in the male as part of a seizure itself.

ALTERATIONS IN SEXUAL DRIVE AND POTENCY

Numerous clinical studies now document the relationship between limbic lesions and alterations in sexual drive (hyposexuality or hypersexuality) and potency. Diminution in drive and subsequent inability to obtain penile erection are described by Johnson (1965) in a man with right temporal lobe astrocytoma. Either impotency or reduction in sexual drive has been described in individuals with temporal lobe lesions or epilepsy by Hierons and Saunders (1966), Blumer and Walker (1967), and Saunders and Rawson (1970). Van Reeth et al. (1958) described heightened sexual drive in four individuals, each with a deep anterior temporal lobe tumor.

Extra-temporal lesions altering potency and drive in man have been described by Meyers (1963) following lesions in the septo-fornico-hypothalamic region and by Heath (1964) who reported penile erection in three patients during electrical stimulation and orgastic response in a female following chemical stimulation of the septal region. Although extra-temporal, these regions are within the limbic system. Genital sensations associated with increased sexual drive, due to an irritative lesion of the right paracentral lobule (genital sensory area), occurred in a woman reported by Erickson (1945).

Sexual drive provides the power for all sexual activity; therefore, heightened sexual drive will intensify the need for approach to an object or, in another sense, will energize the active focus. Phenomena which release sexual drive may thus tend to release approach automatisms, as is true, for example, in the case of Klüver-Bucy syndrome (bilateral temporal lobectomy) in man, described by Terzian and Dalle Ore (1955).

CONCLUSION

An attempt has been made to conceptualize phenomena on both the brain and behavioral levels by the use of models which facilitate cross-correlation. At the brain level the model is the active focus, a specific neural substrate in a state of excitability or of release from inhibition and with the capacity to activate other neural tissue. The second model is a behavioral chain extending from the evoking stimulus to the consummatory act and powered by sexual drive. Such a behavioral model may not do justice to the complexities and nuances of adult sexual behavior or of sexual deviations, but it is useful when cross-correlating with the neural level and, indeed, perhaps should not be underestimated as a universal basic pattern. For sexual behavior must deal with an organism's relationship to an object or to another organism. Neural circuitry must be available to subserve this behavioral chain leading to consummatory action with the other.

The limbic system is an important locus in such neural circuitry. In sexual psychopathology the role of the limbic system stands out in clear relief when there is over-excitation or inhibitory release of limbic mechanisms. Often the release does not merely involve an isolated behavioral chain, for it is known from clinical examples that several deviations may co-exist in the same individual. Further, in certain individuals the release may involve extra-sexual behavioral areas, such as excess aggression and impaired control over perceptual or thought processes, as well as facilitation of erection and ejaculation (Epstein, 1960).

The complexities of adult sexual behavior probably require an extensive brain substrate; one should therefore avoid its overly naïve localization to a specific brain area. For example, mature coital patterns are not described as components of limbic seizures. It is possible that the more simple approach automatisms, with their tendency to employ nongenital effectors for consummation, are manifestations of limbic reflexes, while adult coital patterns, which are based upon learning, require extra-limbic tissue. In this connection the role of frontal areas in human sexual behavior requires delineation. Another unanswered question is whether maleness and femaleness are reflected at the level of brain structure and function. Male sex deviations preponderate in the clinical literature, but it is not clear whether this reflects a sex difference in neural mechanisms or is an artifact.

While recognizing the perils of over-zealous localization, there is sufficient clinical evidence to direct those psychopharmacologists and neurosurgeons seeking to devise therapies for the psychosexual disorders to anterior temporal, septal, and certain hypothalamic loci. Further, if future studies of sexual psychology and psychopathology are to be comprehensive and meaningful, they must take into account the role of the brain and particularly its limbic portions.

REFERENCES

Bieber, I. Olfaction in sexual development and adult sexual organization. In Masserman, J. H. (ed.), *Psychoanalysis and human values, vol. 3, Science and psychoanalysis*. New York: Grune & Stratton, 1960, pp. 201–4.

Blumer, D. Transsexualism, sexual dysfunction, and temporal lobe disorder. In Green, R. & Money, J. (eds.), *Transsexualism and sex reassignment*. Baltimore: The Johns Hopkins Press, 1969, pp. 213–19.

Blumer, D., & Walker, E. Sexual behavior in temporal lobe epilepsy. *Arch. Neurol.* 1967, 16: 37-43.

Clark, L. P. The nature and pathogenesis of epilepsy. *New York J. Med.* 1915, 101: 385-92, 442-48, 515-22, 567-73, 623-28.

Davies, B. M. & Morgenstern, F. S. A case of cysticercosis, temporal lobe epilepsy, and transvestism. *J. Neurol. Neurosurg. Psychiat.* 1960, 23: 247-49.

Denny-Brown, D. *The basal ganglia.* London: Oxford, 1962.

Entwistle, C. & Sim, M. Tuberous sclerosis and fetishism. *Brit. Med. J.* 1961, 2: 1688-89.

Epstein, A. W. Fetishism: a study of its psychopathology with particular reference to a proposed disorder in brain mechanisms as an etiological factor. *J. Nerv. Ment. Dis.* 1960, 130: 107-19.

_____. Relationship of fetishism and transvestism to brain and particularly to temporal lobe dysfunction. *J. Nerv. Ment. Dis.* 1961, 133: 247-53.

_____. Fetishism: a comprehensive view. In Masserman, J. H. (ed.), *Dynamics of deviant sexuality. Vol.* 15, *Science and psychoanalysis.* New York: Grune & Stratton, 1969, pp. 81-87.

Erickson, T. C. Erotomania (nymphomania) as an expression of cortical epileptiform discharge. *Arch. Neurol. & Psychiat.* 1945, 53: 226-31.

Heath, R. G. Pleasure response of human subjects to direct stimulation of the brain: physiologic and psychodynamic considerations. In Heath, R. G. (ed.), *The role of pleasure in behavior.* New York: Harper & Row, 1964, pp. 219-43.

Hiernos, R., & Saunders, M. Impotence in patients with temporal lobe lesions. *Lancet* 1966, 2: 761-64.

Hooshmand, H., & Brawley, B. W. Temporal lobe seizures and exhibitionism. *Neurology* 1969, 19: 1119-24.

Hunter, R., Logue, V., & McMenemy, W. H. Temporal lobe epilepsy supervening on longstanding transvestism and fetishism. *Epilepsia* 1963, 4: 60-65.

Johnson, J. Sexual impotence and the limbic system. *British J. Psychiat.* 1965, 111: 300-3.

Knoll, J. *The theory of active reflexes.* New York: Hafner, 1969.

Kolarsky, A., Freund, K., Machek, J., & Polak, O. Male sexual deviation, association with early temporal lobe damage. *Arch. Gen. Psychiat.* 1967, 17: 735-43.

Krafft-Ebing, R. von. *Psychopathia sexualis.* New York: Physicians & Surgeons Book Co., 1931.

MacLean, P. D. New findings relevant to the evolution of psychosexual functions of the brain. *J. Nerv. Ment. Dis.* 1962, 135: 289-301.

Meyers, R. Central neural counterparts of penile potency and libido in humans and subhuman mammals. *Cincinnati J. of Med.* 1963, 44: 281-91.

Mitchell, W., Falconer, M. A., & Hill, D. Epilepsy with fetishism relieved by temporal lobectomy. 1954, *Lancet* 2: 626-30.

Ovesey, L. The homosexual conflict. *Psychiatry* 1954, 17: 243-50.

Roeder, F., & Müller, D. Zur stereotaktischen heilung der pädophilin homosexualität. *Deutsch. Med. Wschr.* 1969, 94: 409-15.

Saunders, M., & Rawson, M. Sexuality in male epileptics. *J. Neurol. Sci.* 1970, 10: 577-83.

Sherrington, C. *The brain and its mechanism.* London: Cambridge, 1937.

Terzian, H., & Dalle Ore, G. Syndrome of Kluver and Bucy reproduced in man by bilateral removal of the temporal lobes. *Neurology* 1955, 5: 373-80.

Twitchell, T. Early development of avoiding and grasping reactions in man. In Locke, S. (ed.), *Modern neurology.* Boston: Little, Brown, 1969, pp. 333-45.

Van Reeth, P. C., Dierkens, J., & Luminet, D. L'hypersexualité dans l'épilepsie et les tumeurs du lobe temporal. *Acta Neurol. Belg.* 1958, 58: 194-218.

Walinder, J. Transvestism, definition and evidence in favor of occasional derivation from cerebral dysfunction. *Int. J. Neuropsychiat.* 1965, 1: 567-73.

chapter 15

Antiandrogen in the Treatment of Sex Offenders: Mode of Action and Therapeutic Outcome[*]

Ursula Laschet[†]

Antiandrogens belong to the hormone-antagonist group of substances and are part of a relatively young field of research. Only those substances which exert a competitive blocking effect on the corresponding hormone at the receptor can be defined as anti-hormones, that is, not substances which primarily alter the rate of production or secretion of a hormone. Antiandrogens are, therefore, those substances which inhibit competitively the action of endogenous androgens produced by the testes and adrenals in males and the ovaries in females and exogenous androgens administered therapeutically.

*I would like to thank my co-workers, Dr. Leonhard Laschet, head of the hormone laboratories, and Wolfgang Kieser, psychologist. We are extremely grateful to the firm of Schering AG Berlin and to Deutsche Forschungsgemeinschaft for their support of our work.

†Ursula Laschet, Pfälzische Nervenklinik, Landeck, Federal Republic of Germany.

Lerner et al. (1960) and Dorfman and Dorfman (1960) provided the first description of two very weak antiandrogenic substances, A-norprogesterone and Δ^1-testolactone. The first clinical experiments were subsequently done with 17α-methyl-3-nortestosterone. In their search for new progestogens Wiechert and his co-workers at Schering AG Berlin synthesized cyproterone and cyproterone acetate. Cyproterone acetate, the most effective antiandrogen known at present, is shown in Figure 1. It is a steroid ($1,2$ α-methylene-6-chloro-$\Delta^{4,6}$-pregnadien-17α-ol-3,20-dione-17α-acetate) which will probably be introduced into the German market this year under the trade name Androcur. Free cyproterone has only an antiandrogenic activity without any other hormonal side effect. Cyproterone acetate belongs primarily to the antiandrogen group; its partial progestogenic function is of secondary importance to the clinical action under discussion. Because of the cybernetic regulatory mechanism in the endocrine system, however, it is this secondary function which facilitates long-term therapy with antiandrogen.

From the physiological point of view two main factors determine male sexuality, or better, male sexual reaction: the androgen level in the organism and the functional capacity of certain areas of the diencephalon sensitive to androgens, generally designated "mating centers." To reduce or inhibit sexuality one can ; (1) remove the main androgen production centers by castration; (2) attempt to neutralize the hypothalamic receptors by stereotactical operation; (3) reduce the testicular androgen production and secretion of Leydig cells through the inhibition of the gonadotropic function of the pituitary by drugs—treatment with estrogens or progestogens may lead to irreversible damage of the Leydig cell function during high-dosage long-term treatment; or (4) utilize the inhibition of androgenic action by antiandrogens at the target organs.

After Neumann and his team in Berlin found in detailed animal experiments that it was possible to achieve a competitive blocking of the androgen receptors at the mating centers by cyproterone acetate, the first clinical studies in the treatment of male hypersexuality and sexual deviation were instituted in our department in May 1966. One year later we reported the initial results

Cyproterone

Cyproterone acetate

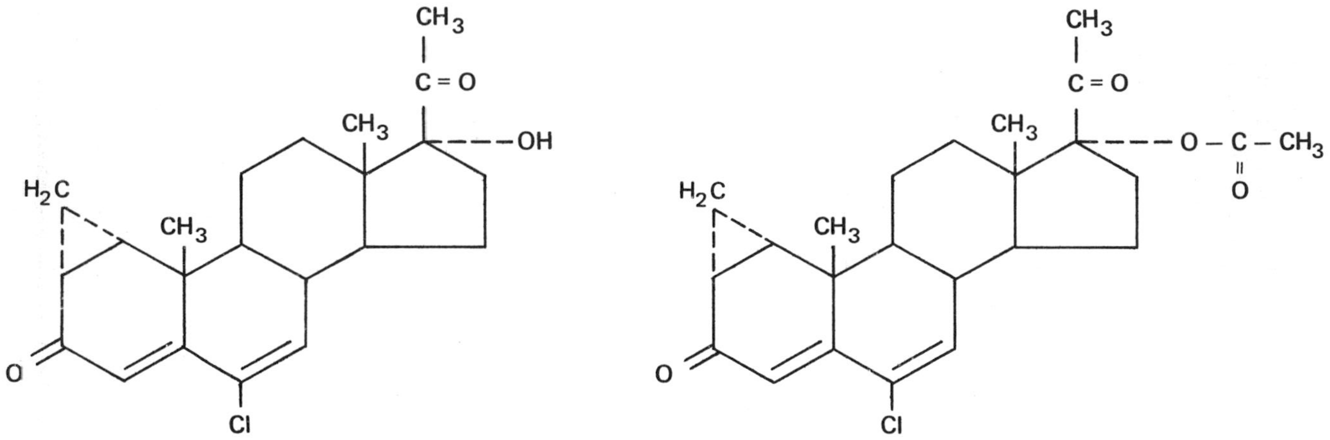

Figure 1

313

on 17 treated men (Laschet & Laschet 1967). We have now achieved results in 120 of 150 men who have been treated for a minimum of 6 and a maximum of 57 months without interruption. The 30 men who were observed for less than 6 months are excluded from this report.

About 50 percent of them are sexual offenders;* the others have never been before a court and came for treatment because of personal, emotional pressure. However, the majority of the non-delinquents, with the exception of the Don Juan type of hyper-sexuality, are considered likely to commit criminal acts and several had been treated for many years with all available therapies, such as sedatives, tranquilizers and other psychopharmacological agents, as well as psychotherapy, but without success. Some of them had attempted suicide more than once, because of their sexual problems.

At the outset of the experiment, the clinical properties of cyproterone acetate and, therefore, its indication in this type of treatment were unknown and our attitude toward its use was somewhat negative. Consequently, although we knew which subjects received treatment, the methodology can be termed blind trials.

The competitive blocking effect of cyproterone acetate at the central target organs reduces male sexuality in the following order: libido, erection, orgasm; reversibility takes place in the same order. In 80 percent of the cases, 100 mg/day cyproterone acetate administered orally is sufficient; 20 percent require 200 mg/day. Generally, 50 mg/day produces a reduction of libido and potency, such as the excessive sexual desire for the partner in Don Juanism or excessive onanism. With the administration of 100 mg/day the patients report a reduction of libido and erectional ability at the end of the first week of treatment. Regardless of the dosage administered the maximum effect is attained between the 20th and the 25th day of treatment. Reversibility of erectional ability can

*In the following report of the results of treatment with cyproterone acetate, the term "sexual delinquent" refers only to *male* sexual delinquents, as defined under the criminal law for sexual offenders in the Federal Republic of Germany. Female sexual delinquents are a rarity, and not only in Germany.

take up to six weeks, depending on the dosage administered and the duration of treatment.

According to results so far available for parenteral administration, the injection of 300 mg cyproterone acetate in an oily solution at intervals of 10 to 14 days has proved to be sufficient. In this case we first test the individual's ability to respond by oral administration, and then when the desired therapeutical effect has been achieved, we change over to intramuscular injection. In delinquents the regularity of treatment can easily be checked at any time by means of a therapy-control card which the therapist signs after giving the injection. However, reversibility of the effect after parenteral therapy may be delayed for pharmacokinetic reasons, particularly after long-term treatment. Cyproterone acetate is mainly stored in fatty tissue, and due to different absorption conditions the depot formation can be more pronounced after intramuscular injection than after oral administration. As a result, the delayed release from the depots can retard the complete reversibility of the effect.

Sexuality can be influenced only partially and under certain circumstances not at all if the disturbance is androgen-independent. For example, if posttraumatic or postencephalitic damage, such as diabetes insipidus or dilation of the 3rd ventricle with symptoms of cerebral pressure, is causally associated with the disturbance of sexuality, the sexual disturbance cannot be modified by treatment with antiandrogens. It is also impossible to influence behavior resulting from psychoses with sexual illusions. Alcoholics among the sexual delinquents are unsuitable for the therapy unless alcoholism is concomitant with the sexual disturbance. The results achieved in geriatric offenses associated with cerebral-sclerotic processes or premature degeneration are also not satisfactory. Therapeutic failure is observed in heterosexual and homosexual pedophilia when the manipulations have become independent in a neurotically fixed form. Despite the inhibition of libido and potency, manipulations are continued, frequently, only to establish interhuman contact with inadequate partners. In doubtful cases considerable importance is to be attached to the result of the psychological test examination.

Table 1 lists the total cases (120) according to the prominent deviation. The second column presents the number of delinquents, both those who were convicted earlier and those who underwent treatment in connection with pending legal proceedings. The third column lists the number of cases which were placed on probation with an order for the therapy. The last column shows the number of delinquents who were treated while serving a sentence in prison or, in cases of diminished responsibility, during confinement in a psychiatric clinic.

In the cases of hypersexuality, the symptoms had led to social disarrangement, with a frequent consequence of proceedings under civil law. By reducing sexuality adjustment was achieved in all cases; a satisfactory sexual partnership and complete social reintegration was produced. The same results were achieved in cases of excessive onany and the combination of the two problems.

Table 1.

	No.	Delinquents	Probation	Imprisonment, §42 b,c
Hypersexuality	13			
+	4			
Excessive masturbation	19			
Homosexuality	7			
+	5	5	3	1
Homosexual pedophilia	15	13	5	5
+	4	2	1	
Heterosexual pedophilia	10	4	3	1
+	2	2		2
Exhibitionism	27	18	8	3
Indecent assault, sexual murder	7	7	1	5
Incest	1	1	1	
Fetichism	1	1		1
Masochism	1			
Sodomie	1			
Other cases	3			
	120	53	22	18

The range of offenses of the treated delinquents included homosexual and heterosexual pedophilia, exhibitionism, indecent assault, sex murder, incest, fetishism, and sodomy. Homosexuals are no longer being treated; since September 1969, homosexuality between adults has not been a punishable offense in the Federal Republic of Germany. The largest group was exhibitionism with 27 cases, including 21 delinquents, 10 of them probationers. The results of therapy in this group is easy to demonstrate. In accordance with Masters and Johnson's definition of the role of the penis as a receptor and converter of sexual stimuli, almost all exhibitionists react to a specific visual stimulus with an erection which is abreacted by exhibitionism and masturbation. The absence of erection in reduced libido interrupts the perverse cycle. Rehabilitation in this group was accomplished particularly quickly, completely, and impressively.

Antiandrogens cannot alter the direction of sexual deviation; they can only reduce or inhibit the sexual reaction. However, it has been demonstrated in 7 cases that the elimination of sexuality with antiandrogens can be accompanied by an effect similar to the extinction of a once deeply rooted conditioned reflex: even when the effects of cyproterone acetate were completely reversed, the patients did not revert to the former sexual deviations. Of these 7 cases only one was a delinquent; the other 6 therefore, had nothing to gain by simulating normal sexual behavior. Similar results were reported by Rothschild (1970) of the psychiatric clinic in Zürich in 2 out of 17 male patients. After experimental discontinuation of treatment, four hypersexual men continued normal sexual behavior. In cases which should be treated by sex education or psychotherapy, the use of antiandrogens to create a sexual "calm" facilitated treatment.

The reform of the criminal law on sexual offenses in the Federal Republic of Germany provides that a sexual delinquent must be at least twenty-five years of age before he can volunteer for castration. Treatment with antiandrogens, therefore, remains as the only possibility of specific, controlled, reversible pharmacotherapeutic treatment for juvenile sexual delinquents.

Cyproterone acetate is tolerated extremely well by the liver. Reversible side effects are produced by the effects of antiandrogens at other receptor sites. During the first weeks of treatment the patient may be easily fatigued, require increased sleep, and present depressive moods similar to those after surgical castration. He may gain weight, particularly with a diet rich in carbohydrates. In about 20 percent of the cases beginning in the sixth to eighth month of treatment, the patient may show slight gynaecomastia, which may be reversible even during continued treatment. There may be an increase of head hair, a decrease of body hair, and a decrease of sebaceous gland secretion. Dose-dependent reduction or inhibition of spermatogenesis with arrest at the stage of spermatogonia or spermatocyts can sometimes become normal again during continued oral therapy with 50 mg/day and with higher doses, is reversible within five months of terminating treatment.

Our clinical and laboratory results have been confirmed by Hoffet (1968a, b), Ott and Hoffet (1968), Seebandt (1968, 1969), Krause (1969), Petri (1969), Horn and Witter (in press), Rothschild (1970), and by numerous personal reports. These reports confirm that male volunteers who are treated with cyproterone acetate learn to control their sexuality; and debiles and imbeciles may be kept on an open ward. The suggestion of Hippius that there is relatively more importance to the controlled psychopharmacological influence of antiandrogens on sexuality than to the pharmacology of an antihormone and therefore the action of this substance on the endocrine system should surely be supported. There is no doubt that considerable importance can be attached to the development of psychopharmacological preparations with a very specific, controlled action.

REFERENCES

Dorfman, R. I., & Dorfman, A. S. *Acta Endocr.* 1960, 33: 308–16.

Hoffet, H. *Praxis* 1968, 57: 221–30. (a)

———. *Schweiz. Z. Strafr.* 1968, 84: 378–94. (b)

Horn, H., & Witter, H. Proceedings of the 7th Congress of the Collegium Internationale Neuro-Psychopharmacologicum, in press.

Krause, W. F. *Materia Medica Nordmark* 1969, 21: 29–35.

Laschet, U. *Saarländ. Ärtztebl.* 1969, 22: 370–71.

Laschet, U., & Laschet, L. *Klin. Wschr.* 1967, 45: 324–25.

———. 13th Symposium der Deutschen Gesellschaft für Endokrinologie. Würzburg: Springer Berlin, 1968, pp. 116-19.

———. In Albrecht, F. J. Ramirez-Sánchez, and H. Willomitzer (eds.), *Simposion Esteroids Sexuales Fundacion para Investigaciones Hormonales.* Bogotá, Columbia: Sala-Druck, 1969, pp. 194-97.

Lerner, L. J., Bianchi, A. & Borman, A. *Proc. Soc. exp. Biol. Med.* 1960, 103: 172-75.

Ott, E., & Hoffet, H. *Schweitz. Med. Wschr.* 1968, 98: 1812-15.

Petri, H. *Nervenarzt* 1969, 40: 220-28.

Rothschild, B. *Schweiz. med. Wschr.* 1970, 45: 1918-24.

Seebandt, G. *Öff. Gesundh.-Wesen* 1968, 30: 66-71.

———. *Bewährungshilfe* 1969, 16(2).

chapter 16

Brain Serotonin and
Male Sexual Behavior

Arthur Zitrin,* William C. Dement,†
and Jack D. Barchas†

Research on the relationship between the brain amines and various
aspects of normal and disordered behavior has burgeoned during
the past ten to fifteen years (Schildkraut & Kety 1967; Himwich
et al. 1967; Jouvet 1969). This paper reviews recent studies of the
effects of experimental alteration of brain serotonin concentrations on sexual behavior in a number of male mammals. The impetus for this line of investigation came principally from two findings: (1) the demonstration that parachlorophenylalanine (PCPA)
was effective in selectively lowering brain serotonin concentrations
through inhibition of tryptophan hydroxylase (Koe & Weissman
1966) and (2) the fortuitous observations that male rats and cats
treated with PCPA seemed to show increased sexual activity.

*Arthur Zitrin, M.D., New York University Medical Center.

†William C. Dement, M.D., Ph.D., and Jack D. Barchas, M.D., Stanford University
School of Medicine.

EXPERIMENTS WITH RATS

Male-Male Interactions

Shillito (1969, 1970) studied the effect of PCPA on social interaction of male rats after she had noticed that treated animals showed a loss of hair and shorter or absent vibrissae, presumably as a result of increased contact among the animals. She injected juvenile and adult rats intraperitoneally with 316 mg/kg of body weight. Single doses, or thrice-weekly administrations of PCPA in longer experiments, in young male rats, resulted in increased social interaction, such as chasing, rolling over, social grooming. In treated adult rats there occurred an increase in mounting behavior. The mounting behavior was reduced or abolished by treatment with 5-hydroxytryptophan, the serotonin precursor which can cross the blood-brain barrier. Shillito concluded that serotonin (5-hydroxytryptamine, 5-HT) inhibits sexual behavior in male rats. She suggested also that the increase in social interaction seen normally in juvenile rats may be the behavioral precursor of adult sexual behavior.

Tagliamonte et al. (1969) were led to study the effects of PCPA on sexual behavior of male rats after a serendipitous observation of "sexual excitement" in treated animals in the course of other work with the drug. They reported that the injection of 100 mg/kg of body weight of PCPA for four days induced "compulsive sexual activity," and that this behavior was enhanced when an injection of 80–100 mg/kg of the monoamine oxidase inhibitor, pargyline, was given with the PCPA. Animals were observed in groups of six for a period of twelve hours. None of the untreated controls exhibited sexual excitement during the observation period. Table 1 summarizes the results of their experiment. When animals treated with PCPA plus pargyline were injected with the serotonin precursor, L-5-hydroxytryptophan (25 mg/kg intravenously) all signs of sexual excitement disappeared within ten minutes. PCPA treatment lowered brain serotonin concentrations to less than 10 percent of those in controls, while norepinephrine and dopamine fell only slightly. The administration of pargyline to animals previously treated with PCPA resulted in accumulation of brain catecholamines but not serotonin. The catecholamine levels rose less than in animals receiving pargyline alone, and the authors

Table 1. *Effect of p-chlorophenylalanine (PCPA) alone and in combination with pargyline on sexual activity in male rats. p-chlorophenylalanine (100 mg/kg) injected intraperitoneally daily for 4 days*

Animals treated (No.)	Animals showing mounting behavior in 12 hours (No.)	Animals mounting at frequencies of		
		1–5 times (No.)	6–10 times (No.)	10 (No.)
p-chlorophenylalanine				
60	16	3	3	10
p-chlorophenylalanine plus pargyline				
80	58	4	16	38

Reprinted from Tagliamonte 1969.

conclude that **PCPA** also affects catecholamine levels to some degree. They postulated that the observed changes in sexual behavior were the consequence of the depletion of brain serotonin and of the secondary imbalance between 5-HT and catecholamine activity in the brain. They subsequently elaborated this view (Gessa et al. 1970) suggesting that both brain serotonin and catecholamines control sexual behavior in male animals, with serotonin inhibiting such behavior and catecholamines stimulating it.

In this later paper Gessa and his associates reported the behavior, in groups, of intact and castrated male rats treated with PCPA, PCPA plus testosterone, or testosterone alone. Testosterone was given as the enanthate (1–2 mg/kg, subcutaneously daily for four to five days). Table 2 summarizes the result of that experiment. They considered as sexually excited those animals that made at least one attempt to mount another male rat during the observation period of three hours. They concluded that the depletion of serotonin is associated with sexual excitement only in the presence of testosterone and, conversely, that testosterone produces little sexual stimulation in the presence of normal levels of serotonin in the brain. Sexual behavior in male animals is seen as activated by the action of testosterone in the central nervous system. However, this hypothesis must be considered in the light

Table 2. *Influence of castration and testosterone on compulsive sexual behavior in rats induced by p-chlorophenylalanine (PCPA)*

Rats	Percentage of animals mounting after treatment with		
	PCPA	PCPA + testosterone	Testosterone
Intact	27.5	100*	12.5
Castrated	0	80	0

*Sexual behavior lasted for several days.
Each drug combination was tested in forty animals.

Reprinted from Gessa 1970.

of the more recent findings by Shillito (1971) that a single inges-tion of PCPA induced mounting behavior in castrated rats as well as in rats which were both castrated and adrenalectomized.

In an experiment in which the conditions of the studies by Tagliamonte et al. (1969) and Gessa et al. (1970) were approxi-mated, Mitler et al. (in press) obtained results the trend of which generally agreed with those of the earlier work. However, even among the rats treated with PCPA plus testosterone, in whom mounting occurred most frequently, the findings were not as im-pressive as previously reported. Mounting frequencies were lower; tandem mounting and other behavior suggesting heightened sexual arousal were not observed. After several hours of post-treatment motor retardation, evidence of an increase in general excitability was seen in the PCPA-pargyline-treated animals. They showed fighting behavior and efforts to escape from the cage. Mitler sug-gests that differences between the results of his experiment and those of Tagliamonte and Gessa might be accounted for by several factors: (1) the small number of animals (six) in each group in his work, (2) differences in experimental design, and (3) differences in strain of experimental animals used.

Ahlenius et al. (in press) made casual observations of groups of male rats which had been treated with PCPA and pargyline in the doses employed by Tagliamonte. They saw no mounting among the males, nor any signs of increased aggressiveness, penile erection, or genital sniffing.

Male-Female Interactions

Sheard (1969) treated male and female rats with single intraperitoneal injections of 320 mg/kg of PCPA and tested specifically for changes in sexual and aggressive behavior. The rat under observation was placed in a cage for a thirty-minute period with a rat of the opposite sex and a white mouse (to test for muricidal tendencies). Beginning several hours after the injection male rats treated with PCPA showed an increase in mounting both with and without pelvic thrusting. Increased mounting activity was also shown by PCPA-treated female rats. An increase in aggressiveness in the animals that received PCPA was observed as well.

Whalen and Luttge (1970) tested the effects of PCPA and PCPA plus pargyline on the sexual behavior of male rats who were sexually experienced and vigorous copulators. Table 3 summarizes the result of their experiment. In satiation tests with receptive

Table 3. *Effects of p-chlorophenylalanine methyl ester (PCPA) and PCPA plus pargyline on the heterosexual behavior of male rats* *

Group	No. per ejaculation		Satiation		
	Mounts	Intro-missions	Mounts (No.)	Intro-missions (No.)	Ejacu-lations (No.)
Control: before PCPA	11.2 ± 1.5	7.1 ± 1.3	72.6 ± 7.3	46.0 ± 5.2	7.0 ± 0.9
PCPA**	11.3 ± 4.0	6.1 ± 1.0	55.2 ± 17.6	29.3 ± 3.8	5.0 ± 0.4
Control: after PCPA	9.0 ± 1.5	7.2 ± 1.0	51.6 ± 7.6	43.7 ± 5.6	6.1 ± 0.5
PCPA plus pargyline**	16.0 ± 5.3	6.8 ± 1.3	63.0 ± 12.6	34.8 ± 8.7	5.0 ± 0.7

*Numbers indicate the mean ± standard error of the number of mounting responses and intromissions which preceded each ejaculation and the total number of mounts, intromissions, and ejaculations which preceded sexual satiation.

**Scores for these tests do not include scores for an individual animal which failed to mate during the first thirty minutes of the test.

Reprinted from Whalen & Luttge 1970.

females neither PCPA nor PCPA plus pargyline increased the number of mounts, intromissions, or ejaculations before satiation was reached. Mean ejaculation frequencies were, in fact, slightly reduced during tests of treated animals, and in each of the two drug tests one male failed to ejaculate at all, a change the authors believe may have been due to the nonspecific stress of the treatment. Ejaculation latencies (the duration of the periods between the initial intromission and ejaculation) were not changed by treatment.

Reserpine has been shown to lower brain concentrations of both serotonin and catecholamines by interfering with tissue-binding mechanisms, exposing released amine to the degradation activity by monoamine oxidase (Schildkraut & Kety 1967). Dewsbury and Davis (1970) studied the effect of this drug on the copulatory behavior of male rats tested with receptive females. They reported that the animals showed a decrease in the matter of intromissions (intromission frequency) before ejaculation, and a shortening of the ejaculation latency in the second ejaculatory series. (A series is the test sequence from the first ejaculation to intromission.) They interpreted these results as indicating that reserpine facilitated copulatory performance and Dewsbury (1971) later suggested that the data are consistent with the hypothesis that high brain monoamine level inhibits ejaculation.

Salis and Dewsbury (1971) obtained results with PCPA treatment of rats similar to the reserpine effects reported from their laboratory. Ejaculation latencies were reduced, particularly in the second series, with a decrease in the intromission frequencies. These findings differ from those of Whalen and Luttge. Satiation tests were not performed, so that a comparison with the Whalen and Luttge experiment cannot be made with respect to that measure of performance.

Ahlenius et al. (in press), using the doses of PCPA and pargyline employed by Tagliamonte and his co-workers, also studied the effects of these drugs on the sexual behavior of rats known to be vigorous copulators. The results of their experiment differed from those of Whalen and Luttge, but were generally consistent with the findings of Salis and Dewsbury. Ejaculation latencies were shortened, while the number of mounts and intromissions preceding ejaculation remained unchanged. The number of intromissions per minute was therefore increased. Tests were discontinued after the first intromission of the second ejaculatory series, so that no data on performance in subsequent series or in satiation tests were obtained for comparison with the earlier work of Whalen and Luttge.

Sjoerdsma et al. (1970) reported an experiment with sexually sluggish male rats treated with PCPA, PCPA plus pargyline and pargyline alone. The animals were tested with receptive females for sixty minutes. A higher percentage (100 percent) of the rats treated with PCPA plus pargyline copulated than did those in the other drug groups. No data on latencies or frequencies of mounts, intromissions, and ejaculations were given.

Morden et al. (1968) divided male rats into groups of low, medium, and high copulators on the basis of consistent performance in baseline testing. Low copulators were treated for five to six days with a dose of PCPA known to markedly lower the concentration of brain serotonin. After the third or fourth day of treatment, these rats showed a significant increase in the mean number of ejaculations for the group in tests with receptive females. Scores before or after this period did not differ from performance before drug treatment. There were no significant changes in ejaculation latencies or intromission frequencies during the thirty-minute test period. The sexual behavior of rats that were medium and high copulators was not altered by PCPA.

EXPERIMENTS WITH CATS

Ferguson et al. (1970) conducted a number of behavioral observations and tests on male cats who were receiving chronic administration of PCPA. They reported that after three to five daily injections of 150 mg/kg of body weight, there was a display of pronounced mounting behavior in many of the animals. Stimulus objects were either intact or anesthetized male cats, or both. No animals were used as controls, but the temporal association of mounting behavior and PCPA treatment led the group to conclude that the drug specifically "released" or "induced" sexual behavior. Brain serotonin concentrations were lowered in the sample of treated cats that was sacrificed.

This conclusion was soon called into question, however, after an experiment on the effects of PCPA on copulatory behavior of male cats tested with receptive females performed by Zitrin and his collaborators (1970). Before PCPA treatment base-line observations were made of the behavior of a group of twelve male cats in separate tests with receptive female cats, intact males, anesthetized males, and a stuffed toy animal. All twelve males copulated with a receptive female within a few hours to several weeks after initial pre-drug testing. Also, prior to treatment with PCPA, ten cats with copulatory experience mounted or attempted to mount both unanesthetized and anesthetized males. The ten cats that displayed this behavior before injection of PCPA did so after drug administration. Two cats that did not mount other males before treatment failed to do so under the influence of the drug. No cat mounted the stuffed toy before or after PCPA.

Table 4 presents intromission frequencies for each of eight male cats on whom such data were obtained during pre-treatment and treatment tests with a receptive female. In the fifteen- or twenty-minute tests, six cats showed essentially no change and two exhibited some decrease under the drug. The difference in group averages was not statistically significant. In ninety-minute tests seven of eight males achieved fewer intromissions after PCPA treatment. Two cats who were "low copulators" before treatment showed no change in sexual behavior after PCPA injection. Other measures of sexual activity, such as time before the male's first grip of the female, mount, or intromission, were not significantly altered by PCPA in any of the twelve cats. Brain serotonin concentrations were determined in six cats and were found to be markedly reduced in all five areas of the brain assayed.

More recently, Aronson et al. (in preparation) gave PCPA to four adult male cats that had never been observed to mount or copulate with receptive females in regular observations over a one- to two-year period. Normal appearing genitalia and penile spines were present. After a series of base-line observations the cats were

Table 4. *Intromission frequencies before and after PCPA*

| Cat # | # Injections | Mean for standard tests | | | | Extended tests | |
| | | Before | | After | | | |
		Tests	Mean	Tests	Mean	Before	After
171	6	3	4.0	2	3.0	10	7
115	6	3	2.3	2	2.5	9	4
114	6	3	3.7	2	2.5	8	2
	8		—		—	10	9
119	6	3	2.7	2	2.5	7	9
118	8	3	1.0	2	1.0	3	2
173	8	3	0.7	2	0.5	1	1
151	8	3	2.0	1	2.0	5	5
150	8	3	2.0	1	2.0	8	7
Mean			2.30		2.0	6.77	5.11
			NS			$p < .05$	

Reprinted from Zitrin 1970.

given seven daily injections of PCPA methyl ester (100 mg/kg of body weight), with treatment tests starting after the third injection. No sexual behavior was induced by PCPA treatment. Following a recovery period 50-mg pellets of testosterone propionate were implanted subcutaneously in each animal. After a three- to four-week delay a second series of PCPA injections was instituted and the cats were retested as before. None of the animals showed any sexual activity or heightened sexual interest after the combined testosterone-PCPA treatment.

In a series of three, single blind validation studies by the Ferguson group other behavioral observations were eliminated in favor of focusing on sexual behavior, with the only test being a fifteen-minute exposure to an anesthetized male cat. Essentially no mounting behavior was observed during the base-line or injection period in PCPA animals or in controls (Dement, personal communication). In the most recent test, a number of elements that were present in their original study were reintroduced. The findings were generally negative, however. The reasons for the discrepancy between these results and those of the earlier experiment are not readily apparent and are the subject of continuing investigation by the group.

Hoyland and co-workers (1970) have administered PCPA orally to male and female kittens and adult cats and observed their behavior in groups. Doses ranged from 200 mg/kg to 600 mg/kg in single doses and 600–800 mg/kg in two divided doses. Two of five male kittens and seven of ten adult male cats started mounting other males between forty-eight and seventy-two hours after the first dose of PCPA. Increased sexual behavior in the treated female adult and kittens was limited to rubbing and treading. When 5-HTP (5 mg/kg) was injected intraperitoneally into the cats treated with PCPA, all unusual behavior of both males and females was reported to have ceased. The authors concluded that serotonin appears to act as an inhibitor of sexual behavior in male cats and, to some extent, in females as well.

EXPERIMENTS WITH RABBITS

Tagliamonte et al. (1969) and Sjoerdsma et al. (1970) have indicated that rabbits are more sensitive than any other animal they have tested to the "sexual stimulant effect" of PCPA. The effects were found to last longer than in rats, and the mounting of other animal species by rabbits treated with PCPA was observed. Quantitative data on the behavior of the rabbits treated with PCPA have not yet been reported by these investigators.

EXPERIMENTS WITH MONKEYS

Perachio and Marr (in preparation) have performed thirteen experiments on five rhesus monkeys in which they studied the effect of a single nasogastric administration of 400 mg/kg of PCPA on the animals' sexual behavior. Rhesus monkeys are multiple mounters with a number of intromissions taking place before ejaculation occurs. The authors' data suggested that a decrease in the sequence duration (time from first mount with intromission to time of the last mount leading to ejaculation) occurred about seventy-two hours after the injection. Shorter intermount intervals also occurred in some animals. The combination of these results was interpreted by the authors as possibly suggestive of an increase in sexual behavior. However, no consistent concomitant increase in the number of intromissions per sixty-minute observation period was observed, nor was there a change in the interval between the start of the test and the first intromission. In addition, with repeated measures on the same animal the effects of PCPA were inconsistent.

In some exploratory work in Dement's laboratory (Dement, personal communication) two male rhesus monkeys were housed individually and studied during eleven days of PCPA treatment. Observations included periodic videotaping of the animals. No change in masturbatory behavior of the monkeys was noted. In another experiment in the same laboratory PCPA was given to one male and two female adolescent monkeys. No changes in sexual behavior or in dominance patterns were observed.

PCPA IN MAN

PCPA has been employed by a number of investigators in the treatment of the carcinoid syndrome (Engelman et al. 1967; Satterlee et al. 1970), a condition in which there is increased production of serotonin. Results of the treatment of sixteen cases have recently been summarized (Sjoerdsma et al. 1970). Using a PCPA-placebo protocol under double-blind conditions Carpenter carefully studied the responses to the drug of seven such patients. A number of behavioral changes occurred with PCPA treatment, including depression, anxiety, restlessness, irritability, crying, and agitation. The investigator regarded them as nonspecific emotional responses. Neither the behavior nor the thought content of the patients suggested heightened sexual interest and there was no change in their self-rated interest in sex during the treatment.

PCPA has also been administered to normal human volunteers (Cremata & Koe 1966, 1968). A variety of symptoms were noted as side effects of the drug including fatigue, dizziness, nausea, uneasiness, fullness in the head, headache, paresthesias, and constipation. There was no report of any increase in sexual interest, although this would be exceedingly difficult to evaluate in the group of prison inmates who comprised the volunteer sample.

DISCUSSION

The studies of PCPA and sexual behavior are impressive and intriguing. However, they present a formidable challenge to the reviewer who attempts to interpret their findings and to reconcile the differences among them.

Even in experiments using the same species each of the studies differs substantially from the others, so that precise comparisons are impossible. Differences include method of assessing sexual performance, age and strain of animals, form and dose of drug used, method of drug administration, previous sexual experience and normal performance levels of the subjects, use of controls, and other design variables.

The data of Tagliamonte et al., Gessa et al., Shillito, and Mitler support the conclusion that PCPA and PCPA plus pargyline increase mounting of adult male rats by treated males tested in groups. Sheard's experiment shows that PCPA-treated male rats will mount female rats, even when the latter are not receptive, and that PCPA may induce the male mounting pattern in the females as well. The work of Dewsbury et al. and Ahlenius et al. provides evidence that in tests with estrous females, PCPA-treated male rats show a decrease in ejaculatory latency and a decrease in intermount intervals. Whether such measures can be considered an enhancement of sexual performance is a matter of definition. So far no workers other than Morden et al. have reported an increase in ejaculatory frequency in rats treated with PCPA. Whalen and Luttge found no change in the sexual performance of rats treated with PCPA plus pargyline; mount, intromission, and ejaculation frequencies were unchanged in satiation tests, and latencies were not significantly altered.

Of the few studies of the effects of PCPA on sexual behavior of cats only the results of Hoyland et al. can now be considered as positive. However, their findings will doubtless stimulate efforts at validation with the use of more sophisticated behavioral techniques than they employed. Lacking in their report is precise information on the ages of their cats, detailed descriptions of the behavior of the treated kittens, adequate base-line observations, and quantitative data of sexual behavior in standardized test situations.

Results from the studies of monkeys are regarded by the authors as preliminary, and further experiments are being done. The few reports of the effect of PCPA on human sexual behavior have been negative.

The hypothesis that brain serotonin inhibits sexual behavior in male animals and that its depletion produces enhanced sexual performance has been proposed by all investigators who have reported positive results with PCPA. Abolition of the behavior after 5-HTP injection has been regarded as strongly supportive of this theory. However, alternative possibilities must also be considered. It is now known that PCPA is not as selective in its action on brain serotonin alone as was formerly believed. Although Koe and Weissman reported only a slight decrease in brain catecholamines after PCPA treatment of rats, Welch and Welch (1967) found a decline in brain noradrenaline concentrations in some strains of mice given the drug. Stolk et al. (1969) have found as much as 20 percent reductions in norepinephrine and dopamine levels in rats treated with PCPA. Whereas norepinephrine turnover was decreased only slightly, brain dopamine turnover was increased by PCPA. However, Volicer (1969) did not find any change in the turnover rate of brain catecholamines in rats after PCPA treatment. There is also suggestive evidence that another compound may be formed in the PCPA-treated animals which might account for the false positive nin-hydrin test for serotonin (Dement, personal communication). There are species differences in the responses to PCPA. The drug does not appear to inhibit brain serotonin synthesis in mice to the degree that it does in rats, and PCPA may have different effects on tryptophan hydroxylase from different tissues (Deguchi & Barchas, in press).

The possibility that PCPA causes behavioral effects unrelated to lowered brain serotonin is suggested by experiments in which the equivalent depletion of brain serotonin levels in rats and mice resulted in a decrease in spontaneous motor activity in the rats only (Volicer 1969). Tenen (1967) had earlier shown that the depression of locomotor activity in rats caused by PCPA could not be reversed by 5-HTP, although such an interpretation is complicated by the fact that 5-HTP itself causes some central nervous system depression.

Stark et al. (1970) have demonstrated a dissociation of the effects of PCPA on brain serotonin and self-stimulation for a reward in rats and dogs with hypothalamus-implanted electrodes. PCPA depressed self-stimulation in both species and the effect was unrelated to the lowering of brain serotonin in those species.

Effects of PCPA on biological systems other than those having to do with sexual behavior have been demonstrated. In some species it may cause a transitory insomnia, while in others it causes no change in sleep patterns. PCPA increases sensitivity of rats to pain (Tenen 1967), the likely basis for the faster acquisition of a conditioned avoidance response after the drug administration in this species. Varying degrees of ataxia in some PCPA-treated cats have been noted by all those who have studied the effects of the drug in this species. The basis for this change is not clear.

The capacity of 5-HTP to cause central nervous system depression raises the question of the degree to which its effect in abolishing the sexual behavior of PCPA-treated animals may be a nonspecific consequence of sedation. The effect is a dose-related phenomenon but one difficult to titrate with accuracy so that an interpretation of the role of 5-HTP in PCPA-treated animals should be made with circumspection.

Unpublished observations made recently by Goldstein (personal communication) of rats treated with phenylethylamine and the monoamine oxidase inhibitor catron bear a resemblance to some PCPA effects. In rats injected intraperitoneally with 20–100 mg/kg of body weight of phenylethylamine plus 10 mg/kg of catron, a variety of symptoms was manifested. These included fighting behavior, tremulousness, piloerection, either increased or decreased motor activity, and spontaneous seminal emissions. The picture was one of general autonomic stimulation and heightened arousal.

Sjoerdsma (1970) studied the acute effect of PCPA metabolites, p-chlorophenylethylamine and p-chlorophenylpyruvic acid, in male rats and observed no sexual excitement in the treated animals. No other effects of these compounds were reported.

The possibility that phenylethylamine is formed as a metabolite of PCPA and is responsible for some of the effects observed after PCPA must be considered. In some situations, as when animals are grouped, the general arousal of the organism may lead to increased mounting frequency. An increase in general responsiveness of the animals may also account for the decrease in ejaculation latencies observed by some workers.

The difficulties in assessing change in sexual performance of animals as a function of a particular variable are frequently under-estimated. In emphasizing the need for methodological care in such studies Beach (1967) has stated: "It is impossible to exagger-ate the importance of establishing 'preoperative norms' in every study that involves manipulation of the nervous system and de-scription of postoperative behavior (p. 307)." The establishment of stable base-line measures and a recognition of the varied be-havior of which a particular species is normally capable are essen-tial. The relative ease with which homosexual behavior or the mounting of other species can be elicited in normal cats under-scores the danger of using the mere display of such behavior as indicators of enhanced sexual performance.

The possibility that subtle forms of experimenter bias may influence the behavior of animal subjects is well illustrated by the experience of Hagamen and Zitzmann (1959). After observing the mounting of different species and inanimate objects by normal male cats, they found: "Our ability to elicit this behavior in-creased sharply once we realized it could occur (p. 388)."

The sexual behavior of normal male rats is not less susceptible to a variety of influences which may easily be overlooked. Larsson (1970), describing the mating of the male rat, observed: "Rela-tively little attention has been paid to the possibility that stimuli other than those emanating from the mating partner influence the sexual behavior. Yet daily laboratory practice suggests that even minor variations in the experimental procedure may greatly influ-ence the mating performance" (p. 339).

The possibility that brain serotonin plays a role in male sexual behavior is clearly supported by some of the animal experiments reported here. But additional studies will be required to establish its crucial function more definitely and to delineate the precise nature of that role.

REFERENCES

Ahlenius, S., Eriksson, H., Larsson, K., Modigh, K., & Sodersten, P. Mating behavior in the male rat treated with *p*-chlorophenylalanine methyl ester alone and in combination with pargyline. *Psychopharmacol* 1971, 20: 383–88.

Aronson, L. R., Cooper, M., & Zitrin, A. The effect of *p*-chlorophenylalanine on non-copulating cats. In preparation.

Beach, F. A. Cerebral and hormonal control of reflexive mechanisms involved in copulatory behavior. *Physiol. Rev.* 1967, 47: 289–316.

Cremata, V. Y., & Koe, B. K. Clinical-pharmacological evaluation of *p*-chlorophenylalanine: a new serotonin-depleting agent. *Clin. Pharmacol. Ther.* 1966, 7: 768–76.

———. Clinical and biochemical effects of fenclonine: a serotonin depletor. *Dis. Nerv. System* 1968, 29: 147–52.

Deguchi, T., & Barchas, J. D. Effect of *p*Chlorophenylalanine on hydroxylation of tryptophan in pineal and brain of rats. *Molecular Pharm.* In press.

Dement, W. C. Personal communication.

Dewsbury, D. A., & Davis, H. N., Jr. Effects of reserpine on copulatory behavior of male rats. *Physiol. and Behavior* 1970, 5: 1331–1333.

Dewsbury, D. A. Copulatory behavior of male rats following reserpine administration. *Psychonomic Sci.* 1971, 22: 177–79.

Engelman, K., Lovenberg, W., & Sjoerdsma, A. Inhibition of serotonin synthesis by para-chlorophenylalanine in patients with the carcinoid syndrome. *New Eng. J. Med.* 1967, 277: 1103–08.

Ferguson, J., Henricksen, S., Cohen, H., Mitchell, G., Barchas, J., & Dement, W. "Hypersexuality" and behavioral changes in cats caused by administration of *p*-chlorophenylalanine. *Science* 1970, 168: 499–501.

Gessa, G. L., Tagliamonte, A., Tagliamonte, P., & Brodie, B. B. Essential role of testosterone in the sexual stimulation induced by *p*-chlorophenylalanine in male animals. *Nature* 1970, 227: 616–617.

Goldstein, M. Personal communication.

Hagemen, W. D., & Zitzmann, E. K. "Hypersexual" activity in normal male cats. *Anat. Rec.* 1959, 133: 388.

Himwich, H. E., Kety, S. S., & Smythies, J. R. (eds.), *Amines and schizophrenia*. New York: Pergamon Press, 1967.

Hoyland, V. J., Shillito, E. E., & Vogt, M. The effect of p-cholorophenylala-nine on the behaviour of cats. *Brit. J. Pharmacol.* 1970, 40, 659–67.

Jouvet, M. Biogenic amines and the states of sleep. *Science* 1969, 163: 32–40.

Koe, B. K., & Weissman, A. p-Chlorophenylalanine: a specific depletor of brain serotonin. *J. Pharmacol. Exp. Ther.* 1966, 154: 499–516.

Larsson, K. Mating behavior in the male rat. In *Development and evolution of behavior.* San Francisco: W. H. Freeman & Co., 1970, pp. 337–52.

Mitler, M. M., Morden, B., Levine, S., & Dement, W. The effects of Para-chlorophenylalanine on the mating behavior of male rats. *Physiol. and Behavior.* In press.

Morden, B., Mullins, R., Levine, S., & Dement, W. Effect of REMS depriva-tion on the mating behavior of male rats. Presentation at the 8th annual meeting A.P.S.S., March 1968, Denver, Colo.

Perachio, A. A., & Marr, L. The effect of p-chlorophenylalanine on primate sexual behavior. In preparation.

Salis, P. J., & Dewsbury, D. A. The effects of p-chlorophenylalanine on copu-latory behavior of male rats. *Nature* 1971, 232: 400–1.

Satterlee, W. G., Serpick, A., & Bianchine, J. R. The carcinoid syndrome: chronic treatment with *para*chlorophenylalanine. *Ann. Int. Med.* 1970, 72: 919–21.

Schildkraut, J. J., & Kety, S. S. Biogenic amines and emotion. *Science* 1967, 156: 21–30.

Sheard, M. The effect of p-chlorophenylalanine on behavior in rats: relation to brain serotonin and 5-hydroxyindolacetic acid. *Brain Res.* 1969, 15: 524–28.

Shillito, E. E. The effect of p-chlorophenylalanine on social interactions of male rats. *Brit. J. Pharmacol.* 1969, 36: 193P–94P.

———. The effect of *para*chlorophenylalanine on social interaction of male rats. *Brit. J. Pharmacol.* 1970, 38: 305–15.

———. Effect of *para*chlorophenylalanine on the behaviour of castrated male rats. *Brit. J. Pharmacol.* 1971, 41: 404P.

Sjoerdsma, A. (moderator), Lovenberg, W., Engelman, K., Carpenter, W. T., Wyatt, R. J., & Gessa, G. L. Serotonin now: clinical implications of in-hibiting its synthesis with *para*-chlorophenylalanine *Ann. Int. Med.* 1970, 73: 607–29.

Stark, P., Fuller, R. W., Hartley, L. W., Schaffer, R. J., & Turk, J. A., Dissoci-ation of the effects of p-chlorophenylalanine on self-stimulation and on brain serotonin. *Life Sciences* 1970, 9: 41–48.

Stolk, J., Barchas, J., Dement, W., & Shanberg, S. Brain catecholamine metabolism following *para*-chlorophenylalanine treatment. *Pharmacologist* 1969, 11: 258.

Tagliamonte, A., Tagliamonte, P., Gessa, G. L., & Brodie, B. B. Compulsive sexual activity induced by *p*-chlorophenylalanine in normal and pinealectomized male rats. *Science* 1969, 166: 1433–35.

Tenen, S. S. The effects of *p*-chlorophenylalanine, a serotonin depletor, on avoidance acquisition, pain sensitivity and related behavior in the rat. *Psychopharmacol.* (Berl.) 1967, 10: 204–19.

Volicer, L. Correlation between behavioral and biochemical effects of *p*-chlorophenylalanine in mice and rats. *Int. J. Neuropharmacol.* 1969, 8: 361–64.

Welch, A. S., & Welch, B. L. Effect of *p*-chlorophenylalanine on brain noradrenaline in mice. *J. Pharm. Pharmac.* 1967, 19: 632–33.

Whalen, R. E., & Luttge, W. G. *p*-chlorophenylalanine methyl ester: an aphrodisiac? *Science* 1970, 169: 1000–01.

Zitrin, A., Beach, F. A., Barchas, J. D., & Dement, W. C. Sexual behavior of male cats after administration of parachlorophenylalanine. *Science* 1970, 170: 868–70.

chapter 17

Psychoanalysis and Physical Intervention in the Brain: The Mind-Body Problem Again

Robert J. Stoller*

For over two millennia the mind (soul)-body problem has stirred philosophers. While not listed as one of the "Critical Issues in Contemporary Sexual Behavior," it still overshadows this meeting. Others here can properly omit a consideration of this problem, but having been assigned this subject, I must continue the discussion.

Recall the centuries of brooding over monism versus dualism, interactionalism, idealism, psychophysical parallelism, double-aspect theory, epiphenomenalism. The dreary history of these ruminations about mind-body demonstrates that a philosopher, like a scientist, not only is driven to ask questions that simply cannot yet be answered but also credits his superb mind with sufficient power to give the answers without using demonstrable data. Magic, rather than the slow, grubby process of collecting

*Robert J. Stoller, M.D., UCLA School of Medicine, Los Angeles, California.

facts, is his exhilarating style. Philosophizing, alone, does not contribute particularly to scientific knowledge.

In our business, the "psychologizers" do this with their cathexes, identifications, and egos while the "biologizers" play the game when they postulate influences of genes yet undiscovered or invent hypothetical centers and functions of the central nervous system. Hidden behind these concepts is our megalomania that we can solve problems by thinking in the absence of hard work, that is, scientific labor. Why cannot both psychological and biological investigators simply collect their exciting new data and forego the temptation of the grand unifying answer?

SCIENCE AND PHILOSOPHY

From this viewpoint of trying to keep brain concepts separate from mind concepts and the nature-nurture issue unresolved until *data* permit linkage, I would thank Dr. Epstein for his fascinating findings that connect fetishism with demonstrable organic brain disease. He forces questions upon us, the answers to which will tell us more about the brain and its mind. We ask him to continue so that in time we shall know better the frequency and variety of disordered brain function that accompany specific manifestations of sexual psychopathology. We shall be restless, however, until he and his colleagues in neurophysiology can show us the location of the brain pathology, its pathophysiological nature, and the direct connections between the pathophysiology and the psychopathology. In the meanwhile, we will be patient, knowing that the answers may lie years and many false turns ahead.

It might be prudent, however, to de-emphasize explanations that do not work without the invention of as yet undemonstrated foci and forces, although these may provide guidelines for further research. For now, it is no small thing that you and others have seen several patients in whom fetishism and a specific brain lesion are closely linked. In these cases we can believe with you that the psychopathology would not have appeared had the brain continued undiseased, that is, physiologically normal. But we become intensely interested in the larger question: Is the usual case of fetishism due to a diseased brain or to a disordered life history?

Perhaps all fetishism, and as Dr. Epstein implied, all sexual psychopathology is rather independent of life experience. He states: "This 'reflex' type of response to the fetish object is a characteristic of all fetishists and is probably, in all instances, related to, even though by no means always overtly, clinical epileptic phenomena." His cases, however, do not confim or even suggest it. They actually suggest that fetishism, transvestism, transsexualism, homosexuality, exhibitionism, or impotence have two possible etiologies: one that is set off inside a scarred brain and one which, of course using the brain, is a response primarily to psychological experience. Dr. Epstein is creeping up on the idea that fetishism is epileptic. If so, what are we to think of the uncounted millions of American males who are turned on by women's breasts—or other cultures wherein the males en masse are not? Until the neurophysiologists show us the foci, distinguish their actions from the actions of other foci, or define the foci's functions, let us leave the question open whether all fetishists have such brain pathology. Otherwise, it is still just the same old philosophy decked out in biological words.

And let no one tell us with ecumenical benignity that for us moderns it is no longer significant to worry if something is produced by the brain or by environmental forces because, of course, both always interact. While we double-aspect folk believe there is no mind without brain and there is no developed neurophysiology without continual environmental impingement, some of us still believe that at times nature predominates (as in epilepsy), and at other times nurture does (as when gentlemen prefer blondes). As Freud (1915) put it: "It is not easy to estimate the relative efficacy of the constitutional and accidental factors. In theory one is always inclined to overestimate the former; therapeutic practice emphasizes the importance of the latter. It should, however, on no account be forgotten that the relation between the two is a cooperative and not a mutually exclusive one. The constitutional factor must await experiences before it can make itself felt; the accidental factor must have a constitutional basis in order to come into operation. To cover the majority of cases we can picture what has been described as a 'complemental series,' in which the diminishing intensity of one factor is balanced by the increasing intensity of the other; there is, however, no reason to deny the existence of extreme cases at the two ends of the series" (pp. 239-40).

It is the style among sophisticates these days to brush aside the nature-nurture controversy as antiquated. Granting that the issue is not an either-or, I still hope we do not wash away the differences. It really is not the same if a man becomes sexually excited by an impulse fired from an electrode sunk in his limbic system, by a pretty girl, or by women's clothes. We all believe that mind cannot exist without brain and that mind can be directly modified by brain stimulation. But I hope no one seriously thinks one's past life does not usually influence one's present behavior. That a medical treatment may quite ignore this past, go directly to the brain and succeed in changing behavior does not disprove the importance of that past experience in producing the behavior. It may only indicate the obvious—that the brain is the final common pathway.

Let my research on the overwhelming desire to be a member of the opposite sex serve as an example. Following Money's lead (Money & Pollit 1964), my colleagues and I have been impressed that an unexpected number of hypogonadal males give histories reaching back into earliest childhood of having wished to be females and, having behaved throughout their lives in a very feminine manner, ultimately requesting sex transformation (Baker & Stoller 1968). On the other hand, we have been equally impressed to find in every one of the most feminine males, children and adults, whom we have studied and who have no demonstrable biological abnormality, the same family dynamics present from infancy on. And we have not found this family constellation in fetishistic cross-dressers, effeminate homosexuals, or people without gross gender abnormalities (Stoller 1968). We presume if we see such precise intrafamily dynamics time after time in these extremely feminine males (transsexuals) and that these dynamics are absent in the controls, these dynamics are etiological. Thus, there may be two very different clusters of causes of a desire to become a member of the opposite sex, one primarily biological and the other primarily psychological. Of course, in the particular patient who wishes he were a female, the neurophysiology of his wishing may use the same chemicals and circuits whether he is an

XXY Klinefelter's or the victim since infancy of a depressed, bisexual, over-loving mother and a psychologically absent father.

So let us not yet decide, on the basis of a few cases in which fetishism and gross brain disease are directly linked, that all fetishists suffer organic brain disease, just as we should not yet believe that all sexual excitement in humans can be explained on the basis of disordered limbic system function alone, or that anxiety is a brain disease, an adrenal disease, or a thyroid disease.

We cannot avoid the mind-body problem just because we are tired of it. But we can be patient, continue to explore the brain and the mind, and let the explorations in each area be the best we possibly can do. Some day the neurophysiologists will probably close the gap, showing us that mind is to brain as, say, movement is to muscle. We probably won't live to see much linkage between the two, but in our disappointment at that probability, let us not press our data too hard to make them look like one piece. The bridges are still too flimsy; every time we step on the newest one it collapses.

SCIENCE AND ETHICS

Dr. Laschet's paper is also dominated by a philosophic problem, this time not scientific but moral—the freedom of the individual. Of all the goals of psychoanalytic doctrine, the most profound may be that psychoanalytic treatment free people from the unnecessary enslavement of unconscious forces. The analyst feels not only that the end result of his treatment may be greater freedom for his patient but also that *the struggle itself*, the painful, grinding, working-through process of the analysis of the transference (that distortion by the past of one's capacity to know present reality), exemplifies a quality—persistent, informed courage—that is perhaps the most admirable a human may attain. That is why we analysts feel a bit defeated when drugs, hypnosis, conditioning, implanted electrodes, or psychosurgery are used to modify thoughts, affects, and behavior. These techniques bypass freedom, that rare and lovely acquisition.

But unfortunately this ideal is often modified; patients' welfare demands short-cuts. Sometimes these are used sparingly only to preserve the atmosphere of analysis, and sometimes they are necessary because analysis is not indicated—experience has shown that it fails with certain patients. I repeat these familiar problems in the art of treatment to emphasize the moral issue of the acquisition and development of free will latent in discussions of treatment choice.

Having now touched on psychoanalysis, I can confront with difficulty the assigned title: "Compatibility of Psychoanalytic Doctrine with Hormonal and Surgical Intervention in Psychosexual Pathology. The problem is with the word doctrine. Does one mean psychoanalytic theory, the moral positions taken by psychoanalysts, doctrine as opposed to science, psychoanalysis as religion and faith, or an opinion that psychoanalysts are doctrinally opposed to the use of physical therapies? Perhaps that title indicates someone's belief—if I can let paranoia light my way—that psychoanalysis is more philosophy than science and that it can take on a defensive fervor when expressing the purity of its humanism. Certainly by temperament as well as by doctrine, most analysts prefer therapeutic results achieved without physical treatments and scientific results without experimentation, in the sense that experimentation is used by most scientists.

More specifically, in the treatment of sexual psychopathologies almost all writings by analysts except Freud presume psychoanalysis is the treatment of choice. I can think of no proclaimed psychoanalytic expert in the perversions as pessimistic about psychoanalytic treatment as was Freud, nor any other expert who so vigorously maintained that perversions and disorders of gender identity have biological origins. Finally, perhaps no other analytic expert besides Freud so truly felt that the future would bring biological treatments to alter the perversions. So I presume that it is not Freud who is the doctrinaire but the psychoanalytic literature since his time. Disagreeing with its consensus that psychoanalysis is the only proper treatment for sexual psychopathology, I believe that there are other treatments which also may help and that in the treatment of those identity disorders called perversions the psychoanalytic literature is rich in dynamics and poor in proof of efficacy. So I am not a fair representative of that doctrine.

Perhaps what the title asks is this: What do you as an analyst think of treating these patients by physical methods? I answer for myself, not for psychoanalysis. If there is a treatment that is alleged to work, let us listen. If it is alleged that the treatment is better than those presently used, let us listen closely. And if it is shown that the treatment is the best, let us use it. Let us never rail against a treatment because it is incompatible with our private beliefs and public theories. In return, we shall also ask of all treators that they not confuse the success of their treatment with the proof of a theory. The two may be related, but then again they may not.

We must respect the vital necessity that out treatment not harm the patient. (We shall hope that the electrodes that we are told are burning out homosexuality are not also burning out too much else.) Then we can begin arguing whether our treatment or someone else's is better; fortunately, time and patience eventually answer that. For the perversions, that is, the organized personality aberrations we call perversions, not the ubiquitous, occasional, perverse behavior with which analysis is often successful, I believe that time has spoken: psychoanalysis has been unsuccessful, except perhaps in a modest, but gratifying number of well-selected homosexuals. It is time now for us analysts to encourage ungrudgingly the use of other therapies, not maintaining that our sophisticated theory gives us the right to look down on other treatments. Obviously, there must be absolutely no breach in the rule that the patient understand the treatment and freely consent to it* and that there must be a real chance of the treatment helping. Let us review conditions in which hormonal and surgical intervention have been recommended. They can be divided into those cases with demonstrable biological abnormality and those without.

Somatic Disorders: Intersexuality

The technique of and indications for hormonal and surgical interventions in the various intersexual conditions, such as Kline-

---

*I shall not dwell on the principle that no one, not even a prisoner, should be forced to submit to treatment.

felter's syndrome, Turner's syndrome, adrenogenital syndrome, testicular feminization syndrome, the various forms of genital hermaphroditism, and the like need not concern us here. More pertinent now is the question: When should we assist in transforming such patients' bodies to conform with one sex or the other? To be brief, I agree with the position of Money et al. (1955): we all feel strongly that the main criterion is the patient's identity. When adequate evaluation of his sense of belonging to the male or female sex and of his masculinity and femininity has been accomplished, what do we conclude the patient thinks of himself? For instance, when he feels himself unequivocally a male, then physical modifications should aim to approximate his body more closely to that sense of maleness, regardless of the physical state. When a gender identity has not yet developed, as in the newborn, then the decision should be made according to which body is easier to create, and the answer to that is usually female. When the years of childhood have passed with no decision made and the child (or adult) feels himself to be neither male nor female but a freakish combination of both, then whatever anatomical changes are made will probably not disturb him unduly.

Non-somatic Disorders

Transsexualism. Rather than reviewing a literature that reveals widespread opinions, I would prefer to state my own. The diagnosis of transsexualism should be reserved only for those males who are the most feminine of males, and those females who are the most masculine of females. The patients should have been this way since earliest childhood, and they should not have wavered in their resolve to change their sex since that time. They should never have found their own bodies, especially their genitals, satisfying; this would include their never having been fetishistic. Picking from the increasing number of patients who announce to us that they are transsexual, only those very few who fulfill the above criteria, I believe, should be permitted to "transform" their bodies to approximate those of the opposite sex. Patients so transformed do well subsequently, though I am uneasy that as the years pass, some may become dissatisfied if not despairing. If there were a psychotherapy that could grant them a gender identity compatible with their bodies, that would be the treatment of choice. However, despite the stance taken by an occasional psychoanalyst that such patients should be analyzed, I believe these patients cannot be; none has been reported.

When one has seen such patients, he will no longer doubt the condition exists and that it can be differentiated from other gender disorders, such as fetishistic cross-dressing and effeminate homosexuality. When one has seen the outcomes of hormonal and surgical intervention in such people, one no longer doubts the treatment is effective. I really do not care if this is "compatible with psychoanalytic doctrine." The decision to assist these desperate people must be made outside of doctrine.

Sexual Deviations. We are now into issues upon which Dr. Laschet touches. Her argument should be this: If the patient, fully informed of the nature of the treatment, its complications, and the possibility of its producing improvement, consents; if it is the patient who has defined what is improvement, not his therapist and not society; if there is evidence of its success independent of placebo effects; if, especially, the treatment does not threaten the patient's physical health, or, if it might, that the induced disorder is reversible; and if other treatments of the condition are not clearly more successful, then the treatment can be used. I believe the above are obvious; our arguments should only arise to the degree that these criteria are not fulfilled.

In presenting ethical concerns and treatment biases, I indicate a belief that where psychoanalysis has not done well enough to establish itself as the treatment of choice, other safe treatments can compete and perhaps be favored. Among those may be Dr. Laschet's. If others, treating larger numbers of patients as she has, are as successful, we shall have a fine new treatment. If time bears her out, we shall be reassured because psychosis, new perversions, or other severe psychic manifestations will not have replaced the old condition; the anti-androgen will not have caused a new somatic disease, such as a disorder of another part of the endocrine system or brain; and its effects will have been shown as reversible as preliminary reports indicate. When it is proven that the destructive perversion is permanently gone, that endocrine function has returned to normal, and that gratifying sexual practices replace the old perversion and do not endanger others or the patient, then a major new psychiatric treatment may be proclaimed. All we can do now is await the necessary extensive studies and hope. If this hope is borne out, even the analyst who is deprived of a few patients will be pleased, for people formerly driven by impulses beyond their control will have regained some of that freedom which is the goal of our ethics.

SCIENCE AND LOGIC

A third philosophic issue is raised by the paper of Dr. Zitrin and his colleagues: logic as a scientific tool. What I shall say now is only an extension of ideas expressed earlier about Dr. Epstein's paper when he moved from a few cases toward a generalized theory of fetishism.

Dr. Zitrin and his colleagues are obviously interested in more than vigorously copulating rats and cats; they are interested in studying man. So some of us prepare to flinch for fear we shall again be told that finding a brain mechanism in an ascending evolutionary scale of animals shows that this mechanism is at work in man; we dread being told that sexual behavior is determined by inborn biological mechanisms and that learning is only an illusory determinant. Once again we worry about workers tempted to save time in the search to find where brain becomes mind; if we can link man's mind with cat's brain, we won't have to face the presently almost insuperable problem of studying the living human brain. But these authors have not said that nor are they habituated to that style in other papers. Instead, their work exemplifies that most admirable quality—the slow, steady, patient, careful exploration of reality that typifies the scientific method.

It is amusing to see the response of my analytic colleagues and I myself at an analytic meeting when someone reads a paper with clear-cut facts. Almost always, this is a friendly, nonanalyst or an analyst doing nonanalytic work, such as observing infants, studying the physiology of dreams, or living amongst alien people. If his data confirm an analytic postulate, there is a sense of pride, admiration, and relief in the audience as compared to the dense, painful, convoluted emotions stirred up by purely analytic papers. We enjoy the rare and heady feeling of honest data. It is too bad that these delights are ours only when the data confirm, not when they challenge, psychoanalytic concepts.

But surely no less addled than some analysts' propensity for speculation are some biologists' compulsion to hide speculations in anatomical or chemical hypotheses. The animal fallacy takes many forms; here is one with which you are familiar. Homosexuality, so they say, is found in many species of animals. This tendency being so widely distributed among the species, one can logically expect that its presence in man is one more instance. Therefore, a theory of homosexuality as learned or due to attempted resolution of childhood conflict is redundant, or, if we are to be really exquisite, supposedly fails the test of Occam's Razor. But when we return to data and stop torturing evolutionary theory, we find that what we call homosexuality in animals is not at all what we see in man. Animals other than man do not choose another of the same sex for intercourse, though they occasionally mount one haphazardly for a moment or languidly lick each other's genitals.

Still, we are confronted with underlying brain mechanisms. REM deprived or PCPA stimulated rats and cats certainly are using something in their brains that propels their homosexual attack. In time we shall demonstrate this capacity in other animals. That done, we shall find the affected brain center in these species, find it in man, and then by stimulating this center drive men to homosexual attacks. Does this prove that homosexuality is a brain disease? If we lower the dosage a trifle, will the brain center produce cruising of tea rooms, limp wrists, interior decorating, poetry, and a preference for passive anal intercourse? In the meantime, I prefer the cautious, modest route Dr. Zitrin and his colleagues take. It is not romantic, but it is careful.

There is no need to summarize. I can end now simply by again asking that, in the area of sexual behavior, where mind and body move each other perhaps more than any other, we diligently collect, examine, and report data and try to forgo the megalomania of premature unifying theory.

REFERENCES

Baker, H. J., & Stoller R. J. Can a biological force contribute to gender identity? *Am. J. Psychiat.* 1968, 124: 1653-58.

Freud, S. Drei abhandlungen zur sexual theorie (3rd ed.). Leipzig and Vienna: Deuticke, 1915. Quoted from: Freud, S. Three essays on the theory of sexuality. In: *The Standard edition of the complete works of Sigmund Freud*, vol. 7. Translated by J. Strachey. London: Hogarth, 1953.

Money, J., Hampson, J. G., & Hampson, J. L. Hermaphroditism: recommendations concerning assignment of sex, change of sex and psychological management. *Bull. Johns Hopkins Hosp.* 1955, 97: 284–300.

Money, J., & Pollit, E. Cytogenetic and psychosexual ambiguity. *Arch. Gen. Psychiat.* 1964, 11: 589–95.

Stoller, R. J. *Sex and gender*. New York: Science House, 1968.

chapter 18

Twenty-five Boys with Atypical Gender Identity: A Behavioral Summary[*]

Richard Green[†]

Transsexualism and homosexuality are two patterns of sexual expression which do not conform to the societal norm. These patterns deviate with respect to the sex role in which one wants to live (opposite to one's genital anatomy) and the sex of one's preferred sexual partner (same. genital anatomy) (Stoller 1968; Green & Money 1969).

Research into the psychosexual development of transsexuals and homosexuals has been fraught with methodologic hazards. The standard research strategy has been the clinical interview during adulthood with the goal of piecing together earlier life experiences through retrospective recall. Data gathered by such techniques are of questionable validity being subject to error by

*Supported by NIMH Research Scientist Development Award K1 MH 31 739 and Foundations' Fund for Research in Psychiatry Grant #G69 471.

†Richard Green, M.D., UCLA School of Medicine, Los Angeles, California.

consciously or unconsciously derived omissions and commissions. For this reason a research strategy is being utilized in which retrospective childhood accounts offered by adults with anomalous psychosexual development are used to identify childhood behavior which may represent harbingers of later atypical sexuality (Green 1973).

During the year 1968–69, thirty adult males contacted our research program requesting sex-reassignment to female status. All dated their compelling drive toward feminine behavior to early childhood. Table 1 summarizes four childhood behavioral variables retrospectively described by these thirty male-to-female transsexuals. Seventeen reported feeling as though they were girls or only equivocally considering themselves to be boys; twenty preferred the playthings of girls; fourteen preferred dressing as a girl; and only one preferred boys as playmates. Other researchers reporting the retrospectively described childhood behavior of 106 male homosexuals state that one-third played predominantly with girls and four-fifths did not participate in competitive group games (Bieber et al. 1962).

The following brief interim report summarizes the presenting behavioral characteristics of the first twenty five subjects in a series of boys behaving similarly to that recalled by most adult male-to-female transsexuals and many male homosexuals.

Sample age range is four to ten years. Although more than half are between seven and ten, all showed a preference for dressing in girls' clothes before their sixth birthday (Figures 1 and 2). Wom-

Table 1. *Retrospectively recalled childhood behavior of thirty males requesting surgery for sex reassignment to female status.*

	Childhood history		
	Male	Male and female equally	Female
Self-concept	13	8	9
Playthings	4	6	20
Clothing preference	11	4	14
Playmate preference	1	12	17

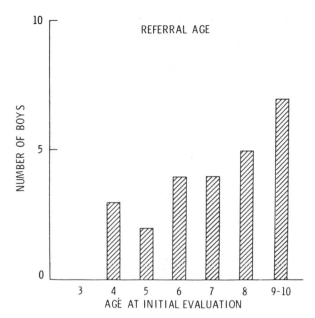

Fig. 1. *Referral age of twenty-five feminine boys.*

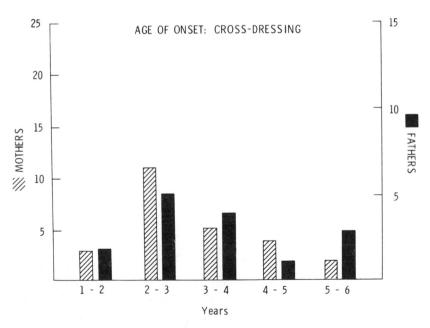

Fig. 2. *Age of onset of cross-dressing of twenty-five feminine boys as observed by their mothers (N=25) and fathers (N=15). (Ten fathers were unavailable.)*

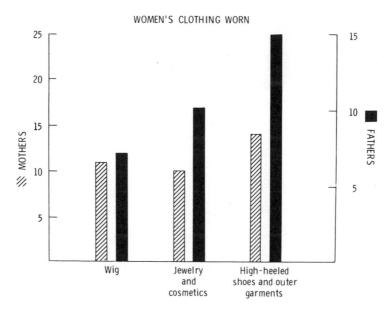

Fig. 3. *Women's clothing and accessories worn by twenty-five feminine boys.*

en's clothing worn includes wigs, high-heeled shoes, jewelry, cosmetics, and outer garments (Figure 3). When denied access to genuine feminine articles, they will create them from other materials: a blanket becomes a skirt, a towel a wig, an adult-sized T-shirt a mini-dress, and felt-tipped pens are used for nail polish, lipstick, and eye shadow.

Feminine mannerisms are frequently displayed by these boys; they are called "sissy" by masculine boys their age and are loners socially. Best friends are girls (Figure 4). Girls' toys are preferred—the "Barbie" doll is a favorite. When playing house or make-believe games they take the role of a female, usually mother or some other woman, such as teacher. They show a considerable interest in play-acting (Figure 5). The majority have said they are or want to be girls. Though of average height and weight, they avoid participation in rough-and-tumble play or participation in sports (Figure 6). Both parents consider the boys emotionally closer to their mothers and more distant from their fathers. In this respect they also differ from our contrast group of masculine boys.

The research methodology here is (1) to record detailed psychologic testing and behavioral observations on these boys and contrast them with masculine male siblings and nonrelated boys of the same age; (2) to conduct detailed interviews of the parents about the boys and themselves; and (3) to make assessments of the parents together and with the feminine boy in structured experimental situations.

The feminine boys briefly described above score similarly to typical girls on several psychological tests and differ from masculine boys. On the It-Scale for Children (Brown 1956) their mean score is similar to published norms for girls and significantly different from our contrast group of masculine boys. On the Draw-A-Person Test, the feminine boys are more likely to draw a female first, as is the case with typical girls, but not boys (Green et al. 1972). In an experimental playroom they spend more time playing

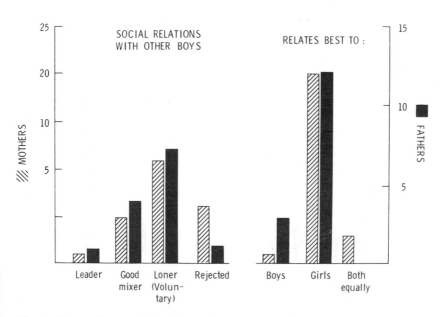

Fig. 4. *Parents' appraisal of feminine boys' social relations with other children.*

with culturally feminine toys, such as a doll, and less time playing with a truck than do masculine boys. Their toy preference is the same as our "control" girls (Green et al. 1972). On the Parent and Activity Preference Test (Green 1971) in which children complete picture story sequences requiring a choice between masculine, feminine, and genderneutral activities, to be performed with either mother or father, again feminine boys and girls score similarly. They select the mother more often than do masculine boys and are more likely to choose feminine activities.

Some attempts at behavioral reorientation are being made and include three approaches: (1) a one-to-one play therapy setting (Green et al. 1972); (2) group meetings with the boys and separately with their parents, and (3) behavior modification based on principles of learning theory. A fourth group is not undergoing systematic intervention. This study is longitudinal. An attempt

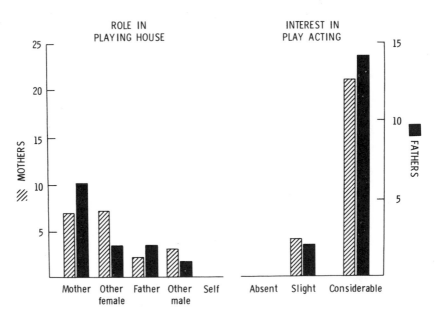

Fig. 5. *a) Role taken by feminine boys when playing "house." b) Parents' estimate of feminine boys' interest in play-acting compared to male sibs and peers.*

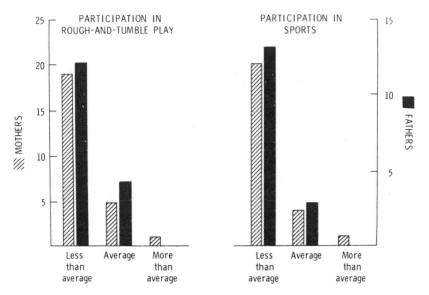

Fig. 6. *Parents' appraisal of feminine boys' participation in rough-and-tumble play and sports.*

will be made to obtain behavioral data on the entire sample of boys as they mature into adolescence and on to adulthood.

REFERENCES

Bieber, I. *Homosexuality*. New York: Basic Books, 1962.

Brown, D. Sex role preference in young children. *Psychological Monographs* 70 No. 14 (Whole No. 421), 1956.

Green, R. Parent and Activity Preference Test. Copyright, 1971, Richard Green, M.D.

———. *Cross-sexed identity in children and adults*. New York: Basic Books, 1973.

Green, R., and Money, J. (eds.). *Transsexualism and sex reassignment*. Baltimore: The Johns Hopkins Press, 1969.

Green, R., Newman, L., & Stoller, R. Treatment of boyhood "transsexualism": an interim report of four years' experience. *Archives of General Psychiatry* 26: 213–17, 1972.

Green, R., Fuller, M., & Hendler, J. Playroom toy preferences of fifteen masculine and fifteen feminine boys. *Behavior Therapy*, 1972, in press.

Green, R., Fuller, M., & Rutley, B. It-Scale for Children and Draw-A-Person Test: 30 feminine vs. 25 masculine boys. *Journal of Personality Assessment*, 1972, in press.

Stoller, R. *Sex and gender*. New York: Science House, 1968.

part V

Sex Education for
the Professional

chapter 19

A Review of
Public Attitudes
on Sexual Issues

Robert Athanasiou*

The 1960s produced a great deal of debate about the so-called "sexual revolution" and gave the impression of widespread changes in public attitudes and private sexual behavior. Data collected in the late sixties and early in 1970 do not, however, show that the United States has as yet experienced a sexual revolution.

On the other hand, there is good evidence for the existence of a sexual renaissance or sexual evolution in which the social issues and interpersonal relations involved in human sexual relationships are taking on a new character. There is a rebirth of pluralism in the style of individual sex ethics. This turn to pluralism is often described by authors for the popular press as an indication of an anomic social system, although it is, in fact, representative of a

*Robert Athanasiou, Center for Social Studies in Human Reproduction, The Johns Hopkins Hospital, Baltimore, Maryland.

polynomic system. It is this growth of pluralism which has sparked such great concern on the part of parents, teachers, health professionals, legislators, and the general public over issues such as sex education, pornography, and premarital sexual behavior.

While it is extremely difficult to survey adequately public attitudes on so sensitive an issue as sex, there has been a good deal of convergence in the findings of a number of major studies done over the past fifteen years. In general these studies have indicated that relative to attitudes, behavior has changed in the past two decades in the direction of greater consistency between attitudes and behavior. There is also some indication that the debates of the 1960s may have provided a prologue for behavior changes yet to come. Most of these studies have confirmed the general hypothesis that variations in sexual behavior may be predicted by knowledge of variations in religious, social, political, ethical, and sexual attitudes.

The first part of this paper will deal with questions of definition, acquisition, function, and measurement of attitudes. The final section of the paper will review data on the specific issues of sex education, pornography, and premarital sex.

DEFINITION OF ATTITUDES

For most social psychologists the study of attitudes constitutes a major portion of their professional activities. Yet when asked to define the concept they usually engage in fancy verbal footwork and change the subject. This avoidance response has its origins not in a lack of knowledge, but in the inability to adequately explain the concept of attitudes in anything less than several hours of conversation or several hundred pages of text. The definition given here, then, is necessarily incomplete and open to further refinement.

Attitudes are generally thought of as relatively "enduring systems of positive or negative evaluations, emotional feelings and pro or con action tendencies with respect to social objects" (Krech et al. 1962, p. 139) or events. Attitudes are based on a substrate of beliefs and values and tend to be interdependent with each other. An example of the syllogistic structure of an attitude might be:

God intended sex for the purposes of procreation. (belief)
Sex divorced from procreation is bad. (value)
Therefore, I will not use contraceptives.

Associated with this attitude there are likely to be (1) negative evaluations of birth control programs; (2) fear, anxiety, or disgust regarding the use of contraceptives; and (3) the possibility of some action, such as petitioning against planned parenthood activities, etc.

In this example, the resultant attitude toward contraceptives is the conclusion resulting from the combination of a major premise (value) and a minor premise (belief). Understanding a subject's behavior or feelings involves the elucidation of these major and minor premises and the (sometimes faulty) logic involved in pro- ducing the attitudes which guide his behavior. The psychothera- peutic technique known as rational-emotive psychotherapy (Ellis 1963), and to a large extent traditional psychoanalysis, pursue this goal with the intent of changing either the belief, the value, or the "logical" system by which they are combined. Ellis and Harper (1961) state, for example, "For *permanent* and *deep-seated* emo- tional changes to be effected, thinking changes (logic), or drastic modifications of the individual's philosophy of life (beliefs, val- ues), appear to us to be necessary in most instances" (p. 21). And, ". . . the theory of (rational-emotive psychotherapy) says that what is essentially done in effective psychotherapy is the changing of the patient's attitudes, especially his attitudes toward himself and others" (Ellis 1963, p. 190).

Regardless of what advertising agencies or psychotherapists would have us believe, attitudes are relatively enduring systems and they are rather difficult to change. Multiplexity is a charac- teristic of attitude components which makes change difficult. When a component of an attitude, a value, or a belief shows a high degree of multiplexity, it contains a large number and variety of separate but related elements. For example, one person may be- lieve that sex can refer to masturbation, petting, pornography, homosexuality, sexual thoughts, religious proscriptions, and so forth. For another, it can refer only to heterosexual genital coitus. In the case of the first individual we might find that in measuring his attitude toward contraception we also had a good indication of his attitude toward abortion, premarital sex, fellatio, masturbation, and pornography. If we were to try to change his attitude toward contraception without separating it from these other topics, that is, without reducing its multiplexity, we would very likely find the attitude quite resistant to change, and any change which did occur might be ephemeral. Because sexual attitudes typically show a very high degree of multiplexity—and because they are interconnected with religion, politics, age, marital status, social position, etc.—they are particularly resistant to change and tend to evoke emotional responses over a wide range of issues.

One of the reasons for this high degree of multiplexity becomes evident when we examine the socialization processes by which sexual attitudes are acquired. Parents, religious institutions, peer groups, dating partners, and mates all influence the acquisition of sexual attitudes by specifying the appropriate beliefs, inculcating the appropriate values, and communicating (sometimes conflicting) expectations for behavior. This variety of inputs, combined with the socially determined curiosity existing prior to puberty and the biological and social necessity for the development of a *personal* code of sexual behavior, virtually guarantees a highly multiplex attitudinal system.

The role of socialization in the acquisition of attitudes should not, however, be overemphasized. In a study of over 20,000 adults, Athanasiou et al. (1970) have indicated that religious preference is a good predictor of sexual attitudes and behavior, but Table 1 shows that *present* religious preference is a better predictor of sex inhibitions than the religion in which subjects were raised.* In this study a very substantial number of subjects indicated that they had changed religions.

In addition to the socialization process, a person's attitudes are often influenced or even created by his behavior. This concept of attitudes following from behavior rather than the reverse has been well documented by researchers in cognitive dissonance theory

---

*Unless otherwise specified, all tabular data in this paper demonstrate a departure from randomness at the 99 percent confidence level or better.

Table 1. *Sexual inhibition by religious preference (partial table)*

Present religious preference:	Atheist	Jew	Unitarian	Protestant	Catholic
Percent of S's saying they were inhibited by religion	12.2	7.4	25.0	23.0	32.2
		$x^2 = 65.9$		C = .20	$\lambda = 4.6\%$
Religious instruction as a child	Atheist	Jew	Unitarian	Protestant	Catholic
Percent of S's saying they were inhibited by religion	13.6	6.8	16.1	19.2	27.3
		$x^2 = 38.0$		C = .14	$\lambda = 0.0\%$

(Festinger 1957; Brehm & Cohen 1964). According to dissonance theory the greatest change in attitude is produced when the *minimum* amount of persuasion required to produce *voluntary* compliance is used. A rather simplified example might be the positive attitude toward sex of a girl who had been seduced, relative to that of one who had been raped. Too great a degree of forced compliance or too great a reward may bring about behavior change but not attitudinal change which will serve to maintain the behavior. Where long-term behavior changes are desired, such as in birth control programs, a minimal amount of persuasion might be indicated.

FUNCTIONS OF ATTITUDES

Having briefly discussed what attitudes are and some of the ways in which they may be acquired, it is now useful to consider some of the functions which attitudes serve. Daniel Katz (1960) has suggested that attitudes may aid an individual in adjustment, ego defense, value expression, and knowledge acquisition and organization. "Attitudes acquired in the service of the adjustment function are either the means for reaching the desired goal or avoiding the undesireable one" (p. 171). A child, for example, may learn that the best way to get along in his family is by developing toward sex an attitude whose affective component contains substantial elements of shame and guilt. If his subsequent toilet or masturbatory behavior are then partially governed by this attitude, he may avoid some instances of censure or at least display appropriately contrite behavior when his transgressions are discovered. Attitudes which serve this function may persist for long periods. This longevity is partially the result of the power of reinforcers utilized, but it may also be due to the effects of variable ratio and variable interval reinforcement patterns during acquisition. Evidence for the functional longevity of such attitudes comes from a study by Mann (1970). In his sample of couples married an average of 17.5 years, many had never discussed sex with each other until participation in a pornography experiment made such nondiscussion dysfunctional. Apparently, sexual adjustment had been achieved without discussing sex. Attitudes which serve an adjustment function represent those codified ways of thinking and feeling about the world which help an individual get along with others—they help to maximize rewards and minimize penalties.

The ego-defensive functions of some attitudes are often very dynamic and somewhat primitive functions. Katz (1960) has stated: "They include the devices by which the individual avoids facing either the inner reality of the kind of person he is, or the outer reality of the dangers the world holds for him. They stem basically from internal conflict with its resulting insecurities" (p. 172). When, for example, a man has strong feelings of sexual arousal and, perhaps, the desire for intercourse with someone other than his spouse, he may project these and his associated guilt feelings onto some convenient minority and restore his ego-ideal by attitudes of superiority to and disdain for that minority. Perhaps the most frequent and blatant example of this attitude is the legendary smut hunters who carefully collect large amounts of sexually explicit material in order to more effectively denounce it, its purveyors, and consumers. We suspect that some of their energy, perhaps most of it, is really directed toward denunciation of their own feelings and restoration of their ego-ideal by telling everyone of their goodness, purity and concern for society's welfare.

Of course, all people employ defense mechanisms, such as rationalization, displacement, denial, etc., at one time or another. Individuals are likely to vary in the degree to which they use them and in their awareness of use. In some cases it seems quite likely that they are unaware of the attitude with which they have been deluding themselves. *It must be emphasized that an attitude is not created by a specific social object, such as pornography, but by an individual's attempts to deal with his emotional conflicts and anxiety concerning the object.* For many social objects or events there are comprehensive social templates contained in a culture which help an individual deal with a specific problem. Most people know, for example, how to behave at a funeral without prior personal experience. It is unfortunate that our culture does not provide adequate templates for dealing with sexual objects and events.

According to Katz (1960), the value expressive function of an attitude is served when an individual "derives satisfaction from expressing attitudes appropriate to his personal values" (p. 170). This expression of values in more or less explicit form is often encountered in assays of public opinion. The values of a society are often contained in its myths and are, therefore, widely known (if not universally accepted) and, because values are often shared, their codification into catch phrases and slogans is quite common. Their public expression, then, is not an attempt to communicate new knowledge but a personal reaffirmation of faith in social myths. The following excerpt from letters to the editor of a college newspaper, The University of Maryland *Diamondback*, illustrates this point:

I can keep silent no longer. There comes a time in every person's life when he can no longer sit and watch everything around him go to pot. It is time for the silent majority to be heard. . . . It is disgraceful to see our young people's minds slowly disintegrate with pornography. . . . It has been proven that an increase in pornography leads to an increase in sex crimes. . . .

Please remember that if you were living in Russia you would not even be allowed a student newspaper.

You always say do not criticize without offering constructive suggestions. My solution? Church every Sunday and an American flag. Think about it.

(a) *Gold Star Mother*

The stereotyped and hackneyed character of value-expressive attitudes often leads the sophisticated observer to discount them as being foolish and amotivational. One must recognize, however, that the popularity of the current vice-president (five out of eight Americans endorse his ideas and actions) is based largely on value-expressive attitudes; people do vote on such a basis, whether the issue is Spiro Agnew, sex education, abortion, or pornography. While our society is indeed pluralistic in terms of the existence of divergent values, we must also remember that most Americans are unpoor, unyoung, unblack, and relatively uneducated, and that the attitudes and values of the majority correspond to these characteristics.

The last function of attitudes to be considered here is the knowledge function which "is based upon the individual's need to give adequate structure to his universe. The search for meaning, the need to understand, the trend toward better organization of perceptions and beliefs to provide clarity and consistency for the individual, are descriptions of this function" (Katz 1960, p. 170). This function is also served when attitudes toward a social object "tell" a person what to believe and the sources of information to which he should subscribe.

An example of this knowledge-sifting function occurred when the President, the Senate, and others were able to reject the report of the Obscenity and Pornography Commission *before* it was published. Still another example is the Gold Star Mother quoted above, whose attitudes would seem to preclude the possibility that facts could change her mind. The knowledge function of an attitude is analogous to that of the runcible spade—an extension of the runcible spoon, a half spoon–half fork—which sifts data as it collects them.

In some instances attitudes may take the place of knowledge. The public's appalling lack of political knowledge, which need not be documented here, is a case in point. Attitudes toward a party or stereotypes can often serve as well (or better) to guide behavior as can knowledge.

The functional approach is useful, but it should not be utilized with procrustean compulsiveness; nor are the functions mutually exclusive. An attitude may serve one or several functions, depending upon the individual. The approach is, however, more than a heuristic one and has proven useful in the empirical study of attitude formation and change.

THE VALUE OF KNOWING PUBLIC ATTITUDES

One might conclude that knowledge about public and individual attitudes would be of very great value in counseling or inducing change or in predicting behavior. Actually, knowledge of attitudes is of dubious value due to problems of reliability, validity, and the social impracticality of some of the solutions which that knowledge would suggest.

Reliability refers to the stability, over time, of individual or group attitudes. It is unfortunately the case that most attitude-measurement devices do not report measures of this stability. Those that do report such measures frequently give correlation coefficients in the 0.80's, that is, only about two-thirds of the variation in scores remains consistent from one time to another. Research has indicated that group attitudes may be somewhat more stable than an individual's. This may be due to an increase in statistical precision when dealing with groups or to a sort of Brownian movement of attitudes within the group. That is, the average attitude score for a group may remain relatively constant, while individuals within the group interchange their attitude positions in a somewhat random fashion (over and above regression effects). It is also possible that the context in which attitudes are assessed may vary from one time to another. One would guess, for example, that attitudes toward extramarital behavior would vary if a subject got married in the period between two measurements. Other reliability problems may be due to differences in sampling or differences in the way in which a question is worded.

It is difficult, therefore, to compare data from two different studies, from different samples, or even from the same sample over time. In survey studies done by major academic research institutions every effort is made to standardize the questions and the actual interview situation, as well as to use carefully chosen probability samples to minimize unreliability from the sources mentioned above.

Validity is a somewhat separate problem from reliability and is a measure of how well our independent variables—usually verbal statements of attitudes—can predict positions on our dependent (criterion) variable. The criterion variable may be a behavior of interest, such as penile intromission time, an assigned status category, such as prisoner, priest, or college student, or the verbal report of behavior or another belief.

We are generally not able to predict each of these criterion categories (behavior, status, verbal report) equally well. Verbal expressions of attitudes may correlate 0.6 or higher with verbal reports of behavior, but rarely account for more than 50 percent of the variation. Status categories are often about as predictable as verbal reports, but are sometimes less so and rarely account for more than one-third of the shared variance. Actual behavior is very difficult to predict and probably averages about 15 percent shared variance with verbal attitudes, although the correspondance is sometimes higher.

Part of the cause of this considerable lack of accuracy lies in the same areas as the causes of unreliability, since reliability sets an upper limit on validity. Another factor in this failure to adequately predict behavior is that the social context in which human behavior occurs is far more likely to shape the behavior than are mere attitudes. For example, Table 2 shows the percentages of males' and females' responses to the question of mate swapping (Athanasiou et al. 1970). From these responses one might conclude that there is a sizable number of people who are interested in mate swapping, that is, who hold attitudes from which one might predict their participation; yet very few have actually participated. It seems likely that the actual behavior is far more a function of opportunity than libido. In this particular case we would

Table 2. *Percent respondents, by sex, to a question concerning mate-swapping*

Have you participated in wife-swapping?

	Males	Females
1. Frequently	1.3	1.5
2. Once or twice	4.2	3.1
3. Not ever, but I might	41.4	21.6
4. Never; would never consider it	53.1	73.8
	100.0%	100.0%

also be trying to predict the behavior of two or perhaps four people from the responses of one person.

There is an additional problem in measuring attitudes and assuming that they will predict behavior. Many people hold attitudes in a general way but apply them in very specific ways. In our survey it was common to find Jewish respondents who held very liberal attitudes toward premarital, extramarital, and group sex, but who did not participate in these activities themselves. In effect, their attitude was: "It is alright for other people to do these things if they wish but I, personally, do not care to participate in them." The respondent's general attitudes are one thing and his personal behavioral preferences are another. This discrepancy between the cognitive and affective components, on the one hand, and the behavioral component on the other, is not very common and the careful design and pretesting of measurement instruments can eliminate some of it.

There is another problem in utilizing information about public attitudes. The majority opinion in the United States often runs counter to some of the very basic and essential values on which our society is built. A recent TV broadcast of a poll conducted by the Columbia Broadcasting System revealed that a majority of Americans did not support half the Bill of Rights and were described as "lukewarm on the other half." For example, in another poll 50.3 percent of the general electorate agreed that "A book that contains wrong political views cannot be a good book and does not deserve to be published"; 36.3 percent felt that under certain conditions "we might have to force people to testify against themselves" (Robinson et al. 1968, p. 174). The wisdom of implementing the opinions of a plurality or majority is often highly questionable to say the least.

ATTITUDES TOWARD SEX EDUCATION

It is even questionable to implement these opinions when professionals feel it would be a "good" thing. Sex education programs in public schools, for example, were approved by 58 percent of the men and 54 percent of the women in a national survey for the Commission on Obscenity and Pornography (COP 1970). An additional 13 percent and 16 percent of men and women respectively, gave qualified approval of such programs. This leaves a sizable minority of 22 to 23 percent of the respondents who were opposed to sex education in the public schools. Even though a clear majority of favorable opinion exists in most school districts, it might be prudent to avoid antagonizing the minority when considering the introduction or the content of sex education programs.

No doubt the etiology of the general positive attitude toward sex education includes a recognition of the short-comings in the existing systems for transmission of knowledge in this area. The survey by Athanasiou et al., (1970) and the later survey by Abelson, Cohen, Heaton, and Suder (cited in COP 1970), asked respondents to indicate what they considered to be the best source of sex education information. They were then asked to name the source from which they had actually received their information. Although the sampling techniques of the two studies differed as widely as possible, their results showed considerable convergence. Table 3 presents both sets of data.

Quite obviously, there is some indication of social dissonance in these data. In both studies the preferred source of information was parents, while the most common actual source was peers. The distribution of these data does not change a great deal when the effect of age is partialled out. Most people did not, and still do not, obtain sexual information in their home from their parents. Most received, and continue to receive, their sex information from a source, friends, which they would not recommend to future generations.

Opposition to sex education often seems to reflect attitudes which are derived from rather questionable beliefs. In the syllogistic paradigm mentioned previously such a belief might take the form: "Sex education involves teaching children how to do it." This belief expressed by one COP commissioner, Mr. Keating (COP 1970), is attached to the value that "a mode of life which imposes on (children). . . . a psychological and moral discipline and privation" (p. 620) is a good thing. This readily leads to the creation of an attitude which is negative toward sex education. Implicit in this analysis is the understanding that if children know "how to do it," they will, indeed, attempt to do it.

Table 3. *Preferred versus actual source of sex education information*

Abelson et al. data*		
Locus	Preferred source	Actual source
Parents	80–90%	25–46%
Family doctor	60	5
School	40	8–9
Church	26	5
Siblings	10	NA
Peers	5	35–53
Athanasiou et al. data[†]		
Locus	Preferred source	Actual source
Parents	48.8%	12.1%
School	22.7	2.8
Church	1.1	0.5
Peers & friends	4.5	53.6
Books	14.0	18.6
Pornography	NA	3.6
Other	8.9	8.8
	100.0%	100.0%

*Figures are approximate and represent combined male-female data; several sources were recorded for each subject; Abelson's data represent a national probability sample.

†Male and female data are combined; respondents were allowed to check only one response. Data represent 20,000 adults who responded to a questionnaire appearing in *Psychology Today* magazine (Athanasiou et al. 1970).

There is ample evidence that people who believe that sex is, per se, a bad thing usually believe that ignorance of reproduction and sexual physiology deters people from engaging in sexual activity. This belief that education destroys innocence, and that the destruction of innocence is bad, is amply illustrated by a homilitic message contained in the minority report of the COP (1970):

(people advocating sex education) . . . are doing something which has been regarded for countless generations as one of the most revolting crimes. They are setting out, with their benevolent voices, their paternal manner, their beautiful arty pictures, even with musical accompaniment, to destroy the innocence of a whole generation of young children (p. 670).

We may hypothesize that one of the functions served by such attitudes is that of value expression, but the ego-defensive function of anti-sex education attitudes should also be considered. When a school district introduces a sex education program it is, in effect, telling the parents in the district that they are poor parents and have done an inadequate job of teaching their own children the facts of life. Parents are not expected to be experts in mathematics or science, but the presence of one or more children may be taken as evidence of at least minimal knowledge of the human reproductive process. It is suggested that one of the best ways to gain support for an innovation such as sex education is to not insult those who will be asked to support it.

The value of sex education programs lies in providing a nucleus of accurate information (beliefs) in a realistic value context which fosters the growth of healthy and functional attitudes toward human sexuality. If subsequent behavior is to be responsible and mature, the development of healthy attitudes is essential.

The long-term effects of sex education are not well known. Data exist in fragmentary bits scattered throughout the literature, and it is virtually impossible to adequately review studies of effects. Kirkendall and Miles (1968) attempted to review the data and were struck by the "amazing paucity of research. . . . The questions are there but data for answering them are not."

Some of the data collected by Athanasiou et al. (1970) tend to indicate (though not at a sufficiently reliable statistical level) that respondents who received most of their sex information from courses in school were less responsive to pornography, even though their exposure rates were about average. The COP report indicates that "58 percent of . . . 35 state departments of education reported their belief that an effective sex education program would reduce interest in pornography; 30 percent said they did not know; and 12 percent felt that it would not" (p. 317). One encouraging study cited in the COP report indicated that subsequent illegitimacy and divorce rates are somewhat lower for those who had taken a marriage and family course in senior high school than for those who had not.

While there is a desperate need for comprehensive long-term research in the area of the effects of sex education programs, this author's somewhat limited personal experience has indicated that some school districts may be very reluctant to consider evaluation of their programs. If there is to be any price which professionals can extract for participation in such programs, it should be the requirement for research and evaluation. We should not accept a change from stumbling about in the dark where sex is concerned, to stumbling about in the light; let us confirm the value of our efforts.

ATTITUDES TOWARD PORNOGRAPHY

Pictorial depiction of sexual behavior is probably as old as the culture of Cro-Magnon man; some pornographic cave drawings (petroglyphs) have been reported by archeologists. Moreover, virtually all the men and most of the women over puberty in this country have seen or read pornographic material at some time in their lives. In one study (Athanasiou et al. 1970) 92 percent of male and 72 percent of female respondents had seen pornography. Wallace et al. (1970) report that 80 percent of their mixed sample of respondents from the Detroit metropolitan area had seen pornography. In a study of men and women members of social, professional, church, etc. groups in Denver, Massey (COP 1970) reported that 83 percent had seen sexually explicit material. In the national sample study in Abelson et al. (COP 1970) approximately 85 percent of the men and 70 percent of the women report having seen sexual materials. The remarkable correspondence among these independent studies, with their different samples, confirms the fact that about four out of five adults in our society have seen pornography. As might be expected, exposure is somewhat more common among men than among women; virtually all males and about half the females are exposed to pornography before the age of twenty-one years. These figures drop somewhat when only recent exposure is considered. In the last two years about 60 percent of the men and half the women in the country have been exposed at least once to pornography and about 25 percent of the male population has had regular frequent exposure to such material (COP 1970). What are the public's attitudes regarding this ubiquitous phenomenon?

A caveat should be inserted here before discussing public attitudes toward pornography. Sensitive public issues have a way of producing "instant attitudes"—just add a poll-taker. The social rhetoric and stereotype which may be elicited by poorly worded questions or inferior interviewing technique may be very misleading.

One must also distinguish between the direction and its intensity. By referring to the brief discussion above concerning the public's attitudes toward the Bill of Rights and civil liberties, it is not at all hard to predict the direction of public attitudes toward pornography. Intensity, however, is another issue, since the Abelson survey found that only 2 percent of the public had feelings intense enough to consider ranking pornography as one of the two or three most important questions facing our society.

Nevertheless, a Gallup poll in May 1969 indicated that 85 percent of the country would "like to see stricter state and local laws dealing with obscene literature sent thru the mails." Further breakdown of these data reveal that respondents with only high school education were more likely to want stricter laws than were those with a college degree (87 to 79 percent); Republicans were stricter than Democrats (90 to 83 percent); and older respondents more strict than the young (89 to 75 percent). These respondents wanted stricter laws on unsolicited mail, even though only 12 percent of the nation reports having "received any sex literature in the mail which (they) found objectionable," and only 8 percent have "ever taken any action to stop the sale of objectionable material." Virtually all magazines sold today use pictures of nude or partially nude females and/or males to sell such products as sanitary napkins, mens aftershave, etc. Yet 73 percent of the country indicated that they, "Would . . . find pictures of nudes in magazines objectionable." One wonders if the sales figures for the products associated with nudes in advertisements suffer accordingly. These figures on nudity vary in a way similar to the issue mentioned above when broken down by politics, age, education, and urban-rural environment.

Public opinion in Denmark prior to the repeal of obscenity laws showed much the same sort of distribution as in America. A 1965 Gallup poll taken in Denmark (quoted by Schindler 1969, pp. 277–82) revealed that 44 percent of the country was in favor of restricting pornography, while 35 percent advocated freeing it;

the remainder had no opinion. Here, too, the effects of age (52 percent of those under twenty-five favored freeing pornography), education, and political attitude were obvious; the young, educated, liberal respondents held attitudes which contrasted with those of the older, less educated, conservative portions of Danish society.

Wallace et al. (1970) have probed into the personal and social dimensions of response to pornography in a study which included a wide variety of respondents. They found that people who enjoyed pornography tended to be young, liberal, nonreligious, and generally well educated. The variable of religiosity accounted for a considerable proportion of the variance on a large number of attitude items and pornography rating scales. Comparing the religious and nonreligious groups, Wallace et al. report:

Another finding supportive of our dichotomy is the relationship between sexual arousal and entertainment. The "church" category obtained a value of $r = -.407$ for this relationship, while the "student" and "Magazine Store" categories obtained values of $r = +.341$ and $r = +.871$ respectively. This indicates that members of the "church" category tend to find sexual arousal resulting from exposure to visual erotica displeasurable or non-entertaining . . . The pervasiveness of the dichotomy which we have found, and the strength to which attitudes forming the basis of the split are held, must be considered when one discusses Contemporary Community Standards of visual erotica (p. 52).

Athanasiou and Shaver (1971) have also found that men's and women's responses to pornography may be used to predict their sexual attitudes, political attitudes, religiosity, religious preference, and political preference. In each case, it is the more tolerant, more liberal elements who are aroused rather than disgusted by pornography. These findings are confirmed, in part, by data from Abelson et al. (COP 1970) which show similar relationships between sexual attitudes and exposure to erotica. Study after study has confirmed the relationship of exposure to and arousal by erotica with general and specific components of a liberal-conservative dimension of attitudes and statuses.

It seems plausible to suggest that the ego-defensive function is the one best served by a negative attitude toward pornography.

Exposure to explicit sexual material does lead to sexual arousal in most people. It is the individual's interpretation and evaluation of this arousal which leads to differential attitudes toward pornography. If a person has been taught that sex is dirty, evil, shameful, harmful, vile, and disgusting, he can hardly enjoy a state of sexual arousal, since those adjectives might then be applied to himself. For example, Mosher (1969) has shown that subjects presenting high ratings on sex guilt tend to react with disgust and increased guilt feelings after exposure to erotica. Presumably, they are not able to accept their sexual arousal as a natural human reaction and instead react to it with guilt. It is then far easier to project these feelings on others than to acknowledge them in oneself and, at the same time, to take measures to avoid future exposure to erotic material. Attitudes which lead a person to avoid unpleasant states or experience may also be said to serve an adjustment function.

It is possible that censorship crusades, which most often seem to be led and organized by highly religious, conservative, older persons, serve both the ego-defensive and value-expressive functions simultaneously. Public denunciation of explicit material may have a cathartic effect and an almost confessional quality. Moreover, it brings public recognition to the censor and may help him to retain his beliefs since public commitment often reinforces private acceptance (Festinger 1957).

It is beyond the scope and intention of this paper to review the effects of pornography, but it is possible to say that the best data available to date indicate that pornography is not a major, or even a relatively important, factor in sexual deviance. A report by Kutschinsky (1970) has carefully analyzed the relationship between sex crime data in Copenhagen and the legalization of pornography. An earlier study by Gebhard et al. (1965) suggested that only certain categories of sex offenders would be responsive to pornography, while criminals in other categories would be relatively unresponsive. Kutschinsky's analysis of the Danish crime data confirm this hypothesis. The rate of sex crimes against children in Copenhagen has shown a dramatic decrease since the legalization of pornography, and his analysis shows that it is "unlikely that more than a fraction of the decrease in indecent acts toward children could be explained by a change in the definition of or the attitudes toward reporting this type of crime" (p. 141). Exhibitionism, voyeurism, and the category of crimes labeled "indecency toward women" have also shown dramatic rate decreases in Copenhagen, but these decreases may be attributed in whole, or in major part, to changes in public attitudes toward these "crimes." It is not true that rate decreases have been the result of new legal definitions of crimes.

It has been said, and probably rightly so, that "the natural human use of reason is to support prejudice, not to arrive at opinions." Rational arguments and scientific data will probably not be sufficient to convince the 35 percent of the population who feel that pornography should be censored, even if it were clearly shown that no socially undesirable relationship existed between pornography and crime. These negative attitudes serve important psychological functions for individuals who hold them. Unless an equally functional attitude is substituted, or the need for the function is modified, there is no reason to expect movement toward change.

The stereotyped public reaction to pornography is based primarily on the unsubstantiated myths and beliefs held, in general, by the more conservative, older, and more religious segments of our society. On the other hand, there is a very substantial number of intelligent, healthy, normal, successful adults who respond to and enjoy sexual arousal resulting from pornography. This distribution of opinions and reactions makes it seem highly unlikely that either group's standards could be successfully imposed on the other. This pluralism of attitudes and norms with regard to behavior associated with pornography is representative of the traditional conflicts concerning the rights of minorities in American society and is not at all indicative of anomie. To some it may indicate a breakdown of morals, while to others it may represent a more rational restructuring of the relationships between sexual drives and attitudes and behavior.

PREMARITAL SEXUAL BEHAVIOR

Data from the June and August 1969 Gallup polls demonstrate the considerable difference of opinion between college students and people in general regarding premarital sex. In both polls, income (or parent's income) predicts attitudes; higher income respondents are more accepting of premarital relations. Political affiliation and orientation also predict sexual attitudes; Democrats are more accepting than Republicans. In the college sample 92 percent of those holding an extremely liberal political position say premarital sex is not wrong, while only 44 percent of extreme conservatives approve.

It is probably this striking example of not only a generation gap but also an income gap, education gap, and political gap in sexual attitudes which captures the fancy of writers and columnists. Here, at last, is a no-nonsense issue along which battle lines may be drawn. Those who wish to put down youth, liberals, or college students can point to the decay of morals, the decline of tradition, and the imminent death of the nuclear family, etc. The devotion to higher values, such as making love and not war, forming a "meaningful relationship," etc., may serve a similar value-expressive function for the under-thirty group.

Based on the Gallup data and on those collected by Athanasiou et al. (1970), it would seem that many people under thirty feel that virginity in the pursuit of virtue would be a vice. The rather broad Gallup question, however, does not adequately deal with the question of standards or norms. When a graded set of alternatives is offered it becomes quite apparent that even a group of young, educated liberals will differ among themselves about the conditions under which premarital sex is permissible. Data from such a group indicated that only 9 percent of the respondents felt thall all premarital sex was wrong and only 3 percent felt it was necessary to wait until the couple was engaged.

Table 4. *Premarital sex attitudes*

| | Percent saying, premarital sex is: | | | |
	Wrong	Not wrong	No opinion	Total
College students	29%	66	5	100%
National sample	68%	21	11	100%

Table 5. *Sex of respondent by premarital attitudes*

What is your opinion about premarital sex?	Males	Females
1. OK for young people and adults	36.0%	22.6%
2. OK for consenting adults	24.2	29.4
3. OK for couples who share affection	19.3	20.4
4. OK for couples who are in love	9.8	14.2
5. OK for couples who are engaged	2.3	3.1
6. It's wrong	8.4	10.3
	100.0%	100.0%
If you tried premarital sex, how do you feel about it now?		
1. Very regretful	2.3%	3.6%
2. Somewhat regretful	5.3	15.0
3. No feelings	16.7	12.7
4. Somewhat glad	23.5	27.7
5. Very glad	52.2	41.0
	100.0%	100.0%

Males and females are still different, at least where attitudes and behavior concerning premarital sex are concerned. Additional data from the study by Athanasiou et al. presented in Table 5 indicate that women have somewhat more conservative attitudes than men. Approximately 37 percent of the women chose a "sex with affection" standard, while 52 percent felt that affection was not a requisite for consenting young people or adults. Men in the sample favored the "consenting adult or young people" position over the "sex with affection" categories by about 60 to 31 percent. It is also interesting to note that when asked to evaluate their feelings after engaging in premarital sex, women are less positive about it than are men by an even greater margin than in the previous question. Almost 19 percent of the women versus about 8 percent of the men were at least somewhat regretful about having tried premarital sex, while 52 percent of the men and 41 percent of the women said they were "very glad" that they had participated.

For both men and women these evaluations were closely related to their response concerning feelings of guilt. As shown in Table 6, guilt was a fairly good predictor of both attitudes and

Table 6. *Feelings of guilt versus attitudes and behavior*

In the past 6 months, how often, on the average, did you engage in sexual intercourse?	*Have (guilt feelings) prevented you from freely expressing your sexuality?*		
	Yes	No	Total
1. Not at all	32.3%	67.7%	100%
2. A few times	33.3	66.7	100
3. Once or twice per month	25.8	74.2	100
4. Once or twice per week	26.3	73.7	100
5. Three or more times per week	25.9	74.1	100
Which of the following describes your experience with sexual intercourse?			
1. Very enjoyable	22.9%	77.1%	100%
2. Mostly pleasant	33.4	66.6	100
3. Occasionally pleasant	31.3	68.7	100
4. Neutral or unpleasant	44.4	55.6	100
If you tried premarital sex, how do you feel about it now?			
1. At least somewhat regretful	48.7%	57.3%	100%
2. No feelings	25.0	75.0	100
3. At least somewhat glad	24.6	75.4	100

behavior. Frequency of intercourse, evaluation of intercourse, and feelings of regret about premarital activities were all related to responses indicating that guilt feelings had inhibited the subjects' sex lives.

It is difficult, if not impossible, to accurately assess changes in sexual behavior over time. Some of the reasons for this difficulty were mentioned in a previous section of this paper. We can, however, make a few guesses based on these cross-sectional, though not necessarily representative, data. For example, Kinsey et al. (1953) reported that about half of their young college-educated respondents had engaged in oral-genital behavior. In our data the figures for both active and passive oral-genital contact are slightly over 75 percent for a comparable group of respondents. We cannot say whether this represents a change in behavior or a change in reporting. Some of the data to be presented below tend to indicate that some behavior changes have taken place.

The locus of premarital sexual intercourse does seem to have changed. The data in Table 7 indicate that a rather substantial portion of our female respondents have had intercourse before marriage. Data collected on college students by Packard (1968) in the mid-1960s indicate that about 40 percent of college females and 60 percent of college males have participated in premarital

Table 7. *Respondent's sex versus premarital sexual behavior*

With whom was your first intercourse?

	Males	Females
Spouse	10.3%	15.3%
Fiance	7.7	19.2
Steady date	29.2	40.6
Someone you had known but not dated	19.9	17.0
Casual acquaintance or stranger	17.0	6.6
Prostitute	13.5	—
Other	2.4	1.3
	100.0%	100.0%

How many times did you again have intercourse with that person?

	Males	Females
Not again	31.0%	12.0%
Once or twice	13.0	8.0
Three to ten times	15.0	19.0
More than ten times	20.0	31.0
More than ten times and still having intercourse	21.0	30.0
	100.0%	100.0%

With how many persons have you had premarital sexual intercourse?

	Males	Females
None (includes virgins and those who waited until marriage)	20.0%	22.0%
One	17.0	26.0
Two	10.0	12.0
Three to six	24.0	21.0
More than seven	29.0	19.0
	100.0%	100.0%

intercourse. Our data would indicate that premarital sex is far more common than that. It must be emphasized, however, that our samples are different. Seventy-seven percent of the subjects in the Athanasiou et al. survey were under thirty-five years old; 89 percent had some college experience; most of them earned more than $15,000 per year; and all were readers of *Psychology Today* magazine. Table 7 shows a rather considerable divergence between men and women in the permanence of their first premarital experience and in the number of premarital partners. Women in our sample seem to have intercourse more often with fewer partners.

An indication for change in the locus of first intercourse may be seen in Tables 8 and 9. These data show that for our respondents who have had intercourse the modal location of first intercourse shifted from the spouse (after marriage) for those now over forty-five years old to a steady date for those under twenty-five years old. Table 9 compares the age at which a respondent first had intercourse and the person with whom he (or she) had it. The shift from spouse to steady date is again very marked. These data seem to indicate that the age of first intercourse is decreasing and that its locus is moving further from the type of partner considered likely to be a marriage choice. This seems consistent with the attitudinal data presented earlier, indicating that a casual approach to sex was endorsed by the respondents in favor of a "sex with affection" standard.

These date must be interpreted with caution and the caveats mentioned previously in this paper should be kept in mind. There

Table 8. *Locus of first intercourse versus current age*

Locus	Age			
	under 25	25–35	35–45	over 45
Spouse after marriage	3.7%	15.6%	27.2%	33.6%
Fiance	13.9	17.3	14.8	17.8
Steady date	51.9	34.6	32.1	21.1
Someone you had known but not dated	21.4	22.7	15.2	19.1
Casual acquaintance	9.1	9.8	10.7	8.4
	100.0%	100.0%	100.0%	100.0%

Table 9. *Locus of first intercourse versus age of first intercourse*

Locus	Age at first intercourse			
	under 17	18–20	21–23	over 24
Spouse after marriage	2.3%	8.6%	31.4%	42.5%
Fiance	7.0	22.5	16.2	11.0
Steady date	47.0	44.1	27.4	21.3
Someone you had known but not dated	29.7	18.2	17.1	16.5
Casual acquaintance	14.0	6.6	7.9	8.7
	100.0%	100.0%	100.0%	100.0%

is also a slight artifact in these data. Namely, the number of subjects under twenty-five who have had their first intercourse with their spouse after marriage is restricted, partly because fewer people under twenty-five are married, relative to those over forty-five. It should be kept in mind that 15 to 20 percent of our respondents have not yet had intercourse with anyone, and most of this subgroup is in the age range eighteen to twenty-five years. It is not the intent of this report to estimate specific population parameters regarding the incidence of premarital intercourse. Rather, the concern here is with understanding the relationships among attitudes, statutes, and behaviors.

If we are correct in this analysis, and if these data can be generalized to at least part of the population, then it would seem that part of the population (the young, educated, liberal, upper middle class) is moving toward the type of Scandinavian norms and moral system described by Christensen (1966) who, five years ago, predicted this movement.

Christensen's data were collected about twelve years ago from both American and Danish college students. His comments at that time indicated that there were considerable differences between Danish and American norms: ". . . Danes do not draw a sharp line to set off technical chastity (as do Americans), but rather regard petting and coitus as belonging together, and see them both as appropriate in a relationship based on love and oriented toward marriage. Today [i.e. late 1950's], this kind of a relationship is most apt to be established with 'going steady' in Denmark but not until the engagement in America" (p. 63). Subjects in Christensen's study would now be in their mid-30s. Our data, shown in Table 8, indicate that about 40 percent of the subjects in the range of thirty to forty years of age had had their first intercourse with either their fiance or spouse. It would seem, therefore, that they were only a bit more liberal than Christensen's subjects. On the other hand, the trend suggested by these cross-sectional data is quite marked and indicates a rather substantial change in norms over time.

Table 10 indicates that there is a considerable amount of consistency between attitudes and behavior. Of those subjects who felt that premarital sex was wrong, more than half waited until after marriage for their first intercourse experience. Forty-five percent of the respondents who thought premarital sex was all right for engaged couples had their first intercourse with their fiance. This correspondence between attitude and behavior is similar to that reported by Reiss (1968). This consistency represents a change from the situation reported by Christensen (1966). In his

Table 10. *Locus of first intercourse versus premarital standards*

What is your opinion about premarital sexual intercourse?	Spouse after marriage	Fiance	Steady date	Someone known but not dated	Casual acquaint-ance	Total
1. It is all right for both young people and adults	7.5	11.1	40.6	27.1	13.7	100.0%
2. . . . all right for consenting adults	15.0	16.2	37.0	21.0	10.7	99.9
3. . . . all right for couples who share affection	9.5	13.8	47.4	19.9	9.5	100.1
4. . . . all right for couples in love	11.4	22.7	45.4	16.8	3.8	100.1
5. . . . all right if engaged	25.0	45.0	22.5	7.5	0	100.0
6. It is wrong . . . should wait until married	55.3	14.0	18.4	7.9	4.4	100.0

early data it was apparent that more Americans had participated in premarital sex than approved of it, whereas more Danes approved of it than had participated. The data in Table 10 indicate that Americans in the late sixties are rather close to Danish standards of the late fifties.

A recent article by Christensen and Gregg (1970) report data collected in 1968, just one decade after the previously cited study, which provide further confirmation for the apparent trend in premarital sexual behavior. Christensen's new data and analysis were unknown to this author at the time that the data presented here were gathered and analyzed, so these two studies may represent independent confirmation of Christensen's earlier observations. In view of the previously mentioned problems associated with comparing data or conclusions from two survey studies, the convergence of the present study with that of Christensen and Gregg is quite remarkable.

Their study confirms the observation that the frequency of premarital sexual experience has increased among young college-educated Americans and that our sexual norms now approximate those popular in Scandinavia about ten years ago. Moreover, the observation that the degree of consistency between attitudes and behavior has increased is common to both studies.

It should be emphasized that this apparent increase in premarital sexual behavior is not the result of a breakdown of standards but rather the natural outcome of the application of a different type of normative system. Young people today may be exploring new and different areas of interpersonal relationships, but they are not lost in a sexual wilderness. As predicted by Reiss (1968) (whose data were collected in the early sixties) ". . . there has been a gradually increasing acceptance of and overtness about sexuality. The basic change is toward greater equalitarianism, greater female acceptance of permissiveness, and more open discussion. In the next decade we can expect a step-up in the pace of this change" (p. 32).

If the data presented here can be generalized, it seems that the most recent changes have tended to bring behavior in line with attitudes. This represents a psychologically stable system, and it seems unlikely that there will be very significant further changes in either sexual attitudes or sexual behavior in the next five to eight years. We may expect to come somewhat closer to male-female equity in occupational choice, status, etc., but the change is likely to be quite slow and class-oriented. The Scandinavian countries today are moving in this direction and I expect that our social norms will follow theirs as our sexual norms have.

These existing and impending changes have strong implications for the role of professionals in the health and guidance fields. There is not one new sex ethic, but many new sex ethics. Our personal code may be only one of many. Rubin (1965) writing on the implications for the education of adolescents vis à vis the transition in sex values has suggested three very timely tasks for professionals. The first is to acknowledge "that major value conflicts exist in our society and that no consensus exists among adults" (p. 189). This clearly necessitates that texts and data in the field be re-evaluated to insure that principles of scientific objectivity are upheld. Moreover, it calls for extensive and thorough research on the effects of value changes, of pornography, abortion, sex education, and other concomitants of change.

Rubin's second point was that we give guidance by education rather than indoctrination; that we "deal with all the known facts and results of research; teach critical judgement in dealing with ethical controversy" (p. 189). This requires that we educate ourselves and carefully examine our own standards, knowledge, and prejudices. It would be best, perhaps, if we did not become apologists for the status quo or community standards by developing a new or nonscientific rationale for the old system.

His last point is that we adopt as the main goal of our research and teaching the inculcation of methods and knowledge which will equip people for "intelligent self determination rather than conformity to procedures which will have no educative effect on their real choices of conduct" (p. 189).

The point of studying public attitudes is not to conform to them or to set norms by popular vote, but to recognize their diversity and thereby to dispel pluralistic ignorance.

REFERENCES

Athanasiou, R., Shaver, P., & Tavris, C. Sex (report to *Psychology Today* readers). *Psychology Today* 1970, 4: 37–52.

Athanasiou, R., & Shaver, P. Correlates of heterosexuals' reactions to pornography. *Journal of Sex Research* 1971, 7: 298-311.

Brehm, J., & Cohen, A. *Explorations in cognitive dissonance*. New York: Wiley, 1964.

Christensen, H. T. Scandinavian and American sex norms: some comparisons with sociological implications. *Journal of Social Issues* 1966, 22: 60-75.

Christensen, H. T., & Gregg, C. F. Changing sex norms in America and Scandinavia. *Journal of Marriage and the Family* 1970, 33: 616-27.

Commission on Obscenity and Pornography, The report of. New York: Bantam Books, 1970.

Ellis, A. *Reason and emotion in psychotherapy*. New York: Lyle Stuart, 1963.

Ellis, A., & Harper, R. *A guide to rational living*. New York: Prentice-Hall, 1961.

Festinger, L. *A theory of cognitive dissonance*. Stanford: Stanford University Press, 1957.

Gallup Opinion Index. Princeton: Gallup International. #48, June 1969, p. 32. #49, July 1969, pp. 16-24. #54, October 1969, p. 24.

Gebhard, P. H., Gagnon, J. H., Pomeroy, W. B., & Christenson, C. V. *Sex offenders: an analysis of types*. New York: Harper and Row, 1965.

Katz, D. The functional approach to the study of attitudes. *Public Opinion Quarterly* 1960: 163-204.

Kinsey, A. C., Pomeroy, W. B., Martin, C. E., & Gebhard, P. H. *Sexual behavior in the human female*. Philadelphia: W. B. Saunders, 1953.

Kirkendall, L., & Miles, G. Sex education research. *Review of Educational Research*, Dec. 1968.

Kreck, D., Crutchfield, R. S., & Ballachey, E. L. *Individual in society*. New York: McGraw-Hill, 1962.

Kutschinsky, B. Studies on pornography and sex crimes in Denmark. *New Social Science Monographs*, Rosenorns Alle 11, 1925, Kobenhavn V. Denmark, 1970.

Mann, J. Effects of erotic movies upon sexual behavior. Paper read at 78th Annual Convention of the American Psychological Association, Miami Beach, Florida, September 7, 1970 (mimeographed).

Mosher, D. L., & Greenberg, I. Females' affective responses to reading erotic literature. *J. Consulting and Clinical Psychology* 1969, 33 (4): 472-77.

Packard, V. *The sexual wilderness*. New York: Pocket Books, 1968.

Reiss, I. How and why America's sex standards are changing. *Trans-Action* 1968, 5: 26-32.

Robinson, J. P., Rusk, G., & Head, K. *Measures of political attitudes*. Ann Arbor: Institute for Social Research, 1968.

Rubin, I. Transition in sex values—implication for the education of adolescents. *Journal of Marriage and the Family* 1965: 185–89.

Schindler, G. (ed.), *A report on Denmark's legalized pornography*. Torrance, Calif.: Banner Books, 1969.

Wallace, D., Wehmer, G., & Podany, E. Contemporary community standards of visual erotica. In *Technical Reports of the C.O.P.*, vol. 9, U.S. Gov't Printing Office, Washington, D.C., in press (also mimeographed).

chapter 20

Co-marital Sex: The Incorporation of Extra-marital Sex into the Marriage Relationship

Lynn G. Smith* and James R. Smith†

Many of our social institutions have been facing the challenge of change, and the institution of marriage has been no exception. Predictions for the future of marriage include a continuation of the trend toward "serial monogamy" or "serial polygamy," as it is alternately designated, as the primary pattern plus an emergent secondary pattern of experimentation with innovations and alternate models of marriage relationship (Farson, Hauser, Stroup, & Wiener 1969). Many of these innovations and alternate models involve a rejection of the monogamic ideal and an incorporation of extramarital sex into the marriage relationship (Otto 1970).

Recently some couples have moved into the public and scientific spotlight who are exploring and practicing a substantial inclu-

*Lynn G. Smith, M.A., University of California, Berkeley.
†James R. Smith, M.A., University of California, Berkeley.

sion of extramarital sex into their marriages. These are the couples who participate in mate-sharing or co-marital sex and who have popularly been labeled "swingers." This practice has been the subject of our research for the past four years, and it is the purpose of this paper to present some of our findings and provide a conceptual framework for understanding this type of marital arrangement.

This paper is based on an exploratory field study undertaken in 1966 in the San Francisco Bay area. After gaining access to the sexual freedom or "swinging" subculture through its member groups, the project involved (1) taped depth interviews with group leaders; (2) behavioral observations at over 150 "sexually liberal" gatherings; (3) informal interviews with over 200 participants; and (4) 503 completed questionnaires.

Initially, let us inquire into the fundamental social characteristics of the target population and ask: Who are these persons and what is the apparent magnitude and scope of their behavior? Virtually all studies, our own included, of those involved in co-marital sex have shown the majority to be middle- and upper-middle-class individuals, many of them highly educated, relatively affluent, and engaged in professional or semiprofessional occupations. Their religious commitment tends to be low, and politically they range from radical to ultraconservative (Smith & Smith 1970). They do not fit popular conceptions of deviant individuals and do not exhibit a high order of deviance. Presumptions of pathology and pathological motivation, so frequently espoused in psychoanalytic literature, have not been supported by any empirical studies to date. One recently completed study employing the Minnesota Multiphasic Personality Inventory (MMPI) found the profiles of participants to be what is sometimes called "disgustingly normal" (Twitchell 1970).

The extent of co-marital sexual involvement in our population is a question which must be approached with caution. Estimates have ranged from one million to eight million couples (Bartell 1971; Breedlove 1964). It is always difficult to obtain reliable incidence figures on deviant forms of behavior, but tentative indicators are now becoming available which begin to provide a more scientifically respectable basis for estimation. In a recent questionnaire survey of sexual attitudes and behavior, the question: "Have

you ever participated in wife swapping?" was included (Athanasiou 1970). Of a national sample of 20,000 respondents 5 percent
of the married respondents indicated that they had participated in
"wife swapping," either "once or twice" or "frequently." Another
one-third of the married respondents indicated that they had not
participated in the past, but that they "might" in the future,
perhaps if the opportunity arose. Findings from this survey are not
presented as directly applicable to the country as a whole as the
respondents were predominantly young (the majority were under
thirty), well educated (median level was college graduate), of relatively high socioeconomic status (almost two-thirds earned over
$10,000), and their religious affiliation was low (nearly one-third
claimed to be atheists or agnostics). However, the authors suggested that their findings were descriptive of a well-educated, intelligent group that "just might be a wave of the future." Our sample
(N=503) drawn from those participating in co-marital sex was
found to exhibit very similar demographic characteristics (Smith &
Smith 1970).

Studies of co-marital sex have found that it is more often the
husband than the wife who instigates such involvement (Bartell
1970; Bell 1970; Schupp 1970; Smith & Smith 1970; Varni 1970).
Similarly, Athanasiou found in his sample that twice as many of
the husbands (41 percent) as wives (22 percent) were interested in
"swapping." Considering only those married respondents in his
sample who had a history of extramarital sex, almost 10 percent
had experienced it in its co-marital form. While still small, this is
perhaps a surprisingly large percentage. Another recent study also
sheds light on the question of the extent of co-marital participation. In a study of extramarital sex among a sample of middle-
class, middle-aged, mid-western couples, a 5 percent level of
co-marital experience was also found (Johnson 1971). These two
studies constitute the best indicators of the extent of actual involvement at the present time. Thus, psychologists and counselors
can no longer simply assume that when adultery occurs, it is carried out in a furtive, clandestine, deceptive manner.* More and

*For the purposes of this paper the term "adultery" is used as synonymous with
extramarital sex. In our culture the former is legally defined by the latter, but the
illegitimacy of adultery is not attached to all occurrences of extramarital sex in other
cultures.

more when the topic of extramarital sex arises, whether it be on a questionnaire (Athanasiou 1970), as the subject of a discussion among professionals (Neubeck 1969), or among individuals in everyday life, the question of knowledge and consent by the spouse is raised and mediates in the resultant responses.

Deception has previously been a characteristic feature of adultery; and the effects of adultery have turned more on the success or failure of the deception than on the omission or commission of the adulterous act itself. Adultery is often accepted when it is practiced with discretion and no one is the wiser, and yet it is the deception which provides a large part of the sting when it is discovered.

We are now witnessing among a seemingly growing minority of our population an acknowledgement of the desire for and occurrence of extramarital sex coupled with a rejection of the deception which has previously permeated its practice. The emphasis of the 1960s on communication—honesty and openness—and the youth culture's rejection of hypocrisy have doubtless been in part responsible for both. And it would seem that participants in co-marital sex have taken the spousal and familial "togetherness" emphasized in the 1950s a step further than anticipated or intended.

FORMS OF ADULTERY

Since there are significant variations in the forms which the contemporary practice of adultery is assuming, some distinctions are in order. We wish to distinguish two basic forms of adultery: *conventional* adultery and *consensual* adultery. The former is characterized by the presence of deception and is unknown to the spouse or known only ex post facto. The latter, consensual adultery, is characterized by a lack of deception and both the knowledge and consent of the spouse. Consensual adultery may or may not involve spousal encouragement and may be undertaken as either an individual or dyadic activity.

Three substantially different forms of consensual adultery have emerged:

Adultery toleration. This is the form of consensual adultery which is most similar to conventional adultery. In this form, spouses simply extend to each other the freedom to engage in extramarital sex individually, usually according to a dyadically developed set of ground rules. This may or may not involve encouragement or acceptance beyond the degree of simple toleration. Such adultery toleration pacts were reported to exist some years ago by Hamilton (1929) and by Lindsey (1928). Recent acknowledgements of adultery toleration pacts among the affluent have been described by Cuber and Harroff (1965). Adultery toleration allows extramarital sex into the marriage relationship on very much the same basis as conventional adultery, except that the partners are relieved of their commitment to sexual exclusivity. As a result, the necessity and rationale for deception are removed. They may still practice extramarital sex in a clandestine fashion, but they have what is sometimes simply called an understanding or arrangement. Adultery toleration may or may not involve both partners, that is, it may be a unilateral or bilateral toleration agreement and, if bilateral, may or may not be actually practiced by both partners.

Co-marital relations. Another form of integration of extramarital sex, one which further incorporates it into the marital relationship, is what is commonly called mate-sharing or swinging. In this form of consensual adultery, both partners participate and they participate as a dyad. We prefer the term "co-marital relations" to refer to this form rather than the popular term swinging, because the latter is vague, misleading, and objectionable to some participants, and because the term swinging is becoming almost exclusively associated with a certain subtype of co-marital sex, that type which has been called "recreational" and which discourages emotional involvements.

Co-marital sex is practiced on both a couple-to-couple basis and on a group basis. In the former case it typically involves one couple meeting with another couple and exchanging partners for sexual activity. Sometimes this acquaintance is made through classified advertisements; sometimes it arises and develops more or less spontaneously from previous friendship relations. The sexual activity may take place in the same room, in different rooms in private in the same house, or in different houses with each couple retiring to separate dwellings with the temporary partner.

In the case of co-marital sex on a group basis, a number of couples meet at the same time and sexual activity may occur among any of those present rather than being limited to a direct switching of partners. In this form one partner may more easily participate sexually while the other does not. It is not a matter of both or neither participating in the sexual activity on any particular occasion, although some groups and many individual couples do set up rules to that effect.* More often than not, there is no formally circumscribed group such as a "swap club," as they have been designated, but rather simply gatherings of friends and recent acquaintances who choose to party together. The spouses in these cases know and interact with the extramarital partners and may well be friends.

Group marriage. A third form of consensual adultery, though one whose incidence is far lower than either of the above-mentioned forms, is group marriage. This, of course, involves going beyond the conventional two-person marital relationship. It is the extreme expression of the incorporation of extramarital sex into marriage, involving a significantly altered form of marriage. In a strict sense, therefore, it does not constitute extramarital relations, for all the parties consider themselves married to each other. This, of course, is not legally recognized, so it constitutes an ambiguous analytic category, but one which should be sociologically recognized nonetheless. Group marriage is a large and amorphous category which will need to be refined further along several dimensions in order to accommodate in a theoretically useful way the large range of involvements and affiliations, from casual cohabitation and casual but steady group liaisons to intimate peer groups and companionate families with a high degree of integration.

These forms of consensual adultery are not necessarily mutually exclusive and cannot be considered to form a typology.† One couple may participate in any or all of the forms, while others limit themselves to one form or another. Our research has been primarily concerned with the co-marital form of consensual adultery, and more specifically with co-marital sex on a group basis.

---

*A rule is a codified form of mutually obligatory expectations intended to regulate behavior.

†There is no specifiable ordering variable that could be taken as reliable at this point.

MOTIVATION PATTERNS

To date, two main motivation patterns have emerged from studies of swingers, and each of these patterns exhibit corresponding styles of expression which have been labeled "recreational" and "utopian" and which transect the co-marital forms mentioned above (Symonds 1967). These are best conceived as opposite ends of a continuum. Though they are only rudimentary descriptive categories, they are currently accepted as useful. A more recent attempt to establish descriptive categories, based on a participant observation study, yielded a five-part classification scheme, including "hard-core," "egotistical," "recreational," "interpersonal," and "communal swingers" (Varni 1970).

Utilizing the currently employed recreational-utopian continuum, which may be viewed as a continuum of isolated-integrated deviance, the "recreational swinger" at one end of the continuum is, as the term indicates, someone who "uses swinging as a form of recreation." These persons usually explicitly discourage emotional involvement with their extramarital partners. They are willing to participate sexually with relative strangers at parties and may do so on an anonymous basis. Address books are sometimes kept alphabetically by first names. Emotional attachment is considered threatening to the marriage, and co-marital relationships are thus kept on a "sex only" basis. Many curtail sexual involvements on an individual basis, such as individual dates or even unilateral involvement at a particular party, thereby attempting to guard against emotional involvement.

Recreational swingers are to a large degree conformists, deviating only in their sexual behavior. In fact, even in their sexual behavior, except that it does not take place on a totally monogamous basis, they are also conformists. They are more inclined to engage in sexual activity in relative privacy and less inclined toward group sexual experiences. They sometimes choose not even to engage in group nudity, retiring to a bedroom in private with a chosen sexual partner, disrobing, engaging in sexual activity, and dressing again before returning to the other couple or group.

The "utopian swinger," at the other end of the continuum, is idealistic and sees swinging (if he employs the term at all) as a part of a new life-style that emphasizes communality and interpersonal depth. Persons of this type do not accept the norms of the conventional social order without question and are more likely to be social-action oriented, though not necessarily radical or militant. Emotional involvement with others is preferred. In this sense, they are not swingers, that is, couples who intend and attempt to limit themselves to casual or anonymous sexual encounters and who discourage and severely restrict emotional attachments to others.

It is important to draw a distinction with reference to the utopian swinger in particular between preference level and acceptance level. The two tend to coalesce in the recreational group but despite the fact that the overt behavior may be similar, the structure of expectations is profoundly different. The utopian swinger prefers a total relationship but under varying circumstances will accept somewhat less. Further, there is a disparity between the two groups in that, as far as sexual involvements are concerned, the recreational type will accept his utopian counterpart, but often feels threatened when invited into a more complex and committed relationship. The utopian will swing, but is less likely to be fulfilled by that type of relationship. Their differing expectation and satisfaction levels are conducive to a pattern of conflict which promotes subgrouping along these differing motivational dimensions. Utopian swingers want to share more than sex. Their interpersonal goals include a measure of sociality and friendship. They speak of intimacy and self-development. And they tend to show interest in alternate forms of social life, sometimes a willingness to share food, shelter, and daily life.

In fact, there appears to be two relatively distinct subcultures which may be suitably distinguished in terms of their value orientations. Subgrouping also occurs along other dimensions, such as marital status, age, level of attractiveness, and type of drug use, but is most prominently exhibited in terms of this fundamental value orientation.

The utopian-recreational distinction to some degree parallels Reiss's distinction in a premarital context between "permissiveness with affection" and "permissiveness without affection" (1960). In the case of the recreational swinger we find "permissiveness without affection" institutionalized. It is their way of reaffirming and securing their commitment to marriage; they remain emotionally monogamous while at the same time rejecting sexual monogamy. Recreational swinging is in this way a functional alternative to the declining practice of patronizing prostitutes, but on an ostensibly equilateral basis. It would appear that they are less secure in their marriages than their utopian counterparts and thus jealously guard against emotional involvements with others as a protective precaution.

In between these two extremes are many who want more than sex from their extramarital or co-marital relationships, but who do not anticipate communal living arrangements. They want to expand their interpersonal relationships to a more intimate level, sensing perhaps or reflecting a relationship between marital satisfaction and the number of close friends and relatives. A recent study (Renne 1970) found that people with few intimate associates were more likely to be dissatisfied with their marriages. It is apparent that the isolated nuclear family is experiencing an interpersonal intimacy impoverishment. Various forms of intimate networks are being therapeutically proposed to relieve this condition (Stoller 1970; Farson 1969). Utopian swinging fits such a pattern and may be considered a natural social experiment with as yet unknown results. Sexual intimacy, heretofore usually presumed to be purely dyadic, purely heterosexual, and purely private, is sought with a variety of persons as a means to establish such networks of intimacy. There is a discernible developmental tendency among participants in co-marital sex who initially adopt a recreational emphasis to move, over time, toward concern with interpersonal relations. One is tempted to suggest that a maturational process occurs.

Viewed from within the putative conventional structure of the social order, the above forms of adultery—conventional and consensual adultery and the three subforms of the latter—show a progression which may be mapped in terms of four separate but related continua. These four continua are: (1) the relative frequency of occurrence in the general population; (2) the extent of incorporation of extramarital sex into the marriage relationship; (3) the degree of sociality of expression; and (4) the degree of sanctions based upon the extremity and visibility of the deviant behavior. The underlying relationship appears to be a positive one between the degree of deviance from the conventional norms of monogamy and the degree of sociality and interpersonal intimacy. This, of course, suggests that despite our theoretical prejudices and cultural biases we live, at least sexually, in a basically anti-social environment,* and that Western Christian social life erects a barrier between group sentiment and sexual expression (Freud, 1960). Recreational swingers maintain this barrier by allowing plural and group sex but restricting plural sentiment and group love.

Consensual adultery in its various forms thus involves an alteration of the marital ground rules in such a way as to incorporate extramarital sex. One result is that extramarital sex becomes subject to greater dyadic control. This appears to be one factor which attenuates a jealousy response. There is no a priori reason to believe that those couples who participate together in extramarital sex and those couples who extend sexual freedom to each other in the form of adultery toleration are any the less committed to their marriages or to the institution of marriage than those who participate in the conventional form of extramarital sex without their spouse's knowledge. In one sense, they are expressing a greater commitment to intimacy in their marriage by refusing to conceal their respective extramarital interests and proclivities. They are attempting to recognize and resolve a problem which has plagued monogamous marriage—the virtually universal sexual desire for persons other than one's spouse (Neubeck 1969)—by agreeing to a mutually acceptable outlet for such desires. In this sense they are creating their own marriage contract by defining it from within rather than simply conforming to preexisting institutional frameworks, though swinging already shows signs of becoming an institutionalized alternative.

*"The great evil of monogamy, and its most seriously weak point, is its tendency to self-concentration at the expense of the outer world. . . . The family is a great social influence in so far as it is the best instrument for creating children who will make the future citizens; but in a certain sense the family is an anti-social influence, for it tends to absorb unduly the energy that is needed for the invigoration of society. It is possible, indeed, that that fact led to the modification of the monogamic system in early developing periods of human history, when social expansion and cohesion were the primary necessities. The family too often tends to resemble, as someone has said, the secluded collection of grubs sometimes revealed in their narrow home when we casually raise a flat stone in our gardens." Havelock Ellis, *Studies in the psychology of sex*, vol. II, p. 570. New York: Random House, 1936.

Sampling inadequacies have prevented any conclusions to date about the relative success and failure rates of such ventures. There are and will be casualties from consensual adultery—the question remains whether there will be greater or fewer casualties proportionately than from conventional adultery. But that such alterations of marital ground rules can be successful is evident from isolated cases of couples who have happily maintained such arrangements for periods of twenty years and more. Whether consensual adultery is or will become a feasible alternative to conventional adultery for any sizable portion of the population is yet to be seen.

PREMARITAL ETHICS AND MARITAL SEXUALITY

If we assume that the attitudes and value orientations which prevail prior to marriage tend to shape expectations for marriage itself, a relationship may be posited between premarital ethics and marital sexuality. We should like to offer a tentative hypothesis that the greater the frequency and degree of premarital permissiveness the greater the likelihood that couples will display tendencies to engage in co-marital relations or adultery toleration. A positive relationship between premarital and extramarital coital experience has previously been reported but has received little attention in recent years (Hamilton 1929; Terman 1938; Kinsey, Pomeroy, Martin, & Gebhard 1953). A reexamination and refinement of the existence of such a relationship would appear to be warranted in the light of the recent proliferation of forms of adultery discussed above.

In the last century, the scientific study of and public concern with sexual activity independent of marriage has progressed from an emphasis on premarital to postmarital relations and only recently to extramarital relations. Attitudes toward premarital and postmarital relations have been modified in the direction of an increased tolerance and acceptance, and though it has long been debated and denied, there appears to be an increase in the incidence level of premarital coitus as well, particularly among females (Christensen 1970). It is likely that a similar shift will occur with respect to extramarital relations (Farsons et al. 1969; Pomeroy

1969). We can appreciate the fact that extramarital relations is the last in this progression to be accorded tolerance and acceptance in that it is in the form of sexual relations independent of marital sanctions which is generally considered the most threatening to marriage itself, since it occurs concurrent with the marital relationship and violates our notions that we cannot love and should not have sexual relations with more than one person at a time (Bowman 1949; Comfort 1966; Freud 1912, 1918).

There has been much controversy during the past few decades over the question of a sexual revolution. One of the confounding factors in such discussions has been the lack of determination of what would constitute a revolutionary as opposed to an evolutionary change and to what particular expressions of sexuality one should look. The premarital realm is still the primary focus of the search for evidence of revolutionary change, though there is some evidence that if there has been a revolutionary change in premarital chastity, it occurred in the 1920's (Van der Bourg 1970). We would do well to examine the effects of such premarital changes on other realms of sexuality, in particular, extramarital relations. Kinsey et al. (1953) found a higher incidence of extramarital sexual experience among females who had a history of premarital sex; an increase of premarital sex among females would suggest that we might well expect a higher incidence of extramarital sex subsequently.

Whether or not we acknowledge a revolution in premarital sexuality, we can now see that an alternate premarital ethic of permissiveness has emerged and is competing with the nonpermissive premarital ethic. Both standards currently receive widespread social support. Employing Reiss's (1960) four-part distinction, "abstinence" and the "double standard" may be seen to constitute the traditional nonpermissive premarital ethical forms, while "permissiveness with affection" and "permissiveness without affection" characterize the newer permissive ethical forms. Premarital nonpermissiveness has led rather naturally to the traditional nonpermissive "closed" form of marriage, defined as a permanent and sexually exclusive union. It may be, however, that a strain is generated by moving from the newer ethic of premarital permissiveness to the traditional nonpermissive marriage and that what we are witnessing is the development of a corresponding alternate marital ethic, that of the more permissive "open" marriage.* Adultery occurs in both marital forms, but the nonpermissive marriage would be expected to generate conventional adultery, whereas the permissive marriage would be expected to generate some form of consensual adultery.

Evidence supportive of a relationship between premarital and marital sexual ethics may be seen in the consistently high incidence of premarital coitus reported to date among participants in co-marital sex.† In one recent study of co-marital participants 93 percent of the married respondents (N=151) reported a history of premarital coitus (Smith & Smith, 1970); in another recent study 91 percent of the experimental group of couples who had engaged in co-marital sex (N=60) reported a history of premarital coitus as opposed to 50 percent of the control group of married couples who had not engaged in co-marital sex (Schupp 1970). Preliminary examination of Athanasiou's data (1970) suggests the following relationships: (1) the greater the number of premarital partners the greater the likelihood of co-marital sex ($\chi^2 = 50$, $df = 21$, $p < .001$); (2) the further from marriage that first intercourse occurred and the lower the degree of commitment to the first coital partner the greater the likelihood of interest in co-marital sex ($\chi^2 = 56$, $df = 12$, $p < .001$); and (3) the greater the liberality of opinion about premarital sexual intercourse the greater the likelihood of co-marital sex ($\chi^2 = 107$, $df = 15$, $p < .001$). However, this data is currently being subjected to more stringent statistical examination, so this evidence must be currently viewed as tentative. This data bears more directly on the hypothesized relationship between the frequency and degree of premarital permissiveness and the tendency to engage in co-marital relations than do sheer incidence levels.

It is not suggested that premarital permissiveness by any means inevitably leads to a permissive marital ethic, but only that it might be considered a predisposing factor. Psychodynamically, what is involved is an acceptance by one's mate of multilateral intimacy, whether previous or concurrent. Those who accept a single standard of permissiveness have thus transcended the traditional fetish of virginity. This means that male and female alike must accept the fact that their prospective mate will not likely be a virgin. A comparison of cross-cultural data gathered in 1958 and 1968 by Christensen (1970) provides evidence of a decrease in preference for marrying a virgin on the part of both male and female college students. This acceptance, if it is genuine, makes other such relationships both more likely and easier to cope with, as long as a basic trust is maintained. Such a trust is the basis for a new perspective on both adultery and infidelity.

THE CONCEPT OF INFIDELITY

The development of permissive as well as nonpermissive marriages and the separation of adultery and deception necessitate a corresponding distinction between adultery and infidelity. For those persons involved in co-marital relations or any form of consensual adultery, adultery is not equated with infidelity. The concept of unfaithfulness for these persons is not wholly inapplicable to the act of adultery, but is considered applicable only within a narrow range, depending not on the simple occurrence of the act itself but on its surrounding circumstances.

From our study it is evident that the circumstances under which consensual adultery constitutes unfaithfulness or infidelity may generally be classified as those which involve (1) deception, (2) a breach of any specific agreement or rule of conduct as defined or accepted by the couple themselves, or (3) a violation of paramount loyalty. It is these same circumstances which generally constitute the basis for equating adultery with infidelity, in that at least one of these circumstances, and usually more, is present in the conventional adultery situation. The alteration in the contemporary use of the concept of infidelity is simply, and quite importantly, a recognition that adultery or extramarital sex can take place without the simultaneous occurrence of any of these circumstances. Adultery does not necessarily involve deception, the breach of an agreement, or a violation of paramount loyalty—just as the realization of these three circumstances does not necessarily imply that the act of adultery has been committed. What constitutes fidelity has been reinterpreted by the actors themselves and is not presumed to be inextricably tied to the omission or commission of the act of adultery.

To a large degree, the effect of extramarital sex depends on the meaning assigned to it by the actors and on the marital ground rules they have established. When the meaning differs between the principals or the ground rules are not clear, conflict ensues. When we assume that the occurrence of adultery implies preference for another or is symptomatic of the fact that the marriage is deteriorating, then extramarital sex tends to mean those things to those involved. Their responses will differ according to the system of agreements between spouses and their respective perceptions of the ways in which those agreements are upheld or violated. As Cuber (1969) has noted, the effect of extramarital sex on the marital relationship depends on several factors: "(a) whether the adultery is carried on furtively or is known by the spouse; (b) whether the marriage partners agree to the propriety or expediency of such behavior; (c) whether one or both participates; and (d) whether the condonement is genuine and based on principle or is simply the result of an ultimatum by one of the parties" (p. 193).

CONCLUSION

Consensual adultery in general and co-marital sex in particular need not be viewed as necessarily destructive of marriage, but may well be an evolutionary development which will turn out to be supportive of marriage—simply one in a series of attempts to reform monogamous marriage (Beigel 1969). The reform in this case

involves the sanctioning of extramarital relations. This incorporation of extramarital sex into the marriage relationship constitutes
a redefinition of marital boundaries.

Whether such alternatives to and redefinitions of monogamic
marriage will be viable in the long run remains to be seen. The
study of consensual adultery and co-marital relations is a relatively
new area of research. It is only beginning to emerge from the
exploratory phase, as indeed are many of the participants themselves. Categorization of motivation patterns and types of involvement, even the vocabulary for analysis, are at this point rudimentary and tentative. To dismiss this behavior as a passing fad or
neurotic obsession would be premature; to conclude that such
behavior is inevitably detrimental or beneficial to marriage would
be an oversimplification. Such judgments must be withheld until
sufficient scientific information becomes available.

In all other spheres of life we acknowledge and recognize the
existence of individual differences and sanction their expression. If
we extend this realization to the marital and sexual sphere, then
we must acknowledge that a proliferation of marital styles and
frameworks may help the individual actor grow, develop, and meet
his or her varying needs. From our perspective the private actions
of consenting adults are best left to the decisions of the individuals
involved. At the same time there is a manifest need for a scientific
understanding which would allow them to make those decisions in
a more rational and humane environment.

REFERENCES

Athanasiou, R., Shaver, P., & Tavris, C. Sex. *Psychology Today* 1970, 4(2):
    37–52.

Bartell, G. Group sex among the mid-Americans. *Journal of Sex Research*
    1970, 6: 113–30.

_____. *Group sex*. New York: Wyden, 1971.

Beigel, H. In defense of mate swapping. *Rational Living* 1969, 4(1): 15–16.

Bell, R. R. "Swinging"—the sexual exchange of marriage partners. Paper pre-
    sented at the meeting of the Society for the Study of Social Problems,
    Washington, D.C., August 1970.

Bowman, C. C. Cultural ideology and heterosexual reality: a preface to socio-
    logical research. *American Sociological Review* 1949, 14: 624–33.

Breedlove, W., & Breedlove, J. *Swap clubs.* Los Angeles: Sherbourne Press, 1964.

Christensen, H. T., & Gregg, C. F. Changing sex norms in America and Scandinavia. *Journal of Marriage and the Family* 1970, 32: 616-27.

Comfort, A. *Sex in society.* London: Duckworth, 1963. (Re-published: New York: Citadel Press, 1966.)

Cuber, J. F. Adultery: reality versus stereotype. In G. Neubeck (ed.), *Extra-marital relations.* Englewood Cliffs, N.J.: Prentice-Hall, 1969.

Cuber, J. F., & Harroff, P. B. *Sex and the significant Americans: a study of sexual behavior among the affluent.* Baltimore: Penguin Books, 1965.

Ellis, H. *Studies in the psychology of sex,* vol. II. New York: Random House, 1936.

Farson, R. E., Hauser, P. M., Stroup, H., & Weiner, A. J. *The future of the family.* New York: Family Service Association of America, 1969.

Freud, S. Contributions to the psychology of love: the most prevalent form of degradation in erotic life (1912). In Freud, S., *Collected papers* 4: 203-16. New York: Basic Books, 1959.

_____. Contributions to the psychology of love: the taboo of virginity (1918). In Freud, S., *Collected papers* 4: 217-35. New York: Basic Books, 1959.

_____. *Group psychology and the analysis of the ego.* New York: Bantam, 1960.

Gilmartin, B. Unpublished data, 1971.

Hamilton, G. V. *A research in marriage.* New York: Albert & Charles Boni, 1929.

Johnson, R. Personal communication, January 5, 1971.

Kinsey, A. C., Pomeroy, W. B., Martin, C. E., & Gebhard, P. H. *Sexual behavior in the human female.* Philadelphia: W. B. Saunders, 1953.

Lindsey, B. B., & Evans, W. *The companionate marriage.* New York: Garden City, 1929.

Neubeck, G. (ed.) *Extra-marital relations.* Englewood Cliffs, N.J.: Prentice-Hall, 1969.

O'Neill, G. C., & O'Neill, N. Patterns in group sexual activity. *Journal of Sex Research* 1970, 6: 101-12.

Otto, H. A. (ed.) *The family in search of a future.* New York: Appleton-Century-Crofts, 1970.

Pomeroy, W. Seminar on adulterous sexual behavior at the 1966 Annual Groves Conference, "Two Clinicians and a Sociologist." In Neubeck (ed.) *Extra-marital relations.* Englewood Cliffs, N.J.: Prentice-Hall, 1969.

Reiss, I. L. *Premarital sexual standards in America.* New York: Free Press, 1960.

Renne, K. Correlates of dissatisfaction in marriage. *Journal of Marriage and the Family* 1970, 32: 54–67.

Rudner, R. S. *Philosophy of social science*. Englewood Cliffs, N.J.: Prentice-Hall, 1966.

Schupp, C. An analysis of some socio-psychological factors which operate in the functioning relationship of married couples who exchange mates for the purpose of sexual experience. Doctoral dissertation, United States International University, 1970.

Smith, J. R., & Smith, L. G. Co-marital sex and the sexual freedom movement. *Journal of Sex Research* 1970, 6: 131–42.

———. (eds.). *Co-marital sex: recent studies of sexual alternatives in marriage*. In preparation. Unpublished research referred to in this paper is scheduled for inclusion in this collection.

Stoller, F. H. The intimate network of families as a new structure. In Otto, H. A. (ed.), *The family in search of a future*. New York: Appleton-Century-Crofts, 1970.

Symonds, C. A pilot study of the peripheral behavior of sexual mate swappers. Master's thesis, University of California, Riverside, 1967.

Terman, L. M. *Psychological factors in marital happiness*. New York: McGraw-Hill, 1938.

Twitchell, J. Unpublished research, 1971.

Van der Bourg. Hugh Gimball Lectures on the Psychology of Sex, University of California Medical School, San Francisco, November 1970.

Varni, C. A participant observer study of sexual mate exchange among married couples. Paper presented at the meeting of the Pacific Sociological Association, Honolulu, April 1971.

chapter 21

Pornography
in the Home:
A Topic in
Medical Education

John Money[*]

RELEVANCE OF PORNOGRAPHY IN A SEX EDUCATION COURSE

I am going to begin my talk for the first part of this session with the question: Why bother with pornography in a sex education course? The answer first of all is that it is a social issue today, a community issue, and so has relevance to the thinking of all of us, especially, I would say, to the thinking people who ought to become community leaders eventually—people who should be able to accept invitations to discuss with church groups, PTA groups, or any other community groups, issues of how they should feel and how they should act, and indeed, how they should act politically with regard to this still very touchy issue of the imagery of sex.

In addition to the problem in the community, and how the community should regulate itself, there is also an even more

[*]John Money, Ph.D., The Johns Hopkins University School of Medicine, Baltimore, Maryland.

touchy problem with regard to the introduction of the imagery of sex or pornography in the home. There is likely to be more and more pornography in the home because of the change that is taking place, particularly with regard to commercial pornography. But it doesn't really matter whether pornography comes into the home in three dimensions, in book form, or movie form. What really matters is that it comes into the home in the minds and the brains of the people who occupy the house. I'm thinking of course, particularly, of the children and the teenagers. The big issue here for parents is: How do we deal with this material—these books that come into the house, or the talk about them? Most parents really are at a loss to know what to do. I know that from some of the parents I've talked to, who don't know even what to do with *Playboy*, although that would seem to most of us here, I think, to be not qualified or not qualifiable as pornography anymore.

In addition to the community and the family, there is a personal relevance of the imagery of sex, of pornography. Each person has his own imagery that turns him or her on the most, with regard to sexual arousal. He may, indeed, be perplexed about it at some time, which may be especially the case in teenagers just over the boundary line of puberty. In addition, the personal relevance of pornography can be related to the actual success of one's own sex life in adulthood. So each person has to make a decision as to where he or she stands with regard to sexual stimulation from sexy pictures or sexy stories.

Another good reason for introducing the topic of pornography into sex education is that imagery is a neglected part of sex education. It is something that does indeed seem to make most people very uncomfortable if they have to discuss it, either in close personal acquaintance or more at a distance, as, for example, between speaker and audience. As it turns out, the productions of commercial pornography are one of the best ways of introducing this topic of imagery into the total context of sex education.

SEX ATTRACTANTS AND LOVE

Let's not forget that it is indeed part of Nature's major and grand design to use perceptual imagery in order to procreate the race.

Or, if I may say that in a more everyday way, boys are girl-watchers. I must be careful if I want to turn that around and say that girls are boy-watchers, because it's not exactly the perfect complement. The point I have in mind here is that, if you think of the insect world and some of the lower mammals, Nature's plan to ensure the procreation of the species is to have the member of one sex attracted toward the other on the basis of the sense of smell through pheromones—pheromones being long-distance activators, chemical attractants that can be transmitted through the air and received by the nose, in much the same way that hormones can be carried in the blood stream from one part of the body to another.

So far as one can tell, Nature didn't have it as part of her planned design for us human beings to be very much reliant on odors or pheromones as sexual attractants to give initial impetus to the procreation of the species. In a way, we could consider ourselves a little more like the birds, where Nature's plan has been to use color, the color of the plumage, in order to establish attraction between the sexes. Here, as happens so often in the realm of the biology of sex, where Nature seems to experiment with every possibility she can, the human being seems to be in the category of creatures where the visual image is important to the male. In the case of the birds, it's the visual image that stimulates the female, and the male is the one who carries the bright color, which is a kind of heraldic design to initiate the courtship ritual of the mating of the birds.

I would like to make a point with regard to this matter of the way in which Nature uses the visual stimulus—and in parentheses I must say also the narrative stimulus as a kind of substitute for the visual one—I would like to make a very special point of the fact that when one gets talking of this particular aspect of things, one really is talking to a certain extent about love, but more about sex and mating. I want to really emphasize this because it's very easy in any discussion of sex education to feel, or to have people feel, that one is leaving out the whole concept of love. I do not like to neglect love.

If you look up most of the books on sex education and check the index, you will find that time and again the word love never appears. There is no chapter on love. There is in fact, practically no mention of love at all. I think there really ought to be two aspects to sex education. One we might call sex education and the other should be called love education. I am not going to dwell on the subject of love education today, because there's enough ground to be covered in this matter of visual imagery, from the more strictly sexual point of view. Let me say it this way. People who are in love can be turned on by the visual stimulus, and people who are not in love also can be turned on by the visual stimulus. I certainly do not want to underestimate the importance of love in human life for, in fact, most people's problems in their sexual lives turn out to be not sexual problems in the literal sense but love problems.

SEXUAL IMAGERY

Now let me go one step further with regard to the importance of imagery in human sexual life and remind you that Nature is her own pornographer, if I may say it that way. Particularly in the case of the male, at the time of puberty, she institutes her own movie shows. I'm referring of course to masturbation fantasies and wet dreams. At the time of puberty, when the young male is confronted with these images, since he has no will power or voluntary choice of them, especially those that appear in his dreams, he learns something about his own capacity for sexual arousal. This indeed can be, for many males who have a problem with regard to psychosexual arousal, the first time that their problem is actually presented to them very vividly.

The matter of sexual fantasy associated with sexual arousal, and the ultimate attainment of orgasm, carries another important aspect that I think we should not forget, and that is, if the ideal materials are not available, as for example in book form, then it's very easy indeed for the human being to improvise a fantasy. I can remind you that the Sears Roebuck catalogue, for a generation past, was a sex manual, at least for masturbation fantasies; I'm referring to the section on women's underwear which has provided many a boy with the necessary stimulus-imagery. I'm mentioning this because the fact is that one doesn't need to get into an argument about the types of books that are considered on the edge of legality or are illegal in the commercial market in order to discuss this issue of pornography with regard to individual lives.

Going one step further, I would like to have something to say about the issue of "hang-ups" with regard to sexual imagery. I read a very fascinating article just a few months ago by Robert Stoller* at UCLA, where he had discovered in the case of a transvestite an exact parallel between his own biography and a book with illustrations of a young man being taken hold of by three very domineering, tightly clothed, high-heeled women who forced him to dress up in their clothes. This for him was pornography. It was the potent imagery that could turn him on sexually and make it possible for him to perform sexually. Stoller's parallel was with the photographs that this man brought in from his family album, and the story that he told from his own biography. Lo and behold, at the time when he was a very young child, before school age, when his mother became chronically sick and eventually died, he was taken care of by his aunt and her teenaged daughter. Both of them took some kind of strange and vicarious delight in forcing him to dress up in girl's clothes, especially on such occasions as parties, or as a practical joke. There was indeed a similarity between the story of his own biography and the type of story in the pornographic literature, or, I had better say, in the books that are put out to appeal to transvestites. I say it that way because, in the quite literal sense, the books that appeal to transvestites in the "adult book stores" do not qualify as pornographic in the eyes of the law, because they do not show naked bodies and they do not show sex organs. The characteristic "hang-up" of the transvestite is, of course, clothing.

Stoller pointed out in his article another important theoretical point, namely, that the appeal of the visual image per se is relatively weak as far as women's pornography is concerned, but that for most women the pornographic material that is most likely to be erotically arousing is, in a way, like that of the transvestite, insofar as it has a story line. There is a romantic and sentimental aspect to the story, which does not necessarily go into minute details about nudity and the sexual act itself. All the pornography laws have been made by men. They have never caught onto the fact that *True Confessions* and *True Love* magazine stories are, in

*R. J. Stoller, Pornography and perversion. *Archives of General Psychiatry* **22** (1970): 490-99.

fact, the genuine pornography of women. So women have been allowed to enjoy themselves pornographically as much as they desire.

I can't resist the temptation, in this audience, to enlarge one step further on the idea that each person has his or her own specific favorite and specially arousing pornography. It can become almost a parlor game to try and image what was the best kind of pornographic material for each of various great historical figures. And so, need I remind you that if Freud had left us any stories of what was pornographic for him, they surely would have been Oedipal. Perhaps that very fact should make us take a second look at the basic validity of the Oedipal theory, and ask the question of whether an ordinary masturbation fantasy was applied with too much generality to all mankind.

TABOO AND PORNOGRAPHY

I would like to go ahead and raise a question: Why the extraordinary taboo that our society has maintained on commercial pornography? I would not like to pretend that I could give all the answers to such a grave and important question in a few sentences, but I would like to bring one particular hypothesis to your attention. This hypothesis dawned on me when I went for the second time to live and work with the Aborigines on the far north coast of Australia, an area which still has not been inhabited by white people, except for those who run the small mission townships, or government townships, where there are hospitals, schools and other facilities for the Aborigines who, under their elders, have decided almost unanimously to come in from walkabout and begin being civilized.

I found that the Aborigines have an extraordinary taboo on to whom one is allowed to talk. If a boy is going to school, and could develop ordinary friendly relationships with a girl, for instance talking together about sharing lessons in school or something as simple as that, and if the girl comes from a totemic clan, so defined that her mother could never possibly under the marriage rules become this boy's mother-in-law later in life, then he is not allowed to speak to that girl. There were sometimes difficulties in the school at its beginning, because youngsters would be sitting together in sulking silence, learning nothing, and saying nothing to anybody in the room. The teachers didn't know why, until they found out that they had forced the breaking of this incredibly strict taboo.

One importance of this taboo is that it makes people guilty about whom they may use their vocal organs with; and this kind of guilt, as one understands a little more of their society, turns out to be an extraordinarily powerful weapon that the older people have in controlling the behavior of the younger ones. So, my imagination led me to the taboos that we have on food or burials in our historical culture, or parts of it, and taboos we have on sex. Since I like to be a good science fictionist, for this is the best way to develop new hypotheses in sciences, I have a kind of image in my mind of, five to seven thousand years or more ago, a conclave of priestly rulers who were extraordinarily clever. They came out of their conclave, having discovered the principle that the way to gain power over their people was to make them guilty about the functioning of the body with regard to sex. The power to make people guilty is also the power to make them conform. Perhaps, if I use my science fiction one step further, I can say that now I can understand why the members of the U.S. Senate voted sixty to five against the Report of the Commission on Obscenity and Pornography before they had even seen it. Perhaps they repudiated it because, being skilled in the politics of power and sovereignty, they intuitively sensed that to give people sexual freedom would take away the leverage of guilt on which governing power is based and which the rulers were not yet willing or able to relinquish. Remember, it's science fiction, but perhaps the senators were more artful than they knew.

DEFINITION

How does one define pornography? What's the difference between what is pornographic as compared with what is considered erotic or sexy? I believe the answer is that there is no definition which can be made a workable one. In fact, all one needs to do is read the reports of trials, when distributors and importers of pornog-

raphy are brought to the court, to realize that the courts themselves are struggling desperately to try and find a workable definition of pornography.

As I suspect many of you know, the present unworkable definition is threefold. To be not pornographic, materials portraying
sexual matters should have some redeeming social value, or to put
it the way it's stated, they should not be utterly without redeeming social value. Also, they should have no appeal to the prurient
interest. Well, it's hard to find anything that really is utterly without redeeming social value for somebody somewhere. Even cancer
has value for the cancer researcher. And, if you try to define what
prurient is, you really never get beyond the etymology of prurient,
which means itchy.

The third criterion in the legal definition of pornography is
that it should somehow or another not completely flout contemporary community standards. Let me remind you that it was in
total agreement with contemporary standards during the Inquisi-
tion that, in Switzerland and nearby Germany, the entire population of females in at least one village and thousands more in other
villages were burned at the stake as witches. There are, indeed,
some times when community standards are so wrong that it is our
duty not to obey them. We have to question the whole moral issue
involved. Therefore, I have decided that the best way to deal with
pornography is not to try and define it as something that's different from the erotic or sexy, but simply to let them all be synonymous with one another. Then, perhaps, make some classifications
so that a parent, let's say, can know what kind of material there
will be in a certain type of book, and that it won't get mixed up
with or overlap certain other kinds of material between the same
covers. In that way we can pilot ourselves and our children
through the issues of visual sex without any more difficulty than
we have in trying to pilot a way through the visual issues of
violence, mutilation, and murder.

My own definition of what gets popularly branded as pornography today is that it is visual erotica which, by whatever criterion, has been forbidden, so that to look at it requires the breaking
of a taboo which, in many people, leaves a feeling of surreptitious
and sneaky, albeit exciting, wrongdoing. In addition, pictorial por-

nography, when it is commercially banned and has no competitive market, tends to be trashy in appearance, because of technical incompetence and shoddy materials. Furthermore, the sexual action portrayed is faked, because the actors are faking. They do so either because they cannot not fake before the camera, or because the camera man is content to hurry through a fake performance. A good actor can fake most human experiences, but not the experience of orgasm.

ALLEGORY

I come now to the section of my talk which has the subheading, allegory—an allegory of the Crucifixion. For nearly two thousand years, many hundreds of thousands, if not millions, of children have been given very detailed instructions on Sundays on how to commit a crucifixion. However, I have not heard of children who come home and play crucifixion games with their dolls or playmates. Of course, the moral of this story is that children are taught about the Crucifixion in a moral context, and they learn not only the operational technique of crucifixion, but they learn also the moral significance of the story to which it pertains. Let me, therefore, remind you that even young children are extremely capable of learning moral lessons, moral precepts, and moral rules in the same way as adults. In fact, I think I would say that when they are given them in the correct context, with honesty, so that they realize that they're not being treated with hypocrisy on one count, and the opposite on another, then they're rather good at learning moral precepts as we suggest them.

Pornography does not automatically have the power to incite behavior. It does not have the power to turn people into sexual maniacs who rush out on the street in order to copulate with the first living thing they see, whether on two legs or four. In fact, it doesn't have the power even to turn you into a "picture freak."

DIRECT CONFRONTATION AND YOUR REACTIONS

In a way it's not a very fair advantage that I have standing here tonight, because I really can predict beforehand that unless you

happen already to have been overly exposed to pornography I will
be able to force the engagement of your emotions and your attention. You will have to have some kind of reaction to this material
which, in general, you've been deprived of seeing, up to this point
in your life. Having had your emotions forcefully engaged, you
then may find that, at least for certain aspects of the materials,
you will experience disgust. I would suspect that every single human being alive is able to feel some kind of disgust at the pornography that is sexually arousing to certain other people, but not
oneself. I'm referring here to those certain people who have rather
peculiar sexual "hang-ups."

You will also have an emotional reaction of some degree of
erotic arousal from some of the materials that are traditionally
classified as pornographic; and, if not, then you probably have a
rather rare disease. There are some people who suffer from sexual
apathy and sexual inertia to such an extent that they do, indeed,
require diagnosis and treatment, if such is known. And there are
some, as I've discovered in my work, for whom it's extremely difficult to find a solution. They are people in a pathetic situation
in life; they're quite capable of feeling the need for affection and
closeness, but they are not able to conduct themselves erotically
and sexually in such a way that the relationship is totally satisfying as a love relationship for and with a partner. It is important to
emphasize that it's normal to be aroused by erotic stimuli, even
when they're in pictures in picture books that you buy in the
sleazy part of town.

It's more important, however, I think, to realize that with
regard to these pictures that come from the "gray market," a
proportion of them are not erotically stimulating at all to most
people, and they're not necessarily disgust-evoking. Their importance to the ordinary person is that they satisfy one's natural curiosity. They do exactly the same kind of job that the freak show
does at the county fair in Nebraska, Iowa, or any of the solid parts
of Middle America. Why do people like to see the bearded lady or
the half-man and half-woman? Well, there's probably no better
answer than to say that, being members of the primate species,
they have curiosity which they like to satisfy. They like to know
that such a thing does or does not exist. But I don't feel that the

good solid farmers of Middle America feel that they are themselves freaky because they go to a freak show. Don't forget, they usually only go once. It's not something that one needs to keep repeating during one's lifetime.

Now, on a somewhat different note, and a positive one, exposure to pornography, and considering one's own reaction to it, does in fact, lead to the possibility of bettering one's own sex life, leading one to have less guilt and fewer "hang-ups," and more honesty and freedom about sex.

It also helps one better to define one's own standards and, therefore, to guide one's own children or other people that one may be responsible for—especially those whose lives are devoted to medical care treatment. One becomes better able to help others by achieving a position, and I want to weigh this word very carefully, of nonjudgmentalism.

If one is obliged to have an emotional reaction in passing judgment on one's patients, with their symptoms and diseases, whether they be somatic or psychologic, one automatically disqualifies oneself from much capacity to help the patient. Nonjudgmentalism in one's approach to patients is a professional attitude which is essential for those in the medical profession. It does not mean that one has to be nonjudgmental with regard to one's own personal standards, but it has its specific application in one's professional competence. In treating syphilis, the physician does not pass judgment on the patient for getting the disease. He gives a shot of penicillin.

SATIATION EFFECT

I can summarize the next section of my lecture, satiation effect, rather pithily by borrowing from nuclear physics, that the half-life of pornography, of a particular type of pornography, is from about two to four hours out of your total lifetime. So I might add to that: perhaps you better make sure you'll enjoy it tonight! I do need to explain a little further. I don't mean that one session of four hours will completely satiate you with all pornography for all time. First of all, I mean that one particular type of pornography does reach its satiation point after you've had about that much exposure to it. If you come to something new and novel, you might find yourself capable of repeating the process. That's very important with regard to the commercial distribution of pornography. The pornography makers and distributors are extremely well aware of the fact that they must constantly strive for a novelty value. The purchasers of pornography include a very small segment of the population that repeats its purchases again and again—the people whom I have sometimes called or heard called "picture freaks." Paraphilia pornographia, perhaps one could say. It's a very special kind of thing with regard to psychosexual functioning. The market would not be able to exist on those purchasers alone. The ordinary people who have a natural curiosity to be satisfied are not going to go back repeatedly and pay $10.00 for a book that's worth the 50¢ price of *Time* magazine, unless it promises to give them something new. Then they very quickly become satiated with that type of pornography. And so it goes that after not too much experience of the various types of pornography one becomes, in fact, totally immune to the tyranny of the stimulus.

Secondly, I mean that one doesn't become numb to sex. What happens is that the stimulus itself loses its tyrannical power to evoke the sexual, erotic reaction. What also happens is that the body's own biological clock turns round and, when it's time to be sexy again, then possibly one could utilize some pictorial material or narrative material as part of the experience of sexual arousal, as an adjunct to it. But what also happens, even more importantly, at this stage of satiation, is that the experience of the reality of the human partnership, of the relationship, and indeed I could say of the love affair, becomes far more important and far more dominant than the visual stimulation per se. In a sense, one may also say that the sense of touch, as well as the sentimental and romantic feelings of closeness, supplants the power of the visual image with regard to sexual and erotic arousal.

MALE-FEMALE DIFFERENCES

At this point, it's very natural to mention the matter of male and female differences with regard to erotic imagery. To begin with, remember that the female at puberty does not have erotic dreams,

wet dreams, in the way the boy does. In fact, if we rely on the
data that Kinsey gathered—as old as they are they still seem to be
good—we can say that the experience of erotic dreaming, with
vivid erotic imagery, for females comes later than puberty and
reaches its maximum somewhere in the decade of the thirties. In
boys, it's at its maximum immediately at the onset of puberty.

Moreover, unless as an aftermath of the Women's Lib movement we have to completely revise our concepts of sex differences
in imagery, the evidence as of the present time, and it does indeed
seem to be evidence that can be repeated in many different ethnic
societies, is that the male is the one who is more responsive to
visual and narrative stimulation, and the female is more responsive
to the sentimental and romantic type of stimulation, perhaps incorporating some visual stimulation, that leads rather rapidly to
the importance of tactile and close body contact stimulation. I can
illustrate this by saying that many women with whom I've talked,
some of whom have given considerable professional time to matters of the scientific investigation of sexual matters, including sexual arousal, have consistently agreed on one issue; it is that, if a
woman sees a sexy picture, for instance even an advertisement for
Coca-Cola, she tends to project herself up onto the screen, onto
the picture, and to imagine what it would be like to be that
woman. Or, if she's seeing a sexy film, or a romantic film, to
project herself into the story and perhaps change it a little to suit
certain circumstances of her own existence, and also to feel that
she's learning a few good lessons from the woman up there. She
will then be able to put the lessons into practice in her own
romantic and sexual life.

As for the male viewer, his reaction is rather different, for he
does not project himself up into the picture of a male on the
screen and imagine what it would be like to be that lucky one with
that good looking girl. He objectifies. He takes the girl down off
the screen and has sex with her on the spot.

SOCIOLOGICAL HISTORY—1960s

Now, for a few words about the sociological history of pornography. Nobody really knows what started the so-called sexual rev-

olution, and nobody is really quite in agreement that there has been a sexual revolution instead of an evolution. It's undoubtedly going to be the verdict of history, however, that something happened, and it happened with great speed during the decade of the sixties.

I happened to become interested in the subject of pornography through a fortuitous chance meeting with an insurance agent in the doctor's dining room. He was able to introduce me to the pornography distributors and dealers of Baltimore. I realized something of which I had not been aware. Something important was happening sociologically with regard to the availability of sexual materials. I've learned from my contact with people in the industry that they have a rather organized method of contributing to, and profiting by the sexual revolution. They engage lawyers and they figure out a strategy of just what might be the limit of testing the law with regard to the next kind of novelty that could be published.

Their motivation primarily is to gain profits, and they do gain fairly good ones, but they spend probably half of them in expenses pertaining to legal issues. They're people who become civil libertarians in spite of themselves. To a certain extent, it does become a game to beat the officials of the regulatory agencies. The result is that during the sixties the type of material that became available on sale, showed more and more exposure of nudity and more and more explicit representation of the sexual acts themselves.

I can tell you why I chose my title "Pornography in the Home." Because the availability of pornography in this era in which we live is becoming greater, it has a greater chance of entering the home. I'm thinking especially of the children. Parents do not know how to deal with pornography. It's our duty, yours and mine, to give them some background and some concepts, and above all some vocabulary.

I have found that even in the very simple matters of the sex education of little children, parents are extraordinarily handicapped by not having the proper vocabulary. How ridiculous it sounds to say that mother and daddy press their bodies close together because they love each other so much. And that makes a baby! Anybody ought to feel ashamed of saying that—the same kind of silliness pertains to pornography—because, in the story of fertilization, it is easy to say that the egg is fertilized by the sperm. One can have a small drawing. Then tell about the swimming race of the sperms and how the penis has to fit into the vagina so that all the sperms, when they're pumped out, have a fair chance to win in the swimming race, and out of three hundred million of them, only one is a winner!

In a way, I want to be able to introduce to you and to any others some of the simple concepts and words with which to talk about pornography, and its use in sex education. I had the recent experience of being able, for the first time, to participate in a sex education course at one of the private prep schools in New England and to introduce, for the first time, the topic of pornography to boys between fourteen and eighteen years of age. I found that it was one of the most successful ways of approaching sex education at that age in which I have yet participated. It was well received in a highly intelligent and appreciative way. It really hit at the place where these boys needed some guidance.

In short form, let me classify the way that I think one can best utilize pornography in sex education, whether in high schools or earlier, should the day come when it can be effectively used at the lower age level. (It certainly can be used, dependent upon the skill of the parents, at any age in sex education in the home.) For constructive use in sex education, it is best to have a classification of pornography, so that people can turn to the kind of pictures that they need in order to discuss the particular issues that have come up in the sex education of their children.

CLASSIFIED TYPES

For example, one large group of pornography is sex education material that is called pornographic simply because it shows the naked sex organs, or it shows the copulatory act itself. This is the portrayal of sexual activity that belongs in a "how to do it manual" of reproductive technique. So far as I'm concerned, it's simply sad that our society has painted itself into the corner of having to consider this kind of material indecent.

The next category that I have assembled and will show you when the slides come up is that which pertains to heterosexual arousal. For most people this is erotically stimulating until they get bored with it. It happens to be the largest category, and has the greatest appeal, because it's the kind of sexual imagery that on the normal curve applies to the greatest number, the vast majority, of people.

Then finally comes the kind of picture which is what most people raise their voices against when they think of something that's nasty, evil, dirty, and so on, and which they tend to lump together as being typical of all pornography. This is material on nonconventional sex. I struggled for a while to find a word for it. I think the best word is kinky. It's the pornography that appeals to people who have a special hang-up in their sexual lives. To ordinary people it has the curiosity appeal that I spoke of—like looking at the freak show on the midway. It happens, however, to have a rather good use in regard to sex education, because it can be used to give a young person some kind of advice and warning on how to plan and regulate sexual activities. For example, the pornography that's specially designed to appeal to homosexuals can be a very useful way of discussing the whole topic of homosexuality with youngsters whom one would like to advise, giving them a road map on their way around the sociological world, so to speak, so that they don't get involved in homosexuality through sheer accident.

Also, this kind of kinky pornography can be of value to individuals, especially teenagers, to give them some clue as to what may otherwise be completely baffling and worrying to them in their own sex lives. It may perhaps lead them to a minor degree of self-diagnosis and give them the courage to refer themselves to someone who can help them.

I've mentioned already one special kink, which one doesn't really need to get worried about, namely, paraphilia pornographia: the person who is to be turned on by pictures only, and cannot be turned on by the experiences of real life. These people are not dangerous and they do not offer any serious threat to any member or age group of society, despite what may be said about them. As a matter of fact, they're probably very safe people because they keep themselves at home with their books.

Then, don't forget that all of this so-called kinky kind of pornography also constitutes the only textbook that the average citizen has from which to learn something about the peculiar ways in which the human psyche can develop. He can look up many other things in the encyclopedias that even *Life* and *Time* magazine put out for him, but it's extraordinarily difficult for the ordinary person to find out anything about the imagery of sexual life. So he's almost forced to go to the "adult book stores," and to the places that do not have too good a reputation. With this, I come to the series of slides, arranged in several sections.

SLIDES

The first is a section on erotic art taken from around the world, and at different times in history, simply to remind you that the portrayal of sexual things is nothing special in our society and nothing new—that it has been with mankind probably for all of mankind's history. The special point about these portrayals of the sexual organs and the nude body by people of artistic competence is that it was illegal to show the penis, flaccid or otherwise, until the era of the sixties when the law was constantly tested. It had been quite legal to show the penis in ancient Greece and in modern times, from the Renaissance onward, it has been quite legal to show female nudity. The only special thing, then, about these pictures from the sequence on erotic art is that some of them show the penis, which would have been illegal formerly. May we have the first set of slides please?

This is from Peru. It's actually a modern fake, but it gives you an idea of the tomb pottery from Peru, which, if any of you have seen the museum in Lima, included practically every position and activity of sexuality that one can think of.

A typical nineteenth-century Japanese painting on silk, which with all of its Baroque flourishes almost hides the sex away. Another one from the same period from Japan where you notice the enlarged size of the penis, which is typical of these drawings. Perhaps it illustrates the intensity of desire at the expense of anatomical accuracy.

A picture from an Australian Aboriginal man, aged twenty-three, produced spontaneously, as a matter of fact in a joking way, in reaction to a *Playboy*-type picture that happened to be on the inside cover of *Time* magazine that week, which surprised him and his mission settlement friends. I'm particularly interested in this drawing because it happens to be the only authentic piece of information I have that the sitting position, which was recorded by the early anthropological investigators, is still the typical and preferred one among the Aborigines today. You notice also the enlargement of the penis, which is fascinating insofar as the artist has not had any contact with Asian art. You notice also, as one anthropologist pointed out to me, the triangle as the symbol for the female vulva, which is a very ancient symbol in the world's art. The artist was of the first generation in from the Stone Age way of life.

Here you can have another example, this time from India, of erotic art. In this next picture you see the little idyllic boat scene. It is a rather ancient Chinese painting on silk which is one of the ten that created the need for a court decision, in Baltimore a couple of years ago, as to whether the Kronhausen collection of erotic art could be brought into this country and shown. The ten pictures were cleared, but it's still hanging on a federal decision as to whether the remaining several hundred of the collection may come in and be shown in a public museum, as they were in North Germany and Scandinavia.

Picasso. Most of his sexual drawings from this series of '68 did not show the sex organs, but here are a couple of them that did.

By a Dutch artist, Theo Schoon, from Indonesia and eventually displaced to New Zealand; and you see here that you don't actually need a sex organ to be able to create the image of it symbolically. Here, by the same artist, you do see what would at that time (the 1940's) have been illegal to put on sale—boy with a penis.

And here a Japanese drawing of the modern era, by Frank Rafter, showing the penis.

Here is the poster by Karel Appel, the very well-known and, I might add, the very expensive Dutch abstract expressionist artist, for the Kronhausen exhibition. I imagine this poster would create a lot of noisy talk in the newspapers of Baltimore if the collection came to the museum here.

I couldn't resist the temptation of this collage, a poster showing a portrait of Sigmund Freud in a compromising position on the belly of a nude. It's also an interesting poster because, as people are beginning to become aware and critical of these days, Freud really had a very strong antifeminist leaning.

A poster of coital positions that was given to me after this lecture last year by some students, in recognition of the lecture—one which was bought in Georgetown, D.C..

That of course is a collage, and it indicates that you can use sex for satire and social comment. The penis hanging out of the fisherman's pants is a cut out added to a Camel cigarette ad.

This is from the medical students' 1968 Pithotomy Show. "Join the Marines and Learn How to Really Fuck." It was one of the first clear revelations to me of how angry the young people were about the Viet Nam war at that early period. By the same artist at the same time, a second satirical poster of war protest.

One day about a dozen years ago, two artists, Billy Hadaway and Glen Walker, came to my office, at the time I was running the art exhibitions in the Medical Residence Hall, and they became, in a jocular way, interested in the Draw-A-Person test. Glen Walker spent ten minutes sketching this version of the Draw-A-Person test. It really packs a good deal of information into one image, with the sex organs of a man and a woman transformed into micromeliac arms, shaking hands.

I would like to have a word to say about the next group of slides that have to do with male-female nudity of the type which I have somewhat irreverently called soft-core pornography, and then sex education pictures. Here I need to refer back again to what I had to say about the legal system. One's right to be able to show human sexual intercourse positions, in books that might be used for the sex education of the public at large, followed only upon the right, established by pornography importers and distributors, to be able to show male-female nudity, with the male and the female together. And also to show soft-core pornography in which the male and the female are in an obviously erotic and sexual pose—but only if the man is impotent. We happen to be at the stage still, in legal history, when the right to be able to show the erect penis, even for sex education purposes, has barely been established, but hasn't been fully tested in the courts. So we are still living in an era in which—and I think this is in a way pathetic, tragic, and funny—the greatest nation, the wealthiest and most powerful on earth, has defined it's sexuality for public purposes as being normal only when its men are flaccid and impotent. Surely we ought to paint ourselves out of this corner as quickly as we can.

The first of these pictures are from nudist camps, early in the sixties, idyllic scenes in which nothing is wrong, and nothing seems wrong until you look close enough to see that the people have no clothes on, and both sexes are there. You notice that it's the female nude that's displayed most in these early days, as in Renaissance paintings. When the male nude first appeared, the sex organs were obscure. But he gradually emerged into the open: here you have him on the front and back cover of the same nudist colony magazine, with his partner, both fully nude.

Now, we come to the soft-core or the impotence group. You see here the preliminary stage, the little story line so to speak, and now you get the bare sex organs with a lot of underclothing which I'm going to have something to say about in a moment. One of the things I've tried to do is to put too many pictures into this series so that you'll begin to feel some of the satiation effect.

This kind of impotence picture made it possible to show the naked sex organs for serious sex education purposes, especially the penis and the female organs, and made it possible in the same magazine, which incidentally is called *Sexual Freedom*. These pictures are taken from it. The magazine itself is taken from the film, "Sexual Freedom in Denmark," which is probably the best sex education film that's ever been made. This book went on sale in 1970. The text always has some redeeming social value, by the way. The question on this slide of intercourse is: What is obscene? The insert picture at the top shows a mutilation scene on the battle field. It does invite a very serious question as to whether the obscenity of violence and mutilation is morally better or worse than the obscenity of the creative act. Again, it's a pretty telling comment on our society that somehow, over the course of history, we have managed to make the reproduction of the race obscene but not the obliteration and destruction of it.

At this same time it became possible also to show pictures of birth. I've discovered to my amazement, after my lecture at around this time last year, when I made comments somewhat similar to this about birth, that, pictorially, there are in fact no books, no flat surfaced books, easily available to teach about birth, and no pictures of it easily available to use for teenagers and young adults about to become young mothers or fathers for the first time. The librarian at our Welch Medical Library came to me and showed me the materials they have. They're good but they're not realistic in the way that a movie can be. There are movies for sex education on birth but they're not easily available to any member of the public. They usually have to be rented and shown in a special session. The point is that so far as the ordinary mass group of high-school-aged and young college-aged people are concerned we still require that a young woman deliver a baby without knowing exactly what she will be going through. I certainly hope that error won't take very long to correct. I think everybody should be able to see a movie of the delivery of a child, and this visual information should be easily available. Certainly there should be picture books on this subject, in high quality color printing, available to anyone who cares to go to the library or to a book store.

I have found, incidentally, that of all the pictures of so-called pornography, the pictures of nudity, those that portray the birth of a child, more than any others, tend to turn the stomachs of men; but they do not thus affect women.

The next series I've labeled "the girlie pictures," the fetish pictures, and the rear-ends. These are pictures in the *Playboy* tradition of having a little sneaky peek. They give that burlesque feeling that you're doing something wrong, because you're always covered up with a bit of clothing. This leads me to say that it's probably correct for us to allow that the normal American male, in the statistical sense, is a fetishist for underclothes. He gets turned on by what the trade calls garters and lace. It's more difficult for him to be turned on by the simple, classic nudity of the human form itself. I don't think there's anything particularly wrong with this, but it is a hang-up in it's own way. It probably indicates that our own obsession with privacy and clothing and fear of nudity allows the peek at the underclothes to itself become a sexual stimulus—which I don't think I would call 100 percent healthy, although I am not going to inveigh against it with great gusto.

It is hard for me to understand why there should be a market for pictures showing ladies' rear-ends. The market doesn't show mens' rear-ends, by the way! Suddenly it dawned on me one day that this is the presentation position for all the primates, other than man. It's no wonder that we inherit something of the primate tendency to be turned on by the rear-end presentation position.

The series begins with some traditional "cheesecake." You see in these first pictures there's always striving for a new effect in pose or accessories. Then the appearance, in about 1968, of the full nude, showing the sexual hair.

Next, a group that shows the contemporary stage of garters and lace. Here's the kind of seductive titilation of, "Maybe you can get those clothes off?" The tease effect! Becoming even quite ridiculous! Then a very blatant step, to be totally without any reserve as far as the spread-legged display of the sexual organs is concerned. Again, around 1968, from the magazine actually called "Dears and Rears," came this rear-end pose.

A group of pictures, now, that cohere together because they all relate to what I've called the phenomenon of the snout-end and the tail-end. For many people this is very difficult to cope with, this matter of oral sex. There are many people who are disgusted by it, and equally so, there are many people who are turned-on by it. So I began asking myself: I wonder why there is this discrepancy, and is it simply a matter of cultural and social conditioning? Well, I think probably there is something more to it than that. I think that we might turn to phylogeny. I would like to point out two things to you.

One I've briefly adumbrated already. In the lower mammalian species, where Nature has designed the sexual relationship to be induced by pheromones or the sense of smell, it is necessary for the male and the female of those species to have a juxtaposition of the snout-end and the rear-end. In these animals, the male is dependent on the odor—this has been shown quite conclusively, only very recently by the way, by Richard Michael in London and Joe

Herbert at the University at Cambridge, in England, to apply to the rhesus monkey. The male is dependent for his turn-on on the hormonally regulated odor that issues from the interior of the vagina. And so he is obliged to be able to do some sniffing around in order to know whether the period of ovulation and the likelihood of fertilization is at hand.

With regard to the female in all species, including the primates up to man, and possibly with the same rule applying sometimes to man, it's not possible for effective delivery to take place without the use of the snout-end in helping to deliver the young. That's in the four-legged species. Or in eating the placenta, which is important with regard to hormonal balance that relates to lactation and maternalism in some species. So, Nature has designed this plan of the juxtaposition of the extremities. Paul MacLean has pointed out in his work on the limbic system of the brain at NIH that the two ends are represented, respectively, in pathways that traverse the amygdala and the septum, which fold around on one another so that snout-end and tail-end are, in fact, in very close anatomical juxtaposition in the brain. So much then for this phenomenon of oral sex with its extraordinary dichotomy of reaction in members of the human race. Perhaps, in view of this dichotomy, there are some people that are closer to their mammalian ancestry than others. I'm not sure whether that's a good explanation or, eventually, if one may have to look further.

This next picture is the book *Sexual Freedom* again, the front cover. I want to remind you that this book only a few months ago established the precedent of legally showing the erect penis. And may I remind you again that the type of heterosexual pose that you see here, which is issued as a sample of the type of thing that was being shown in Denmark at the time, still is not absolutely cleared, in the legal sense, for this country, although pictures showing the erect penis can, in fact, be bought in easy supply in the cities of San Francisco, Los Angeles, New York and, undoubtedly, many others. The quality of the productions is often inferior, because they are frequently pirated photo-offset editions in black and white from the originals in color in Denmark.

I suppose most of you know that in Denmark in July of 1969 it became legal to show and do anything sexual in public, within certain limitations of public decency, of course. This was the era which ushered in the live shows of sexual intercourse, instead of just burlesque shows. Some live shows, incidentally, can be found already in this country in New York and San Francisco.

Here you have more evidence from *Sexual Freedom*: this slide shows sexual intercourse in the context of positions during pregnancy. But in this next picture, one is simply shown what the so-called hard-core pornography of Denmark looks like. This is a good illustration of the point at which we find ourselves in the sociological history of sex in this country—still, as a society, trying to make up our minds about this kind of picture.

Now I will show you a series of pictures from contemporary Danish pornography books which, if on sale in this country, are not legally recognized by the courts. First of all some exhibitions of intercourse and other activities in pairs, which will be followed by some threesomes—again, an illustration of how the striving for novelty is terribly important in order to maintain the market. There was a time when a new legal decision in this country made it suddenly safe to publish soft-core pornography. Then 35 percent of the booksellers went bankrupt. In an open, competitive market they couldn't survive.

And now you see the introduction of a little romance. Quite a large number of these pocket-sized picture books from Denmark do have three or four of the initial pages showing some kinds of preliminary meeting and mating scenes. The point of this particular one is that you should watch out for the photographer at the wedding! He makes a threesome.

This view is rather unique in pornographic pictures, partly because of the striving for effect by showing the ejaculate, which is usually some kind of jelly or cold cream in actual fact; but chiefly because the male shows retraction of the testes, which indicates that he's in an authentic state of arousal to the point of orgasm. It passes unnoticed in most people's consciousness of pornography, that the actual experience in the picture or in the movie is faked, because the people are not able to reach the point of orgasm. One senses in looking at it that it's fake, and yet one doesn't always put that into words. I guess that of all the skills of an actor in portraying human emotions in human situations, the one that cannot be acted is orgasm. That's what is wrong with about 98 percent of pornography books. It's not real. It is in fact extraordinarily difficult to find a good movie to illustrate in a realistic and educational way, possibly let's say for people who are having serious trouble in their own sexual lives, what the sexual relationship should be like. There are not yet many movies made with people who are having an authentic act of intercourse in a sexual relationship.

The next group of slides runs rather more briefly through the historical development of pornography for the homosexual market, which parallels the heterosexual slides that you've just seen. First of all, a word is in order about the etiology of homosexuality and the differentiation between essential homosexuality and optional homosexuality, which really should be called bisexuality. A great deal of the medical and psychiatric literature on homosexuality is wrong because it calls any kind of experience between two members of the same sex homosexual, which is correct, and then generalizes to say that the person or the personality is homosexual, which is not correct. Most often one finds that the person actually has either a bisexual history or a bisexual capacity. It's the ratio between the heterosexual and the homosexual experience that really counts.

The possibility of the optional type of homosexuality occurs frequently throughout the animal kingdom in some degree or another. Despite what you have heard said or read about the idea that homosexuality is exclusively a human phenomenon—it is not.

Another important point here, because it is basic to an underlying fear in many people, is that exposure to pictures or representations, or even actual experiences of homosexuality, will turn a boy or a girl into a homosexual. That is not true. It may allow them to experiment with a homosexual experience, but it will not precipitate their development into an essential or an obligative homosexual. The vast majority of people who in teenage have had some kind of homosexual experience can look back later in life and say that it was just a phase of their lives. It's not something which haunts them for the remainder of their days.

A good deal of argument goes on these days as to whether obligative homosexuality is an illness or, like left-handedness, an alternative mode of functioning. The very word illness implies the need for a cure. Yet physicians have long had to settle for amelioration of suffering in those conditions for which a cure has not been possible, and for rehabilitation when a change, once having occurred, cannot be reversed. In everyday speech, an amputee is not a sick person, but he is one who needs rehabilitation. The obligative homosexual is in a similar situation. His homosexual gender identity may represent Nature's best restorative or reparative attempt after a combination, perhaps, of a noxious prenatal hormonal environment and a noxious postnatal social environment. Restoration to heterosexual status failed, but the failure was not so great as to produce a hermit or an autistically withdrawn isolate. There is a parallel here with a wound that heals to form a keloid instead of an invisible join. Though less than perfect, the keloid is better than no healing at all. To view the obligative homosexual as a person in need not of cure but of rehabilitation as a homosexual makes sense in terms of what a great many homosexuals find compatible with their situation in life. It is also consistent with pragmatism in public health policy, for there are too many hundreds of thousands of homosexuals to provide every one with a personal psychiatrist, even if a cure could be invariably promised, as it certainly cannot.

The first slide shows you the old homosexual pornography of the fifties, which in many ways is kind of indecent because of the blatant way in which the sex organs are brought into focus by being painted out. Then in the middle sixties the homosexual cheesecake pictures came on the market, in which the penis dared to be shown, usually in the context of athletics and weight-lifting and strong-man activities.

And now some samples from the modern age of the homosexual picture books from Copenhagen, in which everything is quite explicit. The presentation of the rear-end, male-to-male, among primates is a gesture of submission. There may be some such phyletic residual in the homosexual who presents his rear-end for anal intercourse, and enjoys it. In the final picture of this group, it is cold cream, not genuine ejaculate on the partner's face. Notice again the interracial partnership, seen also in some of the heterosexual views, earlier.

Finally, the last group of slides falls into the category of "Everyman's Textbook of Psychopathology." May I remind you again that for a great many people these types of picture carry no erotic content and no erotic arousal value. They do stimulate erotic reactions in people who happen to be afflicted with the particular type of disorder in psychosexual functioning portrayed in the picture. For those people, this kind of material would occupy the same place as heterosexual material would for the more commonly occurring type of heterosexual arousal.

I want to have a special word about one of the slides that comes up on pedophilia. There's a very strong feeling of fear and anxiety among many people that anyone who is in any way kinky with regard to sex, and especially anyone who's homosexual, will sooner or later degenerate into assaulting prepubertal children. As a matter of fact, nothing could be further from the truth. There is an extraordinary specificity to kinkiness and, by the same token, an extraordinary specificity to normalcy of arousal with regard to erotic stimulus imagery. It's very difficult to get yourself aroused by some other kind of imagery than that which is specifically yours. It's like your facial features or the dermatoglyphics of your hand. It has to be your own "thing" so far as sexual arousal imagery is concerned.

This pertains also to the pedophiliac, who is really in a pretty tragic position in our society. If he were a gerontophiliac and could only be turned-on by mother or father figures, dependent on sex or on homosexual inclination, then nobody would pay much attention to him so long as the age discrepancy was not too great, so that the older person would seem to be a pedophiliac. But it's when you have a young man in his teens or twenties, who can only be turned-on by children of ten, eleven, or twelve years of age, that the public gets panicky. And so this person really is in a tragic position, since nobody is ready to tolerate his activity with their children, or anyone else's children.

I have an example which helps to explain a little about what goes on here. Also, by generalization it helps to explain something more about the other kinky forms of sex. I'm referring now to a boy who has been under treatment, and reasonably successfully, for the last couple of years. He does indeed teach us a pretty good lesson about our own responsibility in medicine. This is a boy who was a blue baby and had a successful heart operation at the age of ten. Up until that time, he'd been a social isolate because he could not exercise any of his motor functions with the rest of the children. After a successful operation, which, let me remind you, meant the end-result of several thousand dollars invested in this life, the boy went to live out in the country. He had the disadvantage of also having highly disturbed parents, who were very strange in their own behavior and their behavior together. Out in the country he had no friends at all nearby, but eventually he became friends with a boy of sixteen who was a social adolescent misfit.

Part of the older boy's adjustment problem was that he wanted to show his friendliness sexually. So the two children, without any real problem between them emotionally, did get involved in sexual play. The format of the sexual play was that the older boy liked to lie on the younger one and perform interfemoral intercourse, ejaculating between the legs, with no penetration. And so it happened that at age sixteen the boy who had had the successful heart operation was being hunted by the police because he was attacking boys of ten and eleven with a knife and forcing them to submit to him sexually. He was, as it finally transpired, exactly living out in replica the experience he'd had himself as a ten-year-old, driven by a complusion which he himself could not understand.

He was given some treatment, first with antiandrogen injections to help him gain some measure of control over the libido itself, and then he was given some guidance and counseling in psychotherapy. He has not been able completely to leave his homosexuality, but he's been able to leave his feeling, desire, and urge for pedophiliac homosexuality. He has graduated now toward actually having a girlfriend and being able to perform perfunctorily in a heterosexual relationship. It's too early to know whether he will end up bisexual or possibly become completely preferentially heterosexual.

The point of my story then is that, even for something that society views so gravely as pedophilia, there is an explanation, if one looks for it, and a possibility of helping. I mentioned antiandrogen because this is about the newest thing in the treatment of people who are hung-up with kinky sex. It offers a promise which yet remains to be fully tested. It's a method, incidentally, that's being used in Germany and, on a very limited scale, in this country at the present time, because of the bureaucratic slowness of the F.D.A. in releasing new drugs for clinical trials.

The most unusual form of kinky sex that you will see in this series of pictures, the most unusual I've actually come across and been able to get color slides made of, is with regard to zoophilia—which also is very difficult for most people to take. I would like to point out one thing to you, for those of you who are interested in animal behavior and biology. That is that dogs are neurotic too, especially dogs raised in city apartments. They disobey all of the standard rules of biology texts, where animals are supposed to be turned-on only by the cycle of their hormones. Whether they're male or female, they may get to be really turned-on by human beings, too.

The first picture is of an advertisement in a swinger magazine for sadists who want partners. You see them dressed up in some of their paraphernalia. Bondage and Discipline magazines they're called. This is very extreme costuming, this leather body stocking and hooded mask, as far as sadism goes. It can be used by the masochist who wants to be locked away and not know what's going to happen to him, but it also can be used by the sadist. You notice there is a good streak of leather fetishism involved here, as there often is in sadism. Sadism probably has its origins in infantile and childhood punishment. It's often said that it occurs more frequently in England and Germany, especially in the older generation, than it does in other countries, and I would suspect that that may be true. It may be related to the system of corporal punishment of children, especially in schools, since any overwhelming and big emotional experience can flood over into the sexual system, especially in early childhood, and leave its imprint for a lifetime.

Here is the kind of transvestite imagery that I have mentioned already, which is not explicitly sex-organ sex at all, but is erotically arousing to the transvestite whose kink is on clothes.

And now a magazine which, as a matter of fact, has been rather helpful to quite a lot of people, in a way that almost any type of portrayal of normal sexual organs can be helpful to those that have an abnormality of the sexual organs, a congenital abnormality, or a fear that they have something wrong with the size of the genitalia. It's very difficult for people who have a genuine abnormality of the organs to figure out, unaided, whether they will be able to perform normally in sex. So it is, in fact, very helpful for them to see some pictures of what to expect among other members of the human race, and what to expect that a partner would expect of them.

This is obviously a rather strange book on autofellatio and masturbation. It does, however, serve the purpose of giving some examples of penis size. So far as I know, there is no authentic publication in medicine which gives us any measurements about penises or about any aspects of the sex organs on a comparative basis. There should be.

Here is another one on phallic development which really has a kind of idiotic humorous touch when you see all the pages one after another. Some people go to extraordinary extremes: a penis tattoo—"Love it." Such people, incidentally, usually have a psychopathic side to their personalities.

I'd like to point out two or three things about the film that you're going to see now.

FILM

At the University of Indiana, in the use of 8-millimeter movies in the sex education course it was possible to use films that were borrowed from the Kinsey Institute, some of them made by Kinsey and his staff themselves and some of them supplied to the Institute from police confiscations, by a special arrangement that the Institute had with the police in Chicago and New York. I actually had no choice in choosing a film, so I simply relied on an example from the ordinary commercial market in pornography and arranged to have this and another film sent over to me from Copenhagen, sight unseen. I was glad enough to do this because it allows one to get a sense of what's going on in the world around one. Films of this type have not yet been legally cleared for sale on the open market in the U.S., though some are actually produced in this country.

There is a special point about this film, titled "Pornography in the Garden," as far as commercial pornography is concerned: it's fairly good, in the sense that the two young people in the film do really become to some extent sexually involved with one another. Several people who have seen the film say that they feel there is not enough indication of a love relationship between the couple. But there is some kind of sentiment and romantic tenderness going on, which you do not see in a large proportion of commercial pornography films. They are dead-end productions in which the sex act really doesn't come off effectively for the camera. This particular film, therefore, could be used by juxtaposing it against one of the poorer types of film to illustrate to patients, let's say with impotence or with some special problem in their sexual lives, what they might aim for in the way of a happy sexual experience together. The authenticity of the enactment does show the phenomenon of retraction; but since one buys these films by so much for 200 feet, it was cut just before the climactic moment, which makes it a bad scientific example for teaching, but artistically it's good.

There is another defect in that the camera man became more engrossed with the girl's face than the boy's, so that you don't really see the boy's face after the very opening of the film. But he did manage to catch, in two places toward the end of the film, the girl's orgasmic flush as the moment of orgasm approached. This phenomenon of the physiology of sexual climax is something that, so far as I know, was first pointed out to us by Masters and Johnson, just a few years ago. I suppose somebody in the human race knew about it before, but it wasn't recorded in the textbooks. In the same way, the retraction of the testicles was not recorded. So I will simply ask you to watch for these special points in this film, and you can make your own criticisms of it.

EPILOGUE

My epilogue will be brief. I will remind you again of my crucifixion example, in order to remind you that everyone can establish his or her own moral standards. In fact, one can with truth say that pornography is indeed in the mind of the beholder. I'm particularly pleased that again tonight the men and the women are here together, because it makes all the difference to the whole subject of pornography for the sexes to exchange their ideas about it and to illuminate one another.

And may I close by wishing you all many years of a happy and normal sex life—for you, your children, and your patients.

chapter 22

Obstacles to the Ideal and Complete Sex Education of the Medical Student and Physician

Harold I. Lief*

As Athanasiou pointed out, one cannot escape one's own values, interdependent with each other and with a system of beliefs. It is through value-oriented eyes that one perceives the world, interprets it, and makes up his mind about various issues such as sex education, pornography, and sexual behavior in general.

My belief is that sexual relations are enhanced and become much more meaningful by an affiliative interpersonal relationship between the two people involved. Casual sex may be good; besides the bodily pleasure obtained, which is not to be minimized, casual sex may increase one's pride and sense of competence. A person's self-esteem rests on his ability to provide pleasure for himself and others. There is also the individual who has separated sexual asser-

*Harold I. Lief, M.D., Department of Psychiatry, University of Pennsylvania, Philadelphia, Pennsylvania.

tion from tenderness, so that each drive or motivation takes for itself different objects for gratification. The result permits him to experience intense sexual pleasure only in the absence of tenderness or real concern for his partner. However, for most people, especially after numerous repetitions, casual sex may lose its significance as a source of pride and become an almost empty ritual.

Athanasiou has reported, with fairly convincing data, that the educated, curious, probably more liberal, segment of society, represented by the readers of *Psychology Today*, is moving toward the Swedish values, which approve premarital coitus in the context of an affiliative relationship. His data are confirmed by the data accumulated by Ira Reiss (1967), on a more representative sample of the population, about attitudes, indicating that the norm is now "permissiveness with affection," and by Christensen's (1970) study of the Danish and two American cultures, first done in 1958, and repeated in 1968. With some minor qualifications, related to young people who are pushed by social and group pressures to conform to new sexual mores before they are emotionally ready for it, this change in sexual behavior fits in with my own values. On the other hand, the papers by Smith and Smith and Money are somewhat disconcerting. Despite the evident need for these forms of sexual behavior, co-marital sex—essentially a group sexual activity—and pornography, in spite of their utility in certain situations, seem to contribute to dehumanization of sexuality. Smith & Smith point out that many of the people engaged in co-marital sex are seeking an emotional relationship either as a substitute for one they do not have with their spouses or as an addition to the one they find in their own marriages. There is no convincing evidence that the majority of the people succeed in forming intense relationships or that co-marital sex greatly enhances their own marital relations. Based on data derived from a study of 280 housewives, salesmen, lawyers, teachers, and other "swingers" in the Mid-West, Texas, and Louisiana, Bartell (1971) in his final evaluation comes to the same conclusion.

The primary reason for the dropouts among the more sensitive, more intellectually inclined people who enter swinging . . . (is) that the practice of more or less indiscriminate swinging is much too mechanistic; that there is a loss of identity, an absence of commitment; and that this total non-involvement—at least to them—represents the antithesis of sexual pleasure and satisfaction. . . .

Although couples initially report that they want new friends, interests, and activities in addition to purely sexual contact, in reality this is rarely so. Proof is seen in the fact that most couples will see another couple only once. Even on those occasions when social relationships develop with another couple, the social relationship is minimal even when the sexual relationship is maximal [p. 287].

Bartell also concludes that most male swingers are "in effect bartering their women." He points out that they initiate swinging and that they exchange pictures of their nude or semi-nude women with other couples as a kind of come-on. The implicit message is "Look what a luscious tid-bit I have for you. Do you have anything equally good for me?" Bartell considers this "a further indication that swingers generally swing for purely mechanical sexual reasons [p. 288]." His general conclusion is that "in a society of alienated human beings, sex, after all, serves a socially integrating function. Among swingers sex all too often replaces authentic intimacy [p. 291]." "However, their human relationships outside the dyad are not good. Their activities with other couples reflect mechanical interaction rather than an intimacy of relationships (page 292). Bartell's final sentence is one which I endorse—"What we would like to see is a freedom of sexuality, but one more concerned with human relationships, and that these human relationships rather than the sexual relationships become the primary goal."

Overall, pornography does no harm, and in some cases erotica is helpful, but, essentially, pornography also is dehumanizing. In the *New York Times Book Review* (January 31, 1971), Edward Dahlberg wrote, "Pornography is a folly because it is positively asexual; a man who is starved for a female or a wife cannot satisfy his hunger watching nudes in films or privy bedroom erotica [p. 2]." Still, indicating the value conflict within me, I do not wish to be so locked into my value position that I cannot examine new data, new evidence, without prejudice. As John Money has said, medical students and physicians must know the broad spectrum, the enormous diversity of sexual behavior. They must be fully acquainted with group sex and with pornography, among other aspects of contemporary human sexuality. Without this information a medical student or physician cannot truly evaluate the sexual behavior of any patient or couple he wishes to counsel.

Money's position is that an increased awareness of the range of behavior will lead to an increased tolerance of deviant behavior. Exposure to pornography from two to four hours will also lead the medical student to an increased awareness of his own sexual arousal and, therefore, be less alarming when it happens in a clinical situation. It will also lead to an increase in detachment about human sexuality, to an increase in what Reneé Fox and I (Lief & Fox 1963) have called "detached concern," a balance between objectivity and empathy, so essential to the proper functioning of the physician.

Before discussing the obstacles to a complete and ideal sex education for the medical student and physician, it may be worthwhile to take a look at what might constitute an ideal program, even while recognizing the difficulties in achieving consensus. The Center for the Study of Sex Education in Medicine at the University of Pennsylvania is now in the process of surveying sex education curricula in the medical schools of the United States, and there is an enormous variety. The sex education curriculum should be studied from three primary dimensions—namely, information, attitudes, and skills.

INFORMATION

Clearly, human sexuality is an area in which there is an exquisite conjunction of the biological and behavioral sciences. The medical student should become aware of the broad range of sexual behavior and of the various influences affecting sexual behavior, such as the biologic, psychologic, transactional, cultural, and legal. He should have information about sex counseling and therapy, and since most sexual problems arise in the context of marriage, he should know the fundamentals of marriage counseling. It is impossible to separate a sexual relationship from a marital relationship, and that is why, by themselves, behavioral models of therapy of sexual disorders are incomplete. The physician must also know something about the fundamentals of sex education and of family planning. When one includes these dimensions one can begin to see the enormous breadth of the field. Clearly what is required then is a core curriculum to be followed by electives for those students who are particularly interested in special aspects of human sexuality. An example of this core curriculum was recently published by Tyler (1970). The medical student should be helped enormously by the forthcoming volume produced by a special committee of the American Medical Association entitled *A Handbook of Human Sexuality* (in press). This will include much of the basic information we would like to transmit to medical students and physicians.

ATTITUDES

Other than in the care of the dying patient, there is no other place in the medical curriculum where attitudes play such an important role in the management of clinical problems. It is unrealistic to expect a physician to be free of bias. Everyone has a set of beliefs and preferences based on his own experience and judgments. What we must try to develop in every physician is an awareness of his own set of values. If the medical student or physician has a clear concept of just what he believes in, he is much less apt to unwittingly impose his values on his patient or have them affect his judgment and management of the clinical situation. The physician who is unable to countenance premarital intercourse under any circumstances is a poor choice for the single girl who is looking for contraceptive help. An internist may threaten to discontinue treatment for a middle-aged female hypertensive unless she gives up her extramarital affair. A doctor may not prescribe contraception for a woman who is having extramarital sex relations, perhaps feeling that if she does get pregnant this will be a punishment she well deserves. One study, reported in the *New York Times*, showed that in approving abortions, married physicians more frequently approved abortions for married women while single physicians more frequently approved abortions for single women. This is an example of how some physicians project their own particular life experiences into a clinical situation. Occasionally a physician will impose his own more liberal values on a patient who is not emotionally ready for a new sexual experience. A gynecologist treated a married woman who had never had an orgasm and recommended masturbation, without finding out her intense revulsion toward the idea, and lost a patient.

Hopefully, the physician will be as open-minded as possible, so that his beliefs and attitudes may change with experience and the acquisition of wisdom. Clearly this is an area in which tact and delicacy are essential, but shame and false modesty are handicaps. The physician's own embarrassment and anxiety will increase the patient's. The physician feeling comfortable with his subject is probably the most important aspect of his training for handling problems of a sexual nature (the same is obviously true of school teachers involved with sex education). If the physician is comfortable with his own sexuality, he is not only going to be able to do a much better job of counseling, but will be able to elicit information from patients that the embarrassed or anxious doctor will not. Indeed the survey of sexual problems encountered in practice by Burnap and Golden (1967) demonstrates that the physician's comfort with the subject is positively correlated with the frequency of sexual problems in his practice.

In the six regional workshops for medical educators held by the Center for the Study of Sex Education in Medicine, there has been clear recognition that attitude training is the key to education in human sexuality. It is insufficient to teach facts alone. Medical students must go through a process of what Clark Vincent (1968) has called "desensitization," sensitization," and "integration." In desensitization the students become less anxious, less uncomfortable, and there is a decrease in inappropriate defense mechanisms, such as avoidance, embarrassed or sarcastic humor, anger, or superior attitudes. In the process of sensitization the student becomes more aware of his own feelings and responses and, as a consequence, is able to be more sensitive to the feelings and attitudes of his patients. The third stage of attitude training involves the integration of facts with his changed attitudes so that he can become a more effective therapist.

The process of attitude training has created the most controversy among medical teachers. Perhaps this is the first time that medical educators have become clearly involved with this dimension of medical education. Many have been unaware of the importance of attitudes in the training of medical students, even deeming them irrelevant, or they have felt that nothing can be done to modify attitudes. Attitude training does go on in medical education, but until recently it has gone on unconsciously, not only outside the general awareness of the student but outside the awareness of the faculty.

Changes in attitudes have been a spin-off, an accidental development, of medical education. Such attitudes as detached concern, the capacity to deal with uncertainty and to develop responsibility, and those attitudes that affect professional identification and self-image form without any specific or organized attempt to shape them according to an educational model. However, in the training of medical students to become more effective sex counselors, we are now making specific attempts to modify attitudes. This is a still unrecognized revolutionary development in medical education, with enormous implications. There are three major techniques for producing attitudinal changes: consensual validation, confrontation, and implosion.

Consensual Validation. Consensual validation involves the attempt to get medical students to recognize the broad range of attitudes and behavior. One of the more effective ways of doing this is the use of the Sex Knowledge and Attitude Test (SKAT) designed by David Reed and me. This test is now in use in over forty medical schools, and in this academic year we anticipate it will have been given to approximately 3,500 medical students. On the basis of this we will be able to collect a great deal of information about the current knowledge and attitudes of medical students. The preliminary survey of the first 500 medical students in six medical schools we tested this year demonstrated that 22 percent of them still believed that masturbation is etiologically related to mental illness. Fifty-four percent still believed that there were two kinds of physiological orgastic responses in women, one clitoral, the other vaginal. Fifteen percent believed that the condom is the most reliable of the various contraceptive devices, and 20 percent believed that pornography is responsible for much of today's aberrant sexual behavior. It seems that there is still a long way to go in changing attitudes on the basis of new information.

The use of the SKAT enables medical students to compare their own attitudes with those of their peers in a small group setting. The lively discussions of diverse attitudes that ensue permit the student to recognize where he stands with regard to the others. He can then validate whether his attitudes are in the mainstream or at one extreme or the other. This often produces changes in attitudes, especially in increased tolerance for different viewpoints. We are in the process of demonstrating attitude change by pre- and posttesting after courses in sex education which include this type of consensual validation.

Confrontation. The second technique is that of confrontation, in which students are confronted with the wide array of sexual behavior. This serves to "shake them up" and may modify prejudice. There are two major techniques for accomplishing this, through the use of live patients or through the use of film and video tape. Patients with problems such as transsexualism, transvestitism, fetishism, homosexuality, etc., are presented to the group. If patients are unavailable, or better demonstrations have been captured on film or tape, audio-visuals are used. At Hahnemann Medical College active members of the Homophile Action League of Philadelphia have been brought in to discuss homosexuality. Members of the community are used rather than patients, but the goal remains the same. The second technique of confrontation involves the use of the group process. In one technique that we ourselves have employed we ask each member of the class to set forth what sexual attitudes and behavior seem appropriate for his own socioeconomic class and ethnic background, including race and religion. In other words, the student casts aside his own personal idiosyncratic behavioral patterns and presents himself as a stereotype of a person coming from that particular background. This technique enables the group to compare the impact of race, class, religion, and ethnic background in general on attitudes and values and brings into sharp focus differences existing in the student class. Some schools are using variants of "T" groups to create confrontation and attitudinal changes.

Implosion. A third technique is that of implosion in which the students are overwhelmed by sexual stimuli, usually in the form of films and video tapes. This is the technique that has been pioneered by Tyler (1971) of the University of Indiana, Money

(1971) of Johns Hopkins, and by Chilgren (1972) of the University of Minnesota. Chilgren reports significant changes in attitudes after a weekend "marathon" learning experience, but the assumptions on which implosion is based need additional testing. We must find out if attitudinal changes obtained by these methods are stable, and if they carry over to the patient.

SKILLS

The basic skills required of a competent sex counselor are the ability to interview, to take a sexual history, and to use his interviewing skills to produce change. These skills might include some preliminary competence in conjoint couple interviewing, as well as the interviewing of a single patient. If the physician has learned specialized techniques, such as those designed by Masters and Johnson (1970), these would be additional skills adding to his competence. In general, he must learn to apply his knowledge to elicit pertinent information and to create an atmosphere of trust and confidence, which decreases the sexually inhibiting emotions of fear, rage, guilty fear and guilty rage. If he can accomplish this, while creating the possibility of better communication between husband and wife and teaching them behavioral techniques to reduce the common problems of premature ejaculation, impotence, and diminished sexual response in the female, he will be doing a competent job.

OBSTACLES TO SEX EDUCATION

There are several major obstacles preventing the development of this form of educational experience.

1. *Inadequate information.* This is in part related to inadequate information in the field at large, but is really a phony argument—an excuse used as a rationalization for failing to teach human sexuality in medical schools. There are other areas of medicine in which there are large gaps in information, yet adequate education occurs. A more pertinent aspect of this is the relative ignorance of medical educators. Only in the last few years has there been a determined effort to secure a cadre of informed and motivated teachers of sex education in medical schools. This effort

is still going on, and much remains to be done to develop a group of teachers in each and every medical school who can carry on the task.

2. *Faculty reluctance or outright obstruction to the development of programs of sex education.* The reasons for this include the faculty's shame and embarrassment, a lack of confidence in the ability to teach, a wish to avoid controversy, and the recognition that human sexuality cuts across departmental lines so that it requires a coordinated interdisciplinary effort to teach it properly.

3. *Rigid attitudes on the part of students.* Clearly, if students fail to modify guilt-ridden attitudes, their education will be impaired. Some students may punish or humiliate patients whose sexual behavior they scorn. A decade ago, studies of Tulane medical students (Lief 1960, 1971) demonstrated that about one-third had personality characteristics we labeled "adjusted." These were students who were uncomfortable with their own feelings and, hence, uncomfortable with those of patients, even though at superficial levels they were poised and articulate and developed relationships. It is possible that the percentage of students who fall into this category is now decreasing. At any rate, these were students who tended to avoid clinical situations where intense emotion might be evoked. One of the problems of medical education is to decide whether we should attempt to modify the attitudes of all students or just work with those students who have the capacity for becoming sensitized to their own feelings and those of their patients. This is still controversial.

4. *Lack of experience with the wide range of sexual behavior.* Learning this has to be accomplished either through the use of audio-visual or live patients, or through the use of group process with or without the SKAT.

5. *Failure to develop adequate skills.* It is clear that lectures and even small group discussions will not produce the required skills in patient management. This requires more than patient demonstrations, either live or with video tapes. It requires learning by doing, by active counseling, and there are only a few medical schools that can provide the clinical facilities to enable medical students to conduct sex and marriage counseling under close supervision.

6. *Uncertainty about teaching methods.* This not only includes uncertainty about attitude training but involves such practical matters as whether to have a separate course in sex education or to incorporate it into other courses. A lively debate is going on among medical schools with regard to this point. Although our survey of medical schools is still incomplete, we have found twenty-nine medical schools with separate courses and twenty-one with incorporated courses. Some schools have both. Briefly, the argument in favor of incorporated courses is that human sexuality should not be dealt with apart from other aspects of clinical management, such as gynecology, urology, pediatrics, and internal medicine. The argument for separate courses is that unless the course is separate and set apart the experiences that the student encounters are often accidental or happenstance.

A second debate is whether the course should be mandatory or elective. Some argue that every physician should have the basic information and skills in the treatment of these problems. The counter argument is that there are some physicians who are too ill-equipped, because of their personality difficulties or conflicts, to deal with sexual problems which should be reserved for those physicians who, by their own personality development, have some potential aptitude. Many medical schools are developing a short-core program followed by electives for those students who want to develop certain aspects in greater depth.

A third area of argument about teaching is whether sex counseling should be incorporated with marriage counseling, and whether sex and marriage counseling should be integrated with training in family planning. At the Center for the Study of Sex Education in Medicine it is strongly believed that all of these should be integrated into one program of training and that family planning training involves much more than contraceptive education or discussions of abortion and sterilization. Clinically, one cannot justify the separation of family planning from sex and marital relations and the problems involved in these relationships. Therefore, the training should be integrated.

7. *Relative absence of good audio-visual materials.* This is an important obstacle to the development of an ideal program. Some are now being developed. Recognition of this deficiency has moti-

vated a number of medical educators to new developments in this area that look promising.

CONCLUSION

In any program in sex education in medical schools, up-to-date information about sexual attitudes and behavior is an absolute requirement. The papers by Athanasiou and Smith & Smith not only give us additional information about changes in sexual mores, important to the student and physician, but they are important aids in attitude training. It is through the recognition of change and new sexual life styles that the student comes to grips with his own attitudes and behavior, beginning the process of desensitization, sensitization, and integration necessary to the development of a competent sex counselor. Clearly, it is also essential to those physicians who will go into the community and become involved with sex education programs in schools or churches or other social institutions. Physicians seeking counsel for developing such programs can obtain help from the Sex Information and Education Council of the United States (SIECUS).

Money's paper is a direct challenge to those medical educators who wish to test new techniques. It takes some courage to present this kind of material to any group, even medical students. For in a society with intense feelings about pornography it would be easy to label this as one more attempt at "smut peddling" and fail to see the potential value of this pioneering educational program and its possible applications to other areas of medical education.

Speaking as a medical educator who has been so concerned with the development of competent sex and marriage counselors among the physicians in our country, I welcome these three contributions for their enlargement of horizons and their challenges to medical educators to use this information and new educational techniques as appropriately as possible.

REFERENCES

American Medical Association. *A handbook of human sexuality* (to be published).

453   Sex Education of Medical Student and Physician

Bartell, G. D. *Group sex*. New York: Peter H. Wyden, 1971.

Burnap, D. W., & Golden, J. S. Sexual problems in medical practice. *Journal of Medical Education* 1970, 45: 1025-31.

Chilgren, R. A. A process of attitude change in human sexuality. Center for the Study of Sex Education in Medicine Newsletter No. 3, Spring, 1972.

Christensen, H. T., & Gregg, C. F. Changing sex norms in America and Scandinavia. *Journal of Marriage and the Family* 1970, 32(4): 616-27.

Dahlberg, E. *New York Times Book Review*, January 31, 1971, p. 2.

Lief, H. I. A psychodynamic study of medical students and their adaptational problems: preliminary report (with K. Young, V. Spruiell, R. Lancaster, & V. F. Lief). *Journal of Medical Education* 1960, 35: 696-704.

_____. Family planning and undergraduate medical education. *Fertility Control* 1967, 2(2): 16-19.

_____. Sex and the medical educator. *Journal of American Medical Women's Association* 1968, 23(2): 195-96.

_____. Sexual education of the medical student: implications for family planning. In Mary Calderone, (ed.), *Manual of family planning and contraceptive practice* (2nd ed.). Baltimore: Williams & Wilkins, 1970, pp. 171-88.

_____. Personality characteristics of medical students. In R. Coombs & C. Vincent (eds.), *Psychosocial aspects of medical education*. Springfield, Ill.: Charles C Thomas, 1971, pp. 44-87.

Lief, H. I., & Fox, R. C. Training for "detached concern" in medical practice. In H. I. Lief, V. F. Lief, & N. R. Lief (eds.), *The psychological basis of medical practice*. New York: Hoeber-Harper, 1963, pp. 12-35.

Masters, W. H., & Johnson, V. E. *Human sexual inadequacy*. Boston: Little, Brown, 1970.

Money, J. Pornography and medical education. In Vernon W. Lippard (ed.), *Family planning, demography, & human sexuality*. New York: Josiah Macy Jr. Foundation, 1971, pp. 98-109.

Reiss, I. *The social context of premarital sexual permissiveness*. New York: Holt, Rinehart and Winston, 1967.

Tyler, E. A. Introducing a sex education course into the medical curriculum. *Journal of Medical Education* 1970, 45: 1025-31.

Vincent, C. E. (ed.) *Human sexuality in medical education and practice*. Springfield, Ill.: Charles C Thomas, 1968.

Publications of the American Psychopathological Association

Vol. I	(32nd Meeting):	*Trends of Mental Disease.* Joseph Zubin (Introduction), 1945.*
Vol. II	(34th Meeting):	*Current Therapies of Personality Disorders.* Bernard Glueck (ed.), 1946.
Vol. III	(36th Meeting):	*Epilepsy.* Paul H. Hoch and Robert P. Knight (eds.), 1947.
Vol. IV	(37th Meeting):	*Failures in Psychiatric Treatment.* Paul H. Hoch (ed.), 1948.
Vol. V	(38th Meeting):	*Psychosexual Development in Health and Disease.* Paul H. Hoch and Joseph Zubin (eds.), 1949.
Vol. VI	(39th Meeting):	*Anxiety.* Paul H. Hoch and Joseph Zubin (eds.), 1950.
Vol. VII	(40th Meeting):	*Relation of Psychological Tests to Psychiatry.* Paul H. Hoch and Joseph Zubin (eds.), 1951.
Vol. VIII	(41st Meeting):	*Current Problems in Psychiatric Diagnosis.* Paul H. Hoch and Joseph Zubin (eds.), 1953.
Vol. IX	(42nd Meeting):	*Depression.* Paul H. Hoch and Joseph Zubin (eds.), 1954.
Vol. X	(43rd Meeting):	*Psychiatry and the Law.* Paul H. Hoch and Joseph Zubin (eds.), 1955.
Vol. XI	(44th Meeting):	*Psychopathology of Childhood.* Paul H. Hoch and Joseph Zubin (eds.), 1955.

*This volume was published by King's Crown Press (Columbia University). Volumes II through XXVI were published by Grune & Stratton. Volume XXVII was published by The Johns Hopkins University Press.

Vol. XII	(45th Meeting):	*Experimental Psychopathology.* Paul H. Hoch and Joseph Zubin (eds.), 1957.
Vol. XIII	(46th Meeting):	*Psychopathology of Communication.* Paul H. Hoch and Joseph Zubin (eds.), 1958.
Vol. XIV	(47th Meeting):	*Problems of Addiction and Habituation.* Paul H. Hoch and Joseph Zubin (eds.), 1958.
Vol. XV	(48th Meeting):	*Current Approaches to Psychoanalysis.* Paul H. Hoch and Joseph Zubin (eds.), 1960.
Vol. XVI	(49th Meeting):	*Comparative Epidemiology of the Mental Disorders.* Paul H. Hoch and Joseph Zubin (eds.), 1961.
Vol. XVII	(50th Meeting):	*Psychopathology of Aging.* Paul H. Hoch and Joseph Zubin (eds.), 1961.
Vol. XVIII	(51st Meeting):	*The Future of Psychiatry.* Paul H. Hoch and Joseph Zubin (eds.), 1962.
Vol. XIX	(52nd Meeting):	*The Evaluation of Psychiatric Treatment.* Paul H. Hoch and Joseph Zubin (eds.), 1964.
Vol. XX	(53rd Meeting):	*Psychopathology of Perception.* Paul H. Hoch and Joseph Zubin (eds.), 1965.
Vol. XXI	(54th Meeting):	*Psychopathology of Schizophrenia.* Paul H. Hoch and Joseph Zubin (eds.), 1966.
Vol. XXII	(55th Meeting):	*Comparative Psychopathology—Animal and Human.* Joseph Zubin and Howard F. Hunt (eds.), 1967.
Vol. XXIII	(56th Meeting):	*Psychopathology of Mental Development.* Joseph Zubin and George A. Jervis (eds.), 1968.
Vol. XXIV	(57th Meeting):	*Social Psychiatry.* Joseph Zubin and Fritz A. Freyhan (eds.), 1968.
Vol. XXV	(58th Meeting):	*Neurobiological Aspects of Psychopathology.* Joseph Zubin and Charles Shagass (eds.), 1969.
Vol. XXVI	(59th Meeting):	*The Psychopathology of Adolescence.* Joseph Zubin and Alfred M. Freedman (eds.), 1970.
Vol. XXVII	(60th Meeting):	*Disorders of Mood.* Joseph Zubin and Fritz A. Freyhan (eds.), 1972. Also published under Association auspices: *Field Studies in the Mental Disorders.* Joseph Zubin (ed.), 1961.

Index

457

THE JOHNS HOPKINS UNIVERSITY PRESS

This book was composed in Baskerville text by Jones Composition Company, Inc.
It was printed by Universal Lithographers, Inc. on S. D. Warren's
55-lb. Sebago paper, in a text shade, regular finish and bound
by L. H. Jenkins, Inc. in Milbank Vellum cloth.